D0848044

Unmarried Couples, Law,
and Public Policy

Unmarried Couples, Law, and Public Policy

CYNTHIA GRANT BOWMAN

OXFORD
UNIVERSITY PRESS

OXFORD
UNIVERSITY PRESS

Oxford University Press, Inc., publishes works that further Oxford University's objective of excellence in research, scholarship, and education.

Oxford   New York
Auckland   Cape Town   Dar es Salaam   Hong Kong   Karachi   Kuala Lumpur   Madrid   Melbourne
Mexico City   Nairobi   New Delhi   Shanghai   Taipei   Toronto

With offices in
Argentina   Austria   Brazil   Chile   Czech Republic   France   Greece   Guatemala   Hungary   Italy
Japan   Poland   Portugal   Singapore   South Korea   Switzerland   Thailand   Turkey   Ukraine
Vietnam

Copyright © 2010 by Oxford University Press, Inc.

Published by Oxford University Press, Inc.
198 Madison Avenue, New York, New York 10016

Oxford is a registered trademark of Oxford University Press
Oxford University Press is a registered trademark of Oxford University Press, Inc.

Library of Congress Cataloging-in-Publication Data

Bowman, Cynthia Grant, 1945–
    Unmarried couples, law, and public policy / Cynthia Grant Bowman.
        p. cm.
    Includes bibliographical references and index.
    ISBN 978-0-19-537227-4 (hardback) : alk. paper)
1. Unmarried couples—Legal status, laws, etc.—United States. 2. Unmarried couples—Social
aspects—United States. 3. Unmarried couples—Legal status, laws, etc. I. Title.
    KF538.B69 2010
    346.7301'6—dc22   2009041113

1 2 3 4 5 6 7 8 9

Printed in the United States of America on acid-free paper

Note to Readers
This publication is designed to provide accurate and authoritative information in regard to the subject matter covered. It is based upon sources believed to be accurate and reliable and is intended to be current as of the time it was written. It is sold with the understanding that the publisher is not engaged in rendering legal, accounting, or other professional services. If legal advice or other expert assistance is required, the services of a competent professional person should be sought. Also, to confirm that the information has not been affected or changed by recent developments, traditional legal research techniques should be used, including checking primary sources where appropriate.

*(Based on the Declaration of Principles jointly adopted by a Committee of the
American Bar Association and a Committee of Publishers and Associations.)*

You may order this or any other Oxford University Press publication by
visiting the Oxford University Press website at www.oup.com

To Ben

Contents

Preface and Acknowledgments

I BECAME INTERESTED in the subject of this book when I was working in the legal clinic at Northwestern University School of Law. One day, a victim of domestic violence came in and asked me for advice. "What can I take with me?" she asked, if she were to leave a 15-year abusive relationship in which she had given birth to two sons. The couple had never married but presented themselves as married for all purposes. The student to whom I assigned the research returned a few days later to say, "The news is not good. She can take her clothes with her but not much else. If she has custody of the children, she will get child support."

It was in this situation that I discovered that Illinois, the state in which I then lived, did not recognize any claims brought by unmarried cohabitants, although this client would have had substantial remedies if the state had not abolished common law marriage. I began to write on the topic from the perspective of advocating the revival of common law marriage, arguing that it had served to protect the interests of vulnerable parties at the end of unmarried relationships. As states continued to abolish the institution, this argument began to seem increasingly unrealistic. The harms against which I was seeking legal protection can only be remedied today by developing the law applicable to opposite-sex cohabitants. That impulse and the articles it generated were the seeds of this book.

When I began this book, I was myself a cohabitant. Although Ben Altman and I married many years later, I still think of him as my long-term partner; and I'm grateful to him for his unflagging support and for our continuing discussion, both personal and intellectual, of the issues involved in cohabitation.

I have received help and encouragement from many people over the course of the years during which these ideas took shape. I am grateful to both Northwestern University School of Law and Cornell Law School for their support of my research. I owe a great deal to individuals at both institutions who have helped me along the way. I thank Rachel Julis, Kate Shaw, and Al Turco for their excellent research assistance while they were students at

Northwestern University School of Law; Marcia Lehr and Pegeen Bassett of the Northwestern University Law School Library for their help; and Melanie Meerschwam for her translation of various Dutch language materials for me. I'm also grateful to Roald Nashi, Clare Ballard, and Yu Yin at Cornell Law School for their very able editorial and research assistance and to Julie Jones and Amy Emerson of the Cornell Law School Library for tracking down all kinds of sources for me. For their constructive criticism of articles that preceded this manuscript, I thank Andy Koppelman and other colleagues at Northwestern University School of Law, Anne Barlow, Mary Anne Case, and my current colleagues at Cornell Law School. Emily Sherwin deserves special thanks for sharing all her research files on equitable remedies for cohabitants with me. I'm also greatly indebted to Ben Altman and Michael Shoenberger for having shared their editing skills with me so generously.

My knowledge about the legal treatment of cohabitation in other countries benefited enormously from the assistance of Anne Barlow at the University of Exeter; Ian Sumner and Wendy Schrama at the Molengraaf Institute in Utrecht and Kees Waaldijk of the E.M. Meijers Institute of Legal Studies at the University of Leiden, whom I met and interviewed about this subject in The Netherlands in the summer of 2004; and Caroline Mécary, whom I interviewed at her law office in Paris in the summer of 2005.

Portions of this manuscript were previously published in a much earlier form in the *Oregon Law Review*, the *Journal of Law and Policy*, and the *Journal of Law and Family Studies*.[1]

CYNTHIA GRANT BOWMAN
Ithaca, New York
September 2009

---

1. Cynthia Grant Bowman, *A Feminist Proposal to Bring Back Common Law Marriage*, 75 OR. L. REV. 709 (1997); Cynthia Grant Bowman, *Legal Treatment of Cohabitation in the United States*, 26 L. & POL'Y 119, 139 (2004); Cynthia Grant Bowman, *Social Science and Legal Policy: The Case of Heterosexual Cohabitation*, 9 J. L. & FAM. STUD. 1 (2007).

Introduction

OVER THE COURSE OF THE LAST FEW DECADES, a dramatic change has occurred in the way Americans organize their intimate lives. The Census Bureau reported in 2006 that for the first time less than half of all households consisted of married couples.[1] Instead, large numbers of people are choosing to live either in unmarried cohabiting unions, both heterosexual and gay or lesbian, or as single persons. By this behavior, Americans are participating in a trend that has become characteristic of industrialized nations. As a result of this trend, many other countries have changed their laws to reflect the way people now live. In the United States, however, there is resistance to doing so.

While people have changed their living patterns, the law of the fifty states has by and large refused to recognize this new social reality. U.S. family law has made only a few attempts to accommodate these changes, by recognizing contracts between cohabitants or by extending benefits to registered partners that are available as a matter of law to married couples. The reasons for this refusal on the part of the states vary. The most common and most strongly held objections to recognizing cohabitation as a new family form rest upon concerns for the impact upon the institution of marriage and for the autonomy of cohabitants who have chosen not to marry. Within these constraints, the enforcement of contracts entered into by cohabitants has gained acceptance. But extending the rights, benefits, and obligations of marriage to cohabitants has not.

These social changes have occasioned highly politicized debates over same-sex marriage, on the one hand, and arguments raised by the so-called "Marriage Movement," on the other. The campaign to legitimize same-sex marriage has given rise to broad-ranging public discussion—in the media, in

---

1. Sam Roberts, *It's Official: To Be Married Means to Be Outnumbered*, N.Y. TIMES, Oct. 15, 2006, at A22.

1

political campaigns, and in the scholarly literature of law. A high point of the drive for marriage rights for gays and lesbians was reached in 2004, when the Massachusetts Supreme Judicial Court decided, on state constitutional grounds, that same-sex couples must be allowed to marry.[2] Although a number of other states followed suit, a backlash also appears to have developed, with state after state passing Defense of Marriage Acts and constitutional amendments to prevent similar changes on their turf. Or, in the case of California, overturning the state supreme court's decision that same-sex marriage was constitutionally required by means of a popular referendum amending the state constitution.

The Marriage Movement is a reaction not only to the campaign for same-sex marriage but also to the increase in cohabitation and to no-fault divorce.[3] Conservative commentators and the politicians who echo their appeal to values emphasize the importance of marriage as an institution and raise alarms about the dangers posed to it by these trends. A recurrent theme in Marriage Movement literature is that children are best raised by nuclear, two-parent, heterosexual, married couples.[4] Supporters of this movement see marriage as an antidote to delinquency, crime, dependence on welfare, and moral decline in general. Reflecting these concerns, they support making divorce more difficult, for example, by establishing covenant marriages that preclude no-fault divorce.[5] They supported the Bush Administration's strategies for encouraging marriage, which included spending vast sums on marriage promotion initiatives. The Marriage Movement opposes both the extension of marriage or marriage-like benefits to same-sex couples and also any sort of legal recognition for cohabitants, arguing that giving benefits to either group would have a detrimental impact on the institution of marriage.

While the rights of same-sex couples have given rise to a great deal of public debate and scholarly literature, the legal situation of opposite-sex cohabitants has received less extensive consideration by legal scholars and practitioners in the United States, and it is rarely seen as a public issue on the

---

2. Goodridge v. Dept. of Pub. Health, 798 N.E.2d 941(Mass. 2003).

3. *See, e.g.,* Phyllis H. Witcher, *Premarital Cohabitation Increases the Chances of Divorce, in* DIVORCE 63–68 (Christina Fisanick ed., Greenhaven Press 2007) (presenting argument by a pro-marriage activist who founded Protecting Marriage, Inc. that no-fault divorce has led many people to cohabit instead of getting married).

4. A good source for literature of the Marriage Movement is the Web site of the Center for Marriage and Families, *available at* http://center.americanvalues.org/. *See also* Anita Bernstein, *For and Against Marriage: A Revision,* 102 MICH. L. REV. 129, 153–58 (2003).

5. *See, e.g.,* LA. REV. STAT. ANN. § 9.272 (2001) (enacted 1997).

radar of policymakers. The American Law Institute, a group of distinguished judges, lawyers, and law professors, proposed in 2002 to extend a limited number of remedies to cohabitants upon the dissolution of their relationships, but no state has adopted its recommendations.[6] Domestic partnership schemes of differing scope have been adopted by a few states, many localities, and a substantial number of private corporations, but most apply only to same-sex couples. In contrast to other industrialized nations, major changes in the law governing heterosexual cohabitation have been absent from the legislative agenda in the United States, and the courts of most states have been very cautious.

Unlike the legal academy, social scientists have been studying the phenomenon of heterosexual cohabitation for years, analyzing and describing its extent, demography, and impact upon both the adult partners and their children. This burgeoning literature has only begun to make its way into legal scholarship. Nonetheless, for quite some time, a number of U.S. legal scholars have been calling for change in the way American family law deals with cohabiting couples.[7] Their concern is to prevent the substantial injustice that can result when family law diverges from the reality of people's relationships. Cohabitants who have merged their lives for a period of time develop relations of dependency that leave them vulnerable when the union ends in separation or death. This vulnerability affects not only the adults involved but also their children. It affects the wider society as well if one member of the couple must turn to public funds to survive at the end of a long relationship.

Faced with cases raising these issues, courts in the United States have turned to principles of contract or of property law and equity to address perceived injustices arising at the dissolution of cohabiting relationships. Yet the task of protecting individuals involved in intimate relationships is more appropriately performed by the law of domestic relations, and family law is equipped with the appropriate arsenal of legal concepts to do so. Indeed, the dispute over how to treat cohabitants is central to the very purposes of family law in general.

---

6. PRINCIPLES OF THE LAW OF FAMILY DISSOLUTION: ANALYSIS AND RECOMMENDATIONS §§ 6.04–6.05, 4.09–4.10, 5.04 (ALI 2002).

7. *See, e.g.,* Linda C. McClain, *Intimate Affiliation and Democracy: Beyond Marriage?,* 32 HOFSTRA L. REV. 379 (2003); William A. Reppy, Jr., *Property and Support Rights of Unmarried Cohabitants: A Proposal for Creating a New Legal Status,* 44 LA. L. REV. 1677 (1984); Grace Ganz Blumberg, *Cohabitation Without Marriage: A Different Perspective,* 28 UCLA L. REV. 1125 (1981).

I argue that family law in this context should be seen as a set of rules designed to protect individuals who may be harmed when the institution of marriage or other family relationships fail—just as contract law addresses problems when promises are not kept, and tort law provides redress when persons fail to exercise due care. In the context of the family, children are naturally the subject of particular concern, and it is easy to understand why societies feel compelled to regulate families in such a way as to protect them. Apart from these protective functions, it is difficult to see why the state should be involved in regulating intimate relationships at all.

Many of the norms now governing our family law have in fact been inherited directly from medieval religious law and bear the imprint of this derivation.[8] Following the approach embedded in them, family law can be seen as essentially a set of statements by society in favor of a particular ideal—heterosexual marriage and reproduction within the nuclear family—even though that ideal now coexists with widespread different family structures. Under the approach I embrace in this book, family law is called upon to address situations of injustice resulting from the application of this dogmatic philosophy to a changed world—a situation in which the current rules of marriage and divorce do not address problems faced by large numbers of people in family relationships. To this end, it is important to take a dispassionate look at the society in which we live, examining the impact of not recognizing nonmarital unions upon the welfare of both adults and their children, rather than clinging to the traditional, religiously derived underpinnings of marriage.

This book undertakes such an examination. Stepping back from the noisy debate about marriage as an ideal institution under siege, it seeks to evaluate the arguments for and against extending legal recognition to heterosexual cohabitants and imposing legal rights and obligations upon them. What do the many social scientific studies say about these unions? What groups are involved? What are the problems particular to different groups? Is cohabitation detrimental to the welfare of the partners and their children and, if so, in what ways? What are the implications for the law of these findings? And what is the range of legal choices available based on options that have been tried in other countries? Which one might offer a model for the United States at this time?

---

8. *See, e.g.*, Mary Becker, *Family Law in the Secular State and Restrictions on Same-Sex Marriage: Two Are Better Than One*, 2001 U. ILL. L. REV. 1, 17–27 (2001).

In this discussion, I specifically confine myself to the subject of hetero-sexual cohabitation. Legal treatment of heterosexual and homosexual couples often differs both in the United States and abroad. Social scientific examination of the two groups has given rise to a literature about each. I do not undertake to compare and contrast the situations faced by these two groups in a thoroughgoing fashion here. The starkest difference between them, of course, is that heterosexual couples usually have the option to marry (they may not if they are already married or too closely related), while same-sex couples do not have this choice in most states. Thus, while the problems arising on dissolution of a relationship may be similar for the two groups, it does not follow that precisely the same legal treatment will always be appropriate. Gay and lesbian couples may in fact need more, and different, remedies for the legal problems that arise in their relationships.

The paradoxical politics of the marriage debate have made it increasingly likely that gay and lesbian couples may be accorded legal partnership rights or civil union status as a politically acceptable solution short of marriage, while such rights are rarely extended to heterosexual cohabitants. The exten-sion of these rights to opposite-sex couples is seen as more of an attack on the institution of marriage, or at least as a qualitatively different one. For example, some Americans, although a diminishing number, believe that both groups are living in sin. Marrying may cure that sin for opposite-sex couples, but, in the eyes of many, marriage may in fact compound the sin for same-sex couples. Thus, although I believe that the recommendations and remedies I propose in this book are appropriate for all cohabitants regardless of their sexual orientation, I also believe that a separate discussion of heterosexual cohabitation is helpful. In any event, there has been an abundance of discus-sion about same-sex marriage and not yet enough, in my opinion, about cohabitation by opposite-sex couples. I therefore limit my discussion in this book to considering the legal treatment of heterosexual cohabitants.

In Chapter 1, I examine the history of cohabitation and its treatment by the law in the United States. Historically, this legal treatment has been very negative, including criminalization and the denial of any private or public benefits to cohabitants. The one notable exception was the institution of common law marriage, which worked to protect many of the people who would be protected by extending rights to cohabitants today. Unfortunately, only a minority of the jurisdictions in the United States still recognize common law marriage, and the trend is to abolish it. Moreover, given the widespread acceptance and resulting openness of cohabitation today, common law marriage's doctrinal requirement that the partners present one another to the public as their husband or wife prevents it from offering an adequate legal remedy today, when even spouses are sometimes introduced as partners. I use Illinois law as an illustration of the inequities that arise if a state refuses to grant any legal recognition or remedies to cohabitants who would have been treated as married under common law.

Faced with traditional legal standards, judges in some states began to reach out to address obvious injustices—for example, where a relationship of long standing had dissolved and all of the property acquired during it was titled in one party's name. Equitable principles drawn from property and contract law, such as restitution and unjust enrichment, were employed to offer some relief. Yet, while the inadequacy of such remedies has led to calls for legal change in other countries,[9] most courts and legislatures in the United States have been unwilling to take that step, assuming that recognition of cohabiting relationships would somehow privilege unions that were bad for people and deter entry into marriage. The discussion presented in this book challenges these assumptions.

Chapter 2 describes the development of several different legal models governing cohabitation in the United States today. In a famous case involving the actor Lee Marvin, the state of California pioneered a contract approach to remedies upon dissolution of a cohabiting relationship.[10] Almost every state (with the exception of Illinois, Georgia, and Louisiana) now recognizes such agreements among cohabitants, although a few insist that they be embodied in written contracts. By contrast, the state of Washington applies a family law, status-based approach to cohabitants upon dissolution of their relationships but only with regard to a limited number of property issues.[11] Each of these approaches was developed by the courts in response to particular cases of apparent injustice brought to them for resolution.

A number of other states have passed statutes establishing domestic partnerships designed to meet the needs of gay and lesbian couples but also extended to some groups of heterosexuals as well.[12] Limited packages of rights are also bestowed by local ordinances and private companies. All told,

---

9. *See, e.g.,* LAW COMM'N, CONSULTATION PAPER NO. 19, COHABITATION: THE FINANCIAL CONSEQUENCES OF RELATIONSHIP BREAKDOWN (2006), *available at* http://www.lawcom. gov.uk/docs/cp179.pdf.

10. Marvin v. Marvin, 557 P.2d 106 (Cal. 1976).

11. Connell v. Francisco, 898 P.2d 831 (Wash. 1995).

12. CALIFORNIA DOMESTIC PARTNER RIGHTS AND RESPONSIBILITIES ACT, CAL. FAM. CODE § 297 *et seq.*; NEW JERSEY DOMESTIC PARTNERSHIP ACT, N.J. STAT. ANN. § 26:8A-1 *et seq.*

however, the rights and protections given to opposite-sex cohabitants in the United States are very stingy, reflecting assumptions about the necessity of retaining a privileged position for marriage and the dangers of conferring benefits upon an institution that is less than ideal.

Chapter 3 explores the phenomenal increase in heterosexual cohabitation in the United States from 1970 to the present, as well as the differential rates of cohabitation by various economic, racial, and ethnic groups. Over the last few decades, cohabitation has become widespread among all groups of the population, and popular acceptance of it is now broadly based. Given the diversity of individuals who live together without marriage today, the meaning of cohabitation is likely to differ among the groups involved. For many, though not all, the dissolution of such unions by separation or death can result in situations that cry out for a remedy, both to address problems of exploitation of one partner by the other and to protect a long-term cohabitant and his or her children after a relationship of dependency terminates.

Chapter 4 interrogates the literature of social science to see what we now know about cohabitation and its effects. Is cohabitation bad for adults because of the shorter duration of cohabiting unions and its apparent connection to domestic violence? Is it bad for their children? How does it differ from marriage in critical respects? Chapter 4 examines not only the findings of social science with respect to these and other questions but also the implications of these findings for the law. Even if cohabiting unions are less stable and not as beneficial as marriage, I argue that this is not a reason to deny legal remedies to persons involved in them. Indeed, just the opposite may be true.

Chapter 5 discusses the legal treatment of cohabitation in a number of other countries. There is quite an array of models from which to choose: Canada's treatment of cohabitation as a type of common law marriage; the equivalence of rights extended to cohabiting and married persons in Sweden; the domestic partnerships offered to both heterosexual and gay couples in The Netherlands; the more limited package of benefits contained in the Pacte Civile de Solidarité, or PACS, in France; and so on. Our closest legal kin, England, has been engaged in a major debate over the extension of legal remedies to heterosexual cohabitants. Immediately after passage of a Civil Partnership Act providing marriage-like benefits to gay and lesbian couples in 2004, the Law Commission in England undertook an extensive study of what rights should be extended to opposite-sex cohabitants.[13] The experience of

_____

13. Law Comm'n, *supra* note 9.

countries similar in many respects to the United States now provides a good deal of evidence about how well the new and varying legal structures developed to govern cohabiting relationships have been working. Are any of them good models for the United States?

Chapter 6 bites the bullet and makes a proposal for adoption in the United States. I propose a multifaceted legal regime, under which a heterosexual couple initially may choose between marrying or entering into a domestic partnership that extends the rights and obligations of marriage unless they execute a contract between them to avoid those consequences. If they do not do so, after two years or the birth of a child, this quasi-marriage status would be imposed upon them unless they specifically opt out by agreement. Arguments about why this is an appropriate approach include an assessment of how such a legal change would affect both the institution of marriage and the different groups of cohabitants described in Chapter 3. Easy acceptance of the connection between legal recognition for cohabitants and the alleged decline of marriage is a mistake. When the assumptions underlying this connection are deconstructed, and when history and the experience of other countries are examined, fears that extending protections to cohabitants will harm the institution of marriage are revealed to be largely without foundation.

What turns on this? By the date of the 2000 Census, there were more than 3.2 million persons in the United States who had cohabited with a person of the opposite sex for more than two years; and 40 percent of all cohabiting households included children.[14] By 2008, there were 6.8 million opposite-sex unmarried couples and thus presumably 13.6 million individual cohabitants.[15] In short, many people are affected by the manner in which the law treats heterosexual cohabitants, and their numbers are growing rapidly. Without legal change, a long-time cohabitant with children who is abandoned by a

---

14. This data is extrapolated from U.S. CENSUS BUREAU, MARRIED-COUPLE AND UNMARRIED-PARTNER HOUSEHOLDS: 2000 (2003), *available at* http://www.census.gov/prod/2003pubs/censr-5.pdf. The 40 percent figure appears to have remained fairly constant. *See* U.S. CENSUS BUREAU, CURRENT POPULATION SURVEY, 2008 ANNUAL SOCIAL AND ECONOMIC SUPPLEMENT, Table UC3. *Opposite Sex Unmarried Couples by Presence of Biological Children Under 18: 2008, available at* http://www.census.gov/population/www/socdemo/hh-fam/cps2008.html [hereinafter CPS 2008]. The Current Population Survey is an annual survey of about 50,000 households conducted by the Bureau of the Census; the social and economic survey is published in June of each year. *See* http://www.census.gov/cps.

15. CPS 2008 at Table UC1. Opposite Sex Unmarried Couples by Labor Force Status of Both Partners: 2008.

partner has in most jurisdictions no access to the property distribution and maintenance remedies that would be available upon divorce if the couple were married. If, as happens more often in the case law than one would expect, the couple's assets are titled in one partner's name and, as is typical, the two never drew up a contract to govern their relationship, the partner without title will be left without property or support other than child support. If the same cohabiting couple were involved in an auto accident caused by the negligence of another driver, and one of them was grievously injured, in almost every state, the cohabitant witnessing the accident cannot sue for negligent infliction of emotional distress or for loss of consortium (loss of the companionship of his or her partner). If the ambulance takes the injured partner to the hospital, it can be difficult for the other partner to gain access to him or her, and state laws do not list an unmarried partner as a party to be consulted in end-of-life decisions. If death results from the accident, the long-term cohabitant will (with one exception pertinent only to New Hampshire) receive nothing in the absence of a will. Moreover, even though the deceased person may have been the primary wage earner for the family, his or her surviving partner will not receive social security survivors' benefits.

These examples reflect only a few of the consequences that follow upon marital status in the United States today. In each of these situations, the unmarried couple functioning as a family is left without any of the protections of family law. While some might say this was their choice, I question whether this choice is likely to have been either knowing or voluntary in the first place and whether, even if it were, it should deprive both parties of legal protection. My own answer to these questions is clear: it is time to address the social, legal, and economic problems that result from family relationships as they have been restructured in the modern world.

ONE

Cohabitation in the United States: The Past

THE MEDIA DISCOVERED COHABITATION, as though for the first time, when college students began to live together in the 1960s.[1] Far from being invented in the sixties, however, cohabitation has a long history in the United States, and its interaction with the legal system has been uneasy. Most states originally had criminal statutes on the books that applied to cohabitation, often under the rubric of fornication or lewd and lascivious behavior, and some still do. The courts refused to adjudicate disputes between cohabitants if they separated, and the two parties were denied any benefits that turned upon marital status. One exception in many states was for couples who could show that their relationship conformed to the legal definition of common law marriage. In other states, courts faced with instances of hardship, or judges in situations where the common law marriage doctrine did not quite fit, applied equitable notions such as estoppel or unjust enrichment to allocate property at the end of cohabiting relationships. These doctrines applied only in limited circumstances, though, and were difficult to litigate. With the phenomenal increase in cohabitation from 1970 to the present, it has become clear that other remedies are necessary.

This chapter sets the historical context in which the legal treatment of cohabitation must be considered today. That history is one in which the law's treatment of cohabitants has been very negative, and the exceptions to this rule have not been available to many persons involved in unmarried unions. To illustrate, I discuss first the traditional criminalization of cohabitation and its recent decline. I then describe the history of common law marriage in the United States, a doctrine that treated informally married couples for all purposes as though they were married. Indeed, under this doctrine, they *were* married. For a variety of reasons, prime among them that

---

1. *See, e.g.*, Judy Klemesrud, *An Arrangement: Living Together for Convenience, Security, Sex,* N.Y. TIMES, Mar. 4, 1968, at 40.

it has been abolished in most states since 1900, the doctrine no longer works for the majority of persons involved in long-term cohabitating relationships. I use the state of Illinois as an extreme example of a state which, since abolishing common law marriage, has maintained a consistent attitude of nonrecognition of cohabiting unions, thus leaving separating couples who are unmarried without any remedy. I discuss the real-world problems this may cause. Finally, I describe and discuss the inadequacy of the various equitable remedies judges have reached for in an attempt to fill the gap.

🎐 1. Criminalization of Cohabitation

Although they were not illegal at common law, the early American colonies quickly passed statutes criminalizing adultery and fornication (sexual intercourse between unmarried persons).[2] Penalties ranged from imprisonment to fines to public humiliation, including, as anyone who has read Hawthorne in high school remembers, wearing or being branded with the letter "A."[3] The first statute was enacted in Massachusetts in 1692, and in the period from 1760 to 1774, it accounted for 210 of the 370 criminal prosecutions in one Massachusetts county.[4] Other colonies, states, and territories followed suit, though the penalties they visited upon unmarried sex tended to be less severe than in the Puritan colonies, and eventually the prohibition became universal.[5] The purpose of the statutes was clear: to enforce conformity with the moral standards of the community.

The statutes imposing criminal penalties upon consensual heterosexual intercourse varied from state to state, with some describing the forbidden activity simply as fornication; others as sexual intercourse between

---

2. A good source for definitions of these offenses is ROBERT VEIT SHERWIN, SEX AND THE STATUTORY LAW IN ALL 48 STATES 19–21, 48–49 (Oceana Publications 1949). *See also* DONALD E. J. MACNAMARA & EDWARD SAGARIN, SEX, CRIME, AND THE LAW 186 (The Free Press 1977).

3. MORRIS PLOSCOWE, SEX AND THE LAW 144 (Prentice-Hall 1951). *See* NATHANIEL HAWTHORNE, THE SCARLET LETTER (1850).

4. MASS. GEN. LAWS ch. 272, § 18 (2003) (enacted 1692); Melanie C. Falco, *The Road Not Taken: Using the Eighth Amendment to Strike Down Criminal Punishment for Engaging in Consensual Sexual Acts*, 82 N.C. L. REV. 723, 737 (2004); Note, *Fornication, Cohabitation, and the Constitution*, 77 MICH. L. REV. 252, 253–54 (1978) (reporting numbers of cases for Middlesex County, Massachusetts).

5. PLOSCOWE, *supra* note 3, at 144; Falco, *supra* note 4, at 737.

unmarried persons; and others by a series of quaint terms, such as "lewd and lascivious conduct." Included therein, or in many instances prohibited by separate statute, was "lewd and open cohabitation"—living together without being married. There is an obvious relationship between the two types of statutes: presumably those who lewdly cohabit also associate lewdly and lasciviously, that is, engage in sexual intercourse. Yet fornication could, theoretically, be a single instance, while cohabitation was associated with habitual sexual relations; and the statutes typically required that it be "open" or "notorious." Thus, if a cohabiting couple was discreet (or furtive) and/or represented themselves as married, their behavior might not attract the attention of the law. When communities were small and people well known to one another, this would have been difficult.

Virtually every state had criminal sanctions against cohabitation.[6] In addition to the regulation of morality associated with laws against fornication, the criminal statutes against cohabitation were intended to protect the institution of marriage, as well as the state's control over entry into it. In the words of one Wisconsin court as late as the 1930s:

> Lewd and lascivious behavior is a defiance of the usual conventions recognized in our laws as standards of decency. It is a continuing offense, and the willful creation of the reputation of the relation of the parties is an affront to society. It constitutes a disturbing element which the law desires to eradicate.... Lewd and lascivious behavior contains an element of some openness of association under such circumstances. . . . The law seeks in such an instance to prevent a course of conduct which in public estimation constitutes an example detrimental to the morals of the community.[7]

In short, cohabitation was to be punished not only because it violated the community's standards of decency but also because it flaunted that violation, introducing a "disturbing element" which must be "eradicated" lest it lead others, by its very openness, astray. In short, whether charged with fornication or cohabitation, unmarried persons living together risked criminal prosecution.

In the 1960s, the Supreme Court issued a series of opinions developing the right to privacy in cases involving contraception and abortion. *Griswold v. Connecticut*, which struck down criminal laws against the sale of contraceptives

---

6. Martha L. Fineman, *Law and Changing Patterns of Behavior: Sanctions on Non-Marital Cohabitation*, 1981 Wis. L. Rev. 275, 276 (1981).

7. State v. Brooks, 254 N.W. 374, 375 (Wis. 1934), *cited in* Fineman, note 6, at 312–13.

to married persons, extolled the privacy that surrounded sexual relationships between those living in matrimony but was very soon extended to
allow selling contraceptives to unmarried persons as well.[8] *Roe v. Wade* built
upon *Griswold* and the right of privacy to construct a woman's right to abort
a nonviable fetus.[9] After this constitutional right to privacy was established,
state laws against fornication were then challenged on similar grounds, and
the states defending them were required to come up with compelling state
interests served by the legislation.

Ultimately, state courts began to see the applicability of the *Griswold-Roe*
line of decisions to laws against fornication and cohabitation. In 1977, for
example, the New Jersey Supreme Court struck down that state's fornication
statute under the right to privacy contained in the U.S. Constitution.[10] The
state argued that its interests in preventing disease (by regulating the right
to marry and discouraging nonmarital intercourse), preventing an increase
in the numbers of illegitimate children, and protecting both the marital relationship and public morality were compelling, but the court found that these
interests were either not served by the fornication statute or not compelling
enough to justify impinging on the fundamental right to privacy. Most states,
however, simply repealed their statutes against fornication and cohabitation
legislatively, in the face of evidence that the public attitude toward nonmarital
sexual conduct had changed.

One key event in this respect was the publication of the Kinsey Report in
1948, which showed that the behavior criminalized was engaged in by large
sections of the U.S. population.[11] Publication of the initial findings about
male sexual behavior (Kinsey and his associates did not publish their findings about females until 1953) caused one legal commentator to conclude
that:

> The Kinsey Report would seem to require a drastic re-examination of
> our statutes relating to sexual offenses [as] [m]uch of what the law

---

8. Griswold v. Connecticut, 381 U.S. 479 (1965); Eisenstadt v. Baird, 405 U.S. 438 (1972).

9. Roe v. Wade, 410 U.S. 113 (1973).

10. State v. Saunders, 381 A.2d 333, 339 (N.J. 1977). Legal scholars also urged this constitu-
    tional ground for invalidating laws against cohabitation. *See, e.g.,* Kenneth L. Karst, *The
    Freedom of Intimate Association,* 89 YALE L.J. 624 (1980); Note, *supra* note 4, at 266–305.

11. ALFRED C. KINSEY ET AL., SEXUAL BEHAVIOR IN THE HUMAN MALE (W. B. Saunders Co.
    1948).

denounces as crime . . . appears to be relatively normal behavior in the human male.[12]

The drafters of the Model Penal Code and various legal commentators took these findings to heart, recommending that the criminal law not be used to punish either morality-based offenses or victimless crimes. Thus, while the 1955 draft of the Model Penal Code still included a prohibition on cohabitation if it was open and notorious, this provision was deleted from the May 1962 draft.[13]

Yet many states still had statutes against both fornication and/or cohabitation as late as 1978: fornication was a crime in fifteen states and the District of Columbia and cohabitation a crime in sixteen states.[14] These statutes were widely understood to be seldom enforced,[15] and as a result, there was little incentive to change them. A pathbreaking empirical study by Martha Fineman published in 1981 challenged these assumptions.[16] At that time, Wisconsin still had a law against cohabitation, with penalties of up to nine months in prison and/or a $10,000 fine.[17] Fineman sent questionnaires to district attorneys charged with prosecuting this and other laws, as well as to legislators and judges. Their responses showed that although the law was almost never invoked in response to cohabitation *per se*, it was in fact used in a number of other circumstances. It was used against welfare mothers who had men living in their homes, that is, in cases of so-called welfare fraud, and as a substitute charge on which to prosecute cases of domestic violence and child neglect. It provided ammunition for the parties in divorce or custody proceedings. Threat of prosecution for cohabitation was also used to obtain admissions of paternity, thus obviating the need for formal proceedings. Cohabitation charges were brought in connection with charges of other criminal conduct that were harder to prove, or as something for the prosecutor to be able to give away in plea bargaining. Neighbors sometimes filed complaints as well, usually because they had other grievances against the

---

12. PLOSCOWE, *supra* note 3, at 136.

13. Fineman, *supra* note 6, at 277, 282–83.

14. Note, *supra* note 4, at 254.

15. RICHARD A. POSNER & KATHARINE B. SILBAUGH, A GUIDE TO AMERICA'S SEX LAWS (Univ. of Chicago Press 1996).

16. Fineman, *supra* note 6, at 276.

17. Fineman, *supra* note 6, at 278.

cohabitant or cohabitants, such as nonpayment of rent. In short, the cohabitation statute was in fact being used, but for purposes other than those intended, and often as a way to circumvent procedural or evidentiary restrictions attached to other criminal laws.[18]

Responses by legislators to Fineman's questionnaire showed that most of them believed that the statute neither deterred nor punished the conduct represented by cohabitation but were unwilling to vote to repeal the law because of its symbolic importance to their constituents.[19] With the legislators confident that the law was not being used anyway, several attempts at repeal had failed.[20] Fineman's study definitively disproved this assumption, showing that the law was in fact being applied selectively and discriminatorily. In 1983, not long after publication of the Fineman article, the Wisconsin law against cohabitation was repealed.[21]

Laws against fornication and cohabitation were either repealed or overturned by the courts in half the states that still had them between 1978 and 2008. While fornication was a crime in fifteen states in 1978 and cohabitation in sixteen, by January 2009, only seven states (Idaho, Illinois, Massachusetts, Minnesota, South Carolina, Utah, and West Virginia) had fornication statutes, and seven (Florida, Michigan, Mississippi, North Carolina, South Carolina, Virginia, and West Virginia) had criminal laws against cohabitation.[22] Nonetheless, the supreme courts in some of these states still insisted that cohabitation was properly treated, in the words of a 1994 Mississippi

---

18. Fineman, *supra* note 6, at 288–97, 307. Other studies have shown that these laws were used, especially during Reconstruction, as a way to police the behavior of African Americans, especially males. Katherine M. Franke, *Becoming a Citizen: Reconstruction Era Regulation of African American Marriages*, 11 YALE J.L. & HUMAN. 251 (1999).

19. Fineman, *supra* note 6, at 298–99.

20. Fineman, *supra* note 6, at 299.

21. WIS. STAT. § 944.20(3), *repealed by* 1983 Act 17, § 7.

22. Jurisdictions with criminal statutes against fornication as of January 2009 were Idaho (IDAHO CODE § 18-6603 (enacted 1972)); Illinois (720 ILCSA 5/11-8 (enacted 1961)); Massachusetts (MASS. GEN. LAWS ch. 272, § 18 (enacted 1692)); Minnesota (MINN. STAT. § 609.34 (enacted 1967)); South Carolina (S.C. CODE ANN. § 16-15-60 (enacted 1880)); Utah (UTAH CODE ANN. § 76-7-104 (enacted 1973)); and West Virginia (W. Va. CODE § 61-8-3 (enacted 1849)). States with criminal statutes against cohabitation as of December 2006 were Florida (FLA. STAT. ANN. § 798.02 (enacted 1868)); Michigan (MICH. COMP. LAWS § 750.335 (1979)); Mississippi (MISS. CODE ANN. § 97-29-1 (enacted 1848)); North Carolina (N.C. GEN. STAT. § 14-184 (enacted 1805)); South Carolina (S.C. CODE ANN. § 16-15-60 (enacted 1880)); Virginia (VA. CODE ANN. § 18.2-345 (enacted 1950)); and West Virginia (W. VA. CODE § 61-8-4 (enacted 1849)).

case, as "a crime against public morals and decency."[23] Most courts, however, were finding ways around the few cases that came before them, either by imposing trivial sentences or by interpreting the law so as to require an openness and evidentiary support that would be rare. For example, the Virginia Supreme Court in 1973 overturned a conviction for cohabitation based on the fact that the evidence (stark evidence, to be sure) was obtained only because the drawn curtains of one defendant's apartment were blown aside by the wind, allowing a police officer to see into an area that would otherwise have been shielded from the public. The statutory proscription, the court said, "was aimed at conduct which, by its openness and notoriety, tends to affront the public conscience and debase the community morality."[24] But only if it were literally in public view, which this was not.

Another court, in Georgia, used similar reasoning to overturn the conviction of a juvenile for violating that state's fornication statute in a case where two 16-year-olds were caught by the girl's mother in the girl's bedroom. Rather than reinterpreting the state's statute to require that the sex act be performed almost in public, as Virginia had done, the court in *In re J.M.* invalidated the Georgia statute on grounds that it violated the state constitution's right to privacy. The girl had an expectation of privacy in her bedroom, according to the court, and the two had even attempted to bar the door with furniture; thus, the state's interest in "shielding the public from inadvertent exposure to the intimacies of others" was not at issue.[25] (Subsequent Georgia appellate court opinions have limited the Georgia Supreme Court's holding in *In re J.M.* to cases in which the sexual intimacy was between persons legally able to consent, thus not applying if one of them is below the age of consent, which is sixteen in Georgia.)[26]

What is particularly interesting about the Georgia Supreme Court's decision in *In re J.M.* is that it specifically invoked the authority of its own prior case, striking down the Georgia criminal sanction against sodomy in 1998—the same statute which had been unsuccessfully challenged in the Supreme Court

---

23. Davis v. Davis, 643 So. 2d 931, 935 (Miss. 1994).

24. Everett v. Commonwealth, 200 S.E.2d 564, 566 (Va. 1973).

25. *In re* J. M., 575 S.E.2d 441, 444 (Ga. 2003).

26. *See In re* L.A.N., 623 S.E.2d 682 (Ga. Ct. App. 2005); Engle v. State, 659 S.E.2d 795 (Ga. Ct. App. 2008).

in 1986 in *Bowers v. Hardwick*.[27] If the right of privacy protected consensual sodomy between unmarried partners in Georgia, the court reasoned, surely heterosexual sex between unmarried partners cannot be subjected to criminal sanction.

Bowers v. Hardwick was overturned by the United States Supreme Court in 2003. With the decision of *Lawrence v. Texas*, holding criminal laws against sodomy to be unconstitutional, the landscape has changed in what must surely be a decisive fashion. *Lawrence* held that the constitution protected a liberty interest to engage in homosexual relationships in the confines of one's own home, even where a state has historically viewed the practice as immoral (and may still).[28] A case challenging a similar statute reached a state supreme court not long after that decision, and the parties argued that *Lawrence* renders all criminal laws against fornication unconstitutional. In that case, a woman sued her sexual partner for knowing transmission of a sexual disease, and he defended by saying that her injuries could not be recompensed because they were caused by her participation in an illegal act.[29] She countered by challenging the constitutionality of the Virginia fornication statute under *Lawrence*. The Virginia Supreme Court agreed with her, finding no relevant distinction between the circumstances in *Lawrence* and the case before it, and therefore overturned the Virginia fornication statute.

Would it have done so if the Virginia cohabitation statute were at issue instead? Perhaps not, and that statute remained on the books. At least formally there is a distinction that might make a difference between the two; that is, apart from simply performing morally distasteful acts in private, a cohabiting couple is openly violating the state's marriage law by dispensing with a marriage license as a prerequisite for setting up house together. On the other hand, *Lawrence* is widely seen as a case about freedom of intimate association,[30] and subjecting cohabitants to the possibility of criminal sanctions substantially interferes with such freedom.

Were our system of laws simply based on logic, states would have scurried to repeal the remaining laws against both fornication and cohabitation after

---

27. Powell v. State, 510 S.E.2d 18 (Ga. 1998), *cited in In re* J. M., 575 S.E.2d at 442; Bowers v. Hardwick, 478 U.S. 186 (1986).

28. Lawrence v. Texas, 539 U.S. 558, 577–78 (2003).

29. Martin v. Ziherl, 607 S.E.2d 367, 368 (Va. 2005).

30. *See, e.g.,* Lawrence H. Tribe, *"The Fundamental Right" That Dare Not Speak Its Name*, 117 HARV. L. REV. 1893, 1903–04 (2004); Katherine M. Franke, *The Domesticated Liberty of Lawrence v. Texas*, 104 COLUM. L. REV. 1399, 1408 (2004).

the decision in *Lawrence*. But there is no pressure to do so because the laws are so seldom used. Often it takes embarrassing publicity over some current case to provoke a legislature to repeal its statute. For example, on March 25, 2000, an article appeared in the *New York Times* about a prosecution for unlawful cohabitation in New Mexico.[31] Mr. Pitcher and Ms. Henry, recovering from their respective divorces, were living together. Mr. Pitcher's previous wife swore out a complaint with the police and paid a $25 fee, thereby putting in motion a criminal charge of cohabitation against the couple. Although his ex-wife had herself lived with Mr. Pitcher for six years before they married, she had become a born-again Christian and professed to be worried about the moral climate created for their daughter by her ex-husband's cohabitation. Ms. Henry, one of the defending cohabitants, commented that if the law were really enforced, "the whole state would be in jail." The local district attorney agreed with her, saying that his office would likely find some way to dismiss the case. This drama played out in the national press just one month after the Arizona legislature had refused to repeal the cohabitation statute, which a committee chair described as armor against the "decaying fabric of society." Nonetheless, in 2001, the New Mexico statute was repealed, and Arizona followed suit.[32] But unless cohabitation statutes become the subject of embarrassing public attention, they are unlikely to appear high upon the agenda of state legislatures.

Moreover, it is tricky to mount a challenge to fornication and cohabitation statutes. The lack of prosecution under these laws results in the absence of persons with a motive to litigate such a challenge. Moreover, even if someone were prosecuted and convicted, the sentence is likely to be so minor— typically a fine—that it does not pay to undertake the costs of hiring an attorney to appeal. Perhaps most important, though, potential litigants must navigate the shoal of establishing standing to sue. Standing is a constitutional doctrine that requires a litigant to show that he or she will be sufficiently harmed by the law challenged to be allowed to bring the case.[33] One 1986 case challenging the constitutionality of Virginia's laws against fornication and cohabitation foundered upon lack of standing because the laws

31. Jim Yardley, N.M. J.; *Unmarried and Living Together, Till the Sheriff Do Us Part*, N.Y. TIMES, Mar. 25, 2000, at A9.

32. ARIZ. REV. STAT. ANN. § 13-1409, *repealed by* Laws 2001, Ch. 382, § 1; N.M. STAT. § 30-10-2, *repealed by* Laws 2001, Ch. 32, § 1.

33. *See, e.g.*, Frothingham v. Mellon, 262 U.S. 447 (1923).

were so rarely enforced. Evidence showed that the last conviction for fornication in Virginia was in 1849, and none of the police witnesses could recall a cohabitation arrest since 1976. As a result, the court found that the plaintiffs faced only the most theoretical threat of prosecution under the law, which was not a substantial enough harm to confer upon them standing to challenge it.[34] The plaintiff in a subsequent case did succeed in getting the Virginia Supreme Court to overturn the fornication statute but only because lack of standing had not been raised as a defense in the trial court and had thus been waived.[35]

Consequently, as of 2006, a total of sixteen jurisdictions in the United States still had laws against either fornication or cohabitation on the books, although they were probably all unconstitutional. There are obvious dangers presented by their continued existence, for the laws may be used, as they were in Wisconsin, as threats used by prosecutors in effecting other goals. The fact of illegality may also be used as a weapon in custody battles at and after divorce, and their use to show bad character is directed more often against women than against men.[36] Moreover, discrimination against unmarried couples in other arenas is more difficult to combat if these laws remain on the books. In states where cohabitation is illegal, for example, refusals to rent to unmarried couples have been upheld against challenge under local antidiscrimination laws that make discrimination on grounds of marital status illegal.[37]

One scholarly treatment of the interrelationship of sex, crime, and law summed this all up as early as 1977, concluding that "Laws against consensual adult sex . . . are unenforceable, victimize some persons by selective or discriminatory enforcement, are used for harassment . . ., do not discourage the activities . . ., may lead to blackmail and police corruption, and have other ill effects." They also "encourage disrespect for all law."[38]

---

34. Doe v. Duling, 782 F.2d 1202, 1206 (4th Cir. 1986).

35. Martin v. Ziherl, 607 S.E.2d at 368–69.

36. *See, e.g.,* Sullivan v. Stringer, 736 So. 2d 514 (Miss. Ct. App. 1999); Jarrett v. Jarrett, 400 N.E.2d 421 (Ill. 1979); *see also* MacNamara & Sagarin, *supra* note 2, at 187 (discussing the differential impact by gender).

37. *See, e.g.,* N.D. Fair Hous. Council v. Peterson, 625 N.W.2d 551 (N.D. 2001); Cooper v. French, 460 N.W.2d 2 (Minn. 1990).

38. MacNamara & Sagarin, *supra* note 2, at 194, 198.

⁊ 2. Common Law Marriage and Related Fictions

Keeping out of criminal court, however, was only one problem faced by cohabitants in the United States. Now that decriminalization has become the trend, other problems come into more prominence. For couples who live together without marriage, numerous legal dilemmas present themselves. Traditionally, one of the major issues was the status of their children as illegitimate, or bastards, with a stigma attached to the status and without the rights of support, inheritance, or other benefits attendant upon having married parents.[39] Since the 1960s, however, the Supreme Court has struck down almost every distinction based on legitimacy of parentage as violating the Equal Protection Clause.[40] Nonmarital children now clearly have rights to support and other legal remedies, although states may treat them differently than marital children in relation to inheritance.[41] So the stigma of bastardy need no longer be a major impetus to formal marriage.

Numerous other problems remain. What is to happen if the relationship ends in death or separation? Traditionally, and still in almost every state, unmarried partners have no rights to support, division of property, or inheritance. And, no matter how functionally similar their union may be to a married family, they will not be treated as such by the multitude of laws dependent upon marital status—taxation, social security, and tort remedies such as loss of consortium and negligent infliction of emotional distress, for example. Yet many of those involved in informal unions in fact believe that they are entitled to be treated, after a certain period of time, as though they

39. HARRY D. KRAUSE, ILLEGITIMACY, LAW AND SOCIAL POLICY 22 (Bobbs-Merrill 1971). *See also* 1 WILLIAM BLACKSTONE, COMMENTARIES *446–47.

40. Levy v. Louisiana, 391 U.S. 68 (1968) (holding that to deny recovery to nonmarital child for Wrongful Death Act claim for death of mother was unconstitutional); Glona v. Am. Guar. & Liab. Ins. Co., 391 U.S. 73 (1968) (holding that mother could also recover under Wrongful Death for death of nonmarital child); Weber v. Aetna Cas. & Sur. Co., 406 U.S. 164 (1972) (permitting recovery by nonmarital child for death of father under state workers' compensation law).

41. Labine v. Vincent, 401 U.S. 532 (1971) (holding that denial of right of intestate succession to nonmarital child did not violate equal protection or due process); Lalli v. Lalli, 439 U.S. 259 (1978) (holding that it is constitutional to require judicial finding of paternity during unmarried father's lifetime for nonmarital child to inherit); *but see* Trimble v. Gordon, 430 U.S. 762 (1977) (holding that it is unconstitutional to allow inheritance by intestate succession from mother but not from father).

were formally married.[42] One can only understand the persistence of this belief by reference to the history of common law marriage in the United States.[43]

Unlike countries in Europe, which abolished the institution centuries ago,[44] the majority of states in the United States recognized common law marriage well into the nineteenth century.[45] Common law marriage, continuing the ancient tradition of informal marriage, does not require a ceremony or registration by the state. Instead, heterosexual cohabitants who agree to live as man and wife and do so, holding themselves out to the community as spouses, are treated as married for all purposes under law, both state and federal.[46] Some courts simply infer the requisite agreement from the parties' cohabitation and "holding out."[47]

Common law marriage was imported into the law of some of the original American colonies from English law (it was not abolished in England until 1753). Although the courts of some colonies (Massachusetts, for example) interpreted their colony's own marriage statute as abrogating informal marriages, others (New York, for example) held that common law marriages continued to be valid.[48] Common law marriages were often found in the

---

42. Colleagues with experience at legal assistance clinics confirm that female clients typically believe that if they had lived with someone for several years, they were legally married. *See also* Ginny Carroll, *Marriage by Another Name*, NEWSWEEK, July 24, 1989, at 46 (reporting that law students informally surveyed at one law school believe the same); Ellen Kandoian, *Cohabitation, Common Law Marriage, and the Possibility of a Shared Moral Life*, 75 GEO. L.J. 1829, 1862 n.141 (1987) (reporting that those who frequent food pantries in New York City refer to their "common-law" spouses although the state does not recognize that legal status).

43. For a definitive and comprehensive history of the institution of common-law marriage in the ancient and modern world, *see* GÖRAN LIND, COMMON LAW MARRIAGE: A LEGAL INSTITUTION FOR COHABITATION (Oxford Univ. Press 2008).

44. Informal marriage was no longer recognized in the Roman Catholic countries of Western Europe after the Council of Trent in 1563, and England abolished common-law marriage by passage of Lord Hardwicke's Act in 1753. *See* OTTO E. KOEGEL, COMMON LAW MARRIAGE AND ITS DEVELOPMENT IN THE UNITED STATES 22 (J. Byrne & Co. 1922); HOMER H. CLARK, JR., THE LAW OF DOMESTIC RELATIONS IN THE UNITED STATES 22–23 (West Publishing Co. 2d ed. 1988).

45. For a list of states that recognized common-law marriages, *see* Cynthia Grant Bowman, *A Feminist Proposal to Bring Back Common Law Marriage*, 75 OR. L. REV. 709, 715 n. 24 (1996).

46. *See* CLARK, *supra* note 44, at 48, 50.

47. *See, e.g.*, Metro. Life Ins. Co. v. Johnson, 645 P.2d 356, 361 (Idaho 1982).

48. Commonwealth v. Munson, 127 Mass. 459, 460–61 (1879) (holding that common-law marriage had never been valid in Massachusetts); Fenton v. Reed, 4 Johns. 52 (N.Y. Sup. Ct. 1809)

frontier territories and states, where institutions of civil government were inadequate. Indeed, courts and some commentators have attributed the institution of common law marriage in the United States to "frontier conditions," although this thesis is incapable of explaining its persistence in New York City and its absence in Wyoming.[49] The story is much more complicated in this diverse nation, involving legal and popular traditions about marriage in states and territories previously governed by Spain or Mexico, Native American traditions of informal marriage, and the prohibition of marriages between slaves and persons of different races.[50] For our purposes, it suffices to say that recognition of informal marriages was common in states conquered from Mexico, states with large Native American populations, and in former slave-holding states.[51]

Between 1875 and 2009, a total of twenty-three states abolished common law marriage.[52] Their reasons for doing so varied. Certainly the urbanization

---

(holding that common-law marriage was valid under New York law because it had been valid in English common law at time of its reception); *see also* Meister v. Moore, 96 U.S. 76 (1877) (adopting an interpretation similar to that in Fenton v. Reed in a case interpreting Michigan law).

49. *See, e.g.*, McChesney v. Johnson, 79 S.W.2d 658, 659 (Tex. 1934) (attributing the institution of common-law marriage to sparse settlement, difficulty of travel, and lack of persons with the authority to officiate at formal marriages); MICHAEL GROSSBERG, GOVERNING THE HEARTH: LAW AND THE FAMILY IN NINETEENTH-CENTURY AMERICA 69–78 (Univ. of N.C. Press 1985) (attributing informal marriage to spirit of frontier individualism); Roberts v. Roberts (*In re* Roberts' Estate), 133 P.2d 492, 502 (Wyo. 1943).

50. For a detailed description of this variegated heritage, *see* Bowman, *supra* note 45, at 724–31, 737–39.

51. *See, e.g.*, Woodrow Borah & Sherburne F. Cook, *Marriage and Legitimacy in Mexican Culture: Mexico and California*, 54 CAL. L. REV. 946 (1966); Walter O. Weyrauch, *Informal Marriage and Common Law Marriage, in* SEXUAL BEHAVIOR AND THE LAW 302 (Ralph Slovenko ed., Thomas 1965) (suggesting that presence of a large Native American population inclined jurisdictions to recognize common law marriage); LAWRENCE M. FRIEDMAN, A HISTORY OF AMERICAN LAW 496 (2d ed. Simon & Schuster 1985) (commenting that about half of the former slave-holding states recognized common law marriage, which was almost a necessity for them because slaves had not been allowed by the state to marry); MAXWELL BLOOMFIELD, AMERICAN LAWYERS IN A CHANGING SOCIETY, 1776–1876 109–10 (Harvard Univ. Press 1976) (describing how courts recognized previous informal marriages of freed slaves as common law marriages).

52. Eight states abolished common law marriage between 1875 and 1917, and at least fifteen more have done so since 1920, primarily out of fears of fraudulent claims and to protect the institution of marriage. Bowman, *supra* note 45, at 715 n. 24 (1997); *see also* PA. CONS. STAT. ANN. § 1103 (2005); IDAHO CODE ANN. § 32-201 (1996). There is some confusion about the status of common-law marriage in Oklahoma, where statute law seems to prohibit it, but the Oklahoma Supreme Court appears to recognize it. *See* OKLA. STAT. tit. 43, §§ 4, 7; Standefer v. Standefer, 26 P.2d 104 (Okla. 2001).

and industrialization of the country played a role, as the developing economy demanded security of title to property, which could be uncertain if it depended upon marriages that were not registered with the state.[53] Racism, class prejudice, and eugenics were also influential in the movement to abolish common law marriage. Eugenicists in the late-nineteenth century urged formal marriage as a way not only to enforce compliance with health regulations but also to prevent the marriage of undesirables.[54] Common law marriage was seen by the writers of sociological texts as uncivilized and lower class. It was prevalent among African Americans, these authors said, because they were guided by emotion rather than reason or morality and incompletely assimilated into the superior moral standards of European Americans.[55]

Courts (as well as the government commission that recommended abolition of common law marriage in New York State) were also obsessed with the specter of fraudulent claims brought by "gold-digging women," particularly after the death of an alleged common law husband.[56] These fears do not appear to have been very well founded. In fact, the recorded cases indicate that it was more common for women to be deceived by men into believing they were married and then abandoned without any legal remedy, as often

---

53. *See* Bowman, *supra* note 45, at 732–36; Friedman, *supra* note 51, at 496 ("For business reasons—especially the needs of the land market—it would be helpful if marriage was a matter of record, formally created, formally dissolved.").

54. *See, e.g.,* Hesseltine v. McLaughlin (*In re* McLaughlin's Estate), 30 P. 651, 658 (1892) (connecting nonrecognition of common law marriages with society's need to prevent marriages that would lead "to pauperism, crime and transmission of hereditary diseases and defects."); *see also* Ploscowe, *supra* note 3, at 23–24 (arguing against recognition of common law marriage for similar reasons).

55. *See* John Sirjamaki, The American Family in the Twentieth Century 69 (Harvard Univ. Press 1953) (reporting that common law marriages were numerous among lower-class African Americans and whites and in matriarchal families); Meyer F. Nimkoff, Marriage and the Family 219 (Houghton Mifflin Co. 1947) (describing African Americans as unassimilated and governed by sentiment and expedience rather than morals).

56. *See* Bowman, *supra* note 45, at 741–43; *see also* Morone v. Morone, 413 N.E.2d 1154, 1157 (N.Y. 1980) (describing abolition of common law marriage in New York); Collins v. Hoag & Rollins, Inc., 241 N.W. 766, 767 (Neb. 1932) (stating that common-law marriage was abolished in Nebraska because of the "common knowledge that for many years the estates of deceased persons have been despoiled by persons claiming to be a common-law spouse of decedent, or an heir-at-law of decedent, born of a common-law marriage"). *In re* Estate of Erlanger, 145 Misc. 1 (N.Y. Co. Surrogate's Ct. 1932), was the highly-publicized case that led to abolition of common law marriage in New York. *See* Ariela R. Dubler, *Wifely Behavior: A Legal History of Acting Married*, 100 Colum. L. Rev. 957, 974–1009 (2000).

happened in states that did not recognize the institution of common law marriage.[57] It also appears from the case law that the legal standard for common law marriage worked quite well in distinguishing meritorious from nonmeritorious or fraudulent claims.[58]

Two additional concerns that contributed to the abolition of common law marriage have been inherited by those who oppose the extension of legal rights to cohabitants today: the fear of a perceived threat to the institution of marriage and a concern about the administrative burden upon courts and administrative agencies in the absence of marriage formalities. Courts in the past repeatedly warned that recognition of common law marriage would "weaken the public estimate of the sanctity of the marriage relation"[59] and "encourage formation of such relationships and weaken marriage as the foundation of our family-based society."[60] This criticism seems inapt in the context of common law marriage, given that it in fact constituted a legal marriage, although it was entered into without a ceremony and license. To the extent that this is a complaint about the formation of alternative family structures, it mirrors arguments made against legal protection for cohabitants today. But in both cases it is nonrecognition that in fact debases long-term relationships by, for example, allowing one partner to walk away with all of the couple's accumulated wealth should their relationship end. The conclusion that recognition of common law marriage will discourage persons from marrying, moreover, is simply inconsistent with the evidence that the number of licensed marriages in states recognizing common law marriage was in fact higher than that in nonrecognizing jurisdictions.[61]

Concerns about administrative convenience and fraud in relation to government benefits arose with the growth of benefit programs that turned upon marital status—widows' benefits after World War I, for example; social security survivors' claims; and workers' compensation. Informal marriages generated litigation, just as modern-day cohabitants' claims do.[62] A review of

---

57. *See* Bowman, *supra* note 45, at 754–57.

58. *Id.* at 742–43, 750–51.

59. *In re* Estate of Soeder, 220 N.E.2d 547, 561 (Ohio Ct. App. 1966) (quoting Sorensen v. Sorensen, 100 N.W. 930, 932 (Neb. 1904)).

60. Hewitt v. Hewitt, 394 N.E.2d 1204, 1207 (Ill. 1979).

61. Weyrauch, *supra* note 51, at 308–09.

62. *See, e.g.,* Johnson v. Green, 309 S.E.2d 362, 363 (Ga. 1983) (reporting 105 appellate cases on common law marriage in Georgia between 1955 and 1983).

the cases, however, shows that most of them did not involve frivolous claims but rather claims the legal system *should* see as its role to address.[63] In the end, moreover, arguments about administrative and judicial efficiency can be evaluated only by asking whether these concerns are outweighed by other values.

Eleven U.S. jurisdictions still recognized common law marriage as of 2009—Alabama, Colorado, the District of Columbia, Iowa, Kansas, Montana, Oklahoma, Rhode Island, South Carolina, Texas, and Utah.[64] The doctrine is influential beyond the borders of the states that recognize it, however. If a relationship fits the doctrinal criteria and was entered into in a jurisdiction recognizing common law marriage, the marriage will be considered valid in a nonrecognizing state as well.[65] Indeed, some states' courts, such as that of New York, have traditionally bent over backwards to find common law marriages even when a couple has spent relatively brief periods in a recognizing jurisdiction during their union.[66] The persistence of common law marriage in some jurisdictions thus has protected many cohabitants in the event of divorce, inheritance, and the receipt of government benefits, especially women, persons of nonwhite color, and poor people.[67]

Faced with cases in which great hardship might result from failure to recognize a long-term relationship as a marriage, courts have also applied a number of remedial doctrines to protect a vulnerable party in some circumstances. The only one that approaches the protections of marriage is the putative spouse doctrine. Under this doctrine, a party who in good faith believes herself (usually it was a female in this position) to be married but is in fact not legally married because of some irregularity affecting the validity

---

63. Bowman, *supra* note 45, 741–43 (1996).

64. *Id.* at 715 n. 24. Pennsylvania and Idaho have since abolished common law marriage. 23 PA. CONS. STAT. ANN. § 1103 (2005); IDAHO CODE ANN. § 32-201 (1996); *see also* Standefer v. Standefer, 26 P.3d 104 (Okla. 2001) (recognizing common law marriage although Oklahoma statute seems to prohibit).

65. Under the *lex loci*, the validity of a marriage is determined by the law of the state in which it was entered, unless it is against a strong public policy of the forum. *See* CLARK, *supra* note 44, at 47, 57–59.

66. *See, e.g.*, Ram v. Ramharack, 571 N.Y.S.2d 190, 192 (N.Y. Sup. Ct. 1991) (upholding common law marriage where couple visited relatives in the District of Columbia several times a year); Coney v. R.S.R. Corp., 563 N.Y.S.2d 211, 211–12 (N.Y. App. Div. 1990) (upholding common law marriage where couple spent three days with relatives in Georgia).

67. *See* Bowman, *supra* note 45, at 754–70.

of the marriage ceremony or license is treated as though married.[68] The case often used to illustrate this doctrine is that of Mr. Vargas, who had a wife and children in one locale and then went through a marriage ceremony with another woman, setting up a separate household with her in another town; children were also born to this marriage.[69] The second marriage, of course, was invalid because of bigamy. Amazingly, neither woman suspected the deception until Mr. Vargas died, when there were two widows laying claim to his estate. The court deciding the matter held that the second Mrs. Vargas was a putative spouse because she believed in good faith that they were married, and the judge split the estate equally between the two women because all of the Vargas assets had been accumulated during the period when he had been "married" to both.

Although treatment may vary from state to state, a common law spouse may be a putative spouse as well—for example, a wife who believes herself to be validly, though informally, married under common law to a man who never told her he was not divorced from a previous spouse.[70] In this situation, a valid common law marriage would not exist because he was without capacity to enter into a marriage, but the putative spouse doctrine could protect the innocent party.

In short, common law marriage and a variety of other doctrines worked to protect many persons involved in cohabiting unions in the past.[71] All of these depended upon the couple (or one member in the case of a putative spouse) believing themselves to be and holding themselves out to the community as married, for example, by consistently introducing themselves as man and wife. With the greater acceptance of unmarried cohabitation over the last several decades, this has become much rarer. Most cohabitants do not believe themselves to be married in the eyes of the law, and they typically refer to themselves as partners rather than spouses. Thus, the work that the

---

68. The status would disappear once she discovered that the marriage was invalid; it worked only while she was unaware of it. *See, e.g.,* Lassarevich v. Lassarevich, 200 P.2d 49, 55–56 (Cal. Ct. App. 1948) (holding that plaintiff was no longer a putative wife for the period of seven months after she discovered that they had not in fact been married for the previous twelve years).

69. Vargas v. Vargas (*In re* Estate of Vargas), 111 Cal. Rptr. 779 (Cal. Ct. App. 1974).

70. *See, e.g., In re* Estate of Marson, 120 P.3d 382 (Mont. 2005).

71. Courts also used a variety of evidentiary presumptions about the existence of a marriage and, in Tennessee, the doctrine of marriage by estoppel. Smith v. North Memphis Sav. Bank, 89 S.W. 392, 397 (Tenn. 1905).

common law marriage doctrine performed in the past is a load it can no longer carry.

🎗 3. Denial of Benefits to Cohabitants: A Case Study of Illinois

With the abolition of common law marriage in state after state, the traditional position was that cohabitants simply had no rights at all vis-à-vis one another or third parties. Three states—Illinois, Georgia, and Louisiana—still adhere to this position.[72] I will use the case law of Illinois to illustrate the situation in which cohabitants may find themselves in such a jurisdiction.

The case invariably used to illustrate the Illinois position is a stark one, *Hewitt v. Hewitt*.[73] Victoria and Robert Hewitt began their relationship as students at Grinnell College. When Victoria got pregnant, Robert told her "that they were husband and wife and would live as such, no formal ceremony being necessary, and that he would 'share his life, his future, his earning and his property' with her," an accurate description of the agreement required for a common law marriage, which was and is recognized in Iowa.[74] Not long after, the couple moved to Illinois, where he went to dental school (for which her parents paid) and eventually established a lucrative practice; she served as homemaker and mother to their children, while assisting him in building his practice, including working in his pedodontia office and depositing her pay into their common account. After fifteen years, they separated. Mrs. Hewitt, apparently believing that they were married (by common law), initially sued for divorce.[75] The trial court dismissed the divorce action; and

---

72. *See* Katherine C. Gordon, Note, *The Necessity and Enforcement of Cohabitation Agreements: When Strings Will Attach and How to Prevent Them—A State Survey*, 37 BRANDEIS L.J. 245, 253–54 (1998-99) (describing states which offer no recognition to express or implied contracts or equitable remedies for cohabitants). Oddly, Georgia did recognize a contract partitioning property between two lesbian cohabitants in Crooke v. Gilden, 414 S.E.2d 645 (Ga. 1992).

73. Hewitt v. Hewitt, 394 N.E.2d 1204 (Ill. 1979).

74. *Id.* at 1205.

75. A common law marriage validly entered in Iowa should have been recognized by the Illinois court as a marriage; however, the Hewitts apparently left Iowa and returned to Illinois very soon after their agreement so that it would have been difficult to show that they lived together in Iowa. ELIZABETH H. PLECK, SHACKING UP: COHABITATION AND THE SEXUAL REVOLUTION 1962 TO 1990, unpublished manuscript on file with author.

when she amended to add alternative causes of action in contract and for unjust enrichment, seeking one half of the couple's accumulated property, it dismissed that complaint as well, on the grounds that any such claim required a valid marriage.[76] The appellate court reversed, and Mr. Hewitt appealed to the Illinois Supreme Court. In its opinion, that court reasoned that to give Mrs. Hewitt any rights at all would denigrate the institution of marriage and in effect bring back common law marriage, which Illinois had abolished in 1905.[77] Thus, the Supreme Court held, Mrs. Hewitt was entitled to no remedy at all and specifically not to any property distribution or support payments. In short, after a 15-year period of reliance upon and contribution to a relationship that resembled a conventional marriage in every way, Mrs. Hewitt was left without anything. The principle of upholding traditional marriage was more important than her rights, said the court:

> Of substantially greater importance than the rights of the immediate parties is the impact of such recognition upon our society and the institution of marriage. Will the fact that legal rights closely resembling those arising from conventional marriages can be acquired by those who deliberately choose to enter into what have heretofore been commonly referred to as "illicit" or "meretricious" relationships encourage formation of such relationships and weaken marriage as the foundation of our family-based society? In the event of death shall the survivor have the status of a surviving spouse for purposes of inheritance, wrongful death actions, workmen's compensation, etc.? And still more importantly: what of the children born of such relationships? What are their support and inheritance rights and by what standards are custody questions resolved? What of the sociological and psychological effects upon them of that type of environment?[78]

In short, after pointing out all the problems, including those posed for the spouse and children of a Mr. Hewitt in the absence of legal recognition of their relationship, the court opted to deny any claims based on Mrs. Hewitt's quasi-marital status because "We cannot confidently say that judicial recognition of property rights between unmarried cohabitants will not make that alternative to marriage more attractive by allowing the parties to engage in

---

76. *Hewitt*, 394 N.E.2d at 1206.

77. *Id.* at 1209–11.

78. *Id.* at 1207–08.

such relationships with greater security."[79] In other words, giving Mrs. Hewitt compensation for her contributions to this relationship (which she in fact regarded as a marriage) might lead many others to dispense with marriage and enter cohabiting unions instead.

Hewitt was followed and, indeed, extended in *Ayala v. Fox* in 1990.[80] In this case, two heterosexual cohabitants built a house together. Based on his oral promise of joint tenancy and half the equity if they ended their relationship, she undertook the mortgage and paid the majority of the principal, interest, taxes, and insurance. Ten years later, the couple separated, and the title was discovered to be in his name only. She sued, alleging breach of contract and unjust enrichment, only to be denied recovery based upon *Hewitt*'s nonrecognition of property rights for cohabitants.

The only exception Illinois courts are willing to make is for situations where the claims of a cohabitant can be seen as independent of the non-marital and "meretricious" relationship of the parties. In one case, for example, the plaintiff during her six-year cohabitation with defendant had provided most of the funds to purchase two automobiles and two motorcycles which were then titled in the defendant's name because he said the insurance premiums would be cheaper that way.[81] She sued to recover. Under these circumstances, the court did find that to allow the defendant to keep all the vehicles would constitute unjust enrichment, and it imposed a constructive trust upon the property, which was to be regarded as held in trust for the benefit of the other party. Thus, the plaintiff's claim was recognized in this case—but only because, as the *Hewitt* court itself had recognized, unmarried cohabitants are not precluded "from forming valid contracts about independent matters, for which sexual relations do not form part of the consideration."[82] In short, the specifically identifiable monetary investments one partner may make in property that appears to be separate from the meretricious nature of their relationship—as motorcycles apparently are but homes are not—may be recognized and compensated. Ordinary housewives like Mrs. Hewitt are out of luck.

---

79. *Id.* at 1209.

80. 564 N.E.2d 920 (Ill. App. Ct. 1990); *but see* Spafford v. Coats, 455 N.E.2d 241 (Ill. App. Ct. 1983) (recognizing claim under constructive trust theory for several automobiles registered in partner's name because plaintiff had furnished most of the consideration and obtained financing).

81. *Spafford*, 455 N.E.2d 241.

82. *Id.* at 245.

Results in these cases may depend, of course, upon the individual judge's conclusions about the nature of the investment made by the contributing cohabitant—a subjective judgment leading to seemingly inconsistent results. In 2000, the Illinois appellate court was presented with another case in which a cohabitant had contributed to a mortgage on property titled in her partner's name. Rather than directly paying the mortgage on a monthly basis, as in *Ayala*, she gave all of her savings to her partner when he asked for it, saying that it would be a "safe investment" and that he would pay it back when the property was sold.[83] He paid off his mortgage on his house with it but refused to return the $47,188.38 when she moved out a year later. Even though the plaintiff had cohabited with him and served as a homemaker, doing shopping, making meals, and taking care of both the house and the yard, the appellate court interpreted this situation differently from that in *Ayala*. It distinguished the case before it because the plaintiff was asking for the return of a lump sum, "money had and returned," under a theory of either implied contract or quasi-contract.[84] As a result, even though the money was for the home in which they cohabited, the court saw this as a contract severable from their relationship as cohabitants—a distinction that might not make a difference to ordinary folks.

Lest there be any doubt whether cases like this have made inroads upon the essential holding of *Hewitt*, the 2006 decision in *Costa v. Oliven* showed that *Hewitt*'s extremely negative treatment of cohabitants is still the law in Illinois. On May 17, 2006, the Appellate Court for the Second District, whose jurisdiction covers the mostly affluent suburbs to the west of Chicago, decided a case brought by a male cohabitant who had lived with a woman for twenty-four years while she created her own corporation, acting as a stay-at-home parent for their daughter, whom he home-schooled while running the household in order to allow his partner to work full time.[85] Title to almost everything the couple possessed was listed in Ms. Oliven's name when she demanded that he vacate their home in 2004. Because Mr. Costa's contribution to their very long-term partnership was that of a homemaker, the court held that the case was controlled by *Hewitt* and denied him any remedy. Perhaps the reversal of gender roles influenced its decision as well.

---

83. Kaiser v. Fleming, 735 N.E2d 144 (Ill. App. Ct. 2000).

84. *Id.* at 147.

85. Costa v. Oliven, 849 N.E.2d 122 (Ill. App. Ct. 2006).

In short, states like Illinois refuse to extend any recognition to cohabitants because to do so, they believe, would somehow harm the institution of marriage. This reasoning is open to dispute, of course. Just the opposite may in fact be true. To deny property and support rights to cohabitants in fact creates an incentive for unscrupulous individuals to *avoid* marriage—Mr. Hewitt, Mr. Fox, and Ms. Oliven were all able to extract the benefit of their partners' contributions and get away with all of the couple's accumulated wealth.

The Illinois cases discussed thus far dealt primarily with the equitable distribution of property at the end of long-term cohabiting relationships. Other remedies available to married couples are also denied to cohabitants in Illinois. Alimony, or maintenance, is not available. This rule led to an unintended ironic result in one case. The question at issue was whether a divorced woman who was cohabiting with another man could continue to receive alimony from her prior spouse.[86] At the time of this case, the Illinois Marriage and Dissolution of Marriage Act provided, as does the law of many states, that alimony payments from an ex-spouse terminate upon remarriage of the spouse receiving the alimony. As a consequence, an appellate court held in 1984 that, because common law marriage was invalid in Illinois, cohabitation would not constitute grounds to terminate alimony.[87] The legislature rushed to change the statute so as to overturn the case law which would have permitted support payments to a cohabiting ex-wife to continue.[88] The act was changed to provide, as it still does, that "the obligation to pay future maintenance is terminated upon the death of either party, or the remarriage of the party receiving maintenance, *or if the party receiving maintenance cohabits with another person on a resident, continuing conjugal basis.*"[89] In short, logic—in the form of a consistent recognition that cohabitation should have no legal consequences comparable to marriage—briefly interfered with the state's determination to treat cohabitants as negatively as possible, for cohabitants could continue to receive alimony until the statute was amended.

With the addition of the provision that alimony should terminate upon cohabitation "on a resident, continuing conjugal basis," the focus of the cases has shifted to what is and what is not resident, continuing, and conjugal.

---

86. Atwater v. Atwater, 309 N.E.2d 632 (Ill. App. Ct. 1974).

87. *Id.* at 640.

88. *See In re* Marriage of Sappington, 462 N.E.2d 881, 883 (Ill. App. Ct. 1984).

89. 750 ILL. COMP. STAT. ANN. 5/510(c) (West 1999) (emphasis added).

Residence 50 percent of the time was held in one case to be noncontinuous,[90] while six weeks full-time residence with a formally married man was found to be enough to terminate alimony in another case.[91] Sexual intercourse between the cohabitants is a necessary element, though, so if the new partner is impotent, alimony will not cease.[92]

Unless seen simply as reflecting the state's determination to treat cohabitation negatively in every respect, this case law makes little sense. Why should it matter if the new partner is impotent if he is in fact contributing financially to the ex-spouse's support? On the other hand, if alimony is intended to relieve the financial need of a prior spouse, her economic situation can be assessed independently, rather than using cohabitation as a proxy. The economics of the situation are unlikely to bear much relationship to the precise amount of time she spends with the new cohabiting partner or whether they have a sexual relationship regarded as normal (no impotence) in the eyes of the court. And if, as a number of scholars now opine, alimony is a form of compensation for contributions to a past marriage,[93] cohabitation is certainly not relevant to that. Nonetheless, the courts of Illinois have consistently adhered to this position, with its underlying implication that women are simply handed over economically from one man to another.

Reason does seem to have prevailed, however, with respect to cohabitation and the custody of children, at least in the long run. Jacqueline Jarrett had the misfortune to have hers be the first case to reach the Illinois Supreme Court after *Hewitt*. At her divorce in 1976, Mrs. Jarrett had received custody of her three children, only to be served with a petition for change of custody seven months later, on the grounds that her boyfriend had moved in with her.[94] She did not intend to marry him, she testified, because it was too soon and because the divorce decree required her to sell the family home within six months after remarriage and her children wanted to live there. The circuit court accepted her ex-husband's argument that her living arrangements created an environment that was not good for the moral and spiritual welfare of their three daughters, although they were doing well in every other respect, and transferred custody of the girls to their father. As in *Hewitt*, the appellate

---

90. Schoenhard v. Schoenhard, 392 N.E.2d 764, 768 (Ill. App. Ct. 1979).

91. *In re* Marriage of Roofe, 460 N.E.2d 784, 785 (Ill. App. Ct. 1984).

92. *In re* Marriage of Sappington, 462 N.E.2d at 882–84.

93. *See, e.g.,* Ira Mark Ellman, *The Theory of Alimony*, 77 CAL. L. REV. 1, 40–77 (1989).

94. Jarrett v. Jarrett, 400 N.E.2d 421 (Ill. 1979), *cert. denied*, 449 U.S. 927 (1980).

court reversed, finding that the trial court judge had improperly transferred custody based upon his own personal moral beliefs.[95]

Mr. Jarrett appealed, citing Roman Catholic moral teachings in his brief, while his ex-wife quoted census statistics to the effect that 1.1 million households were composed of opposite-sex cohabitants in 1978, and a quarter of them included at least one child—rather modest numbers compared with those today.[96] These "dueling briefs" led one commentator to see the *Jarrett* case as symptomatic of the culture wars of the '80s.[97]

The case was soon back before the same court that had decided *Hewitt* one year earlier. Relying upon its recent opinion in *Hewitt*, as well as upon the state's criminal statute against cohabitation and "open and notorious" fornication, the Illinois Supreme Court reversed the appellate court and affirmed the trial court's removal of custody from Mrs. Jarrett, commenting that:

> Jacqueline's disregard for existing standards of conduct instructs her children, by example, that they, too, may ignore them and could well encourage the children to engage in similar activity in the future. That factor, of course, supports the trial court's conclusion that their daily presence in that environment was injurious to the moral well-being and development of the children.[98]

In short, it was unnecessary to prove that the children had been harmed by living with their mother and her partner; the court could simply assume that.

A shudder of fear went through the divorced mothers of Illinois, as their ex-husbands were handed a weapon which they could either use to gain custody or employ the threat of doing so as a tactic to defend against petitions to increase alimony or child support. Lesbian mothers, especially, could never be secure in their custody, for none of their post-divorce relationships could ever be more than nonmarital cohabitation. Application of the *Jarrett* precedent by the courts during the 1980s, moreover, revealed a bias against cohabitation by mothers, while overlooking comparable behavior by their ex-husbands.[99] Mothers were supposed to be asexual, at least in the eyes of

---

95. Jarrett v. Jarrett, 382 N.E.2d 12, 16 (Ill. Ct. App. 1978).

96. *Id.* at 424.

97. PLECK, *supra* note 75.

98. *Id.* at 424.

99. *See In re* Marriage of Thompson, 449 N.E.2d 88 (Ill. 1983) (awarding custody to father who had openly cohabited with child in residence); *see also In re* Marriage of Lawver, 402 N.E.2d

their children, while fathers were not. As noncustodial parents for the most part, fathers also have more opportunity to be sexual beings.

The courts of Illinois quickly drew back from the most extreme implications of *Jarrett*, pointing out that the best interest of the child was always paramount in custody decisions, not the living arrangements of their mothers, and holding that petitions for change of custody, in particular, require proof of changed circumstances that endanger the welfare of the child.[100] Indeed, the Illinois Supreme Court soon distanced itself from its own extreme position, stating in a 1983 case (seemingly contrary to a sensible reading of the language in *Jarrett*) that, "The *Jarrett* case does not establish a conclusive presumption that, because a custodial parent cohabits with a member of the opposite sex, the child is harmed."[101] The Illinois Marriage and Dissolution of Marriage Act now provides that courts should "not consider conduct of a present or proposed custodian that does not affect his [sic] relationship to the child."[102] In other words, there must be a nexus between a parent's cohabitation and some demonstrated adverse effect on his or her child to justify a denial of custody on that ground. Thus, although cohabitation is no longer *per se* evidence of unfitness for custody in Illinois, it remains in the case law as a factor that may be considered in the custody determination. A trial court may find some slight evidence of harm, or other grounds upon which custody might be transferred, in cases involving cohabitation without revealing its real motivation for doing so; and the appellate court is likely to uphold its finding.

Mothers fearing loss of custody have been quick to distinguish their own situations from that of the unfortunate, or incurably honest, Jacqueline Jarrett, by arguing that their cohabitation was not as "open and notorious" as Jarrett's was and/or that they, unlike Jarrett, had plans to marry their

---

430 (Ill. App. Ct. 1980) (refusing to apply *Jarrett* to limit overnight visitation with father, though he was living openly with an unmarried woman); *In re* Marriage of Hanson, 445 N.E.2d 912 (Ill. App. Ct. 1983) (vacating restriction of father's visitation rights in case where father lived in a two-bedroom trailer with unmarried woman). Treating cohabitation by mothers and fathers differently was apparently not uncommon in other states as well. *See* Donald H. Stone, *Just Molly and Me and Baby Makes Three—Or Does It? Child Custody and the Live-In Lover: An Empirical Study*, 11 PACE L. REV. 1, 3, 36 (1990–91).

100. *See* Brandt v. Brandt, 425 N.E.2d 1251, 1259–64 (Ill. App. Ct. 1981).

101. *In re* Marriage of Thompson, 449 N.E.2d at 93.

102. 750 ILL. COMP. STAT. ANN. 5/602(b) (West 1999).

partners in the future.[103] Yet as the years have passed, the case law in Illinois—even in cases involving lesbian mothers—has become more favorable to mothers who continue to have sex lives.[104] One commentator surmises that this is because "More judges [a]re under 50, divorced, women, or had cohabited themselves. They tend[] to reclassify immorality as a matter of personal freedom or personal privacy."[105]

Cohabitation may affect other areas of life as well. Cohabitants may find it more difficult to rent housing than married persons do. If so, they can sue for housing discrimination based on marital status if they live in Chicago, but until relatively recently they could not do so if they resided outside the city. When one couple in DuPage County (a suburban county to the west of Chicago) applied for and was refused housing because the landlord would not rent to unmarried couples, they sued under the Illinois Human Rights Act, which by its terms prohibited discrimination based on marital status (among other things). Citing both *Jarrett* and *Hewitt*, the appellate court held in 1990 that the prohibition against discrimination on the basis of marital status in the statute referred to the plaintiffs' individual marital status (e.g., single, married, divorced, or widowed), not to the nature of their relationship.[106] The statute did not, therefore, cover the landlord's refusal to rent to unmarried persons, the court held, because to interpret it in that way would have placed it in conflict with the criminal prohibition against cohabitation and fornication that was in effect at that time.[107]

Cohabitants refused housing in the city of Chicago have long had more legal remedies than those residing elsewhere in the state. An unmarried couple suing under the Chicago Fair Housing Regulations in 1997, for example, obtained relief in the form of damages when a landlord refused to rent to them out of his religious belief that sexual relations outside of marriage were sinful.[108] The appellate court in that case found that the earlier DuPage

---

103. *See In re* Marriage of McKeever, 453 N.E.2d 1153, 1157 (Ill. App. Ct. 1983) (affirming award of custody to father nonetheless); *In re* Marriage of Cripe, 538 N.E.2d 1175, 1179 (Ill. App. Ct. 1989 (reversing transfer of custody to father).

104. *Compare In re* Marriage of Diehl, 582 N.E.2d 281 (Ill. App. Ct. 1991) (affirming denial of custody to cohabiting lesbian mother) with *In re* Marriage of R.S. and S.S., 677 N.E.2d 1297 (Ill. App. Ct. 1996) (denying petition to transfer custody from mother, based on relationship to live-in lover).

105. PLECK, *supra* note 75.

106. Mister v. A.R.K. P'ship, 553 N.E.2d 1152, 1156 (Ill. App. Ct. 1990).

107. *Id.* at 1157.

108. Jasniowski v. Rushing, 678 N.E.2d 743 (Ill. App. Ct. 1997).

County case did not control the outcome, for several reasons. The Illinois legislature had decriminalized cohabitation (though not fornication) since the time of the earlier opinion. More important, the Chicago ordinance was broader in its protections than the Illinois Human Rights Act. It included sexual orientation as a ground upon which landlords or realtors could not discriminate, and for this reason the City Council must have understood unmarried cohabitants to be protected because all same-sex couples would fall into that category.[109] Although this resulted in a conflict with the landlord's right to free exercise of religion, the court held that his right was outweighed by the city's compelling interests in prohibiting discrimination and in making housing available to all Chicago residents and upheld the trial court's award of damages and attorneys' fees to the disappointed lessors.[110]

In most other matters, however, Illinois law hews strictly to the line that cohabitants should receive no favorable treatment from the court system or the state. They are denied damages for loss of consortium, thus denying them compensation, for example, in cases where medical malpractice deprives them of the sexual and other companionship of their partner.[111] Health care decision making can also be an important issue for cohabitants. Although they may execute power of attorney for health care documents to designate one another in advance as the person to make decisions in the event of incapacity, including life and death decisions, most cohabitants fail to do so.[112] To address this common failure to make provision in advance, states have passed health care surrogate statutes that list, in order of priority, the family members entitled to make health care decisions, beginning with a spouse and extending to more distant relatives, and some states include domestic partners in such a list.[113] The Cook County State's Attorney's task force drafting legislation on this issue considered whether to include domestic partners in the list of designated persons in the Illinois act but intentionally excluded them, for fear that the bill would be politically unacceptable to the legislature.[114]

---

109. *Id.* at 746–47.

110. *Id.* at 751.

111. *See, e.g.,* Medley v. Strong, 558 N.E.2d 244 (Ill. App. Ct. 1990).

112. Jennifer K. Robbennolt & Monica Kirkpatrick Johnson, *Legal Planning for Unmarried Committed Partners: Empirical Lessons for a Preventive and Therapeutic Approach*, 41 ARIZ. L. REV. 417, 446 n.144 (1999).

113. *Id.* at 426 n.69.

114. Michael L. Closen & Joan E. Maloney, *The Health Care Surrogate Act in Illinois: Another Rejection of Domestic Partners' Rights*, 19 S. ILL. U. L. J. 479, 491 (1995).

Finally, although Illinois courts will recognize a common law marriage entered into in another state which does recognize common law marriage,[115] they are stingy in extending this recognition. If someone moves to Illinois after marrying and residing in a recognizing jurisdiction, the common law marriage will be considered valid. However, unlike courts in New York State, decisions in Illinois do not allow common law status to be established by persons domiciled in Illinois based upon time they have spent in recognizing jurisdictions at various periods during their union.[116] The public policy of the state is so strong and so clear in this respect that it led one otherwise liberal federal judge in 1988 to deny any remedy at all to an elderly woman in the most compelling circumstances—denying social security survivors' benefits to a 65-year-old woman who had lived with the decedent for almost forty years and borne him three children, despite their sojourns in recognizing jurisdictions.[117]

In short, it is risky for a cohabitant to make any investment in a nonmarital relationship in a state like Illinois. One may only surmise whether *Hewitt v. Hewitt* would come out the same way if it were decided today, but it is still the law in the state (though it has been cited with decreasing frequency over the years.)[118] More important for purposes of this book, however, a review of the way in which *Hewitt* was interpreted and applied during the 1980s provides a stark vision of the situation of cohabitants if no legal protection at all is extended to them.

4. The Inadequacy of Equitable Remedies

By contrast, courts in other states have been unwilling to tolerate inequitable consequences such as befell Mrs. Hewitt, who invested for fifteen years in what

---

115. *See, e.g.,* Allen v. Storer, 600 N.E.2d 1263 (Ill. App. Ct. 1992).

116. *See, e.g.,* Stahl v. Chuhak (*In re* Estate of Stahl), 301 N.E.2d 82 (Ill. App. Ct. 1973); Corder v. Cont'l Ill. Bank & Trust Co. of Chicago (*In re* Estate of Enoch), 201 N.E.2d 682 (Ill. App. Ct. 1964).

117. Lynch v. Bowen, 681 F. Supp. 506, 511 (N.D. Ill. 1988) (Shadur, J.) (citing Hewitt v. Hewitt*).* These days, the federal court in Illinois is more likely to support its decision with citations to literature from the Marriage Movement rather than relying either on *Hewitt* or on hard social science, but the result is the same—to deny benefits to heterosexual cohabitants. *See* Irizarry v. Bd. of Ed. of City of Chicago, 251 F.3d 604, 607–08 (2001) (citing articles and books by Linda J. Waite, Maggie Gallagher, and David Popenoe).

118. *Hewitt* was cited twenty-one times in the 1980s but only seven times in the 1990s.

would historically have been recognized as a common law marriage, and Ms. Ayala, who, after a 10-year relationship, lost both her house and the payments she had made on the mortgage, taxes, and insurance. When the courts of Minnesota were presented with facts similar to those in *Hewitt*, they reached a quite different conclusion. In one case, for example, Laura Carlson and Oral Olson had lived together for twenty-one years, during which she had stayed at home to raise their son. When the couple separated and she brought suit to partition their property, the trial court awarded her a one-half interest in both their real and personal property.[119] The Minnesota Supreme Court affirmed that decision, commenting that:

> The doctrine of common-law marriage would have covered the parties here; however, its demise as a legal entity left a void and necessitates the creative application of traditional common-law and equitable principles to this situation. The elimination of common-law marriage obviously did not eliminate the institution, but only the rules which must be applied to it.[120]

In other words, the Minnesota court was not willing to tolerate the unjust outcome that might follow, given the void left by the abolition of common law marriage.

Writing at about the same time, one commentator pointed out that recovery in such circumstances had traditionally been denied but that, with the increase in cohabitation, pressure was mounting upon the courts to find some remedy in these cases.[121] While courts were likely to turn to the equitable remedies of restitution and unjust enrichment to do so, he thought this approach was not appropriate. Restitution is a remedy designed to address circumstances where one party has conferred an economic benefit upon another which cannot justly be retained by that party—for example, transfers in reliance upon broken promises of marriage, fraudulent misrepresentation about a party's marital status, mistaken beliefs, and the like. Modern cohabitants simply do not fit the requirements of this equitable remedy: they have not entered into their relationship because of fraud, duress, or mistake

---

119. Carlson v. Olson, 256 N.W.2d 249, 249–50 (Minn. 1977).

120. *Id.* at 251.

121. Robert C. Casad, *Unmarried Couples and Unjust Enrichment: From Status to Contract and Back Again*, 77 MICH. L. REV. 47 (1978).

but rather as a matter of choice.[122] More recent commentators such as Emily Sherwin have developed this argument.[123]

Nonetheless, courts in many states use the doctrine of unjust enrichment to address the increasing number of cohabitants' claims that come before them. Situations like that of Ms. Ayala are most readily compensated. It seems eminently unjust not to reimburse cohabitants who had poured their own savings and earnings into houses titled in the name of a partner who was either dead or from whom they were separated.[124] Who would make such an investment without expectation of return? What strikes a reader of these cases is the variety of reasons cohabitants have for agreeing that property be titled solely in the name of one partner even though they have contributed substantially to it themselves—tax advantages, hiding property from welfare authorities or from an ex-spouse paying alimony, or obtaining more favorable financing, for example.[125] The other thing that strikes one is the naïve trust that leads people not to insist upon being listed in title documents—a trust that seems so foolish in retrospect but is apparently common in intimate relationships, as evidenced by the number of cases. The fact that so many cases involve violated trust of this sort illustrates the need for legal protection for cohabitants.

Many states do recognize equitable claims for unjust enrichment in cohabitant cases, most readily in cases where a couple has obtained a divorce and then simply resumed living together without remarrying.[126] Courts are

---

122. *Id.* at 55.

123. Emily Sherwin, *Love, Money, and Justice: Restitution Between Cohabitants*, 77 U. COLO. L. REV. 711, 724 (2006); *but see* HANOCH DAGAN, THE LAW AND ETHICS OF RESTITUTION 164–83 (Cambridge Univ. Press 2004).

124. *See, e.g., In re* Estate of Ericksen, 337 N.W.2d 671 (Minn. 1983) (creating constructive trust of one-half interest in home to prevent unjust enrichment of estate of deceased cohabitant); Sullivan v. Rooney, 533 N.E.2d 1372 (Mass. 1989) (conveying tenancy in common in house under theory of constructive trust).

125. *In re* Estate of Ericksen, 337 N.W.2d 671 (titling the property in name of one partner for reasons having to do with his divorce and her receipt of AFDC benefits); *Sullivan*, 533 N.E.2d 1372 (titling property in name of partner who was in military to obtain favorable financing from the Veterans Administration); Salzman v. Bachrach, 996 P.2d 1263 (Colo. 2000) (en banc) (titling property in name of female cohabitant for reasons having to do with tax advantage to male cohabitant and continuation of her alimony from ex-husband).

126. *See, e.g.*, Pickens v. Pickens, 490 So. 2d 872 (Miss. 1986) (involving couple who were married for fourteen years, divorced, and then began living together a year after divorce for a period of twenty years); Wooldridge v. Wooldridge, 856 So. 2d 446 (Miss. 2003) (involving couple who were married for ten years, divorced, and resumed living together a month later for eleven more years).

also much more likely to grant equitable relief that involves investments in property than to compensate domestic services and are more likely to divide interests in property if the cohabitant in whose name it is not titled can provide documentary evidence of his or her direct monetary contributions to its acquisition.[127] Judges may also be able to appreciate the injustice of an enrichment more easily when the cohabitant who has been deprived is male. A comparison of two cases coming before the New York Court of Appeals (the highest court in New York State) within one four-year period is instructive in this respect. One involved a relationship of some twenty-five years, in which the couple had two children and were known to the community as husband and wife. The woman alleged an implied contract under which she had "performed domestic duties and business services at the request of defendant with the expectation that she would receive full compensation for them."[128] Although holding that New York would recognize a claim based on an express contract, the Court of Appeals dismissed the implied contract claim, saying that "it is not reasonable to infer an agreement to pay for the services rendered when the relationship of the parties makes it natural that the services were rendered gratuitously," that is, as a gift.[129] But in another case involving a male plaintiff, a farmer who had transferred the deed to his property to a younger woman companion who refused to marry him, the court found a "classic example of a situation where equity should intervene."[130] The justices found it "inconceivable that plaintiff would convey all of his interest in property which was not only his abode but the very means of his livelihood without at least tacit consent upon the part of the defendant that she would permit him to continue to live on and operate the farm."[131] In short, while the Court of Appeals found it entirely plausible that a woman would live with a man, bear and raise his children, and perform all manner of domestic and business services for him without any thought of return, the idea that the farmer would have made a gift of his property to a woman he loved was "inconceivable." "It was for just this type of case," the judges opined,

---

127. *See, e.g.,* Waage v. Borer, 405 N.W.2d 92 (Wis. Ct. App. 1994) (holding that household services not directly traceable to the accumulation of assets are not compensable); Evans v. Wall, 542 So. 2d 1055 (Fla. Dist. Ct. App. 1989) (reimbursing for funds, labor, and material invested in construction but denying all claims based on spouse-like services).

128. Morone v. Morone, 413 N.E.2d 1154, 1155 (N.Y. 1980).

129. *Id.* at 1157.

130. Sharp v. Kosmalski, 40 N.Y.2d 119, 123 (N.Y. 1976).

131. *Id.* at 124.

"that there evolved equitable principles and remedies to prevent injustices."[132] If so, the rules of equity evolved with the needs and customs of men in mind and not of women. At any rate, the outcomes of cases based on equitable theories are likely to be both inconsistent and unpredictable.

Even when a court decides that unjust enrichment is available as a reme-dial theory, relief may be hard to obtain or pitifully small. The history of a case that is often seen as a leading precedent for granting equitable relief to cohab-itants shows that relief may prove difficult to come by even in states that are liberal in their approach to these issues. *Watts v. Watts* is the case in which the Supreme Court of Wisconsin responded to the *Hewitt* case by rejecting the Illinois court's approach as harsh and held that very similar facts (the woman had quit her job, borne two children, served as a homemaker, child caregiver, and hostess, as well as working in the man's office) stated a claim for recovery based on unjust enrichment. Indeed, Justice Shirley Abrahamson noted that, "allowing no relief at all to one party in a so-called 'illicit' relationship effec-tively provides total relief to the other, by leaving that party owner of all the assets acquired through the efforts of both . . . contrary to the principles of equity."[133] The *Watts* case was then remanded for decision under the new Wisconsin standard, and the jury's award of $113,090.08 to Mrs. Watts was reinstated. This amount, however, constituted only about 10 percent of the increase in the couple's net assets over the twelve years of their relationship, instead of the 50 percent Mrs. Watts had requested under a theory of implied contract, which the court rejected.[134]

Let us look at what has happened to cohabitants in recent Wisconsin cases pleading the precedent of *Watts*. In one, involving a cohabitant of eight years' standing, the court denied her claim, holding that *Watts* does not recog-nize compensation for housekeeping or other services unless they have been embodied in assets accumulated during the course of the cohabitation.[135] In other words, if a cohabitant's contributions cannot be traced into assets, but rather have been consumed by the couple and their children during the

---

132. *Id.* at 123; *see also Salzman,* 996 P.2d 1263 (involving male cohabitant who had contrib-uted his skilled services to design a home for himself and his partner and paid part of the purchase price; the court had no trouble seeing unjust enrichment here).

133. Watts v. Watts, 405 N.W.2d 303, 314 (Wis. 1987).

134. Watts v. Watts, 448 N.W.2d 292 (Wis. Ct. App. 1989), *cert. denied,* 451 N.W.2d 297 (Wis. 1990).

135. Waage v. Borer, 525 N.W.2d 96, 98–99 (Wis. Ct. App. 1994).

relationship, she may still end up with nothing. If a couple has accumulated little property, this equitable remedy will be useless.

In yet another Wisconsin case, one from 1998, a female cohabitant had undertaken responsibility for the couple's living expenses over a four-year period in order to allow her male counterpart to save for the down payment on a house, which was titled in his name. Thereafter, he paid the mortgage and taxes while she paid for utilities, groceries, and household items over the eight years they lived in the house, during which its value appreciated. When they separated, a trial court jury awarded her $45,000, half the equity in the house, but the appellate court reversed, returning to her only the down payment.[136] The court gave three reasons for this reversal. First, she had continued to work, and the couple had kept their finances separate. Second, the increase in value of the house was due to market factors. Third, her payments for utilities and groceries could be seen as offset by her nonpayment of rent. Thus, although most married partners both work nowadays and many keep their finances separate, commingling of accounts was seen as necessary to the application of *Watts*; without it, the court was unwilling to conclude that there was a committed and sharing relationship. Thus, although Wisconsin is often seen as the prime example of a state where cohabitants may receive compensation for their contributions to a long-term relationship, the unjust enrichment doctrine is applied in such a restrictive fashion that relief may effectively be unavailable or trivial compared to the partner's contribution.

Moreover, even in states that do award compensation for domestic services that cannot be traced into the acquisition of some asset, this liberal treatment may not result in relief that is substantial. The Mississippi Supreme Court, for example, has stated that:

> As any freshman economics student knows, services and in kind contributions have an economic value as real as cash contributions. In such situations, where one party to the relationship acts without compensation to perform work or render services to a business enterprise or performs work or services generally regarded as domestic in nature, these are nevertheless economic contributions.[137]

---

136. Ward v. Jahnke, 583 N.W.2d 656 (Wis. Ct. App. 1998).

137. Pickens v. Pickens, 490 So. 2d 872, 876 (Miss. 1986); *see also* Goode v. Goode, 396 S.E.2d 430 (W. Va. 1990) (recognizing claim for homemaker services that contribute to family's economic well-being, allowing male cohabitant to work full time and thereby amass assets).

But how are domestic services evaluated when the Mississippi courts compensate them? They begin with the replacement cost for seventy hours per week of domestic work at the market rate for such labor (the rate at which a cleaning person or maid would be paid) and then subtract the cost of the wife and mother's rent, food, and other expenses, arriving at a figure of less than $6,400 a year in a 1998 case.[138] Housewives come cheap. Thus, at the end of a long-term relationship during which one of the partners performed all of the domestic work, cooking, keeping the house, raising the children, entertaining, and the like, thus enabling the other partner to focus on work paid in the market, the partner employed in the market could accumulate large amounts of income and property. So long as he paid off the other partner at rates he might otherwise have paid a babysitter or caterer, he would be able to keep all of the accumulated property for himself.

An additional problem with equitable remedies is that they may be very complicated to plead and to prove, particularly in jurisdictions that attempt to adhere to the traditional limitations on the doctrine. Thus, while cohabitants are theoretically entitled to seek relief based on unjust enrichment in both Alabama and Florida, they are likely to fail if they cannot present adequate evidence of one of the following: a confidential relationship (a relationship in which one party trusts the other to look out for his or her interests, which many states will not presume from the fact of cohabitation); mistake; fraud; or some other egregious misbehavior.[139] In one gender-reversing Florida case, for example, a man who had cohabited for many years with a woman supplied all of the purchase price for their home but had transferred title to the property into her name. When she died, he sought to impose a constructive trust on the residence and two bank accounts held in her name but used for operation of his business. In the absence of proof of fraud, misbehavior, or mistake, the court found that the transfers were gifts and not subject to the imposition of any remedial trust.[140] He therefore lost both the home he had paid for and lived in and the balance in his business accounts to his long-term partner's estate—that is, to her blood relatives—upon her death.

Based upon evidence like this, equitable doctrines such as unjust enrichment simply cannot be relied upon to provide relief for cohabitants at the

---

138. Wooldridge v. Wooldridge, 856 So. 2d 446, 453 (Miss. Ct. App. 2003).

139. *See* Jordan v. Mitchell, 705 So. 2d 453 (Ala. Civ. App. 1997); Arwood v. Sloan, 560 So. 2d 1251 (Fla. Dist. Ct. App. 1990).

140. *Arwood*, 560 So. 2d 1251.

end of a relationship. Experience with them in this context has led commentators in other common law countries to this conclusion. The Law Commission charged with considering the financial consequences of the breakdown of cohabiting relationships in the United Kingdom reported in 2006 that this body of law appeared to many commentators to be unfair, uncertain, and both substantively and procedurally too complex to offer an adequate remedy.[141] Equitable remedies, the Law Commission concluded, also fail to recognize economic sacrifices of persons who gave up paid employment to raise children, as well as the value and long-term economic impact of nonfinancial contributions and sacrifices such as parenting.[142] Experience in Australia and New Zealand has led to similar conclusions. Commentators report that litigation based on equitable remedies there requires lengthy, complex, and expensive legal services; and the uncertainty of the outcome makes it very difficult both for attorneys to advise clients and to negotiate settlements. These difficulties have led New Zealand and many Australian states to pass laws providing status-based remedies to deal with the property relationships of "de facto couples."[143]

In sum, common law marriage is no longer generally available and may not apply to the situation of modern cohabitants even if it is; this has left a gap which courts have attempted to fill with equitable remedies. Scholars like Hanoch Dagan argue that restitution and unjust enrichment can work well to prevent abuse of trust between cohabitants without assimilating them to the equal sharing imposed by marriage.[144] But real-life experience with these remedies in the courts of the United States and other countries shows that they simply do not work to achieve this result in any effective and consistent manner.

---

141. LAW COMM'N, CONSULTATION PAPER NO. 179, COHABITATION: THE FINANCIAL CONSEQUENCES OF RELATIONSHIP BREAKDOWN ¶¶ 4.1–4.13 (May 31, 2006), *available at* http://www.lawcom.gov.uk/docs/cp179.pdf.

142. *Id.*

143. *See* Ian Kennedy, *The Legal Position of Cohabitees in Australia and New Zealand*, INT'L FAM. L., Nov. 2004, at 238–43. *See* Chapter 5, *infra*.

144. DAGAN, *supra* note 123, at 164–83.

TWO

Legal Treatment of Cohabitation in the United States Today

AS RATES OF COHABITATION CLIMBED DURING THE 1970s, the courts in California began to search for a different approach to the issues presented by the increasing number of cohabitant cases coming before them. They experimented with equitable remedies such as those described in the preceding chapter and, briefly, with analogizing cohabitants' property rights to those of married couples, ultimately settling on a contract approach that has proved influential throughout the United States. This chapter describes the variety of legal approaches taken in different areas of the country, ranging from rights based on contract to a number of remedies based on a quasi-marital status, as in Washington, or on domestic partnership arrangements for which cohabitants may register, with differing legal consequences for that registration in different jurisdictions. Both contract-based remedies and the status-based treatment under Washington law apply only to the rights of the two cohabitants vis-à-vis one another, but some domestic partnership regimes extend rights to cohabitants against third parties as well. In addition, many states have begun to address the differing issues raised by cohabitants' cases against third parties on a case-by-case basis, with a few states deciding to include cohabitants within the protection of the state unemployment compensation system, for example, or to allow unmarried partners to sue for loss of consortium. Finally, some legal issues remain with respect to cohabitants and their children.

✺ 1. Cohabitants' Rights Based on Contract

With the exception of Illinois, Georgia, and Louisiana,[1] almost every state will now recognize contracts between cohabitants, although they differ as to

---

1. *See* Hewitt v. Hewitt, 394 N.E.2d 1204 (Ill. 1979); Long v. Marino, 441 S.E.2d 475 (Ga. Ct. App. 1994); Schwegmann v. Schwegmann, 441 So. 2d 316 (La. Ct. App. 1983).

whether the contracts must be express instead of implied, oral or in writing. (An express contract is an agreement, or exchange of promises, between two parties, either in writing or verbally; an implied contract is implied by the court from the conduct of the parties toward each other.) This almost universal recognition of contracts between cohabitants required the break-through of the *Marvin v. Marvin* "palimony" case in 1976.[2] Prior to that time, cohabitants' contracts were generally considered to be unenforceable because they rested upon meretricious consideration (that is, resembled prostitution in their exchange of value for sex). The *Marvin* court held that cohabitants could enter into a number of types of contracts with one another, oral and written, express and implied, just as noncohabiting adults could do.[3]

Michelle Triola lived with the well-known movie actor Lee Marvin (*Cat Ballou, The Dirty Dozen*, etc.) from 1964 to 1970, officially changing her last name to Marvin. At the beginning of their relationship, Lee Marvin was not yet divorced; the relationship ended six years later when he evicted her from the beach house they shared in Malibu and suddenly married his childhood sweetheart.[4] When Lee stopped the support payments he was giving to Michelle after a year and a half, she contacted the flamboyant Hollywood divorce lawyer, Marvin Mitchelson. The result was a lawsuit against Lee Marvin, in which Michelle alleged that he had entered into a contract to support her for the rest of her life in return for her giving up her own career and serving as Marvin's "companion, homemaker, housekeeper, and cook." Marvin responded that such a contract was unenforceable under California law. The district court agreed and dismissed the complaint, whereupon Michelle appealed.

Prior to this time, the California Supreme Court had long recognized the rights of cohabitants to enter into legally enforceable contracts with one another concerning property but only if they did so in express agreements that were separate and distinct from their "meretricious relationship."[5] If a court could find such an express property agreement, a cohabitant might recover a share of the couple's accumulated property at the end of their relationship but could not recover if the property interest alleged was

---

2. Marvin v. Marvin, 557 P.2d 106 (Cal. 1976).

3. *Id.* at 122–23.

4. Elizabeth H. Pleck, Shacking Up: Cohabitation and the Sexual Revolution, 1962 to 1990, unpublished manuscript on file with author.

5. *See* Trutalli v. Meraviglia, 12 P.2d 430 (Cal. 1932).

based solely upon the contribution of services by the non-income-producing party.[6]

In 1973, one California appellate court came up with a dramatically new approach to cohabitant cases.[7] The *Cary* case involved facts that are by now familiar to the reader. Janet and Paul lived together as though they were married for eight years, during which they had four children; Janet stayed at home to care for the house and children while Paul worked. When they separated, the trial court divided their property equally between them, and the appellate court upheld this disposition, although on rather peculiar grounds. It analogized the situation to that involving a putative spouse, even though Janet and Paul both knew they were not married.[8] Pointing out that the just-enacted no-fault divorce law evinced an intention on the part of the California legislature to disregard fault or guilt when adjudicating the termination of a family relationship, the court baldly announced that "[t]he relationship between Paul, Janet and their children must reasonably be deemed that of a Family, coming within the broad purview of the Family Law Act."[9] The court then held that the trial judge had appropriately divided the properly equally between the two under the community property system applying to marital property in California. (California is one of nine U.S. states in which all property acquired during a marriage, apart from gift or inheritance, belongs in equal shares to each spouse, regardless of who contributed to its acquisition.) In short, the *Cary* court applied a status-based approach to the resolution of cohabitants' rights, analogizing the couple's relationship to a marriage and then assimilating it to marriage for purposes of legal treatment upon its dissolution. Despite its dubious derivation (the California legislature was clearly not thinking about the rights of unmarried couples when it passed the no-fault law), a few courts did follow the *Cary* decision; others rejected this approach, thus inviting the California Supreme Court to address the question.[10] The case presenting that court with the opportunity to do so was *Marvin v. Marvin.*

---

6. *See* Herma Hill Kay & Carol Amyx, Marvin v. Marvin: *Preserving the Options*, 65 CAL. L. REV. 937, 942–45 (1977).

7. *In re* Marriage of Cary, 109 Cal. Rptr. 862 (Cal. Ct. App. 1973).

8. *Id.* at 863–64.

9. *Id.* at 863.

10. Kay & Amyx, *supra* note 6, at 953.

In *Marvin*, Justice Matthew Tobriner firmly rejected the *Cary* approach but held that Michelle could state a claim based on express contract under California law and remanded the case to the trial court to give her an opportunity to prove that such a contract had existed and its terms. He also said, although it was not necessary to decision of the *Marvin* case, which was predicated upon the existence of an express oral contract, that cohabitants could also make claims against one another based on implied contracts or equitable principles of constructive trust similar to the suits for unjust enrichment described in the previous chapter. In ruling against Lee Marvin on these grounds, the Supreme Court thus established the validity in California of a broad cause of action based on contract or quasi-contract between cohabitants. The *Marvin* case was attended by a great deal of publicity, and feminist commentators applauded it as giving couples freedom to opt out of traditional marriage and experiment with new lifestyles.[11]

On remand, however, after an 11-week hearing in 1979, the trial court found that no express contract had existed between Michelle and Lee Marvin and that no contract could be implied from their conduct.[12] Thus, the *Marvin* case in fact resulted in no recovery at all for the plaintiff; it simply established the principle that cohabitants' rights in California could be based upon express or implied contracts and that the consideration for them could include homemaking services.

While many states adopted the *Marvin* approach, other states reacted with alarm to the long and messy *Marvin* litigation, especially because it required the court to examine and weigh highly intimate details of the couple's relationship. The Illinois court in *Hewitt v. Hewitt* declined to adopt similar contract-based rights;[13] other states moved to accept *Marvin* but to limit its application. New York, for example, restricted so-called *Marvin* rights to those based on express contracts but refused to recognize implied contracts between cohabitants.[14] Minnesota and Texas went further, passing statutes of frauds that require cohabitants' contracts to be in writing.[15]

---

11. Kay & Amyx, *supra* note 6, at 973.

12. Marvin v. Marvin, 5 FAM. L. REP. 3079 (Cal. Ct. App. 1979).

13. 394 N.E.2d 1204 (Ill. 1979).

14. *See* Morone v. Morone, 413 N.E.2d 1154 (N.Y. 1980).

15. MINN. STAT. §§ 513.075–513.076 (2002); TEX. BUS. & COM. CODE ANN. § 26.01(b)(6) (2005); *see also* Posik v. Layton, 695 So. 2d 759, 762 (Fla. Dist. Ct. App. 1997) (pointing out that the Statute of Frauds (FLA. STAT. § 725.01 (1998)), requiring contracts made upon consideration of marriage to be in writing, should apply to "nonmarital, nuptial-like agreements").

Indeed, the application of the *Marvin* case has been quite limited even in California. In *Friedman v. Friedman*, the California Court of Appeal attracted a good deal of attention when it denied relief in 1993 to a disabled woman after a cohabiting relationship of twenty-five years and two children.[16] Terri and Elliott Friedman began to live together in 1967, when they were in their twenties, bought a house to which they took title as husband and wife, signed joint tax returns, and lived as a fairly conventional family, with Terri staying home to care for their children and Elliott going to law school and eventually prospering economically. By the time she sued in 1992, however, Terri (who was disabled and could hardly walk) sought spousal support from Elliott. The case seemed to be a good one for the application of *Marvin* remedies; compared to *Marvin*, the relationship was longer in term, more conventional, and included the birth of children. Nonetheless, Elliott argued that he had never made a commitment to support Terri if their relationship terminated, and the court found that the couple's course of conduct did not support an implied contract to that effect.[17]

The outcome of the *Friedman* case leads one to question the efficacy of contract remedies in general, so long as one party denies the contract. (Of course, if that were not so, that party would simply pay or divide the property, and there would be no litigation at all.) Oral contracts are notoriously difficult to prove because they are not usually made in front of witnesses and their proof pits the word of one party against that of the other. Moreover, in *Friedman*, the proof of an implied contract was rejected because the conduct of the parties did not specifically indicate an agreement by Elliott to provide spousal support upon termination of their relationship.[18] From this outcome, one may infer that cohabitants are only slightly more likely to obtain "palimony" in California than in New York if the claim rests upon an implied contract, and at least the courts in New York are more candid about disallowing such claims. In fact, California courts are inconsistent in this respect, with the result depending upon the discretion, and perhaps the personal prejudices, of the judge. As with the equitable remedies described in the previous chapter, the more like a "male" business deal the parties' contract appears, the more likely the service is to be compensated.

---

16. 24 Cal. Rptr. 2d 892 (Cal. Ct. App. 1993); *see also* Ira Mark Ellman, *"Contract Thinking" Was Marvin's Fatal Flaw*, 76 NOTRE DAME L. REV. 1365, 1370–72 (2001).

17. *Id.* at 898–900.

18. *Id.* at 899.

A much more profound problem with the use of contract principles to redress inequities that may arise on termination of a cohabiting relationship is that cohabiting couples—like married couples—typically do not make contracts; they simply proceed trusting that their relationship will endure and that each party will treat the other fairly. One empirical study of Minnesota residents who self-identified as being in a committed unmarried relationship found that only 21 percent had written agreements about property; of these, 52.1 percent had a provision for dividing property if the relationship were to end, but only 35.4 percent set up duties of support upon termination.[19] Most cohabitants simply proceed under vague agreements to pool resources and make no provision for remedies upon termination.[20]

It is hard to know what to make of the absence of a contract, whether to infer a caring relationship that would have resulted in provisions for property and support upon dissolution if the parties had thought about it, or to infer that the parties (or at least one of them) intended not to undertake such responsibility to one another. Much may depend upon the group of cohabitants under consideration. Some couples, like the Friedmans, fall into a cohabiting relationship that then persists, leaving them in circumstances neither would have envisaged when their union commenced. Terri Friedman, for example, gave up her goal of obtaining a college degree in the course of their relationship because of the sickness of one of their children.[21] Other couples may explicitly desire to stay unmarried because of objections to involving the state or church in what they regard as a private relationship yet still intend a caring and mutually supportive relationship. In the case most observers worry about, one or both may specifically intend to avoid any monetary commitments to one another. The implications of cohabitation are likely to differ for each of these groups, thus affecting the expectations that accompanied the cohabitants' living together and the likelihood of an implied contract between them. In short, even though contracts between cohabitants are now enforceable in most states, both the probability that such a contract can be proved and the likelihood of inferring one from the conduct of the parties may vary, with the result that few cohabitants will in

---

19. Jennifer K. Robbennolt & Monica Kirkpatrick Johnson, *Legal Planning for Unmarried Committed Partners: Empirical Lessons for a Preventive and Therapeutic Approach*, 41 ARIZ. L. REV. 417, 435–36, 439, 441 (1999).

20. Grace Ganz Blumberg, *Cohabitation Without Marriage: A Different Perspective*, 28 UCLA L. REV. 1125, 1164–65 (1981).

21. *Friedman*, 24 Cal. Rptr. 2d at 895.

fact find a remedy in contract for the vulnerable situation they confront upon the ending of their relationship.

In sum, a contractual approach to cohabitants' rights returns to them the rights and remedies they would have had as individuals to enter into contracts of various sorts with one another, in a sense commodifying their relationships. The more the arrangement looks to the court like a business deal, the more likely it is to be recognized and compensated. By contrast, women's traditional contributions to relationships continue to be underrecognized and uncompensated. Although postrelationship support is theoretically available under a contract doctrine, it needs to have been a quite explicit expectation of the parties. Thus, contractual remedies may not protect the Victoria Hewitts and Terri Friedmans of this world, whose partners either never intended a caring and supportive relationship or—more likely—no longer recall their earlier intentions at the acrimonious point when the relationship is ending.

Moreover, contract theories of cohabitants' rights are severely limited in scope, applying only to rights of the two parties vis-à-vis one another, and cannot create any rights against third parties. Thus, for example, inheritance, tort claims based on injury to the relationship, or government benefits cannot be derived from a theory of contract. For this, a status-based theory of cohabitants' rights is required, although some status-based laws may also not provide such a wide range of benefits.

2. Cohabitants' Rights Based on Status

Dissatisfied with many of the limitations of contract-based remedies, a number of states have instead conferred rights upon cohabitants based upon their quasi-marital status as such, the approach that was rejected by the *Marvin* court.[22] There are two general types of status-based regimes applicable to heterosexual unmarried couples in the United States—the "meretricious relationship" doctrine in Washington and a variety of domestic partnership regimes in a number of states and local communities. These domestic partnerships have typically been established in response to the demand of gay cohabitants for same-sex marriage, but some of these arrangements have been extended to heterosexual cohabitants as well.

---

22. *Marvin*, 557 P.2d at 119–22.

2.1. Meretricious Relationships in Washington

Courts in Washington, like those in California and other states, struggled for some time to address the inequities common at the end of a cohabiting relationship. The traditional rule in Washington, called the *Creasman* presumption, held that the property of cohabitants was presumed to belong to the party in whose name it was titled.[23] When this led to clearly unjust results in individual cases coming before them, judges would reach for a variety of doctrines to adjust the equities: implied partnership, contract, unjust enrichment and constructive trust, and other legal and equitable concepts.[24] In 1984, the Washington Supreme Court, sitting *en banc* (all of the justices, not just the smaller panel that typically decides cases), struck down the *Creasman* presumption in a divorce case, where the parties' marriage had been preceded by a period of cohabitation during which certain property was acquired.[25] Rather than engaging in a presumption of separate property, the court held that the trial court must examine the nature of the meretricious relationship involved in the case and the property accumulated during it and then make a just and equitable distribution of the couple's property. In *Lindsey*, this resulted in a remand to the trial court to determine the nature of the property acquired during the couple's period of premarital cohabitation.

For a period, it was unclear whether this approach would be applied only to cases of premarital cohabitation or also to cases in which the cohabitants never married. The Washington Supreme Court, in another *en banc* decision, definitively resolved this question in *Connell v. Francisco*, which it decided in 1995, and set out a model for how the state's courts should go about analyzing these cases.[26] Richard Francisco and Shannon Connell cohabited from 1983 to 1990, during the last four years in the state of Washington, where they jointly managed an inn on Whidbey Island. At the beginning of their relationship, Francisco's net worth was about $1.3 million, while Connell had virtually nothing. During their relationship, Francisco acquired substantial real estate and other property, so that by 1990, when they separated, his net worth was more than $2.7 million, a net increase of almost $1.4 million during the period they lived together. They were viewed by the local community as married, and Francisco executed a will in 1987 leaving the bulk of his estate to Connell.

---

23. *See* Creasman v. Boyle, 196 P.2d 835 (1948).

24. *See In re* Marriage of Lindsey, 678 P.2d 328, 330–31 (Wash. 1984) (*en banc*).

25. *Id.* at 331.

26. Connell v. Francisco, 898 P.2d 831 (Wash. 1995) (*en banc*).

When the parties separated, Connell sought a just and equitable distribution of the property acquired during their relationship; the trial court agreed that she was entitled to such a distribution but limited the amount to be divided to property that would have been community property if they had been married. (The community property system in Washington is a bit different from that in California, where 50/50 ownership is presumed. By contrast, in Washington, the community property of a married couple is simply to be "justly and equitably distributed" upon divorce and, under the statute in effect at that time, the court could consider a party's separate property in making this distribution.[27]) The Washington Supreme Court affirmed the trial court's decision, holding that all income and property acquired by either party during a meretricious relationship (but not separate property) was to be equitably divided between them.

There is, of course, a good deal of irony in the Washington court's use of the term "meretricious" to describe relationships deserving of property division when they end. While the common understanding of meretricious is that the relationship is similar to prostitution and thus not deserving of legal protection, the term is used in *Connell v. Francisco* instead to describe a relationship that is functionally similar enough to a traditional marriage to qualify for favorable treatment upon its termination. Ironically, meretricious relationships are to be rewarded, while nonmeretricious ones are not.

At the end of such relationships, the trial court was directed to undertake a multipart inquiry. First, it was to determine whether the couple were in fact in a meretricious relationship, defined as "a stable, marital-like relationship where both parties cohabit with knowledge that a lawful marriage between them does not exist."[28] The Supreme Court instructed judges to consider the following factors, among others, in making this determination:

1. continuous cohabitation
2. duration of the relationship
3. purpose of the relationship
4. pooling of resources and services for joint projects
5. the intent of the parties[29]

---

27. *Id.* at 835 n.3.

28. *Id.* at 834.

29. *See Connell*, 898 P.2d at 834; *Lindsey*, 678 P.2d at 331.

After making this determination, the trial court must evaluate the interest each party has in the property acquired during the relationship, and specifically whether it would have been classified as community property if they were married, and then make a just and equitable distribution of it, as in a divorce proceeding. While all property acquired during a meretricious relationship is presumed to be in the nature of community property (or quasi-community property), this presumption may be rebutted. *Connell v. Francisco* was therefore remanded to the trial court to decide whether Francisco could overcome the presumption that all the income and property acquired during the years they were together was quasi-community property or establish, for example, that it was purchased with funds that would have been characterized as separate property if the couple had been married.[30]

In short, the courts in Washington, unlike those in most other states, have rejected a contract approach to the thorny legal issues presented upon dissolution of cohabitant relationships and adopted instead a status-based approach accompanied by limited remedies (it only applies to property distribution, not to support). The inquiry under a status-based cohabitant regime of this type is not whether the couple had any kind of agreement for property or support (although their intent may be relevant to the inquiry). Instead, the court inquires whether their conduct has been such as to place them within the state-prescribed definition of a meretricious relationship. If a couple in a long-term marriage-like relationship do not wish to undertake this kind of economic commitment to each other, they need to contract *out* of such obligations in the state of Washington. By contrast, in California and other states following the approach in *Marvin*, obligations are undertaken by specifically contracting *into* them. Because no form of registration with the state is required, Washington residents who are not well-versed in the law may have an unpleasant surprise upon ending their nonmarital relationships, finding that they have commitments they did not anticipate.

Evaluated in terms of protection for vulnerable parties, the status-based approach taken in Washington appears to be an improvement on contract schemes in some respects. It imposes upon cohabitants who have become interdependent an obligation to share their accumulated property when terminating their relationship without requiring them to prove the existence of a contract to do so. On the other hand, the Washington approach is limited in several ways. First, unlike contractual or quasi-contractual remedies,

---

30. *Connell*, 898 P.2d at 837.

it only applies to property distribution and does not extend to support payments at the end of the relationship. If a couple have consumed all their income and thus have not accumulated property, or have not accumulated it during the period they were together, the remedy is worthless. Second, the Washington approach, like a contract approach, pertains only to rights of the cohabitants against one another, thus excluding any type of remedy sought from a third party. So, for example, cohabitants lack standing for tort claims and the plethora of government benefits tied to marital status. Third, the Washington remedy is activated only upon termination of the relationship by either dissolution or death; the pseudo-community property does not attach during the relationship.

There have also been significant problems in the application of the meretricious relationship doctrine by the Washington courts. It only applies if the trial court first makes a finding that the parties' relationship fits the factors listed in *Connell v. Francisco*—it must be stable, continuous, involve pooling of resources, and generally look to the court like a marriage. If there are periods of separation breaking the continuity of a cohabiting relationship, some courts will find that the relationship is nonmeretricious. Trial courts' decisions about cases that do or do not qualify for this status appear to be inconsistent, unpredictable, and inequitable as a result.[31] Depending as it does on weighing a list of subjective factors, the decision in a particular case may, of course, bear a strong relationship to the individual judge's biases as well. The standard also imposes a very heavy administrative burden on the courts, requiring intrusive examination into factors that qualify a relationship as "marital-like" in an era when no-fault divorce laws have dispensed with an examination of the dynamics of marital relationships at their demise.

The *Connell v. Francisco* rule governing property distribution in cohabiting relationships has been extended by the Washington Supreme Court to same-sex couples and applied to situations where a couple's relationship has been terminated by death.[32] The inclusion of property distribution upon death is important. Studies have shown that a majority of both opposite- and same-sex cohabitants express a preference that at least a substantial share,

---

31. *See* Gavin M. Parr, *What Is a "Meretricious Relationship"?: An Analysis of Cohabitant Property Rights under Connell v. Francisco*, 74 WASH. L. REV. 1243, 1264–69 (1999). *See also In re* Marriage of Pennington, 14 P.3d 764 (Wash. 2000) (*en banc*).

32. *See* Vasquez v. Hawthorne, 33 P.3d 735 (Wash. 2001).

if not all, of their estates go to their surviving partners upon death.[33] Thus, inheritance can be an important issue for cohabitants. With only a few exceptions, cohabitants are excluded from inheriting under the intestacy law of every state.[34] Unless they make wills, which most do not, especially if they are opposite sex,[35] cohabitants receive no property upon the death of their partners. If the couple were married, on the other hand, a portion of the decedent's assets would go directly to the surviving spouse by operation of law. If the cohabitants live in Washington and qualify under the definition of a meretricious relationship, the surviving partner may be awarded an equitable share—perhaps even all—of the couple's accumulated property at his or her partner's death.[36]

Despite its limitations, the approach taken to cohabitants' rights in Washington provides some important protections to individuals who have become economically interdependent in the course of a longstanding relationship. Although it is limited to property distribution and does not include provision for postrelationship support if there is no property to distribute, in the absence of contract it offers the most far-reaching protection available in the United States for heterosexual cohabitants. It is interesting that the system is not very well-known because it has been in place since 1984 (although not extended to gay and lesbian couples until 2001) yet apparently has not occasioned widespread public controversy.

The American Law Institute (ALI) has recommended that a somewhat similar but expanded scheme be adopted in all states. The 2002 ALI *Principles of the Law of Family Dissolution* suggest that the same rules that ALI recommends for property division at the divorce of married persons be applied to cohabitants if they qualify as "domestic partners" within the meaning of that status as defined by state statute.[37] The proposed ALI rules

---

33. Mary Louise Fellows et al., *Committed Partners and Inheritance: An Empirical Study*, 16 LAW & INEQ. 1, 9 (1998).

34. New Hampshire provides a form of common law marriage applicable only at death. *See* N.H. REV. STAT. ANN. § 457: 39 (2001) (providing that persons cohabiting and reputed to be husband and wife for three years before the death of one party shall be deemed to have been legally married). Domestic partnership statutes in California, the District of Columbia, New Jersey, and Maine also provide cohabitants with inheritance rights.

35. Fellows et al., *supra* note 33, at 54 (finding that same-sex partners are more likely to have made a will than heterosexual cohabitants are).

36. *Vasquez*, 33 P.3d 735.

37. AM. LAW INST., PRINCIPLES OF THE LAW OF FAMILY DISSOLUTION §§ 6.04–6.05 (2002).

pertaining to divorce presume equal division of property acquired during the relationship and also provide for compensatory payments—alimony or spousal maintenance—to dependent parties in long-term unions.[38] Individuals would be presumed to qualify as domestic partners under the ALI scheme either if they have cohabited continuously for a state-defined period and act jointly with respect to household management or if they have a common child; if not, they are entitled to establish a domestic partnership by proof of a number of factors having to do with financial interdependence, intimacy, and reputation as a couple.[39]

The proposed ALI *Principles* have given rise to criticisms similar to those leveled at the meretricious relationship doctrine in Washington, most especially that they require a cohabiting couple to fit into a very traditional model.[40] Whereas a contemporary married couple may well maintain separate bank accounts, even separate residences, violate traditional divisions of labor within the family, and perhaps not even be monogamous, cohabitants do not have the freedom to deviate from traditional models of marriage in such ways, and thus lack the ability to experiment with new forms of relationships.

Although ALI formulations have been influential upon state law in the past, thus far no state has moved to adopt the ALI's recommendations on domestic partnership.

2.2. Domestic Partnership Laws

Many states and localities have adopted laws or ordinances establishing a domestic partner status for which qualified persons may register. The initial impetus for such schemes arose out of the demand of gay and lesbian couples for equal treatment, but quite a few domestic partnership laws allow opposite-sex couples to register as well. These laws now form an important part of the landscape for cohabitants' rights in the United States. This is a landscape that changes rapidly, with some jurisdictions adding partnership laws or expanding their protection and others altering them in response to changes in the availability of civil unions or same-sex marriage for gays and lesbians.

---

38. *Id.* at §§ 4.09, 5.04.

39. *Id.* at § 6.03.

40. *See, e.g.,* Martha M. Ertman, *The ALI Principles' Approach to Domestic Partnership*, 8 DUKE J. GENDER L. & POL'Y 107, 114–16 (2001).

By 2009, the domestic partnership arrangements that had been established varied substantially in their provisions. Many were limited to same-sex couples and are thus beyond the scope of this discussion, unless some future equal protection clause challenge to the exclusion of opposite-sex couples should succeed. Equal protection challenges have been mounted against exclusion of opposite-sex couples from domestic partnerships limited to same-sex couples, challenging the disparate treatment as unconstitutional discrimination based on sex, sexual orientation, or marital status. These lawsuits have met with little success thus far, as courts find that the two groups of cohabitants are not similarly situated or that the distinction is not based on a protected status (classifying it as based upon marital status rather than upon sex).[41] If so, the discrimination between the two groups is unconstitutional only if it is not rationally related to a legitimate government purpose; the Seventh Circuit Court of Appeals has found that discriminating between same- and opposite-sex couples is rationally related to the state's interest in confining costs and ease of administration.[42]

A few domestic partnership laws, often called "reciprocal beneficiary acts," are limited to persons, gender-neutral, who are not legally allowed to marry. Hawaii's law, passed in response to the constitutional amendment overturning the Hawaii Supreme Court case that allowed same-sex marriage, is of this type, applying to opposite-sex persons who cohabit but only if they face some impediment to marriage (for example, they are too closely related and thus forbidden to marry under state law).[43] Vermont's scheme is similar, and both are very limited in the protections they offer.[44] This type of partnership law is not relevant to the topic under discussion, which concerns the rights of opposite-sex cohabitants who are legally capable of marrying but do not. Current domestic partnership laws also differ dramatically in the breadth of the benefits and obligations they contain, ranging from some that include only hospital visitation and health care decision making to ones that extend

41. *See* Foray v. Bell Atlantic, 56 F. Supp. 2d 327 (S.D.N.Y. 1999); Cleaves v. City of Chicago, 68 F. Supp. 2d 963 (N.D. Ill. 1999). *But see* Ayyoub v. City of Oakland, No. 99-02937 (Cal. State Labor Comm'r, Oct. 27, 1997) (ordering city to extend benefit given same-sex partners to opposite-sex partners), *available at* http://www.scribd.com/doc/9170076/Ayyoub-v-City-of-Oakland. *See also* Paul R. Lynd, *Domestic Partner Benefits Limited to Same-Sex Couples: Sex Discrimination Under Title VII*, 6 WM. & MARY J. WOMEN & L. 561 (2000).

42. Irizarry v. Bd. of Educ. of Chicago, 251 F.3d 604 (7th Cir. 2001).

43. HAW. REV. STAT. ch. 572C.

44. VT. STAT. ANN. tit. 15, §§ 1301–1306.

all the rights and obligations of marriage under state law to partners who register.[45]

Finally, domestic partnership laws not limited to same-sex couples differ sharply as to the category of opposite-sex couples who may register, with some (those in Maine and the District of Columbia, for example) open to all heterosexual cohabitants over the age of eighteen[46] and others limited to couples in which one member is sixty-two or older (California, New Jersey, and Washington).[47] In the face of so much variety and constant change, I will focus on a few examples to illustrate the types of protection that may be available to opposite-sex cohabitants under domestic partnership laws and limit any extended discussion to systems that are available on a state-wide basis. That is not where the story of domestic partnerships in the United States must begin, however.

The earliest domestic partnership schemes were established in municipalities where large numbers of cohabitants, both gay and straight, lived. Many such programs provided merely a system of registration and dissolution, with no attendant benefits except for municipal or county employees, who might receive family leave, family medical insurance, and other employment benefits tied to marital status.[48] Domestic partners could also present evidence of their registration to private employers in case partner benefits were available to them at work. Some local programs started out in this limited fashion but were gradually extended to include more protections. San Francisco's was among the earliest.

In 1989, San Francisco established a partnership registry for both same-sex and opposite-sex couples, defined as "two adults who have chosen to share one another's lives in an intimate and committed relationship of mutual caring, who live together, and who have agreed to be jointly responsible for basic living expenses incurred during the Domestic Partnership."[49] Except with respect to city employees whose benefits were within its control (most important benefits are determined by state or federal law), the benefits the city provided were limited, such as mandating that cohabitants be

---

45. *Cf.* ME. REV. STAT. ANN. Tit. 22.2 § 2710 *with* CAL. FAM. CODE §§ 297–299.6.

46. ME. REV. STAT. ANN. Tit. 22.2 § 2710; D.C. MUN. REGS. tit. 29, § 8000 *et seq.*

47. CAL. FAM. CODE §§ 297–299.6; N.J. STAT. ANN. § 26:8A; WASH. REV. CODE § 26.60.

48. Craig A. Bowman & Blake M. Cornish, *Note, A More Perfect Union: A Legal and Social Analysis of Domestic Partnership Ordinances,* 92 COLUM. L. REV. 1164, 1192 (1992).

49. SAN FRANCISCO ADMIN. CODE, § 62.2.

given hospital visitation rights; city employees were also to be provided with paid bereavement leave, health insurance for registered partners, and the like.[50] In 1996, however, San Francisco passed an ordinance requiring private contractors doing business with the city to extend benefits to domestic partners of their employees.[51] The ordinance was challenged by a number of companies but ultimately upheld by the federal courts, although limited to the contractors' operations located in San Francisco and to contractors with respect to whom the city was acting as an ordinary consumer of goods and services, not as a regulator or monopolist.[52] By November 1999, over 2,500 contractors with the city of San Francisco offered domestic partner benefits, including medical insurance, retirement plans, and leaves of absence.[53]

Local domestic partnership ordinances have proliferated, driven by employees' desire to obtain benefits. Many private employers have also provided domestic partner benefits without government mandate, out of their interest in retaining employees. Though the benefits to be obtained may be somewhat limited, eligibility for domestic partner status is typically quite strict, requiring nonrelationship, indefinite commitment, common residence, and an agreement to joint responsibility for basic living expenses.[54] Moreover, domestic partner benefits such as health or life insurance, unlike those provided to married couples, have been subject to federal income taxation.[55]

The 2000 census showed that California was the state with the largest numbers of residents living in unmarried partner households—591,378 households of opposite-sex couples and 92,138 of same-sex couples.[56] Not surprisingly, the demand for equal benefits was not limited to San Francisco. In 2001, the California legislature passed its first domestic partnership law, under which domestic partners received the right to sue for damages for a partner's wrongful death, as well as to make health care decisions for one another, to

---

50. Jonathan Andrew Hein, *Caring for the Evolving American Family: Cohabiting Partners and Employer Sponsored Health Care*, 30 N.M. L. Rev. 19, 35–37 (2000).

51. *Id.*

52. *See* Air Transport Ass'n v. City of San Francisco, 992 F. Supp. 1149 (N.D. Cal. 1998), *aff'd*, 266 F.3d 1064 (9th Cir. 2001).

53. *San Francisco Human Rights Commission, Overview, available at* http://www.sfgov.org/site/sfhumanrights_page.asp?id=5921.

54. *See* Bowman & Cornish, *supra* note 48, at 1192–95.

55. David L. Chambers, *What If? The Legal Consequences of Marriage and the Legal Needs of Lesbian and Gay Male Couples,"* 95 Mich. L. Rev. 447, 475 (1996).

56. *See Census 2000 Special Reports: Married-Couple and Unmarried-Partner Households* 4 (Table 2), *available at* http://www.census.gov/prod/2003pubs/censr-5.pdf.

receive sick leave and unemployment benefits for reasons related to a partner, to adopt a partner's child as though a stepparent, and to administer a partner's estate.[57] Opposite-sex couples were included in the California domestic partnership statute if one member of the couple was over the age of sixty-two—old enough to qualify for social security and thus vulnerable to losing social security or pension benefits from a prior spouse if he or she remarried.[58] The reason for including this group of heterosexuals in a statute clearly intended to benefit gay and lesbian couples appears to have been strategic: to gain more widespread support for passage of the legislation by expanding the group who would benefit from it to include a sizeable population with political clout.[59]

From the perspective of family law theory, inclusion of opposite-sex cohabitants only if they are over the age of sixty-two is difficult to explain. There is no reason to believe that older cohabiting couples are more likely to be economically interdependent than younger cohabitants are. Indeed, they are probably less interdependent because their age makes it unlikely that there are children in the household. One commentator has described the early California domestic partnership law as providing "marriage lite" for older straight couples, allowing them to receive some benefits of marriage without losing rights that a surviving or divorced spouse would lose upon remarriage.[60] Because inheritance rights were not included in this initial partnership law in California, registration as domestic partners also did not interfere with older couples' typical desire to leave their assets to children of a previous relationship.

In September 2003, California passed a second partnership act, the Domestic Partner Rights and Responsibilities Act, which went into effect in January 2005 and greatly expanded both the rights and the obligations of domestic partners.[61] The new act gave extensive rights to cohabitants, providing that:

> Registered domestic partners shall have the same rights, protections, and benefits, and shall be subject to the same responsibilities, obligations, and

57. DOMESTIC PARTNER REGISTRATION ACT, CAL. FAM. CODE § 297 (2000); *see also* Christopher D. Sawyer, *Practice What You Preach: California's Obligation to Give Full Faith and Credit to the Vermont Civil Union*, 54 HASTINGS L. J. 727, 742–43 (2003).

58. CAL. FAM. CODE § 297(a)(5)(B) (2000).

59. Megan E. Callan, *The More, The Not Marry-er: In Search of a Policy Behind Eligibility for California Domestic Partnerships*, 40 SAN DIEGO L. REV. 427, 458 (2003).

60. J. Thomas Oldham, *Lessons from Jerry Hall v. Mick Jagger Regarding U.S. Regulation of Heterosexual Cohabitants or, Can't Get No Satisfaction*, 76 NOTRE DAME L. REV. 1409, 1431 (2001).

61. DOMESTIC PARTNER RIGHTS AND RESPONSIBILITIES ACT, CAL. FAM. CODE § 297.5 (2005).

duties under law, whether they derive from statutes, administrative regulations, court rules, government policies, common law, or any other provisions or sources of law, as are granted to and imposed upon spouses.[62]

Thus, since 2005, a partnership regime with rights equivalent to those given married couples has been available to a subset of opposite-sex couples in California for all purposes of state law, except joint filing status on tax returns. (Joint state tax filing was later added to the statute.)[63] The obligations of married couples toward one another—community of property and the duty of support, for example—were also imposed upon them. Because of the large change the new statute would make in their legal status, all registered domestic partners in California were given notice that unless they dissolved their partnerships by December 31, 2004, the rights and obligations they had toward one another would be radically changed. At least one observer saw this as providing a real-life laboratory to test whether domestic partnerships would be as attractive to cohabitants if they imposed obligations upon them as well as offered benefits.[64]

By the end of 2004, just before the shift from the first to the second partnership law, a total of 29,272 couples had registered as domestic partners in California.[65] Although the state does not keep statistics concerning how many of these are same-sex couples and how many are opposite-sex couples, it has been estimated that heterosexual couples made up five percent to six percent of the total.[66] By the end of 2004, dissolutions of these unions jumped to an all-time high of 2,513, more than triple that in any previous year, with 1,188 of them occurring in December, the last month during which one could terminate a partnership without becoming subject to the expanded partnership statute.[67] Individuals' reasons for dissolving their unions do not appear

---

62. *Id.* at § 297.5(a)–(c).

63. SB-1827, Sept. 30, 2006, effective Jan. 1, 2008.

64. *See* Cynthia Grant Bowman, *Legal Treatment of Cohabitation in the United States*, 26 LAW & POL'Y 119, 139 (2004).

65. The annual number of domestic partner registrations in California is *available at* http://www.law.ucla.edu/williamsinstitute/publications/Couples%20Marr%20Regis%20Diss.pdf.

66. *See* Gary J. Gates et al., *Marriage, Registration and Dissolution by Same-Sex Couples in the U.S.* at 14, *available at* http://www.law.ucla.edu/williamsinstitute/publications/Couples%20Marr%20Regis%20Diss.pdf.

67. *Id.* at 14; Rona Marech, *California Partners Law Now Prompts Caution: Many Gay Couples Opt Out, Citing Legal Uncertainties*, SAN FRANCISCO CHRON., Mar. 28, 2005, at B1. There were about 25,525 active partnerships of same- and opposite-sex couples left at the end of

to have been to avoid more extensive obligations to their partners, however. Interviews revealed that many were confused about the effect of the new law on benefits they anticipated, about its interaction with federal law, and the potential loss of public benefits or of scholarships if a partner's income were taken into account.[68]

The dissolution proceedings necessary to end a domestic partnership under the new California act are equivalent to divorce, but because divorce is available in California on pure no-fault grounds, they are not particularly onerous. As under California divorce law, a simplified procedure is also provided, by which shorter-term (five years or less) relationships without children, real property, or many assets may be terminated by mutual consent. However, a formal judicial proceeding is required to terminate many, if not most, domestic partnerships, at which property issues will be decided under California's community property rules, support will be considered, and all issues concerning custody and support of children adjudicated.[69] In an attempt to avoid the conflict of laws problems that might arise if another state did not recognize the validity of their partnerships, the California legislation requires couples entering domestic partnerships to agree to continuing jurisdiction by the California courts over dissolution of their relationship, even if one or both should move out of the state.[70]

Another major legal change occurred in California when the state's supreme court held in May 2008 that it was unconstitutional to prohibit same-sex couples from marrying.[71] Between June 16, 2008, when same-sex marriage became available in the state, and November 4, 2008, when the electorate passed Proposition 8 amending the state constitution to prohibit same-sex marriage, approximately 18,000 same-sex couples married in California.[72] Same-sex domestic partners were nonetheless advised not to

---

December 2004. *Id. See also* Enrique A. Monagas, *California's Assembly Bill 205, The Domestic Partner Rights and Responsibilities Act of 2003: Is Domestic Partner Legislation Compromising the Campaign for Marriage Equality?*, 17 HASTINGS WOMEN'S L.J. 39 (2006).

68. *See* Kathleen Pender, *New Financial Aid Rules for Domestic Partners*, SAN FRANCISCO CHRON., Jan. 30, 2005, at E1; *see also* Partner Task Force for Gay & Lesbian Couples, *Domestic Partner Registration: The California Approach*, Jan. 6, 2007, *available at* http://www.buddybuddy.com/d-p-cali.html.

69. CAL. FAM. CODE § 299.

70. *Id.* at § 299(d).

71. *In re* Marriage Cases, 183 P.3d 384 (Cal. 2008).

72. *See* John Schwartz & Jesse McKinley, *Court Weighs Voters' Will Against Gay Rights*, N.Y. TIMES, Mar. 6, 2009, at A12.

dissolve their partnerships because other states might recognize their domestic partnership but not their marriage.[73] The 2005 domestic partnership act remained on the books, for the benefit of opposite-sex couples sixty-two and older and any same-sex couples who might prefer domestic partnership to marriage, with its traditional stigma in some gay and lesbian circles. The domestic partnership declarations filed between May and November 2008 varied between 292 and 386 a month, by contrast with figures of 500 and 600 per month during 2006 and 2007.[74] Presumably the reduced number of domestic partner registrations reflected primarily (although not exclusively) registrations by opposite-sex partners.

There is also a domestic partnership statute in New Jersey, and since 2004 it has been available only to opposite-sex couples. The New Jersey legislature, influenced in part by the dilemmas of cohabitants who lost their partners in the World Trade Center bombing on September 11, 2001 and in part by the same-sex marriage case wending its way up through the state's courts, passed a Domestic Partnership Act that went into effect in July 2004.[75] The act, like that in California, allows cohabitants aged sixty-two and older to register, but it provides many fewer benefits than are available to domestic partners in California. New Jersey does keep records of domestic partner registrations by sex, however. During 2005, the first full year after passage of the act, a total of eighty-four opposite-sex couples registered as domestic partners in New Jersey, compared to 2,034 same-sex couples, about four percent of the total.[76] One can only surmise why this is lower than the estimate of six percent in California—most likely because the benefits given by the New Jersey law are so few.

---

73. Lisa Keen, *California Statistics Show Gay Marriage Rush, available at* http://www.sgn.org/sgnnews36_27/mobile/page5.cfm.

74. Monthly figures are extrapolated from an Excel spreadsheet obtained by e-mail from Sandra L. Snell, program analyst in the office of the California Secretary of State, Domestic Partners Registry, on May 19, 2009, a copy of which is in possession of the author.

75. New Jersey Domestic Partnership Act, 2003 N.J. Ch. 246, (codified at N.J. Stat. Ann. § 26: 8A-1 *et seq.* (West 2009)). *See also* Lewis v. Harris, 875 A.2d 259 (N.J. Super. Ct. App. Div. 2005) (affirming judgment of the trial court to dismiss the action for failure to state a claim), 908 A.2d 196 (N.J. 2006) (affirming the intermediate appellate court's ruling that New Jersey's marriage laws did not contravene New Jersey's statutory substantive due process guarantee but reversing its ruling that the laws did not violate New Jersey's equal protection guarantee and holding that same-sex couples must be afforded the same rights and benefits enjoyed by opposite-sex couples).

76. Figures are extrapolated from *New Jersey Health Statistics, 2005: Marriages, Divorces, and Domestic Partnerships, available at* http://www.state.nj.us/health/chs/stats05/marrdp05.pdf, Table MD10.

Couples filing for domestic partner status in New Jersey receive exemption from inheritance taxes and a limited state income tax deduction, along with hospital visitation rights for a hospitalized partner, health care decision making authority for an incapacitated partner, and protection against discrimination in employment, housing, and credit. However, only same-sex couples who are state employees receive health and pension benefits. If opposite-sex couples want those benefits, the legislature opined in the text of the act, they should get married.[77] The New Jersey statute provides no other benefits against third parties or the state and specifically rejects equitable distribution of property and support payments on dissolution of the relationship.[78] Nonetheless, domestic partners in New Jersey are required to go through a judicial dissolution proceeding to terminate their relationships, on grounds virtually identical to those for divorce in that state (adultery, desertion, extreme cruelty, alcoholism or addiction, institutionalization for mental illness, imprisonment, or irreconcilable differences after an 18-month period of separation).[79] In short, domestic partnerships in New Jersey have quite stringent requirements for both entry and exit and very few benefits.

Not surprisingly, same-sex couples continued their campaign for the right to equal benefits in New Jersey, eventually succeeding in the New Jersey Supreme Court but ending up with civil union status instead of marriage when the court gave the legislature a choice between the two.[80] Unlike California when same-sex marriage became available, the New Jersey legislature prohibited registration of domestic partnerships by same-sex couples after the effective date of the Civil Union Act (February 19, 2007), although continuing to allow opposite-sex couples sixty-two and older to register as partners. The partnerships of same-sex couples who entered civil unions were automatically terminated, although those who had previously registered as partners and did not enter civil unions remained protected.[81] While 2,373 same-sex couples entered into civil unions in 2007 and 1,127 in 2008, the number of domestic partnerships registered fell to 109 in 2007 and 32 in 2008, after civil union status became available, with those in 2008 entirely

---

77. N.J. STAT. ANN. § 26:8A2 (d)–(e).

78. N.J. STAT. ANN. § 26:8A-10(a)(3).

79. N.J. STAT. ANN. § 26:8A-10; *cf.* N.J. STAT. ANN. § 2A: 34-2.

80. Lewis v. Harris, 908 A.2d 196 (N.J. 2006); NEW JERSEY CIVIL UNION ACT, N.J STAT. ANN. § 37:1-28 *et seq.*

81. N.J. STAT. ANN. § 26:8A-4.1.

limited to opposite-sex couples.[82] In sum, domestic partnerships in New Jersey are now available solely to older heterosexual cohabitants, but the protections they offer are negligible.

The jurisdiction in which opposite-sex cohabitants are offered the most extensive protection is the District of Columbia. It is the most extensive for several reasons. First, there are more cohabitants per capita there than elsewhere in the United States. Unmarried partner households made up 20.8 percent of all coupled households in D.C. in 2000 (versus 10.4 percent in California), 15.7 percent opposite-sex couples and 5.1 percent same-sex couples.[83] Second, the rights extended to domestic partners in the District apply to all opposite-sex couples, not just to those sixty-two or older.[84] Finally, although the D.C. domestic partnership ordinance was initially limited to a guarantee of hospital visitation rights and health care insurance for partners of employees of the District of Columbia government when it went into effect in 1992, it was extended by the Domestic Partnership Equality Amendment Act of 2006 to give domestic partners rights and responsibilities similar to those of married couples with respect to a large number of issues, including inheritance, spousal immunity, spousal support and property distribution upon the termination of their relationships, and the right to sue for damages for wrongful death.[85] It accomplishes this simply by striking the phrase "husband and wife" or "spouse" throughout the D.C. Code and replacing it with "spouse or domestic partner." In short, although the total number of rights which the government of the District of Columbia can confer on its residents may be limited, it has to the greatest extent possible attempted to assimilate cohabitants of whatever sexual orientation into the status of married couples.

In sum, the legal landscape for cohabitants has become quite complicated with the passage of new partnership statutes and other status-based regimes with varying provisions, varying benefits, and a variety of interstate recognition schemes. California, for example, has what can only be described

---

82. Numbers of civil unions and domestic partnerships are taken from an Excel spreadsheet obtained from Darren Goldman, New Jersey Department of Health and Senior Services, Center for Health Statistics, via e-mail, May 18, 2009, a copy of which is on file with the author.

83. *See Census 2000 Special Reports: Married-Couple and Unmarried-Partner Households* 4–7.

84. *See* D.C. Mun. Regs. Tit.29, § 8000 *et seq.*

85. Domestic Partnership Equality Amendment Act of 2006, D.C. Law 16-79, effective Apr. 4, 2006.

as a hybrid legal regime for cohabitants. For most heterosexuals (those younger than sixty-two), cohabitants' rights rest upon and are limited by contract, although a number of rights against third parties may be available from a domestic partnership ordinance if there is one in the city or county in which they live and it applies to opposite-sex couples. (Same-sex couples who do not register as domestic partners are also limited to contract-based rights under *Marvin*.) By contrast, all of the benefits of marriage under state law are available to those who register as domestic partners. For those persons only, the California system fulfills the family law purpose of protecting vulnerable parties to the same extent as the state's marriage and divorce law performs this function; it serves the state's interest in the privatization of support as well.

However, unlike meretricious relationships in the state of Washington, domestic partner status must be deliberately chosen by going through the procedure for registration. Thus, if one member of a couple desires to register and the other does not, no protection is available; and couples are left to whatever other protections may be offered by a state's law on cohabitants' rights. The benefits of state domestic partnerships are also limited to those that can be conferred by state law, which is a substantial limitation. By one estimate, in 1996 there were 1,049 different federally based benefits given to people because they are married.[86]

✎ 3. Rights Against Third Parties

Although contractual remedies or status as a couple in a meretricious relationship in Washington may confer many benefits upon cohabitants against one another, neither enables them to seek remedies against parties outside their relationship. Rights against third parties may be very important to working-class and middle-class cohabitants who have not acquired substantial amounts of property and thus would gain little or nothing from rights to property distribution at the conclusion of their relationships.[87] As we have seen in the previous section, a few of these rights have been conferred by domestic partnership statutes in California, New Jersey, and the District of Columbia.

---

86. *See* http://www.gao.gov/archive/1997/og97016.pdf.

87. *See* Blumberg, *supra* note 20, at 1126–27.

In addition to rights against third parties available to registered domestic partners in the few jurisdictions that offer that status to opposite-sex couples, a number of remedies against third parties are available to heterosexual cohabitants who live in states without domestic partnership laws or who fail to register as partners in ones that do have them. In some states, benefits against third parties may be conferred upon cohabitants by a mélange of rights derived from case law, statute, or ordinance. In this section, I describe a few of these, limiting the discussion to illustrative examples in three areas: (1) benefits from the state, such as workers' compensation, unemployment insurance, and taxation; (2) tort claims against third parties, such as claims for wrongful death, negligent infliction of emotional distress, and loss of consortium; and (3) health-related benefits, such as insurance and health care decision making power. Again, this is an area in which the law has been changing, so these examples are not intended to be comprehensive but simply to illustrate the issues posed for cohabitants in each area of the law. Many of these examples come from California and New Jersey, the states in which many of these issues were addressed by the legislature and courts at a relatively early time.

3.1 Benefits from the State

One way in which third-party benefits for cohabitants may be derived is by the development of case law that embraces a functional definition of the family for purposes of certain state statutes. This has happened in some states with respect to workers' compensation and unemployment insurance law. Workers' compensation statutes are typically written so as to cover "dependents" of a worker who has died or been injured in a workplace accident. The legislative intent of such statutes is to provide for dependent family members who have lost the wage earner upon whom they depend. This underlying purpose of workers' compensation laws would seem to dictate that a dependent cohabitant should qualify for benefits, but many courts have refused recovery by cohabitants on grounds of public policy.[88] This may be changing, at least in some areas. In California, opposite-sex cohabitants have been recognized as eligible for workers' compensation survivors' benefits since 1979 if they can show that they were dependent upon the worker at the time of his

---

88. *Id.* at 1141.

or her death.[89] Oregon has reached a similar result by passing a workers' compensation statute that provides that unmarried opposite-sex couples may also claim benefits if they have lived together for more than one year prior to the accident and have children:

> In case an unmarried man and an unmarried woman have cohabited in this state as husband and wife for over one year prior to the date of an accidental injury received by one or the other as a subject worker, and children are living as a result of that relation, the surviving cohabitant and the children are entitled to compensation under this chapter the same as if the man and woman had been legally married.[90]

Rather than requiring the court to determine if the cohabitant and children were in fact economically dependent on the worker, Oregon has thus opted to rely on duration of the relationship and the birth of children as proof that this is probably so.

Similarly, although California courts in the past denied unemployment insurance benefits to cohabitants who relocated for reasons related to their partners' needs, subsequent case law in the state supports an award of benefits in these circumstances as well. The court may undertake a somewhat searching investigation into the nature of the relationship, however, perhaps injecting its own values into that determination. Unemployment insurance is only available if an employee is dismissed or resigns for certain recognized reasons; following a spouse to a new job in another location has long been recognized as such a reason. In 1983, the California Supreme Court faced the question whether leaving a job to follow a cohabitant also qualified as good cause to resign.[91] In that case, Mary Norman resigned to be able to move to Washington to follow the man with whom she was living; the couple averred that they had plans to marry but had not set a date, and they had not married by the time of the oral argument two years later. The court found that this did not constitute good cause under the statute for a number of reasons, including the state's strong public policy favoring marriage and interest in promoting it, difficulties of proof without the bright line of a marriage license, and the intrusiveness of requiring administrative agencies to investigate the

---

89. *See* State v. Workers' Comp. Appeals Bd., 156 Cal. Rptr. 183, 186 (Cal. Ct. App. 1979).

90. OR. REV. STAT. § 656.226.

91. *See* Norman v. Unemployment Ins. Appeals Bd., 663 P.2d 904 (Cal. 1983) (*en banc*).

nature of a relationship. It held out the possibility that in some future case cohabitants might be able to establish good cause.[92]

The hypothesized case came before the same court the following year. Patricia MacGregor had lived with her male partner for three years, and the couple had a child in common; the reason her partner was moving was to look after his ailing father in another state.[93] This, the court held, did constitute good cause—a cause that would reasonably motivate someone to give up paid employment and become unemployed. Central to the court's decision was its finding that MacGregor was moving to New York "in order to maintain and preserve their family unit."[94] The longevity of their relationship and the birth of a child were sufficient indicia of the importance and permanence of their family unit even in the absence of marriage and sufficient, as well, to address the problems of proof that had seemed so important in *Norman.*[95]

Future cohabitants bringing such claims know what they need to allege in order to shift a court's attention away from a policy to disfavor nonmarital relationships,[96] reminiscent of the Illinois courts, to its concern for protecting "family units." The holding in *MacGregor* indicates that the duration of a cohabiting relationship and the birth of a child to the couple play an important role in courts' decisions whether to extend legal protections to them. A couple with a relationship of long duration and a child is a family unit considered worthy of protection, unlike a childless unmarried couple.

The California domestic partnership legislation now guarantees eligibility for workers compensation and unemployment insurance benefits to older heterosexual couples who register with the state (who may in fact be retired and thus less likely to need them), but the case law above extends these benefits to a much larger group of cohabitants. The courts of Massachusetts follow the same approach.[97]

---

92. *Id.* at 909–10.

93. *See* MacGregor v. Unemployment Ins. Appeals Bd., 689 P.2d 453 (Cal. 1984) (*en banc*).

94. *Id.* at 455.

95. *Id.* at 456–59.

96. *Norman*, 663 P.2d at 909.

97. *See* Reep v. Comm'r of Dep't of Employment and Training, 593 N.E.2d 1297 (Mass. 1992) (holding that lack of marriage to partner with whom woman had cohabited for thirteen years did not preclude eligibility for unemployment benefits when she resigned to relocate with him).

Many of the most significant government benefits are universally unavailable to cohabitants, however, because they derive from federal law. Social security survivors' benefits are available only to those who qualify as spouses as defined by state law.[98] Common law spouses are eligible under this provision (although same-sex spouses are excluded by the federal Defense of Marriage Act's provision that "[t]he federal government may not treat same-sex relationships as marriages for any purpose, even if concluded or recognized by one of the states").[99] Cases challenging the denial of social security benefits to cohabitants have been unsuccessful, on the ground that the wage-earner was never legally required to support his or her surviving cohabitant.[100] In theory, this rationale should no longer apply to registered domestic partners in California or the District of Columbia, who do have a legal duty to support one another.

Cohabitants also cannot file joint federal income tax returns, claim one another as dependents, or take advantage of spousal exclusions from federal estate and gift taxation.[101] Although states with comprehensive domestic partnership arrangements extending to opposite-sex cohabitants initially excluded spouse-like treatment under state income tax laws as well, apparently in order to maintain the same filing status on both state and federal returns, California has amended its domestic partnership law to extend favorable treatment on state tax forms as well. Domestic partners may also file jointly in New Jersey and the District of Columbia.[102] In addition, a state statute allows cohabitants in Arizona to claim one another as dependents on their state tax forms.[103]

3.2 Tort Claims Against Third Parties

Standing to bring a variety of tort claims—for the wrongful death of a partner, for negligent infliction of emotional distress, and for loss of consortium, for example—is also available to cohabitants in a few states. Wrongful death

---

98. SOCIAL SECURITY ACT, 42 U.S.C. § 416(h) (2003).

99. 1 U.S.C. § 7.

100. *See* Blumberg, *supra* note 20, at 1114–45.

101. *See* Chambers, *supra* note 55, at 472–75.

102. Gates, *supra* note 66, at 31 (App. 4).

103. ARIZ. REV. STAT. ANN. § 43-1001 (2002).

suits are intended to compensate a victim's survivors for the economic benefit that they would have received if the deceased person had not died as a result of the defendant's conduct.[104] The right to sue for wrongful death is derived entirely from statute and thus depends upon the wording of the state's wrongful death statute; traditionally, that language (for example, "heir," a term referring to a specified list of persons under state intestacy law) has ruled out recovery by cohabitants.[105] In some states, such as California, this law was changed by passage of the domestic partnership act, which conferred the right to sue for wrongful death upon registered partners, and the state's wrongful death statute has been revised so as to include registered domestic partners among the list of parties entitled to sue.[106] In a few other states, a wrongful death action may be available to cohabitants depending on the language of the state wrongful death statute and its interpretation by the courts—specifically, whether it defines the parties entitled to sue to include, more generally, persons dependent upon the deceased person at the time of his or her death.[107]

Actions for negligent infliction of emotional distress and for loss of consortium, by contrast, are derived from the common law rather than from statute. Their availability to cohabitants is fought out in the case law, with different states reaching opposing conclusions. Tort claims for negligent infliction of emotional distress (NIED) provide a good example. NIED damage claims are available in both California and New Jersey to family members who are at the scene of an accident caused by the negligence of a third party and who witness the death or serious injury of a close family member.[108] So, for example, a mother witnessing her son's gruesome death trapped in a malfunctioning elevator is entitled to sue not only for damages for his death

---

104. Anne E. Simerman, *The Right of a Cohabitant to Recover in Tort: Wrongful Death, Negligent Infliction of Emotional Distress and Loss of Consortium*, 32 U. LOUISVILLE J. FAM. L. 531, 532 (1993–94).

105. *Id.; see, e.g.*, Garcia v. Douglas Aircraft Co., 184 Cal. Rptr 390 (Cal. Ct. App. 1982); Harrod v. Pacific Southwest Airlines, Inc., 173 Cal. Rptr 68 (Cal. Ct. App. 1981).

106. CAL. CODE CIV. PRO. § 377.60 (2005). Wrongful death actions are available to registered domestic partners in New Jersey and the District of Columbia as well. *See* Gates et al., *supra* note 66, at 31 (App. 4).

107. *See, e.g.*, HAWAII STAT. ANN. § 663-3 ("by any person wholly or partly dependent upon the deceased person"); ALASKA STAT. ANN. § 09.55.580 ("by a spouse or children, or other dependents"); W. VA. CODE § 55-7-6) ("any persons who were financially dependent upon the decedent at the time of his or her death"). *See* Simerman, *supra* note 104, at 533.

108. *See* Dillon v. Legg, 441 P.2d 912 (Cal. 1968); Portee v. Jaffee, 417 A.2d 521 (N.J. 1980).

but also for emotional damage inflicted directly upon her by the experience of observing his injury.[109] The rationale underlying this tort has to do with the foreseeability that extreme emotional distress will be caused by an experience like this, due to the closeness of the relationship between the victim and the person observing.

But when a heterosexual cohabitant in California brought such a claim after witnessing his partner's death in an auto accident, recovery was denied on the familiar grounds that granting cohabitants such rights would interfere with the state's interest in promoting marriage.[110] The court was also determined to draw a bright-line rule that would not require courts to inquire into the details of an intimate relationship and would also prevent extension of NIED claims to large numbers of people.[111] This rule, of course, was changed with respect to some California cohabitants by passage of the domestic partnership statute that conferred upon registered partners all the state law benefits available to married parties, but apart from older couples registered as domestic partners, opposite-sex cohabitants cannot bring NIED claims in California.

By contrast, when a similar case arose in New Jersey, the court rejected a bright-line approach based upon marriage and allowed recovery for NIED by cohabitants who could show that they were in an intimate and familial relationship, tested by its duration, mutual dependence, and the like.[112] In that case, Eileen Dunphy's fiancé Michael was helping a friend change a tire on the highway; Eileen and Michael had been living together for about two years at that time. A negligent driver struck and either dragged or propelled Michael's body 240 feet. His fiancée was standing about five feet away when this happened, saw the whole accident, and ran to Michael, trying to assist and comfort him until the ambulance arrived. After he died the next day, Eileen suffered, not surprisingly, from depression and anxiety for which she required psychiatric treatment.

The New Jersey Supreme Court held that Eileen Dunphy was entitled to recover from the driver who had hit Michael for negligent infliction of emotional distress. The court said that it was confident that trial courts would be able to identify relationships that entitled the parties to such entitlement

---

109. Portee v. Jaffee, 417 A.2d 521 (N.J. 1980).

110. *See* Elden v. Sheldon, 758 P.2d 582, 586–87 (Cal. 1988).

111. *Id.* at 587–88.

112. Dunphy v. Gregor, 642 A.2d 372 (N.J. 1994).

and disagreed with the California court that extension of this right would in any way damage the state's interest in protecting marriage. The prospect of tort recovery in such a disastrous case, it pointed out, would be unlikely to figure into anyone's decision whether or not to get married.[113] The inquiry the court must undertake to determine whether the couple is in a marriage-like relationship is similar to that for identifying meretricious relationships in Washington, requiring it to determine "the duration of the relationship, the degree of mutual dependence, the extent of common contributions to a life together, the extent and quality of shared experience, and . . . 'whether the plaintiff and the injured person were members of the same household, their emotional reliance on each other, the particulars of their day to day relation-ship, and the manner in which they related to each other in attending to life's mundane requirements.'"[114] New Hampshire courts have also adopted this analysis, extending the cause of action for NIED to cohabitants in that state as well.[115] In Ohio, the courts appear willing to do the same but only in cases where the cohabitant was directly involved in the accident and not purely an observer, thus treating cohabitants differently from spouses for purposes of this cause of action.[116]

A claim for loss of consortium, though often brought together with an NIED claim, is one for damages for being deprived of the companionship of a family member. Originally derived from an old English action to recover for the loss of a servant and then extended to loss of a wife, the modern tort has been reinterpreted as one for loss of companionship, both emotional and sexual.[117] As of 2009, the only state willing to extend this claim to persons who are unmarried has been New Mexico.[118] In *Lozoya v. Sanchez*, Sara Lozoya had lived with Ubaldo Lozoya for at least fifteen years in a relationship that

---

113. *See Dunphy*, 642 A.2d at 379 (quoting *Elden*, 758 P.2d at 586 (Broussard, J., dissenting)).

114. *Id.* at 378 (quoting the appellate court opinion).

115. Graves v. Estabrook, 818 A.2d 1255 (N.H. 2003).

116. Binns v. Fredendall, 513 N.E.2d 278, 281 (Ohio 1987).

117. *See, e.g.*, Alisha M. Carlile, *Like Family: Rights of Nonmarried Cohabitational Partners in Loss of Consortium Actions*, 48 B.C.L. REV. 391, 395–96 (2005).

118. *See* Lozoya v. Sanchez, 66 P.2d 948 (N.M. 2003). *Contra* Feliciano v. Rosemar Silver Co., 514 N.E.2d 1095 (Mass. 1987) (denying cause of action for loss of consortium for couple who had lived together "as a *de facto* married couple" for twenty years before workplace accident causing injury); Lennon v. Charney, 797 N.Y.S.2d 891 (N.Y. Sup. Ct. 2005) (deny-ing claim to partner registered under the New York City Domestic Partnership Law).

would have qualified as a common law marriage if the state still recognized that status; they had three children and all shared the same surname. The New Mexico Supreme Court held that Sara could bring a claim for loss of consortium despite the fact that they were not married, stating that:

> We must consider the purpose behind the cause of action for loss of consortium. A person brings this claim to recover for damage to a *relational* interest, not a legal interest. To use the legal status as a proxy for a significant enough relational interest is not the most precise way to determine to whom a duty is owed. Furthermore, the use of legal status necessarily excludes many persons whose loss of a significant relational interest may be just as devastating as the loss of a legal spouse.[119]

In reaching this conclusion, the New Mexico court relied heavily upon the New Jersey Supreme Court's opinion in *Dunphy v. Gregor*, although that case concerned a claim for negligent infliction of emotional distress rather than loss of consortium, and held that New Mexico courts should apply the *Dunphy* test for proving an intimate familial relationship. The plaintiff would start with the benefit of a presumption of such a relationship, however, if the couple were either married, engaged, or would have met the test for common law marriage if it were still recognized.[120]

Ironically, the courts in the state that decided *Dunphy* do not agree with this conclusion, although they have yet to set out a comprehensive and reasoned decision explaining why this is so. The issue was first raised as a question of New Jersey law by a federal court deciding an admiralty case pertaining to New Jersey residents. Although there was no state court precedent, the federal court held that the New Jersey courts would be likely to recognize a loss of consortium claim brought by a cohabitant because to do so was consistent with the New Jersey courts' views about the compensatory purposes of tort law in general, with their recognition of an implied contract cause of action between cohabitants, and with the development of the loss of consortium tort into one protecting a relational rather than a property interest.[121] Within two years, however, courts in New Jersey repudiated the federal

---

119. *Lozoya*, 66 P.2d at 955 (emphasis in original).

120. *Id.* at 957–58.

121. Bulloch v. United States, 487 F. Supp. 1078 (1980).

court's opinion in this respect and held that the right to recover for loss of consortium depended upon marriage.[122] It is therefore hard to predict what the post-*Dunphy* New Jersey Supreme Court would conclude more than two decades later. In the meantime, New Jersey is inconsistent in its treatment of NIED and loss of consortium claims, extending the first but not the second to cohabitants, although both can be seen as claims brought to compensate harms deriving from a close relationship, harms which, as many have pointed out, cannot be identified by the existence of a marriage license or its absence.[123] Law students writing notes or comments for law journals see no reason why loss of consortium should not be extended to cohabitants, perhaps because they are writing in a period when cohabitation has become so common.[124]

To sum up, the right of cohabitants to sue third parties for injuries to their relationships is still very limited and depends upon the state in which they live. Given the courts' insistence upon limiting these claims to cohabitants whose relationships mirror conventional models of marriage, it is ironic that the majority of unmarried couples who are now protected under these circumstances are same-sex couples—a result, apparently, of publicizing and personalizing their plight after 9/11 in New Jersey and the case in which Diane Whipple witnessed her partner's death from being attacked by their neighbor's dog in California.[125]

3.3 Health-Related Benefits

Another area in which a number of benefits are available on a variety of noncontract-based, nonstatus-based grounds is health care. As described previously, health insurance coverage of cohabitants of domestic partners is

---

122. *See* Leonardis v. Morton Chemical Co., 445 A.2d 45 (N.J. Super. Ct. 1982); Childers v. Shannon, 444 A.2d 1141 (N.J. Super. Ct. 1982).

123. *See, e.g.,* Simerman, *supra* note 104, at 543.

124. *See* Simerman, *supra* note 104; Carlile, *supra* note 117.

125. The bill giving domestic partners the right to sue for wrongful death in California was introduced as a response to public outcry over the plight of Diane Whipple's lesbian partner, who witnessed the savage attack by their neighbor's dogs. *See* Michael Jay Gorback, *Negligent Infliction of Emotional Distress: Has the Legislative Response to Diane Whipple's Death Rendered the Hard-Line Stance of* Elden *and* Thing *Obsolete?*, 54 HASTINGS L.J. 273, 275–76 (2002).

increasingly offered not only by municipalities and counties to their employees but also by private companies throughout the United States, especially high-tech companies, those in the entertainment industry, and academic institutions, particularly on the east and west coasts.[126] The cost of providing this benefit has been fairly low, given the low participation rate, which apparently results from the fact that cohabitants are more likely than married couples to each be employed and thus have separate health insurance.[127] Moreover, the net economic cost of the insurance is greater to cohabitants than to married couples because the benefit is currently taxed as income to the unmarried, a disincentive to enrolling.[128] Challenges to exclusion of cohabitants from family health insurance coverage as discrimination based on either marital status or sexual orientation have generally failed, on the grounds that married and unmarried couples may be treated differently because the latter have no legal duty of mutual support.[129] Although the court in one Alaska case found that denial of coverage to the gay male partner of an employee constituted discrimination on the basis of marital status, courts deciding the mirror image case (claiming discrimination against heterosexual cohabitants) have disagreed.[130] The health insurance issue may become even more pressing in the face of the health insurance crisis in the United States and the massive number of persons who are uninsured—a problem that would not arise if the United States had universal health insurance that covered persons as individuals, as all other major Western democracies do.

Decision making about health care in an emergency can also present an important issue for cohabitants. While cohabitants may execute documents to designate one another in advance as the person to make such decisions,

---

126. *See* Hein, *supra* note 50, at 28–34.

127. *Id.* at 32.

128. *See* Chambers, *supra* note 55, at 475.

129. *See e.g.*, Phillips v. Wisconsin Pers. Comm'n, 482 N.W.2d 121 (Wis. Ct. App. 1992); *see also* Craig W. Christensen, *Legal Ordering of Family Values: The Case of Gay and Lesbian Families*, 18 CARDOZO L. REV. 1299, 1375–79 (1997).

130. *See* Tumeo v. Univ. of Alaska, No. 4FA-94-43 Civ., 1995 WL 238359 (Alaska Super. Jan. 11, 1995); *cf.* Irizarry v. Bd. of Education, 251 F.3d 604 (7th Cir. 2001) (finding that board of education policy extending health benefits only to same-sex domestic partners was rationally related to the board's legitimate goals and did not violate equal protection). *See also* Holguin v. Flores, 18 Cal. Rptr. 3d 749 (Ct. App. 2004) (finding that statutory distinction between registered domestic partners and unmarried heterosexual cohabitants for purposes of wrongful death action had a rational basis and thus did not violate the equal protection clause).

most fail to do so; and, as described in Chapter 1, most state health care surrogate statutes do not include domestic partners in the list of persons authorized to make these decisions, and at least one prioritizes them lower than adult children.[131] Unprotected by statute, cohabitants are left to the courts if they desire to assert rights in this respect. Thus, a cohabitant may face a legal battle if her partner is, for example, incapacitated in an accident and critical decisions need to be made about his care, particularly if the partner is opposed by hostile family members.[132] Of course, exclusion of cohabitants from health care surrogate statutes and by legal battles with the partner's other family members defeats the underlying purpose of substituted decision making in general, for the partner is the person most likely to know what the incapacitated individual would have wanted if he or she were able to express a preference. Opposite-sex cohabitants who register as domestic partners in Maine, California, New Jersey, and the District of Columbia are now protected under these circumstances.[133]

🌺 4. Cohabitants and Their Children

Finally, significant legal consequences can attach to cohabitation with respect to children. The situation differs depending upon whether the children are the biological offspring of the two cohabitants, as about 50 percent are,[134] or of only one of the two, with the other cohabitant in a position similar to a stepparent. Where the children are theirs jointly, many of the traditional legal consequences of being unmarried no longer pose problems. A major breakthrough in this respect was the Supreme Court's 1972 decision in

---

131. *See* Robbennolt & Johnson, *supra* note 19, at 455 & n. 144, 426 & n. 69

132. *Cf. In re* Guardianship of Kowalski, 478 N.W.2d 790 (Minn. Ct. App. 1991) (describing eight-year struggle of lesbian cohabitant to be appointed guardian of her severely incapacitated partner in the face of opposition from the partner's family of origin, occasioned both by their homophobia and differing conceptions of the potential capacities of handicapped persons).

133. *See* Gates et al., *supra* note 66, at 31 (App. 4).

134. *See, e.g.*, Gregory Acs & Sandi Nelson, "Honey, I'm Home." Changes in Living Arrangements in the Late 1990s, Urban Institute New Federalism National Survey of America's Families B-38; Rose M. Kreider & Jason Fields, Living Arrangements of Children:2001 5 (Table 2) (U.S. Census Bureau 2001).

Stanley v. Illinois.[135] Joan and Peter Stanley lived together over a period of eighteen years and had three children. When Joan died, following provisions of a state statute, the children were considered to be without any legal parent and thus were removed from Peter's custody and made wards of the state. He successfully challenged this action on equal protection grounds, arguing that the statute treating unmarried parents differently from married parents in this respect summarily deprived him of a fundamental right (to raise his children) without any finding that he was an unfit parent. The Supreme Court agreed, pointing out in its decision that to take children away from their surviving biological parent without any finding that he was unfit was not in their best interest. The decision in *Stanley* thus guarantees that a fit biological but unmarried parent has a right to custody, at least in a case where he, the mother, and the children have all been living together.

If both of the cohabiting parents are alive and seeking custody, this decision will be made after a hearing based on the best interest of the child standard, and a right to visitation on the part of the noncustodial parent will be assumed to be in the child's best interest. Subsequent Supreme Court cases, arising in the context of unmarried fathers asserting a right to object to adoption of their biological child by the mother's new husband have qualified this right in situations where the biological father had not lived with the child, failed to support it, and neglected to seek a declaration of paternity prior to the stepparent adoption.[136] Thus, cohabiting parents' relationships to their biological children are recognized and protected so long as they have not in some way abandoned them. Otherwise, each biological parent's rights to custody and visitation and their obligations of support will parallel those of married parents.

Cohabitants in the position of stepparents to their partner's child from another relationship (or by adoption), however, will confront substantial obstacles to continuing their relationship to the child if the natural parent dies or their relationship dissolves. Even married stepparents have traditionally been given no rights at the end of their marriage to a child's biological parent, but rights to visitation and sometimes even to custody are gradually

---

135. 405 U.S. 645 (1972).

136. *Cf.* Caban v. Mohammed, 441 U.S. 380 (1979) *with* Quilloin v. Walcott, 434 U.S. 246 (1978); Lehr v. Robertson, 463 U.S. 248 (1983). *But see* Michael H. v. Gerald D., 491 U.S. 110 (1989) (departing from this principle where the mother was married to another man at the time the child was conceived and born).

being extended to them in some jurisdictions.[137] By contrast, the second parent in a cohabiting relationship is typically denied the rights of a stepparent and must struggle even to obtain visitation upon dissolution of the relationship. In one Iowa case, for example, a woman had served in the role of a child's mother on a daily basis while she lived with his father, who was a truck driver often away from home.[138] When their relationship ended after five years and the birth of two additional children, she was denied visitation even though this would also result in severing the boy's bond with his two half-sisters and despite the court's own belief that visitation was in the child's best interest. Nonetheless, the Iowa Supreme Court held that it had no authority to grant visitation to a nonparent in the face of the biological parent's opposition. The result was similar, though with the genders reversed, in a 2001 New York case, in which the nonbiological parent had lived with the child and his mother for six years, during which they had formed a close and loving relationship; the court nonetheless found that the nonbiological father had no standing to seek custody.[139] Some petitions for visitation are dismissed, like this one in New York, based on lack of standing, which can prevent even a hearing concerning the interests and merits involved in the particular case. Others founder on the requirement, if visitation is opposed by the biological parent or parents, that a nonbiological parent show that denial of visitation would clearly be detrimental to the child or that other extraordinary circumstances exist, a difficult standard to overcome.[140]

Some states have passed statutes that allow visitation by third parties, usually inspired by grandparents' desire for visitation after the death or divorce of their grandchild's parent. Some of these statutes are limited by their terms to grandparents and stepparents, but others define the third parties broadly enough to include former cohabitants. The statute regarding visitation by unmarried persons in Minnesota, for example, provides that:

> If an unmarried minor has resided in a household with a person, other than a foster parent, for two years or more and no longer resides with the

---

137. *See, e.g.*, David R. Fine & Mark A. Fine, *Learning from Social Sciences: A Model for Reformation of the Laws Affecting Stepfamilies*, 97 DICK. L. REV. 49, 49–58 (1992); June Carbone, *The Legal Definition of Parenthood: Uncertainty at the Core of Family Identity*, 65 LA. L. REV. 1295, 1311–14 (2005).

138. *In re* Marriage of Freel, 448 N.W.2d 26 (Iowa 1989).

139. Multari v. Sorrell, 731 N.Y.S.2d 238 (N.Y. App. Div. 2001).

140. *See, e.g.*, Stockey v. Gayden, 280 Cal. Rptr. 862 (Cal. Ct. App. 1991); Cooper v. Merkel, 470 N.W.2d 253 (S.D. 1991).

person, the person may petition the district court for an order granting the person reasonable visitation rights to the child during the child's minority. The court shall grant the petition if it finds that:

(1) visitation rights would be in the best interests of the child;
(2) the petitioner and child had established emotional ties creating a parent and child relationship; and
(3) visitation rights would not interfere with the relationship between the custodial parent and the child.

The court shall consider the reasonable preference of the child, if the court considers the child to be of sufficient age to express a preference.[141]

Thus, in Minnesota, cohabitants of at least two years duration are entitled to a hearing on the question of visitation and are then entitled to visitation if they can show that they have bonded closely with their former cohabitant's child; that visitation would be in the child's best interest; that it would not interfere with the child's relationship to its biological parent; and that, if the child is old enough, the child wants to continue the relationship with the former cohabitant.

A similar right appears to be available from the language of the Arizona statute regarding any person who has been "*in loco parentis*," meaning "a person who has been treated as a parent by the child and who has formed a meaningful parental relationship with the child for a substantial period of time."[142] This, like other nonparental visitation statutes, however, has been reinterpreted in light of the Supreme Court's 2000 decision about grandparental visitation.[143] In *Troxel v. Granville*, the Court found that Washington's visitation statute was unconstitutionally broad because it did not defer to a fit parent's determination that visitation was not in the child's best interest. Interpreting its own statute in light of *Troxel*, the Arizona appellate court, in a case involving visitation by a nonbiological lesbian parent, essentially read a so-called parental presumption into the visitation section, holding that "the court should apply a rebuttable presumption that a fit parent's decision to deny or limit visitation was made in the child's best interests."[144] It also

---

141. MINN. STAT. ANN. § 257C.08(4).

142. ARIZ. REV. STAT. § 25-415 (C).

143. Troxel v. Granville, 530 U.S. 57 (2000).

144. Egan v. Fridlund-Horne, 211 P. 3d 1213, 1224 (Ariz. Ct. App. 2009).

reaffirmed the Arizona courts' holding, in a case involving opposite-sex cohabitants decided prior to passage of the visitation statute, that Arizona had never adopted the *de facto* parent doctrine as a matter of common law.[145] Other states that have third-party visitation statutes with definitions broad enough to cover cohabitants include some form of the parental presumption in their text, but it is unclear whether the presumption can be rebutted simply by evidence of the former cohabitant's relationship to the child, such as previous financial support or status as primary caretaker.[146]

Cohabitants unable to take advantage of a third-party visitation statute have asserted standing based on the *de facto* parent doctrine, on their status *in loco parentis*, as a psychological parent, or on other equitable doctrines. These doctrines have been developed most extensively and successfully in the context of cases involving lesbian couples who have had children by artificial insemination of one of the partners. If they separated, the nonbiological mother was often denied any standing to seek custody or visitation even though she had participated in the decision to have a child and coparented the child for some period.[147] More recently, however, courts in some states have been awarding visitation and in a few cases even custody to the nonbiological mother based on one of these equitable doctrines.[148] One of the first cases to hold that a court had equitable powers to grant visitation to a lesbian in a parent-like relationship with her partner's child was decided by the Wisconsin Supreme Court in 1995.[149] In it, Justice Shirley Abrahamson provided a structure of analysis that has been borrowed by courts in other states, holding that the court should decide whether visitation is in the best interests of the child if the petitioner proves four elements:

> (1) that the biological or adoptive parent consented to, and fostered, the petitioner's formation and establishment of a parent-like relationship with the child; (2) that the petitioner and the child lived together in the same household; (3) that the petitioner assumed obligations of parenthood by

---

145. *Id.* at 1221, reaffirming holding in Hughes v. Creighton, 798 P.2d 403 (Ariz. Ct. App. 1990).

146. *See* Nev. Rev. Stat. Ann. 125C.050(2),(4),(6); Or. Rev. Stat. § 109.119(1),(2),(4).

147. *See, e.g.,* Alison D. v. Virginia M., 569 N.Y.S.2d 586 (N.Y. 1991).

148. *See, e.g.,* Jones v. Boring Jones, 884 A.2d 915 (Pa. Super. Ct. 2005); E.N.O. v. L.M.M., 711 N.E.2d 886 (Mass. 1999); Mason v. Dwinnell, 660 S.E.2d 58 (N.C. Ct. App. 2008).

149. *In re* Custody of H.S.H.-K. (Holtzman v. Knott), 533 N.W.2d 419 (Wis. 1995).

taking significant responsibility for the child's care, education and development, including contributing towards the child's support, without expectation of financial compensation; and (4) that the petitioner has been in a
parental role for a length of time sufficient to have established with the
child a bonded, dependent relationship parental in nature.[150]

Significantly, in finding that the courts had this power, Justice Abrahamson
relied upon her prior decision in *Watts v. Watts*, the opposite-sex cohabitant case described in the previous chapter, in which the court held that it
had equitable powers to decide property disputes between unmarried
cohabitants.[151] Other courts following Justice Abrahamson's analysis in
same-sex parent visitation cases have also specifically stated that, although
the case before them arose in the context of a same-sex relationship, the
same standard would govern a case involving unmarried opposite-sex
couples as well.[152] Still others believe that the Supreme Court's decision in
Troxel prevents such a conclusion, whether the former partners were of the
same or opposite sex.[153] In sum, cohabitants who seek to continue their relationship with a former cohabitant's child will face significant legal problems
if the state in which they live has no third-party visitation statute or has not
adopted some version of the *de facto* parent doctrine. Even if it has, they may
confront problems raised by the *Troxel* decision.

Courts have been unsure about the exact scope of the holding in *Troxel*,
which was carefully drafted to fit the circumstances of the case before the
Supreme Court, one in which grandparents were seeking visitation, not
cohabitants, stepparents, or other third parties. Although some have applied
the holding and rationale from *Troxel* to cases involving former cohabitants,
there are many good reasons to distinguish the two situations. In a typical
case involving grandparents, like *Troxel*, the relationship the grandparents are

---

150. *Id.* at 421.

151. *Id.* at 431; Watts v. Watts, 405 N.W.2d 303 (1987).

152. *See, e.g.*, V.C. v. M.J.B., 748 A.2d 539, 541 (N.J. 2000) ("the standard we enunciate is applicable to all persons who have willingly, and with the approval of the legal parent, undertaken the duties of a parent to a child not related by blood or adoption").

153. *See, e.g.*, Janice M. v. Margaret K., 948 A.2d 73, 86–87, 93 (Md. Ct. App. 2008) (refusing to
follow pre-*Troxel* Maryland case and holding that court erred in granting visitation
to nonbiological lesbian mother on the grounds that she was *de facto* parent without
finding either that the biological mother was unfit or that exceptional circumstances
overcome the parental presumption).

seeking to maintain is one in which they receive visits from their grandchildren, as they had done prior to their child's divorce from the grandchild's other parent or before their child's death. This situation is not really comparable to one involving cohabitants. One has only to recollect the facts in the Iowa case described earlier to see the difference. There, the former cohabitant seeking visitation had not only lived with the child but also essentially served as the child's mother (as almost a single parent) for some five years.[154] The interests and emotions involved are quite different in such a case from ones involving grandparents unless the child was actually living with and being raised by the grandparents.

Despite these substantial obstacles, cohabitants have in a few cases succeeded in asserting standing to seek visitation.[155] This, of course, does not end the two-step proceeding; the former cohabitant must then go on to convince the court that visitation is in the child's best interest, and he or she is unlikely to succeed if there is another biological parent or parent figure of the same sex in the picture. Thus, in a Connecticut case decided the same year as one extending standing under the state's third-party visitation statute to a cohabitant,[156] the same court denied visitation to a man who had believed he was a child's biological father from birth and had served as his primary caretaker while he lived with the mother.[157] Now, however, the mother was living with another man who was alleged to have stepped into the role of psychological parent to the child.[158] The previous cohabitant thus lost any right to contact with the child he had always regarded as his own.

Although courts have been quick to assert that they would apply the same approach in cases involving same- and opposite-sex cohabiting couples, one may also question the strength of the analogy to lesbian second-parent jurisprudence. Two lesbians typically decide to have a child together, although only one of the two can give birth to it. Unless the egg of one woman is implanted in the other, the child will have a biological relationship only to one of them. But the courts are beginning to develop a concept of parenthood by

---

154. *In re* Marriage of Freel, 448 N.W.2d 26 (Iowa 1989).

155. *See, e.g.,* Barker v. Briggs, 544 A.2d 629 (Conn. 1988).

156. *Id.; see also* CONN. GEN. STAT. § 46b-59.

157. Temple v. Meyer, 544 A.2d 629 (Conn. 1988).

158. *Id.* at 632.

intent in cases involving artificially assisted reproduction,[159] and this doctrine fits the lesbian or gay situation nicely. The child would not exist without the intentional acts of the two parties, who may also draw up a coparenting agreement.[160] In a lesbian case, moreover, both parties are women and thus are likely to have cared for the child coequally rather than according to the unequal gendered division of labor common to many heterosexual couples, where one partner is the primary wage earner and the other takes care of the home and children. Also, because the child is typically produced by artificial insemination from an anonymous donor, there is no other potentially competing parent involved. These factual differences may affect courts deciding cohabitant cases, at least as factors in the consideration of the best interest of the child.

If cohabitants face substantial problems in the visitation context, they face even more daunting obstacles if seeking custody. First of all, third-party visitation statutes often set a higher standard for custody than for visitation, requiring, for example, proof that "it would be significantly detrimental to the child to remain or be placed in the custody of either of the child's living legal parents who wish to retain or obtain custody."[161] The only cases in which courts even consider granting custody to a former cohabitant involve quite extraordinary circumstances, close to abandonment of the child by its biological parent. In one North Carolina case, for example, a cohabitant had mothered her former partner's diabetic young daughter from the age of four to ten, often with little assistance from the child's father.[162] When the father sent the girl to live instead with his parents in Puerto Rico, she ended up in the hospital because of the elderly grandparents' inability to care for her diabetes. The court found the father's conduct to be "inconsistent with his constitutionally protected status as a parent" and held that his former cohabitant had standing to seek, and should be granted, custody based on the best interest of the child.[163] The far more frequent answer from courts faced with a petition for custody by a former cohabitant, however, is an

---

159. *See, e.g.*, Johnson v. Calvert, 851 P.2d 776 (Cal. 1993) (*en banc*) (holding that mother who provided egg that was implanted into surrogate was the natural mother because she intended to procreate the child).

160. *See, e.g.*, Mason v. Dwinnell, 660 S.E.2d 58, 60–61 (N.C. Ct. App. 2008).

161. Ariz. Rev. Stat. § 25-415A(2). *See also* Or. Rev. Stat. § 109.119(4)(a),(b).

162. Ellison v. Ramos, 502 S.E.2d 891 (N.C. Ct. App. 1998).

163. *Id.* at 896–97; *see also* Price v. Howard, 484 S.E.2d 528 (N.C. 1997) (holding that father who had been told, falsely, that he was the child's biological father and whose mother

almost peremptory denial.[164] Alternately, the court may require the former cohabitant to show that the child's welfare *requires* that the nonbiological parent receive custody.[165]

Is there any way for cohabitants who want to ensure a continuing relationship with their partner's child to protect themselves? The approach that many lesbian nonbiological mothers have taken is to pursue a second-parent adoption. Adoption requires that a child's biological parent either voluntarily relinquish his or her parental rights or have them terminated by a court. In the case of a cohabitant attempting to adopt his partner's child, there will typically be another parent in the picture (unless the child has been adopted by the partner or born by means of artificial insemination from an anonymous donor), and that parent may not want his rights terminated. Second-parent adoption is a device that gets around the necessity of terminating the other parent's rights in an adoption. New York now allows second-parent adoption by both lesbian and heterosexual cohabitants.[166] This allows the unmarried partners of biological mothers, whether of the same or opposite sex, to adopt their partner's child without terminating the rights of the biological parent.

However, some states prohibit unmarried couples from adoption in general. Courts in these states may not allow persons of the opposite sex who are living together to make use of this procedure either to jointly adopt a child or to effect a second-parent adoption by the person in the position of a stepparent.[167] Moreover, second-parent adoption procedures are costly,

---

essentially abandoned the child to his care for several years may be given custody based on best interest of the child).

164. *See, e.g.,* Engel v. Kenner, 926 S.W.2d 472 (Mo. Ct. App. 1996); *In re* Custody of Dombrowski (Dombrowski v. Goodright), 705 P.2d 1218 (Wash. Ct. App. 1985); Van v. Zahorik, 597 N.W.2d 15 (Mich. 1999); *In re* Nelson, 825 A.2d 501 (N.H. 2003).

165. Buness v. Gillen, 781 P.2d 985 (Alaska 1989). *See also* Lawrence Schlam, *Third-Party "Standing" and Child Custody Disputes in Washington: Non-Parent Rights—Past, Present, and . . . Future?,* 43 GONZ. L. REV. 391, 445–46 (2007–08) (discussing approach of different states).

166. *In re* Jacob, 600 N.E.2d 397 (N.Y. 1995). *See also In re* Adoption of Carl, 709 N.Y.S.2d 905 (N.Y. Fam. Ct. Queens Co. 2000); *In re* Adoption of Joseph, 684 N.Y.S.2d 760 (N.Y. Surr. Ct. Oneida Co. 1998).

167. *See, e.g., In re* Meaux, 417 So.2d 522 (La. Ct. App. 1982); *In re* Jason C., 533 A.2d 32 (N.H. 1987) (Souter, J.). If either of these states wants to reconsider, neither of these cases is strictly on point. In *Meaux,* the parents seeking to adopt alleged that they were in fact the child's natural parents; in *Jason C.,* the petitioner was the divorced husband seeking to complete a joint adoption of a foster child which he and his wife had initiated before their divorce.

intrusive, and risky; and a successful outcome results in a family in which the coparents are legal strangers to one another, while many family benefits depend upon spousal status.[168]

Adoption is a right governed entirely by statute, and most adoption statutes provide that a single person or married couple jointly may adopt; they say nothing about joint adoptions by unmarried couples. Some judges have urged that courts should simply assume that "single person" includes its plural, thus including unmarried couples; other states have revised their statutes to make this clear.[169] Yet others have specifically ruled out adoption by unmarried couples, either in cases interpreting the state's statute or in the language of the statute itself. The Utah statute, for example, previously contained a specific finding by the legislature "that it is not in a child's best interest to be adopted by a person or persons who are cohabiting in a relationship that is not a legally valid and binding marriage under the laws of this state."[170] Commentators saw this provision as aimed not only at preventing adoptions by polygamous or same-sex couples but also at attempting to assure that children would be placed in homes that were likely to be permanent and stable—that is, with married rather than unmarried couples.[171] In 2008, however, the Utah statute was revised; that language was removed, and it appears now to focus solely upon the best interest of the child standard.[172] It is too soon to tell if adoption investigators and courts will continue to find that placement with unmarried couples is generally not in the best interest of children.

If an unmarried couple is not allowed to adopt, of course, one of the two may still be able to adopt as a single person. This may be necessary to

---

168. *See* Susan E. Dalton, *Protecting Our Parent-Child Relationships: Understanding the Strengths and Weaknesses of Second-Parent Adoption, in* QUEER FAMILIES, QUEER POLITICS: CHALLENGING CULTURE AND THE STATE 211–15 (Mary Bernstein & Renate Reimann eds., 2001).

169. *See In re* Jacob, 620 N.Y.S.2d 640, 641 (1994) (dissenting judges), *rev'd, In re* Jacob, 600 N.E.2d 397 (N.Y. 1995); CONN. GEN. STAT. § 45a-724 ("any parent of a minor child may agree in writing with one other person who shares parental responsibility for the child with such parent that the other person shall adopt or join in the adoption of the child, if the parental rights, if any, of any other person other than the parties to such agreement have been terminated").

170. Scott H. Clark, *Utah Prefers Married Couples*, 18 ST. THOMAS L. REV. 215, 215–16 (2005).

171. *Id.* at 222–25; *see also* William C. Duncan, *Marital Status and Adoption Values*, 6. J. L. FAM. STUD. 1 (2004).

172. *See* UTAH CODE ANN. § 78B-6-137.

adopt internationally.[173] If so, the child will be denied the many advantages of having two legal parents, which include benefits such as social security and insurance benefits in the event of the nonbiological parent's death, eligibility for coverage under both parents' health insurance, and the right to economic support from more than one person.[174] Moreover, if the couple separates, the nonadoptive partner may be out of luck if there is a conflict over custody or visitation.[175]

Finally, cohabiting couples experiencing fertility problems may not be able to have access to artificially assisted reproductive technology. Some states do not allow unmarried couples to use artificial insemination, although it is hard to see how any state could police this restriction; and states that allow surrogate motherhood contracts generally permit only married couples to engage in the practice—a prohibition that discriminates against gay couples desiring to have a biological child, as well as against cohabitants if the infertile member of the couple is the female.[176] Moreover, male cohabitants who consent to artificial insemination of their partners are not entitled to the presumption of paternity given to husbands in this situation and may encounter problems if they seek parental rights upon the termination of the cohabiting relationship, even if the two had entered into a contract purporting to grant such rights.[177] In sum, the relationship of cohabitants to children with whom they live may prove insecure.

As should be clear from the discussion in this chapter, the law concerning cohabitants' rights in the United States varies immensely from state to state and does not provide adequate protection for them in any state. As judges have felt uneasy when presented with cases involving injustices arising at the end of cohabiting relationships, they have tried to protect vulnerable cohabitants. During the late 1970s and 1980s, this unease led to the

---

173. *See, e.g.,* Janice M. v. Margaret K., 948 A.2d 73, 75 n.2 (Md. 2008).

174. *In re* Jacob, 636 N.Y.S.2d at 718; *In re* Tammy, 619 N.E.2d 315, 320 (Mass. 1993).

175. *Cf.* Janice M. v. Margaret K., 948 A.2d 73 (Md. 2008) (reversing grant of visitation to former partner of lesbian mother who had adopted a child during their 18-year committed relationship).

176. *See* Richard F. Storrow, *Rescuing Children from the Marriage Movement: The Case Against Marital Status Discrimination in Adoption and Assisted Reproduction*, 39 U.C. DAVIS L. REV. 305, 310–16 (2006).

177. *See* Dunkin v. Boskey, 98 Cal. Rptr. 2d 44 (Cal. Ct. App. 2000).

extension of cohabitants' rights based on contract, an approach that proved inadequate as other courts insisted upon finding express contracts and refused to imply contracts in the absence of direct evidence of agreement. The state of Washington's meretricious relationship doctrine is better in this respect, looking first for the characteristics of a relationship of interdependence and then imposing property distribution remedies upon cohabitants at the end of their relationships, even if they are unwilling. Neither approach, however, addresses rights against third parties, whether it be the state or an employer or a tortfeasor, which are often more valuable than rights *inter se*.

In addition, the campaign for same-sex marriage has spawned many and varied legislative schemes to set up domestic partnerships, ranging from the limited remedies contained in Hawaii's Reciprocal Beneficiaries Act to extension of all the benefits and obligations of marriage to registered domestic partners in California. The result of all this activity is a rather confusing legal situation in which cohabitants' rights are based upon a mixture of remedies that not only vary from state to state but also result in legal regimes within a single state based on different legal theories.

THREE

Cohabitation in the United States Today

DESPITE THE MANY LEGAL PROBLEMS COHABITANTS FACE, their numbers have burgeoned over the past several decades. The skyrocketing statistics have been accompanied by a rapid change in attitudes toward nonmarital cohabitation. It is difficult to discern which is cause and which is effect. Do people report feeling more favorable toward cohabitation because it is so much more common and thus familiar to them? Or has it become more frequent as a result of a change in popular attitudes, the so-called sexual revolution? Surely it is some combination of the two. Whatever the cause and effect, however, there has been a substantial change in living patterns over a short period of time, and U.S. family law has not kept pace.

This chapter will discuss these changes in attitudes and numbers over time, beginning with a vignette from the 1960s to illustrate how dramatic the changes have been. It then examines the picture as it exists in the early twenty-first century, describing the groups who cohabit and exploring why they do. This section is broken down into a discussion of different groups of cohabitants in the United States today, exploring variations by age, income, race, ethnic group, and prior marital status.

✄ 1. The 1960s

I begin with a story from the late 1960s, the era of flower children and sexual freedom, a story I personally observed with keen interest as a graduate student at Columbia University. An undergraduate at Barnard College named Linda LeClair moved in with her boyfriend in an off-campus apartment in 1967; this constituted a violation of Barnard's housing rules.[1] Barnard, the

---

1. An excellent source for a thick description of the 1968 Linda LeClair case is ELIZABETH H. PLECK, SHACKING UP: COHABITATION AND THE SEXUAL REVOLUTION, 1962 TO 1990, unpublished manuscript on file with author.

sister school to Columbia, was one of the "Seven Sisters"—the elite women's colleges regarded as the female counterpart of the Ivy League. It is directly across the street from Columbia, on the Upper West Side of Manhattan. The Barnard administration found out about Linda's deception when Linda and her boyfriend, Peter Behr, gave an interview that appeared in the March 4, 1968 *New York Times* under the title "An Arrangement: Living Together for Convenience, Security, Sex."[2] Although the names of the three student couples interviewed were disguised, the Barnard administrators quickly guessed that it was Linda and brought charges against her.[3]

The charges against Linda LeClair were considered by the Barnard judicial board, a group that included faculty members, at an open hearing; and the board recommended that she be deprived of her cafeteria privileges as a sanction.[4] This was generally regarded as a mere slap on the wrist and brought the wrath of numerous Barnard College alumnae down upon President Martha Peterson in the midst of a $7.5 million fundraising campaign.[5] Peterson decided to overrule the judicial board and sent Linda a letter stating, "It is my inescapable conclusion that no useful purpose can be served by your continued enrollment at Barnard College."[6] Ultimately, Linda did not return to Barnard in the fall, and she later graduated from another university.[7]

The remarkable thing about the LeClair scandal was that it was covered extensively and prominently in the *New York Times* and other newspapers throughout the nation. There were daily articles in the *Times* under headlines such as "Father Despairs of Barnard Daughter" and "Sex and the Single College Girl."[8] These were mild in comparison to coverage in the tabloid newspapers, and Linda was followed and photographed.[9] Reporters repeatedly

---

2. Judy Klemesrud, *An Arrangement: Living Together for Convenience, Security, Sex*, N.Y. TIMES, Mar. 4, 1968, at 40.

3. Deirdre Carmody, *Barnard Protest Follows 'Affair'*, N.Y. TIMES, Mar. 15, 1968, at 42.

4. Fred M. Hechinger, *Sex and the Single College Girl*, N.Y. TIMES, Apr. 21, 1968, at E9.

5. PLECK, *supra* note 1.

6. Deirdre Carmody, *Barnard President Delays Action on Defiant Girl*, N.Y. TIMES, May 9, 1968, at 42.

7. Deirdre Carmody, *Co-ed Disciplined by College Becomes a Dropout at Barnard*, N.Y. TIMES, Sept. 4, 1968, at 51; *see also* PLECK.

8. John R. Fenton, *Father Despairs of Barnard Daughter*, N.Y. TIMES, Apr. 20, 1968, at 27; Hechinger, *supra* note 4.

9. Laura Kavesh, *An Unmarried Couple's Memories of a Scandal*, CHICAGO TRIB., July 3, 1983, § 15, at 1, 4.

telephoned her parents for interviews, and one *Times* reporter even went to her home town in rural New Hampshire, did research in Linda's high school yearbook, interviewed people at the local public library about their reactions, and wrote a lengthy article describing the small town, its inhabitants, and activities there.[10] Letters arrived not only for the president of Barnard but also in Linda's and Peter's mailboxes, containing nasty messages such as "You are only a cheap tramp"; "You are better off dead than to have to face the world as you are"; and "Linda LeClair is nothing but a common WHORE and you a common PIMP!"[11]

The spring of 1968 was also the period of intense protests over the war in Vietnam, the assassination of Martin Luther King and ensuing riots, and student protests at Columbia that resulted in takeovers by students of several buildings on campus, bringing the university to a virtual halt. The president of Columbia called in New York's Tactical Police Force, who arrested students occupying the buildings and attacked the many other students who were observing the police action in the middle of the night. Linda LeClair and Peter Behr were in the thick of the action that spring, beginning with their intense involvement in the draft resistance movement (Peter turned in his draft card and refused induction into the army) and culminating with their arrest on campus on the night of April 30, 1968.[12]

The political techniques at use in the antiwar movement were adapted to protest the Barnard administration's actions against LeClair for her violation of the student housing rules. There were large demonstrations; a huge percentage of the student body signed a petition on her behalf; and fellow students signed declarations that they too had violated the housing rules.[13] LeClair herself saw the issue less as one about sexual freedom than about her own freedom, having reached the age of majority, to live wherever she liked.[14]

In a sense, the "affaire LeClair" became a composite of the many movements of the period—feminism, draft resistance, student rights, and the

---

10. Fenton, *supra* note 8.

11. *See* PLECK, *supra* note 1.

12. *Id.*

13. *Id.; see also* Kathleen Teltsch, *Barnard Students Demonstrate for a Bigger Role in Policy*, N.Y. TIMES, May 11, 1968, at 20.

14. Carmody, *Coed Disciplined, supra* note 7.

new counterculture. As Elizabeth Pleck, author of a forthcoming book about changing attitudes toward cohabitation, puts it: "College student cohabitation was part of the late sixties protest, communal living, the counterculture, draft resistance, the sexual revolution, and the growth of feminism."[15] Activists from the newly formed National Organization for Women came to campus to protest the continuing double standard that allowed men to live off campus but cabined women students with curfews, elaborate rules about signing in and out, and prohibitions against male students visiting in female students' rooms except under the most restricted of circumstances.[16]

The LeClair case probably struck such a strong theme with the media and the public, moreover, because it was seen as an emblem of this confrontation between the authority of one generation and the freedom asserted by the next. I have chosen to begin with this story because it is almost unfathomable that anything like it could occur at any Ivy League college today. Current Columbia and Barnard students agree if the headline of a 2008 article in the *Columbia Daily Spectator* is any indication, referring to the LeClair incident as having happened "in another era."[17]

The hullabaloo that Linda LeClair's case occasioned is also striking because cohabitation had been around for some time. It had led to the expulsion of a male graduate student from Cornell in 1962 and had occasioned a number of articles in popular journals during the mid-1960s.[18] The phenomenon was not confined to university campuses, the young, or the middle class. But its discovery and construction as a social problem apparently required that it be found among the children of the privileged classes, in the safety of their most elite institutions. Since then, colleges have changed their housing rules (Barnard began to do so as a result of the LeClair case),[19] and living together has become commonplace.

15. PLECK, *supra* note 1.

16. *Id.*

17. Maggie Astor, *In Another Era, a Barnard Student Makes National Headlines After Moving In With Boyfriend*, COLUM. SPECTATOR, Apr. 27, 2008, *at* http://columbiaspectator. com/2008/04/27/another-era-barnard-student-makes-national-headlines-after-moving-boyfriend.

18. Robert S. Gabriner & Rita P. Padnick, *University Ousts Student In Violation of Code*, CORNELL DAILY SUN, Oct. 9, 1962, at 1; *see, e.g., Unstructured Relations*, NEWSWEEK, July 4, 1966.

19. Deirdre Carmody, *Barnard Eases Its Rules For Off-Campus Housing*, N.Y. TIMES, Aug. 23, 1968, at 41.

✄ 2. Change over Time

2.1. Statistics

The number of cohabitants in the United States grew at a startling rate between the 1960 and the 2000 census—from fewer than 500,000 opposite-sex cohabiting couple households in 1960 to 4.9 million (almost 10 million individuals) in 2000.[20] This was an increase of almost 1000 percent over 40 years, an extremely rapid social change. Opposite-sex unmarried-partner households made up about 9 percent of all coupled households by 2000 (coupled households were 57 percent of all households).[21] As of 2008, the total number of opposite-sex unmarried couples had increased to 6.8 million (13.6 million individuals) according to the Census Bureau.[22] Part of this change can be accounted for by what sociologists and demographers call age cohort replacement—that is, cohabitation was embraced with enthusiasm by younger persons and then, as each birth cohort ages, cohabitation spreads into older groups within the population as well:

> [W]e see the dramatic role of cohort replacement as the cohorts on the leading edge of the shift to cohabitation have progressed through the age structure. For example, the proportion of 40–44 year olds who had ever lived in a cohabiting relationship increased by about one half as younger

---

20. Pamela J. Smock & Wendy D. Manning, *Living Together Unmarried in the United States: Demographic Perspectives and Implications for Family Policy*, 26 L. & POL'Y 87, 88 (2004); U.S. CENSUS BUREAU, MARRIED-COUPLE AND UNMARRIED-PARTNER HOUSEHOLDS: 2000 1 (2003).

21. *Id.* at 3. The census is assumed to undercount cohabitants. First, it counts households rather than couples, so that if two unmarried-partner couples reside in the same household, only one would be counted, and if a son and his unmarried partner resided with his married parents, only a married household would be counted. *Id.* at 2. Second, qualitative research demonstrates that cohabitants do not always understand that "unmarried partner" refers to their living arrangement. Wendy D. Manning & Pamela J. Smock, *Measuring and Modeling Cohabitation: New Perspectives From Qualitative Data*, 67 J. MARRIAGE & FAM. 989, 1000 (2005) (drawing on 115 in-depth interviews with young working-class cohabitants).

22. U.S. CENSUS BUREAU, CURRENT POPULATION SURVEY, 2008 ANNUAL SOCIAL AND ECONOMIC SUPPLEMENT, Table UC1. *Opposite Sex Unmarried Couples by Labor Force Status of Both Partners: 2008*, available at http://www.census.gov/population/www/socdemo/hh-fam/cps2008.html [hereinafter CPS 2008].

cohorts aged into this category. By 1995, half of the women in their thirties had cohabited . . .[23]

As we have seen in the last chapter, these dramatic statistics about the increasing prevalence of cohabitation began to make an impression upon courts in the late 1970s.[24]

Not surprisingly, attitudes toward cohabitation changed rapidly over this period as well. Ever since cohabitation gained wide acceptance among young people in the 1980s and 1990s, the trend has been toward ever broader endorsement of nonmarital cohabitation among other groups in the population as well.[25] By 1997–98, 59.1 percent of women and 66.9 percent of men thought living together was a good idea, compared to only 33 percent of women and 46.9 percent of men in 1976–77.[26] There were cross-generational and gender differences of opinion on the issue, although the direction of change was consistently upward for both genders and generations. While 23 percent of mothers agreed that living together was all right in 1980, 44.4 percent of their daughters and 59.4 percent of their sons agreed; by 1993, 32.6 percent of mothers, 64.2 percent of daughters and 71.8 percent of sons approved of cohabitation.[27]

Some studies indicate that this attitude change was due at least in part to respondents' increased familiarity with cohabitation. In particular, once individuals have cohabited themselves, they continue to view cohabitation favorably thereafter, whether they go on to marry or not.[28] Adults who are divorced also view cohabitation with favor, leading the authors of one study to conclude that "few, if any, factors will operate as a brake on the increasing

---

23. Larry Bumpass & Hsien-Hen Lu, *Trends in Cohabitation and Implications for Children's Family Contexts in the United States*, 54 POPULATION STUD. 29, 31–32 (2000) (based on NSFH, as updated by the 1995 cycle of the National Survey of Family Growth).

24. *See, e.g.,* Marvin v. Marvin, 557 P.2d 106, 122 (Cal. 1976); Beal v. Beal, 577 P.2d 507, 508 n.2 (Or. 1978) (en banc).

25. Arland Thornton & Linda Young-DeMarco, *Four Decades of Trends in Attitudes Toward Family Issues in the United States: The 1960s Through the 1990s*, 63 J. MARRIAGE & FAM. 1009, 1023–25 (2001). *See also* William G. Axinn & Arland Thornton, *The Transformation in the Meaning of Marriage, in* THE TIES THAT BIND: PERSPECTIVES ON MARRIAGE AND COHABITATION 147, 156–57 (Linda J. Waite ed., Aldine de Gruyter 2000).

26. Thornton and Young-DeMarco, *supra* note 25, at 1024 (Table 5).

27. *Id.*

28. Mick Cunningham & Arland Thornton, *The Influence of Union Transitions on White Adults' Attitudes Toward Cohabitation*, 67 J. MARRIAGE & FAM. 710, 719 (2005).

acceptability of cohabitation."[29] In a Gallup/USA Today poll taken in September 2007, only 27 percent of the respondents said that they disapproved of men and women living together without being married.[30] About 60 percent of couples now live together prior to marriage.[31] Thus, far from being deviant behavior, cohabitation is now the normal way to initiate unions.[32]

2.2. Rate and Age of Marriage

Over this same period, the median age of first marriage rose dramatically— from twenty-three for men at first marriage and twenty for women in 1966, to twenty-seven for men and twenty-five for women by 1996, and appears to have remained steady in the following years.[33] The total rate of marriage—that is, the percent of all those ever married—has declined from about 95 percent in the 1950s to hover around 90 percent today.[34] This decline may be explained in part by the changing age structure of the population, so that fewer persons are of prime marriage age than in earlier periods; but the rate still falls when one corrects for that.[35] Nonetheless, about 70 percent of men and 78 percent of women in the United States have married at least once by the time they are thirty-four; about 80 percent of men and 84 percent of women have done so by the time they are thirty-nine; and about 86 percent of men and 88 percent

---

29. *Id.*

30. Data provided by the Roper Center for Public Opinion Research, University of Connecticut. Poll was conducted by the Gallup Organization on September 7–8, 2007 with a national adult sample of 1,028.

31. In 1970, cohabitation preceded 11 percent of marriages and 56 percent in the 1990s, an increase of 600 percent in less than 30 years. Michael Svarer, *Is Your Love in Vain? Another Look at Premarital Cohabitation and Divorce*, 39 J. HUM. RESOURCES 523, 531 (2004).

32. *See, e.g.*, Scott M. Stanley et al., *Maybe I Do: Interpersonal Commitment and Premarital or Nonmarital Cohabitation*, 25 J. FAM. ISSUES 496, 514 (2004).

33. R.S. Oropesa & Bridget K. Gorman, *Ethnicity, Immigration, and Beliefs about Marriage as a "Tie That Binds,"* in THE TIES THAT BIND, *supra* note 25, at 188; U.S. CENSUS BUREAU, NUMBER, TIMING, AND DURATION OF MARRIAGES AND DIVORCES: 2001 4 (2003). *See also* U.S. CENSUS BUREAU, ESTIMATED MEDIAN AGE AT FIRST MARRIAGE, BY SEX: 1890 TO THE PRESENT, Table MS-2 (2006).

34. Andrew J. Cherlin, *The Deinstitutionalization of American Marriage*, 66 J. MARRIAGE & FAM. 848, 852–53 (2004).

35. Joshua R. Goldstein & Catherine T. Kenney, *Marriage Delayed or Marriage Forgone? New Cohort Forecasts of First Marriage for U.S. Women*, 66 AM. SOC. REV. 506, 508 (2001).

of women by the time they are forty-nine.[36] Some commentators have concluded that cohabitation has substituted for the lost or postponed marriages; and increased rates of cohabitation by divorced persons definitely seem to account for decreases in the rate of remarriage among them.[37]

The changes in the age and rate of marriage may not be as drastic as recent statistics suggest, however. The oft-used baseline of 1966 is not the best one for purposes of comparison. The median age of marriage was unusually low in the 1960s, having fallen from twenty-six for men and twenty-two for women in 1900.[38] The 95 percent marriage rate of the 1950s was also an anomaly; 90 percent is closer to what the rate was at the beginning of that century.[39] The 1950s and early 1960s were a period when the generation returning from war rushed to marry and have children (the "baby boom"), a movement accompanied by a new cult of domesticity.[40] The 1950s and 1960s in the United States were also an era of prosperity perhaps never to be revisited; historically, during difficult economic times, the rate of marriage has dropped.[41] In short, although this change in age of marriage may have seemed drastic to people coming to adulthood in the 1960s and 1970s and their parents, it loses its startling quality if viewed in historical perspective.

Nor is this a trend one should want to reverse. Marriage at a young age is tied to a high risk of divorce, and later ages of marriage also are associated with higher levels of education, especially for girls, surely a positive development.[42] In current society, where premarital intercourse is widely accepted and effective contraception available, the later age of marriage does increase the likelihood of nonmarital cohabitation.

---

36. U.S. Census Bureau, Number, Timing, and Duration of Marriages and Divorces, Table 3:2004.

37. Larry L. Bumpass et al., *The Role of Cohabitation in Declining Rates of Marriage*, 53 J. Marriage & Fam. 913, 924, 926 (1991).

38. Cherlin, *supra* note 34, at 852.

39. *Id.*

40. *See* Betty Friedan, The Feminine Mystique (1963).

41. Valerie Kincade Oppenheimer, *The Continuing Importance of Men's Economic Position in Marriage Formation, in* The Ties that Bind, *supra* note 24, at 283, 287.

42. *See, e.g.,* R. Kelly Raley, *Recent Trends and Differentials in Marriage and Cohabitation: The United States, in* The Ties that Bind, *supra* note 25, at 19, 31 (Fig. 2.7); Jay D. Teachman, *The Childhood Living Arrangements of Children and the Characteristics of Their Marriages,* 25 J. Fam. Issues 86, 88 (2004).

2.3. Predictions

Cohabitation is now clearly established as an institution in which families live in the United States. The number of unmarried partner households most likely will continue to increase. Between 2000 and 2008, they grew by almost 39 percent, an average of 237,500 households per year. Simple cohort replacement will continue to drive this increase, as the proportion of unmarried cohabitants increases with each successive age cohort. So-called intergenerational transmission also plays a role in this increase. Studies have shown that children of parents who have either divorced or cohabited are more likely to cohabit, and rates of both divorce and cohabitation have soared.[43] Thus, children who have experienced the increasing divorce rates of their parents' generation[44] or lived in the increasing number of unmarried-partner households will swell the number of cohabitants.

In addition, as I will discuss in more detail, postponement of marriage and cohabitation are linked in many groups with economic insecurity.[45] A dramatic economic turn-around might increase the rate of marriage, but there has been a relatively long-term decrease in the number of jobs for young males in the United States, especially for those who are not highly skilled.[46] Nearing the end of the first decade of the twenty-first century, widespread economic security seems to be an ever more elusive goal in the United States.[47] So an increase in marriage based on prosperity also seems unlikely.

---

43. *See, e.g., id.* at 97; Axinn & Thornton, *supra* note 25, at 161–62; Mick Cunningham & Arland Thornton, *Direct and Indirect Influences of Parents' Marital Instability on Children's Attitudes Toward Cohabitation in Young Adulthood*, 46 J. DIVORCE & REMARR. 125 (2007). *See also* ARLAND THORNTON ET AL., MARRIAGE AND COHABITATION (Univ. of Chicago Press 2007) (reporting on a study of numerous intergenerational influences in a limited sample).

44. Bumpass has described the divorce rate as growing at a virtually constant level since 1860, from 7 percent in 1860 to 50 percent-plus by the 1980s. Larry L. Bumpass, *What's Happening to the Family? Interactions Between Demographic and Institutional Change*, 27 DEMOGRAPHY 483, 485 (1990). The Census Bureau reports that the divorce rate increased sharply between 1970 and 1975 but has been stable since the late-1970s. NUMBER, TIMING, AND DURATION OF MARRIAGES AND DIVORCES, *supra* note 33, at 4.

45. *See infra* at 107–08.

46. Kathryn Edin, *What Do Low-Income Single Mothers Say About Marriage?*, 47 SOC. PROBS. 112, 127 (2000). For all but highly educated males, real income has declined since the early 1970s. Pamela J. Smock & Wendy D. Manning, *Cohabiting Partners' Economic Circumstances and Marriage*, 34 DEMOGRAPHY 331, 332 (1997). *See also* Oppenheimer, *supra* note 41, at 298–99 (describing downward pressure on wages of unskilled workers).

47. As of January 2009, the unemployment rate in manufacturing was 10.9 percent; one million jobs had also been lost in construction between January 2007 and January 2009,

Finally, the population of the United States is itself changing over time. Over the next fifty years, it is estimated that the Anglo-American percent of the population will drop from 70 percent to 59 percent of the total and that the Latino population will rise to 20 percent, with the African American population remaining at about 12 percent.[48] The high rates of cohabitation prevalent in the African American and Latino communities will be discussed below.[49] As these groups become a larger percentage of the population as a whole, this will also increase the rate of cohabitation. For all of these reasons— age cohort replacement, intergenerational transmission, economic insecurity, and changing demographics, a continuation of the trend toward higher rates of cohabitation appears to be inevitable. It would be unwise to expect that cohabitation is something we can deter or to base our laws upon such an assumption.

𝍐 3. Who Cohabits and Why?

One knows little about cohabitation from looking at it based solely on aggregate statistics. To understand this growing phenomenon, it is necessary to break down the widely varying groups of cohabitants within the U.S. population into subgroups and discuss what functions these nonmarital unions serve for each group. In this section, I discuss the following topics: cohabitation among the young; variations in the rate and motivation for cohabitation by income, race, and ethnicity; and cohabitation among divorced persons and the elderly.

3.1. College Students and Young Dating Singles

Although cohabitation is spreading through other groups of the U.S. population, a large proportion of those who live together are still relatively young. In 2008, according to the July 2009 Current Population Survey by the U.S. Census Bureau, 46.7 percent of female cohabitants and 38.5 percent of male

---

resulting in an 18.2 percent unemployment rate in that sector. BUREAU OF LABOR STATISTICS, ECONOMIC NEWS RELEASE: EMPLOYMENT SITUATION SUMMARY (Jan. 2009).

48. R.S. Oropesa & Bridget K. Gorman, *Ethnicity, Immigration, and Beliefs About Marriage as a "Tie That Binds," in* THE TIES THAT BIND, *supra* note 25, at 188, 188–89.

49. *See infra* at 111–17.

cohabitants were under the age of thirty; 27 percent of the women and 17.4 percent of the men were under twenty-five.[50] These statistics tell us very little, however, about who these persons are. This age group would include, for example, low-income mothers in the inner city and Latinas, with their particular motivations for cohabitation,[51] as well as students and young single persons who now live together under circumstances where they might previously have been simply dating.

Although cohabitation among college students and other young people first attracted the popular imagination, this category is perhaps the least interesting from my perspective because it does not involve the reliance and interdependence attached to unions between a man and a woman with established lives, children, and perhaps assets. Cohabitation among the young, whether entered into simply for convenience or as a form of trial marriage, is also very likely to be short-term and thus not to implicate the underlying purposes of family law. A brief discussion of the apparent motivation for cohabitation among this group will suffice.

The *New York Times* interview that alerted Barnard that Linda LeClair was flouting its housing rules elicited information about the reasons college and graduate students were living together in the late 1960s, summing them up as "convenience, security, sex."[52] Students spoke of the emotional security they derived from living together during a period in their lives when they were otherwise extremely insecure. They also touted the convenience of not having to walk home to their own dormitory or apartment late at night; indeed, in one case the couple said they moved in together "for the sake of their four cats," two of whom would be left untended whenever they stayed overnight at either person's apartment.[53]

Similar reasons motivated the young adults that one sociologist interviewed in the New York area in 2000–01.[54] These respondents, who had moved in with one another in their late teens or early twenties, mentioned the convenience of having all one's belongings in one place rather than going

---

50. Percentages extrapolated from statistics provided in CPS 2008, *supra* note 22, Table UC3. *Opposite Sex Unmarried Couples by Presence of Biological Children Under 18, and Age, Earnings, Education, and Race and Hispanic Origin of Both Partners: 2008.*

51. *See infra* at 111–17.

52. Klemesrud, *supra* note 2, at 40.

53. *Id.*

54. Sharon Sassler, *The Process of Entering into Cohabiting Unions*, 66 J. MARRIAGE & FAM. 491 (2004).

from one apartment to another during an intimate relationship; they also emphasized the scarcity and expense of housing in New York City, which made sharing the cost of a single living space attractive.[55]

During both periods, many of those interviewed also spoke of cohabitation as a trial of compatibility for marriage, one that was more thorough and "honest" than just seeing one another when all dressed up for a date and on one's best behavior. "When you live with somebody, you get to know them an awful lot better," said one young woman.[56] Apparently most young people today agree that a trial period is a good idea, for almost 60 percent do live together before marriage.[57] It does seem eminently reasonable that one should seek to know another person very well before marrying and that living with someone yields more knowledge than simply dating. Yet this trial marriage hypothesis has in fact come under a great deal of attack in the scholarly literature.

In the early 1990s, social scientists began to note a correlation between cohabitation and subsequent divorce, concluding that persons who cohabited prior to marriage were more likely to divorce than those who entered marriage without cohabiting beforehand. Thus, they concluded, cohabitation was not a good screening device for marriage candidates; indeed, perhaps the experience of cohabiting made one less likely to be successful at marriage in the future.[58] This has become a major theme of Marriage Movement literature: if you cohabit, you raise your risks of divorce.[59]

A closer look at the studies about the relationship between cohabitation and divorce, however, shows that the situation is not quite so simple. First of all, the comparison used in the oft-cited 1992 DeMaris and Rao study was

---

55. *Id.* at 498–99. *See also* Galena H. Rhoades, A Longitudinal Study of Cohabiting Couples' Reasons for Cohabitation, Relationship Quality, and Psychological Well-Being, Ph.D. Dissertation, University of Denver, Dept of Psychology, Aug. 17, 2007, at 94 (describing results of a survey of 120 cohabiting couples who reported that they lived together so as to spend more time together, for financial reasons and convenience, to test the relationship, and because a small minority did not believe in marriage).

56. *Unstructured Relations*, NEWSWEEK, July 4, 1966, at 78.

57. In 1970, cohabitation preceded 11 percent of marriages and 56 percent in the 1990s, an increase of 600 percent in less than 30 years. Svarer, *supra* note 31, at 531.

58. *See, e.g.,* Alfred DeMaris & K. Vaninadha Rao, *Premarital Cohabitation and Subsequent Marital Stability in the United States: A Reassessment*, 54 J. MARRIAGE & FAM. 178 (1992).

59. *See, e.g.,* MIKE MCMANUS & HARRIET MCMANUS, LIVING TOGETHER: MYTHS, RISKS & ANSWERS 49 (Howard Books 2008); *see also* THE NATIONAL MARRIAGE PROJECT, THE STATE OF OUR UNIONS 2007 (2007), at 20, *available at* http://marriage.rutgers.edu/Publications/SOOU/TEXTSOOU2007.htm.

between married persons who previously cohabited and married persons who had not done so; by definition, this sample excludes cohabitants who broke up without marrying, presumably the ones who had tested their relationship and decided that it would not sustain a marriage—what one scholar calls the "divorces avoided."[60] Second, if the data are broken down into individuals who have cohabited with more than one partner and those who cohabited only with the person they married, they look quite different. The correlation between cohabitation and divorce is not very significant for those who cohabit, as the vast majority do, only with the person they subsequently marry.[61] Later studies have confirmed that premarital cohabitation with the subsequent spouse is not associated with a higher risk of divorce.[62] The implication is that only persons who engage in multiple cohabiting relationships prior to marriage are a bad risk.

Studies from other countries show that initial findings of correlation between cohabitation and subsequent divorce may also have been tied to the fact that cohabitation was not as widespread when those studies took place as it is today; perhaps a certain iconoclastic personality was required to flout the norm, amounting to what sociologists call a selection effect. In other words, persons who were individualistic, nonconventional, and not interested in long-term commitments would be more likely both to cohabit than to marry and also to divorce if married. However, in areas where cohabitation has become broadly accepted and is now characteristic premarital behavior, the correlation between cohabitation and subsequent divorce disappears or even becomes negative.[63] In Denmark, Sweden, Norway, Austria, West Germany, Belgium, Greece, and New Zealand, for example, there is a negative correlation between premarital cohabitation and subsequent divorce.[64] In short, cohabitation seems to be working as a screening

---

60. *See* Felix Elwert, Cohabitation, Divorce, and the Trial Marriage Hypothesis, Ph.D. dissertation, Harvard University, Dept of Sociology, Nov. 8, 2006, at 15.

61. *See* Demaris & Rao, *supra* note 58, at 179; Elizabeth Thomson & Ugo Colella, *Cohabitation and Marital Stability: Quality or Commitment?*, 54 J. MARRIAGE & FAM. 259 (1992).

62. Jay Teachman, *Premarital Sex, Premarital Cohabitation, and the Risk of Subsequent Marital Dissolution Among Women*, 65 J. MARRIAGE & FAM. 444, 453 (2003).

63. Svarer, *supra* note 31, at 533–34 (2004). *See also* Celine Le Bourdais & Évelyne Lapierre-Adamcyk, *Changes in Conjugal Life in Canada: Is Cohabitation Progressively Replacing Marriage?*, 66 J. MARRIAGE & FAM. 929, 937 (2004) (reporting that couples in Quebec who cohabited prior to marrying have marriages that are as stable as others who did not).

64. Svarer, *supra* note 31, at 532.

device for marital partners in those countries; it appears to improve a couple's chance of avoiding divorce. A study that divides respondents into birth cohorts gives every indication that a change from a positive to a negative correlation may be occurring in the United States as well; it shows that the correlation between marital dissolution and prior cohabitation begins to disappear for younger age cohorts and even to be negative for those born in 1953–57, the last cohort studied.[65]

3.2. Variations by Income

Although academic attention was first drawn to cohabitation by college students and other young people, when large-scale longitudinal statistical data became available, it showed that students were in fact latecomers to the practice.[66] Although cohabitation spread rapidly among students and more widely during the 1970s, the initial rise came both earlier and among other groups in the population, especially among those who were less well educated:

> [A]mong the birth cohorts of the 1930s—who reached their mid-twenties in the late 1950s—cohabitation in young adulthood was restricted to a small minority in the lower educational groups. And it is among these same groups that the rise in cohabitation began in the late 1950s. By the 1960s, when the birth cohorts of the 1940s entered adulthood, the rise was under way among all groups. Then there was an acceleration in the 1970s of the rate of growth of cohabitation among nearly all educational groups.[67]

Early statistical studies showed that cohabitation was most likely among persons who did not complete high school and those whose families had received welfare while they were growing up, both indicators associated with low income.[68] The connection between low income and cohabitation remains

---

65. Robert Schoen, *First Unions and the Stability of First Marriages*, 54 J. MARRIAGE & FAM. 281 (1992).

66. Bumpass et al., *supra* note 37, at 918. Similarly, working class families appear to have modeled what has been styled the "postmodern," dual-income, divorce-extended family as well. *See* JUDITH STACEY, BRAVE NEW FAMILIES: STORIES OF DOMESTIC UPHEAVAL IN LATE TWENTIETH CENTURY AMERICA 252–53 (1990).

67. Bumpass et al., *supra* note 37, at 917–18.

68. Larry L. Bumpass & James A. Sweet, *National Estimates of Cohabitation*, 26 DEMOGRAPHY 615, 624 (1989).

of continuing importance, leading some scholars to describe cohabitation as the "poor man's [and woman's] marriage."[69] A graphic indication of this may be the geographic distribution of cohabiting opposite-sex couples reported in the 2000 census: the places with the highest percentage were in the older industrial and now depressed areas of the Northeast—Paterson, New Jersey; Manchester, New Hampshire; and Rochester, New York.[70] As of 2008, 56 percent of male cohabitants and 70 percent of female cohabitants earned less than $30,000 per year, and 37 percent of the men and 53 percent of the women made less than $20,000 per year.[71]

There are a number of reasons why cohabitation is common in lower-income groups. Qualitative research reveals that marriage, although much revered in lower-income communities, is seen by many as appropriate only when a couple's economic situation is secure, a situation that may not happen quickly for some groups, if ever.[72] Interviews with working- and lower-middle-class cohabitants suggest that they believe marriage should not occur until financial stability has been reached, including not only the resources for a large wedding but perhaps also for home ownership.[73] Edin and Kefalas's 2005 book, *Promises I Can Keep*, explores why, based on numerous interviews over a five-year period in the Philadelphia area.[74] The young women with whom they talked, all of them poor, repeatedly spoke of how much they revered marriage and did not believe in divorce.[75] These very beliefs led them to cohabit rather than marry. They were convinced that it

---

69. Larry Bumpass & Hsien-Hen Lu, *Trends in Cohabitation and Implications for Children's Family Contexts in the United States*, 54 POPULATION STUD. 29, 32 (2000); Marin Clarkberg, *The Price of Partnering: The Role of Economic Well-Being in Young Adults' First Union Experiences*, 77 SOC. FORCES 945, 947 (1999) (describing cohabitation as appealing to males from disadvantaged groups), quoting Nancy S. Landale & Renata Forste, *Patterns of Entry into Cohabitation and Marriage among Mainland Puerto Rican Women*, 28 DEMOGRAPHY 587 (1991).

70. U.S. CENSUS BUREAU, MARRIED-COUPLE AND UNMARRIED-PARTNER HOUSEHOLDS: 2000 7 (2003).

71. Percentages are based upon statistics provided in CPS 2008, *supra* note 50.

72. Kathryn Edin, *What Do Low-Income Single Mothers Say about Marriage?*, 47 SOC. PROBS. 112, 120 (2000); Pamela J. Smock et al., *"Everything's There Except Money": How Money Shapes Decisions to Marry Among Cohabitors*, 67 J. MARRIAGE & FAM. 680 (2005).

73. *Id.* at 687–90. *See also* Christina M. Gibson-Davis et al., *High Hopes But Even Higher Expectations: The Retreat From Marriage Among Low-Income Couples*, 67 J. MARRIAGE & FAM. 1301 (2005).

74. KATHRYN EDIN & MARIA KEFALAS, PROMISES I CAN KEEP: WHY POOR WOMEN PUT MOTHERHOOD BEFORE MARRIAGE (Univ. of California Press 2005).

75. *See, e.g., id.* at 6–9.

was necessary to monitor their partners (in most cases, their children's fathers) over a period of years, to ensure that they would be faithful, pay their share of the bills, not be violent to them or the children, become addicts, or get in trouble with the law.[76] They also feared that their men would, upon marriage, seek to control and dominate them; the only antidote for this was for the woman to have sufficient earnings and assets so that she could credibly threaten to leave.[77] A large and costly wedding was a sign that the couple was financially secure and also that they planned to get married only once.[78]

In the meantime, cohabitation is a rational choice economically for many of these women. Most cohabitants make some type of in-kind contribution to the household economy, perhaps paying part of the rent or contributing food; and their income is less likely than that of husbands to be taken into account in calculating government benefits.[79] One study, basing its conclusions on four different datasets, showed a significant rate of cohabitation among women on the former welfare program, Aid to Families with Dependent Children—as high as 26 percent, but noted that these unions were more likely to form part of a series of such relationships than to be premarital.[80] They are a survival strategy.

A developing literature about rural women shows that cohabitation is an economic survival strategy for single mothers in nonmetropolitan areas as well.[81] Even if male cohabitants cannot contribute very much in direct economic assistance in rural areas, they "may provide access to housing and also contribute child care, car and home repair, access to a car, provisioning through hunting, and access to larger social support networks of kin and friends," all of which may be more important to women in these regions than welfare benefits.[82] Welfare programs based on work requirements, as they have

---

76. *Id.* at 120–23, 126–27.

77. *Id.* at 114–19.

78. *Id.* at 115.

79. Robert A. Moffitt et al., *Beyond Single Mothers: Cohabitation and Marriage in the AFDC Program*, 35 DEMOGRAPHY 259, 264–65 (1998).

80. *Id.* at 260, 272.

81. *See, e.g.,* J. Brian Brown & Daniel T. Lichter, *Poverty, Welfare, and the Livelihood Strategies of Nonmetropolitan Single Mothers*, 69 RURAL SOC. 282 (2004).

82. Anastasia R. Snyder & Diane K. McLaughlin, *Economic Well-being and Cohabitation: Another Nonmetro Disadvantage?*, 27 J. FAM. ECON. ISS. 562, 580 (2006).

been since the Clinton Administration, are unlikely to benefit women in rural areas from which opportunities for employment have largely vanished.[83]

It is not only at the lower end of the economic scale that resources may relate to the choice whether to cohabit or to marry. The economist Gary Becker posited that marriage is a rational choice when there are benefits to both partners from the specialization of labor.[84] According to Becker's economic theory of marriage, women who were employed and earning money on their own would be less likely to marry. In addition to economies of scale, Becker theorized that both parties benefit from a traditional gender-based division of labor, with the wife working primarily within the home.[85] If specialization of labor was the economic bargain that Becker's marriage seekers were trying to strike, one would assume that men's economic resources would correlate positively with marriage and those of women would not. Family law rules then protect the parties' joint investment, and the law's failure to give comparable protection to cohabitants makes any specialization and investment in their unions risky.[86] According to Becker and theories following Becker, women's economic independence, resulting from their entry into the workforce, has been a major cause of the decline in the marriage rate.[87]

The problem with Becker's theory is that it has largely been disproved by the facts. Initial statistical studies showed that women's economic resources appeared to have little correlation with their probability of marriage.[88] Further investigation has shown that women who earn more are in fact more rather than less likely to marry.[89] Indeed, many studies have now shown that both high-wage men and high-wage women are more likely to marry than their lower-income counterparts.[90]

---

83. Brown & Lichter, *supra* note 81, at 299.

84. *See, e.g.,* Julie Brines & Kara Joyner, *The Ties That Bind: Principles of Cohesion in Cohabitation and Marriage,* 64 AM. SOC. REV. 333, 333–34 (1999); Marin Clarkberg, *The Price of Partnering: The Role of Economic Well-Being in Young Adults' First Union Experiences,* 77 SOC. FORCES 945, 948 (1999).

85. *See, e.g.,* GARY S. BECKER, A TREATISE ON THE FAMILY 14–37 (1981).

86. Brines & Joyner, *supra* note 84, at 335–36.

87. Becker, *supra* note 85, at 230–31, 248–49; Clarkberg, *supra* note 84, at 964.

88. Pamela J. Smock & Wendy D. Manning, *Cohabiting Partners' Economic Circumstances and Marriage,* 34 DEMOGRAPHY 331, 338 (1997).

89. EDIN & KEFALAS, *supra* note 74, at 199.

90. *See* Robert A. Moffitt, *Female Wages, Male Wages, and the Economic Model of Marriage: The Basic Evidence* 302–19, *in* THE TIES THAT BIND, *supra* note 25. *See also* Smock et al., *supra*

The world has changed a good deal, for both married couples and cohabitants, since Becker's treatise about the family was published in 1981.[91] Women, including the mothers of small children, have entered the workforce in record numbers.[92] By 1997, only one quarter of all couples had a single wage earner.[93] Most families today depend for their basic welfare upon the income of both partners.[94] In married couples, wives contributed 26.6 percent of the family income in 1970 and 35.2 percent by 2003.[95] Intra-household specialization, in the sense of a wife working at home and her husband in the market economy, is decreasing even more among recent birth cohorts.[96] In short, the gender-specialized marriage, for reasons both of economics (the difficulty of supporting a family on one income) and of ideology (the increasing belief in gender equality), seems rapidly to be disappearing.[97] The specialization that takes place in most marriages is now confined to women's performance of the "Second Shift."[98]

Given how difficult it can be to survive economically these days, it would be surprising if men did not welcome the added income of a well-paid spouse.

---

note 72, at 682–83 (2005) (Table 1) (summarizing studies of effects of economic variables on marriage).

91. Andrew J. Cherlin argues that this changed world calls for the replacement of the Becker "gains-to-trade" paradigm with one of bargaining, with women in a stronger bargaining position than previously. Andrew J. Cherlin, *Toward a New Home Socioeconomics of Union Formation, in* THE TIES THAT BIND, *supra* note 25, at 126, 139.

92. The percentage of women in the U.S. labor force went from 43.3 percent in 1970 (versus 79.7 percent of men) to 59.2 percent in 2004 (versus 73 percent of men). *See* U.S. DEP'T OF LABOR, BUREAU OF LABOR STATISTICS, WOMEN IN THE LABOR FORCE: A DATABOOK 8 (Table 2) (2005), *available at* http://www.bls.gov/cps/wlf-databook2005.htm.

93. Linda J. Waite, *The Family as a Social Organization: Key Ideas for the Twenty-first Century*, 29 CONTEMP. SOC. 463, 464 (2000).

94. *See* Smock & Manning, *supra* note 88, at 338 (1997), and articles cited therein (documenting the growing importance of women's earnings to married couples).

95. U.S. DEP'T OF LABOR, *supra* note 92, at 65 (Table 24). *See also* Carolyn Vogler, *Cohabiting Couples: Rethinking Money in the Household at the Beginning of the Twenty First Century*, 53 SOC. REV. 1, 9 (2005) (reporting that market participation of women in the United Kingdom in 2002 was 74 percent, compared to 84 percent for men and that they contributed one-third of the average couple's income).

96. Audrey Light, *Gender Differences in the Marriage and Cohabitation Income Premium*, 41 DEMOGRAPHY 263, 266 (2004).

97. *See, e.g.*, Thornton & Young-DeMarco, *supra* note 25, at 1014–16, 1032 (noting increasing endorsement of gender equality in the American population).

98. The reference is to women's performance of a disproportionately large share of household labor in addition to their work in the market economy, as described by Arlie Hochschild in her book THE SECOND SHIFT (Avon Books 1989).

The fact that the rate of marriage is currently highest for high-income and highly educated women demonstrates that "increases in female economic independence are not leading women to 'buy out' of marriage. . . . [M]arriage levels . . . [are] . . . highest for those women who are, in theory, most able to live well alone. . . ."[99] In short, if Becker's marriage bargain based on economic specialization was once true, the relationship of the economic resources of the male and female partners to their propensity to marry appears to have changed.

3.3. Variation by Race and Ethnic Group: African Americans

The economic prospects in some communities are dire. Many African American males, for example, are very loosely connected to the workforce and subject to massive unemployment.[100] In-depth interviews with inner-city African American women show that they are wary of forming permanent connections with men who are not economically productive, who may draw resources away from a woman and her children or endanger them in other ways.[101] Women interviewed by sociologist Kathryn Edin reported that they did not want to bring men into the household whom they could not easily evict if necessary—for example, if the man's source of income brought danger to the family or if a more productive male became an option.[102]

As of 2007, 33 percent of African American males were not in the formal labor force, and 3 percent were incarcerated,[103] creating a scarcity of marriageable males within the community.[104] Not surprisingly, marriage

---

99. Joshua R. Goldstein & Catherine T. Kenney, *Marriage Delayed or Marriage Forgone? New Cohort Forecasts of First Marriage for U.S. Women*, 66 AM. SOC. REV. 506, 517 (2001).

100. The unemployment rate for black males sixteen years and older in 2004 was 11.1 percent, but 33.3 percent of the black male population sixteen years and older were not in the labor force at all. U.S. DEP'T OF LABOR, BUREAU OF LABOR STAT., 52 EMP. & EARNINGS 199 (Table 3) (Jan. 2005) (employment status of the civilian noninstitutional population by age, sex, and race).

101. Edin, *supra* note 72, at 117–18.

102. *Id.* at 119.

103. BUREAU OF LABOR STATISTICS, EMPLOYMENT STATUS OF THE CIVILIAN NONINSTITUTIONAL POPULATION BY AGE, SEX, AND RACE: 2007; BUREAU OF JUSTICE STATISTICS, PRISON STATISTICS: 2007.

104. William Julius Wilson attributed the rise of female-headed families in the African American community to this factor. WILLIAM JULIUS WILSON, THE TRULY

rates among African Americans have fallen much more steeply than for other groups.[105] The Centers for Disease Control (CDC) reported in 2002 that:

> Since 1950, the marital patterns of white and black Americans have diverged considerably. About 91 percent of white women born in the 1950s are estimated to marry at some time in their lives, compared with only 75 percent of black women born in the 1950s.[106]

By contrast, cohabitation is more common among African Americans than among non-Hispanic whites; it is also shorter in duration and less likely to lead to marriage.[107]

High rates of nonmarital unions, female-headed families, and child-bearing outside of marriage by African Americans have been portrayed by some observers and policymakers as a type of cultural pathology.[108] At best, these nonnormative patterns have been seen as caused by history and economic deprivation. Slaves were prohibited from marrying, so that any union between them was at best a common law marriage.[109] In the era of antimiscegenation laws after the Civil War, interracial unions were prohibited in many states as well.[110] Common law marriage was frequent among

---

DISADVANTAGED: THE INNER CITY, THE UNDERCLASS, AND PUBLIC POLICY 81–92 (Univ. of Chicago Press 1987). *See also* R. Kelly Raley, *A Shortage of Marriageable Men? A Note on the Role of Cohabitation in Black-White Differences in Marriage Rates*, 61 AM. SOCIOL. REV. 973 (1996).

105. Edin, *supra* note 72, at 114. Whereas only 19 percent of black women never married in 1970, 57 percent never married in 1993. Smock & Manning, *supra* note 88, at 331.

106. U.S. DEP'T OF HEALTH AND HUMAN SERVICES, CENTERS FOR DISEASE CONTROL AND PREVENTION, NAT'L CENTER FOR HEALTH STATISTICS, COHABITATION, MARRIAGE, DIVORCE, AND REMARRIAGE IN THE UNITED STATES: DATA FROM THE NATIONAL SURVEY OF FAMILY GROWTH 4 (2002) [hereinafter CDC].

107. *See, e.g.*, Susan L. Brown & Alan Booth, *Cohabitation Versus Marriage: A Comparison of Relationship Quality*, 58 J. MARRIAGE & FAM. 668, 673 (1996); CDC, *supra* note 106, at 13 (Figure 6).

108. *See, e.g.*, OFFICE OF POLICY PLANNING AND RESEARCH, U.S. DEP'T OF LABOR, THE NEGRO FAMILY: THE CASE FOR NATIONAL ACTION (the "Moynihan Report") (1965).

109. MAXWELL BLOOMFIELD, AMERICAN LAWYERS IN A CHANGING SOCIETY 1776–1876 108–09 (Harvard Univ. Press 1976); LAWRENCE M. FRIEDMAN, A HISTORY OF AMERICAN LAW 496 (2d ed. Simon & Schuster 1985).

110. By 1916, 28 states and territories had laws against intermarriage of the races. KERMIT L. HALL, THE MAGIC MIRROR: LAW IN AMERICAN HISTORY 157 (Oxford Univ. Press 1989).

African Americans after Emancipation.[111] Scholars in the mid-twentieth century saw the prevalence of common law marriage among this group as an uncivilized custom giving "evidence of the incomplete assimilation of the race to American standards" and, in particular, a sign that African Americans were guided by "sentiment and expediency rather than by a moral code."[112] Racist sentiments such as these played a role in the abolition of common law marriage in many states.[113]

Modern scholarship tells a different story, "reenvisioning" cohabitation by African Americans as reflecting a long history of alternative family relationships "born out of necessity and grounded in the rich cultural past of African slaves" and also as exemplifying the leading edge in the "search for a new cultural narrative about courtship, marriage, and childbearing."[114] Although African Americans have not beaten an "ideological retreat from marriage," Andrea Hunter points to the simultaneous coexistence of African American women's "value of and healthy cynicism about marriage," as documented in classic texts about the Black family, such as Carol Stack's 1974 volume *All Our Kin*.[115] E. Franklin Frazier's 1939 book *The Negro Family in the United States*, which analyzed the period from slavery to the urban migration of the early twentieth century, also described what Hunter calls the "diverse repertoire of partnering" in the African American community, which Hunter sees as having "created ways of living that support survival and challenge dominant cultural narratives about marriage, childbearing, and the ideal social organization of families."[116] In this interpretation, nonmarital cohabitation has long constituted a family form among African Americans, whether as a result of historical, legal, or economic necessity or as a cultural form that is

---

111. *See, e.g.*, Walter O. Weyrauch, *Informal Marriage and Common Law Marriage*, in SEXUAL BEHAVIOR AND THE LAW (Ralph Slovenko ed., Thomas 1965), at 323–26.

112. MEYER F. NIMKOFF, MARRIAGE AND THE FAMILY 219 (Houghton Mifflin 1947); *see also* JOHN SIRJAMAKI, THE AMERICAN FAMILY IN THE TWENTIETH CENTURY 69 (Harvard Univ. Press 1953).

113. Cynthia Grant Bowman, *A Feminist Proposal to Bring Back Common Law Marriage*, 75 OR. L. REV. 709, 744–46 (1996).

114. Andrea G. Hunter, *(Re)Envisioning Cohabitation: A Commentary on Race, History, and Culture, in* RACE, WORK, AND FAMILY IN THE LIVES OF AFRICAN AMERICANS (Marlese Durr & Shirley A. Hill eds., Rowman & Littlefield Publishers 2006).

115. *Id.* at 91 (discussing CAROL STACK, ALL OUR KIN: STRATEGIES FOR SURVIVAL IN A BLACK COMMUNITY (Harper & Row 1974).

116. *Id.* at 89–90.

both traditional and perhaps also a forerunner of future family forms—or as a result of some combination of all these influences.

3.4. Variation by Race and Ethnic Group: Latino/as

Persons of Latin American or Caribbean descent in the United States also have high rates of cohabitation. The Census Bureau found that in 2008, unmarried opposite-sex couples in which either one or both partners were Hispanic accounted for about 20 percent of all cohabiting couples.[117] This is not surprising given that consensual unions are very common in many Latin American societies, especially in Central America and the Caribbean; they outnumber formal legal marriages in the Dominican Republic, El Salvador, Honduras, Nicaragua, and Panama and constitute 25 to 50 percent of all unions in Cuba, Guatemala, Colombia, Ecuador, Paraguay, Peru, and Venezuela.[118] A large proportion of these unions (30–45 percent) are long-term in duration, lasting ten years or more, and they have been an "integral component of the family system for centuries."[119]

Historically, there was a high rate of common law marriage in the states and territories taken by the United States from Mexico.[120] Mexican law has officially required civil marriage since 1859 but, in response to the persistence of informal unions, gives some limited recognition to a status called "concubinage," granting a right of inheritance to women who have cohabited in a monogamous relationship for five years preceding the death of their male cohabitant, or for less time if the couple had children.[121] Mexico has been a major source of immigration to the United States. One 1965 study of welfare families with children in California showed that the largest group in "common law marriages" (a status California law did not then recognize) was

---

117. Percentage extrapolated from statistics in CPS 2008, *supra* note 50.

118. Teresa Castro Martin, *Consensual Unions in Latin America: Persistence of a Dual Nuptiality System*, 33 J. COMPARATIVE FAM. STUD. 35, 38 (2002).

119. *Id.* at 44, 49.

120. *See* Bowman, *supra* note 113, at 726–28.

121. *See* John A. Flood, *The Rights of a Mexican Concubine Under Arizona Workmen's Compensation Law*, 1 ARIZ. J. INT'L & COMP. L. 259, 263 (1982). *See also* Woodrow Borah & Sherburne F. Cook, *Marriage and Legitimacy in Mexican Culture: Mexico and California*, 54 CAL. L. REV. 946, 969, 973 (1966).

of Mexican-American derivation.[122] A similar study carried out by other researchers in California showed that the proportion of Mexican-American women in common law marriages was almost 28 percent among those born in the United States, although only 15 percent for women born in Mexico, contrasted with 6 percent among Anglo-American women in the same welfare files.[123] In short, the women who were immigrants had a higher rate of informal unions than those who remained in Mexico, and both groups had a much higher level than did Anglo-American women on welfare.

These data are in sharp contrast to more recent evidence that shows Mexican Americans exhibiting marriage behavior similar to that of non-Hispanic white Americans.[124] This is sometimes referred to as the paradox of nuptiality among Mexican Americans, who, in contrast to other groups, have relatively high rates of marriage despite poor socioeconomic conditions.[125] Studies comparing attitudes across groups show that Mexican Americans are more tolerant than Anglo Americans of informal unions, but only as a precursor to marriage.[126] Scholars attempt to explain this anomaly by references to Mexican-American Roman Catholic culture and socialization of girls,[127] but it is difficult to see how this influence differs substantially from the culture affecting persons from other countries in Latin America. Perhaps Mexican Americans, having been in the United States longer than other groups from Latin America, are simply more assimilated to Anglo-American patterns in this respect.

In contrast to current U.S. patterns, however, premarital cohabitation does not seem to be associated with subsequent marital disruption among this group: "[I]f anything, cohabitation before marriage appears to be associated with increased marital stability among Mexican Americans."[128] One explanation

---

122. Jacobus TenBroek, *California's Dual System of Family Law: Its Origin, Development, and Present Status*, 17 STAN. L. REV. 614, 618–19 (1965).

123. Borah & Cook, *supra* note 121, at 987–88 (reporting on a study of the welfare files in Santa Clara County, California).

124. R.S. Oropesa, *Normative Beliefs About Marriage and Cohabitation: A Comparison of Non-Latino Whites, Mexican Americans, and Puerto Ricans*, 58 J. MARRIAGE & FAM. 49, 50 (1996).

125. *Id.*

126. *Id.* at 59.

127. *Id.* at 59–60.

128. Julie A. Phillips & Megan M. Sweeney, *Premarital Cohabitation and Marital Disruption Among White, Black, and Mexican American Women*, 67 J. MARRIAGE & FAM. 296, 309 (2005).

given is that cohabitation may have a different meaning for many Anglo Americans, who see it as a trial marriage, while the institution functions as a substitute for marriage among many Hispanic groups.[129]

The ethnic group with perhaps the highest rate of nonmarital unions in the United States is comprised of Puerto Ricans living on the mainland. Studies of Puerto Rican women carried out in the New York area in 1985–86 revealed a particularly high rate of cohabitation among this group. Among Puerto Rican women aged fifteen to twenty-nine years old, 61 percent had entered into a first coresidential union—54 percent of those into marriage and 46 percent into an informal union.[130] Although this community is among the most disadvantaged economically, that fact alone is not adequate to explain its high rates of cohabitation.[131] Rather, Puerto Ricans are heirs to a long tradition of consensual unions, which have been regarded as a form of marriage for centuries; while they are becoming less common in Puerto Rico itself, they are very common among Puerto Ricans in the mainland United States[132] These couples act in their childbearing, employment, and division of labor as though they were married and are likely to define themselves as such, even to census takers, although their unions are less stable than marriage.[133] The meaning of cohabitation for this group is clearly different from that given it by college students living together, young middle-class adults in a trial marriage, or many of the low-income mothers described earlier.

Finally, immigrant groups differ by generation in their propensity to cohabit. Although cohabitation was not acceptable among many early groups of immigrants, it has increased in importance among second and third generation immigrants today.[134] The reasons for cohabiting may differ between generations, however. Second-generation immigrants often delay marriage as they pursue higher education and upward mobility, and they may also have a difficult time meeting their family's expectation of marrying

---

129. *Id.* at 298.

130. Nancy S. Landale, *Patterns of Entry into Cohabitation and Marriage Among Mainland Puerto Rican Women*, 28 DEMOGRAPHY 587, 593 (1991).

131. Nancy S. Landale & Katherine Fennelly, *Informal Unions Among Mainland Puerto Ricans: Cohabitation or an Alternative to Legal Marriage?*, 54 J. MARRIAGE & FAM. 269, 278 (1992).

132. *Id.* at 271.

133. *Id.* at 278–79.

134. *See* Susan L. Brown et al., *Generational Differences in Cohabitation and Marriage in the U.S.*, 27 POPULATION RES. & POL'Y REV. 531 (2008).

someone from the same ethnic group and so cohabit as a substitute, at least for a period of time.[135] Subsequent generations, being more assimilated, cohabit at about the same rates and presumably for the same reasons other women in the United States do.[136] Hispanic immigrants from countries where consensual unions are common may not show a generational change, but immigrants from regions such as Asia, where cohabitation is rare, display dramatic change, especially by the third generation, when their rates of cohabitation have risen and approach those of other groups.[137]

In sum, the propensity to cohabit clearly differs by race, ethnic group, and immigrant status within the United States, but both the meaning of cohabitation and motivations for embracing this status can differ widely by group. It is impossible to disaggregate the statistics into every group that may be relevant in this respect, but it should also be clear that it is impossible to understand the dynamics of cohabitation without doing so to some significant extent.

3.5. Divorced Persons

People who are divorced make up a large proportion of opposite-sex unmarried couples in the United States. In 2007, in 28 percent of the total number of cohabiting couples, both cohabitants had been previously married; and in 51.5 percent of the total, either one or both were married before.[138] Indeed, divorced persons are one of the groups that led the trend to cohabitation in the United States: 60 percent of those who remarried between 1980 and 1987 cohabited before remarriage, 46 percent with the person they ultimately married.[139] Apart from being previously married, of course, this group naturally distributes itself throughout other categories discussed in this section, varying by age, income group, race, and ethnicity.

Understandably, people who have been divorced may be wary because of their prior experience with marriage and the tribulations of divorce and thus determined either to avoid the institution altogether or to screen their next

---

135. *Id.* at 546.

136. *Id.*

137. *Id.* at 546–47.

138. Percentages have been extrapolated from statistics in U.S. CENSUS BUREAU, CURRENT POPULATION SURVEY, 2007 ANNUAL SOCIAL AND ECONOMIC SUPPLEMENT, Table UC4 (July 2008).

139. Bumpass et al., *supra* note 37, at 918.

partner very closely and for a longer period. For this group, again, cohabitation may have a different meaning and a different function. About two-thirds
of divorced women and three-fourths of divorced men eventually remarry,
70 percent of them within four years.[140] Cohabitation does delay the timing of
remarriage; and if the divorced person cohabits with multiple partners,
remarriage is delayed even more, thus contributing to the decline in the rate
of marriage in the United States.[141] For some of these couples, cohabitation
thus functions as a courtship or trial marriage between marriages; for others,
especially those without children, it may prove to be an attractive long-term
alternative to marriage.[142]

3.6. The Elderly

Older persons in general now form a distinct group of cohabitants, especially
in Sunbelt retirement communities.[143] This is a group that has grown quickly.
In 1990, there were at least 407,000 cohabitants over the age of sixty, up from
almost none in 1960.[144] The 2000 census reported that 1.2 million persons
aged fifty and older were cohabiting.[145] Further Census Bureau statistics, for
2008, reported that 14.7 percent of the women in unmarried opposite-sex
couples were fifty or over, and 18.4 percent of men in such couples; 2.8 percent
of women and 3.6 percent of men in these couples were over sixty-five.[146] The
trend toward increasing numbers of cohabitants of older ages is predicted to
intensify with the aging of the Baby Boom generation, as cohorts with more
experience of both divorce and cohabitation enter this age group.[147]

---

140. Xiaohe Xu et al., *The Role of Cohabitation in Remarriage*, J. MARRIAGE & FAM. 261, 261–62
(2006).

141. *Id.* at 270.

142. Sharon Sassler & James McNally, *Cohabiting Couples' Economic Circumstances and Union
Transitions: A Re-examination Using Multiple Imputation Techniques*, 32 SOC. SCI. RES.
553, 575 (2003).

143. Albert Chevan, *As Cheaply as One: Cohabitation in the Older Population*, 58 J. MARRIAGE
& FAM. 656, 664 (1996).

144. *Id.* at 659.

145. Valarie King & Mindy E. Scott, *A Comparison of Cohabiting Relationships Among Older
and Younger Adults*, 67 J. MARRIAGE & FAM. 271, 271 (2005).

146. Percentages extrapolated from CPS 2008, *supra* note 50.

147. Chevan, *supra* note 143, at 664 (pointing out that 11 percent of the forty to fifty-nine year
old unmarried group were cohabiting in 1990); King & Scott, *supra* note 145, at 271.

For this group of older adults, past the age of bearing and raising children, cohabitation has a different function and meaning than for other groups. Older adults may be motivated to take advantage of economies of scale in their living arrangements during retirement, while also responding to certain disincentives to marry, such as the loss of alimony or social security benefits from a divorced spouse.[148] There clearly are economic gains from moving in together if both partners have some resources to contribute to the household, and the structure of some entitlement programs may provide an additional economic incentive.[149] For example, eligibility for Medicaid, with its requirement of spending down your assets before getting assistance, means using up a spouse's assets and savings, but cohabitants can get around this requirement.[150] Adult children also may discourage remarriage out of pecuniary motives (to protect their own inheritance); and other relatives and friends often have a negative reaction to the idea of marrying at an advanced age.[151]

Cohabitants in this age group are primarily persons who have been divorced or widowed, and they tend for a variety of reasons not to be interested in remarriage, reasons extending beyond economic incentives and family pressures.[152] The reasons they give for cohabiting include "companionship, to test the relationship, emotional security, stability, find self-fulfillment, practical convenience, have sex regularly, avoid loneliness, and have somebody to grow old with."[153] Many are confronting the problems of aging—surviving on a low income, health problems, and social isolation, as friends and family die or are busy with the activities of another stage of life.[154] For them, "a cohabiting partner may be a critical resource, providing help in times of

---

148. Chevan, *supra* note 143, at 660–61.

149. REBECCA GRONVOLD HATCH, AGING AND COHABITATION 29–30 (Garland Publishers 1995).

150. *Id.* at 29–30.

151. *Id.* at 27.

152. Susan L. Brown et al., *Cohabitation Among Older Adults: A National Portrait*, 61B J. GERONTOLOGY S71, S71–72 (2006).

153. HATCH, *supra* note 149, at 33–34.

154. *See* Brown et al., *supra* note 152, at S72–73; Susan L. Brown et al., *The Significance of Nonmarital Cohabitation: Marital Status and Mental Health Benefits Among Middle-Aged and Older Adults*, 60B J. GERONTOLOGY S21, S22–23 (2005).

need, material support that alleviates the strains of poverty, and emotional support to assuage loneliness."[155]

Interestingly, older cohabitants report higher levels of relationship quality than younger persons, despite their lack of plans to marry.[156] Scholars opine that this may be because of a maturity and patience gained in later life but also point out that these unions are subject to many fewer stressors than those of younger couples, who cope with the stresses of children, midlife career demands, and work-life balance pressures.[157] The cohabiting relationships of older persons are more stable, longer in duration, and serve as an alternative to marriage rather than a prelude to it.[158]

One indication of the growing size and power of this group of cohabitants is the fact that when California in 2001 began to offer a statewide system of domestic partner registration in response to the needs of same-sex couples, it included opposite-sex couples over the age of sixty-two; and the support of this group has been regarded as central to passage of the domestic partnership act.[159] One prominent student of cohabitation among the elderly urges that these unions should be treated by the law as though they were marriages, in order to privatize caregiving, placing responsibility for it in the hands of the unmarried partner.[160] This level of obligation may not be what cohabitants of this age want from their relationship. Some scholars opine, for example, that older female cohabitants enter a cohabiting relationship primarily for companionship and want to escape the burdens of the gendered exchanges traditional in marriage.[161]

---

155. Brown et al., *supra* note 152, at S78.

156. King & Scott, *supra* note 145, at 282–83. Interestingly, one study seems to show that cohabitation appears to relieve depression for women in this age group but not for men; the authors surmise that men may be in the relationship expecting to be the recipients of caregiving and anticipate needing the type of gendered care a wife traditionally gives, while women are in it for companionship and desire to escape the burdens of the gendered exchanges traditional in marriage. Brown et al. (2005), *supra* note 154, at S28.

157. King & Scott, *supra* note 145, at 273.

158. *Id.* at 282–83.

159. Megan E. Callan, T*he More, The Not Marry-er: In Search of a Policy Behind Eligibility for California Domestic Partnerships*, 40 San Diego L. Rev. 427, 453–54 (2003).

160. Hatch, *supra* note 149, at 132.

161. Brown et al. (2005), *supra* note 154, at S28.

3.7. Other Characteristics

Social scientists have subjected cohabitants to a great deal of scrutiny about other characteristics—their attitudes to traditional lifestyles, their religiosity, and their political orientation, for example.[162] Although these characteristics were shown in early studies to correlate with cohabitation behavior, the effect of these determinants has varied over time. As cohabitation has become more common and accepted by most groups within the population, these correlations have faded. Thus, whereas political activism, liberalism, and low religiosity once strongly correlated with cohabitation, the predictive power of these characteristics has decreased as cohabitation diffused and has been low for cohorts reaching young adulthood after the mid-1970s.[163] Western European studies also show that the influence of a variety of demographic characteristics has disappeared with respect to recent cohorts of cohabitants.[164]

Even education appears to be disappearing as a predictor of cohabitation among some groups. Brenda Wilhelm's 1998 article analyzing responses from a representative sample of 2,253 U.S. citizens born between 1943 and 1964 showed that, while having less than a high school education increased the odds of cohabitation for those in the oldest cohort, the effect of education disappeared for the youngest cohort.[165] Another scholar, working with a sample of 1972 high school graduates, found no association between cohabitation and educational attainment.[166]

In fact, education may have a much more nuanced relationship to cohabitation than first assumed. There are some indications that educated and high-achieving women may prefer cohabitation, as a lifestyle that allows them to pursue careers and avoid the traditional gender division of labor associated with marriage.[167] The author of one study drolly comments that

---

162. *See, e.g.*, Brenda Wilhelm, *Changes in Cohabitation Across Cohorts: The Influence of Political Activism*, 77 Soc. Forces 289 (1998).

163. *Id.* at 296, 310.

164. Dorien Manting, *The Changing Meaning of Cohabitation and Marriage*, 12 Eur. Soc. Rev. 53, 63 (1996).

165. Wilhelm, *supra* note 162, at 297, 308.

166. Clarkberg, *supra* note 69, at 960.

167. Marin Clarkberg et al., *Attitudes, Values, and Entrance into Cohabitational Versus Marital Unions*, 74 Soc. Forces 609, 624; *see also* Clarkberg, *supra* note 69, at 958 (1999).

there are good reasons for high-earning women to be attracted more to cohabitation than to marriage because it is hard for them to attract a "wife":

> Women appear to be simply less able than men to trade high earnings for the household labor of a spouse, given the pervasive social expectations that wives will specialize in the household sphere of labor. To preserve their earnings, high-wage women may be looking for another type of bargain—a union with less specialized roles and expectations.[168]

On the other hand, wealthier and more educated groups within our society still have the highest rates of eventual marriage, with all the attendant implications for the transmission of inequality between generations.[169]

In sum, while there are some patterns about cohabitation behavior, those patterns are made up of multiple designs; and many of them are changing with the passage of time. As a result of the large amount of demographic research now available, we know that multiple and differing groups are included within the aggregate data on cohabitation in the United States. Those groups, in summary, include but are not limited to the following:

1. young "dating" singles, often sharing quarters for reasons of convenience and economy
2. young adults cohabiting prior to marriage, either with no plans to marry or as some sort of trial marriage which may succeed or fail
3. working-class couples without the resources for a wedding ceremony or home ownership
4. low-income mothers making rational use of cohabitation to support themselves and their children
5. Puerto Rican couples in consensual unions, often with children of the union
6. divorced persons either screening candidates for remarriage or seeking an alternative to marriage
7. older persons cohabiting for companionship and economic reasons or because they have no particular reason to marry

---

168. Clarkberg, *supra* note 69, at 957.

169. Goldstein & Kenney, *supra* note 35, at 517 (describing the advantages to children of married parents in higher-income families).

An individual may belong to more than one of these groups at different points in his or her life. There are cross-cutting categories as well—cohabitants with and without children, for example, and unions of longer and shorter duration.

It is important to note that these categories contain, although they are not coextensive with, some of the most vulnerable groups in our society—low-income mothers, economically distressed ethnic groups, and the elderly.

FOUR

Social Science and Cohabitation

THE DISCOVERY OF COHABITATION as a subject for academic study occurred in the early 1970s. This chapter describes both the pioneering years of that study and the main trends in the literature since that time. By now there is a very large body of literature, much of it by demographers and sociologists. After documenting the frequency of cohabitation and exploring the groups likely to cohabit, scholars turned to discussion of a number of issues of concern to them and to policymakers, such as the average duration of cohabiting unions; the economic relationships between the partners; the quality of their relationships, including the frequency of domestic violence; and the impact of cohabitation on children residing in these households. My interest in reviewing the social scientific studies is to draw out the implications of their findings for the legal treatment of cohabitation.

% 1. The Pioneers

The academic study of cohabitation was fraught with risks in the early 1970s. The career of Eleanor Macklin illustrates these risks.[1] Macklin published one of the first scholarly treatments of cohabitation in 1972.[2] According to one author:

> She did for cohabitation what Kinsey did for other sexual behaviors . . . she showed that cohabitation was common. If it was common it was also

---

1. Information about Eleanor Macklin is taken from ELIZABETH H. PLECK, SHACKING UP: COHABITATION AND THE SEXUAL REVOLUTION, 1962 TO 1990, unpublished manuscript on file with author.

2. Eleanor D. Macklin, *Heterosexual Cohabitation Among Unmarried College Students*, THE FAMILY COORDINATOR, Oct. 1972, 463–72. The very first article published was probably Judith L. Lyness et al., *Living Together: An Alternative to Marriage*, J. MARRIAGE & FAM., May 1972, 305–11.

normal rather than deviant, and if a behavior was normal, it could not be punished as deviating from the norm.[3]

Eleanor Macklin was a lecturer at Cornell University in the mid-1970s when her research on cohabitation became widely publicized. She began her study by interviewing students in her course in adolescent development in the College of Human Ecology, in response to an invitation to give a presentation on cohabitation among college students at a prestigious 1971 conference.[4] She discovered from her interviews and subsequent questionnaires that a new sexual norm was emerging among college students and that it was much more widespread than news stories such as those about the Linda LeClair case would indicate. She saw this as a normal and healthy trend and began to organize conferences about cohabitation; she also founded and published *The Cohabitation Newsletter.* Macklin spoke widely on the topic, and her prominence led to an invitation to appear on the Phil Donahue show in 1975.

The publicity about Macklin's research led to dramatic responses from both the public and her employer. Like Linda LeClair, she received hate mail. After an article she wrote appeared in the popular journal *Psychology Today,* letter writers told her that she was "a sick, frustrated sex-starved, evil old woman getting your kicks in advocating such immoral actions."[5] (Macklin was in fact a relatively conventional 41-year-old married woman with two sons at the time.)[6] Another letter, an anonymous one, said "PHD Eleanor Macklin who are you to ruin our childrens [sic] lives? I could gladly choke that silly face, weak mouth. Any one looking and listening to you would know you weren't fit to teach a dog, let alone our children. It seems that colleges are full of such trash as you."[7]

The reaction from senior members of Macklin's department had serious consequences for her future. One senior scholar, Urie Bronfenbrenner, told her that cohabitation would lead to the downfall of the family and that longitudinal studies needed to be conducted before any more research about it

---

3. *Id.*

4. *Id.* This was the 1971 Grove Conference on Marriage and Family, an invited gathering of an elite group of family studies researchers. *Id.*

5. *Id.*

6. *Id.*

7. *Id.*

should be published.[8] Another told her that cohabitation was "not an appropriate area for inquiry" and that professors in the human ecology department "studied 'normal' human ecology, with the implication that cohabitation was not normal."[9] The university and department both received angry letters after Macklin's television appearance.[10]

Eleanor Macklin failed to obtain a tenure-track position and was required to leave Cornell in 1975, occasioning student protests about the school's failure to retain her.[11] She had a difficult time finding another academic position and commuted to untenured positions at other universities before becoming a marriage and sex therapist and obtaining a tenured position at Syracuse University, training therapists until her retirement in 1998. After 1983, she published nothing more about cohabitation, giving up research in the field because "being the center of controversy" was exhausting her.[12]

Nonetheless, by the mid-1980s, cohabitation had become a popular topic for research by social scientists, although the approach they took to it tended to be more conservative than Macklin's, that is, they tended to emphasize its downside rather than seeing it as a healthy step in human development.[13] It is a great irony that some of the prominent scholars of cohabitation today have an academic home in the College of Human Ecology at Cornell University.[14]

⚜ 2. Trends in the Literature

The earliest studies of heterosexual cohabitation were small-scale, nonrepresentative surveys of college students or residents of university towns, in which high percentages of the respondents proclaimed that they had cohabited or

---

8. *Id.*

9. *Id.*

10. Jim Myers, *Popular, Controversial Teacher Loses Job*, ITHACA J., Mar. 4, 1975.

11. *Id.*

12. PLECK, *supra* note 1.

13. *Id. See, e.g.*, Alfred DeMaris, *A Comparison of Remarriages with First Marriages on Satisfaction in Marriage and Its Relationship to Prior Cohabitation*, 33 FAM. RELATIONS 448 (1984); Alan Booth & David Johnson, *Premarital Cohabitation and Marital Success*, 9 J. FAM. ISSUES 255 (1988); Kersti Yllo & Marray A. Straus, *Interpersonal Violence among Married and Cohabiting Couples*, 30 FAM. RELATIONS 345 (1981).

14. Daniel Lichter, Sharon Sassler, and Elizabeth Peters. for example.

would do so and that they did not disapprove of it.[15] Often, the definition of cohabitation used or implied in them was merely that a couple was sleeping together on a regular basis.[16] These were not rigorously scientific studies, and they excluded most of the groups described in the previous chapter as especially likely to cohabit, such as divorced persons, the elderly, persons with children, and persons from lower-income and racially subordinate groups. The early research about college students was of limited significance apart from starting a trend in academic research. Although students touted cohabitation as either trial marriage or an alternative lifestyle, studies based on their responses said more about the sexual revolution and countercultural lifestyles of the 1960s than about the institution of any new type of family structure.

Heterosexual cohabitation could not be reliably studied (as Urie Bronfenbrenner had told Macklin) until large-scale surveys and longitudinal studies were undertaken. It was only with the construction and publication of two major datasets that serious analysis could begin. One was a nationwide longitudinal study of the high school senior class of 1972, with follow-up interviews every several years until 1986; the birth cohorts interviewed would therefore have been born in approximately 1954.[17] Because it did not include high school students who did not graduate, this dataset clearly undercounted minorities and poor people.[18] The other major empirical study in these years was the National Survey of Families and Households (NSFH), which took place from 1987–88 (thus presumably involving birth cohorts from as late as 1970), with a second wave of interviews from 1992–94.[19]

---

15. *See, e.g.*, Ibithaj Arafat & Betty Yorburg, *On Living Together without Marriage*, 9 J. SEX RES. 97 (1973); Lyness et al., *supra* note 2.

16. Macklin herself appears to have defined cohabitors as "heterosexual couples who spent four or more nights together over a three-month period." PLECK, *supra* note 1.

17. The National Longitudinal Study of the High School Class of 1972 was based on interviews of high school seniors in 1972, who were reinterviewed in 1973, 1974, 1976, 1979, and 1986, at which time there were still 12,841 respondents. *See* Ronald R. Rindfuss & Audrey VandenHeuvel, *Cohabitation: A Prescursor to Marriage or an Alternative to Being Single?*, 16 POPULATION & DEV. REV. 703, 707 (1990).

18. *See* Nancy S. Landale & Katherine Fennelly, *Informal Unions Among Mainland Puerto Ricans: Cohabitation or an Alternative to Legal Marriage?*, 54 J. MARRIAGE & FAM. 269, 271 (1992).

19. The first wave of NSFH data was collected from 1987–88 from 13,008 respondents, of whom 80 percent, or 10,008, were reinterviewed from 1992–94. This was thought to be the largest representative sample of cohabitants, with 678 in the first wave. *See* Susan L. Brown, *Union Transitions Among Cohabitors: The Significance of Relationship Assessments and Expectations*, 62 J. MARRIAGE & FAM. 833, 837 (2000).

A seminal article by demographers Larry Bumpass and James Sweet, describing the NSFH results and documenting the rapid increase in cohabitation since 1970, was published in 1989.[20] The 1990 census was the first one to add questions about living with an unmarried partner; by now we have two rounds of official statistics and are poised for the flurry of studies that will doubtless accompany publication of results from 2010.[21]

After these datasets were available, cohabitation became a frequent topic for study by sociologists and demographers and made its way onto the agendas of professional meetings.[22] Of the over 200 social science articles I reviewed for this project, three-quarters of them were published since 1995 and the vast majority since the year 2000.

It is important to note that commentators about cohabitation in law reviews and other outlets rely heavily on studies based on these early datasets, even though the increase in cohabitation has led to its diffusion from lower-income groups and college students to almost every group in the population since those studies began. Bumpass and Sweet's 1989 article is frequently cited, even in law review articles published as late as 2003.[23] Yet many of its conclusions have been modified somewhat or reinterpreted in light of what we now know to be an international and apparently irreversible movement that has changed the way the majority of people form sexual and conjugal unions.[24]

The topics studied by social scientists in this field have varied over the years.[25] Initially, articles noticed, named, and measured the phenomenon.[26] It was important to establish that cohabitation was common before it was

---

20. Larry L. Bumpass & James A. Sweet, *National Estimates of Cohabitation*, 26 DEMOGRAPHY 615 (1989).

21. Prior to 1990, estimates were based on the number of households containing two and only two unrelated adults of the opposite sex. LYNNE M. CASPER ET AL., HOW DOES POSSLQ MEASURE UP?: HISTORICAL ESTIMATES OF COHABITATION 4 (1999).

22. *See* Macklin, *supra* note 3, at 53.

23. *See* William C. Duncan, *The Social Good of Marriage and Legal Responses to Non-Marital Cohabitation*, 82 OR. L. REV. 1001, 1005 n. 24 (2003).

24. *See, e.g.,* Michael Svarer, *Is Your Love in Vain? Another Look at Premarital Cohabitation and Divorce*, 39 J. HUM. RESOURCES 523, 531 (2004) (reporting that 60 percent of couples live together prior to marrying).

25. *See* Pamela J. Smock, *Cohabitation in the United States: An Appraisal of Research Themes, Findings, and Implications*, 26 ANN. REV. SOCIOL. 1 (2000).

26. *See, e.g.,* Richard R. Clayton & Harwin L. Voss, *Shacking Up: Cohabitation in the 1970s*, 39 J. MARRIAGE & FAM. 273 (1977); Bumpass & Sweet, *supra* note 20.

taken seriously. After the NSFH data became available, more sophisticated analysis was possible, including breaking down the statistics into subgroups by income and race.[27] Scholars then turned to closer examination of the unions formed by these groups, exploring how long they tended to endure, their similarities to and differences from marriage, and their likely effect upon that institution.[28] In the late-1990s, economic issues began to be explored, with scholars examining whether cohabitants pooled their income,[29] how they compared with married couples regarding division of labor within the household,[30] and the effect of cohabitation on the economic well-being of the family unit.[31] More recently, the focus of study has been the impact of cohabitation upon the children who grow up in the increasing number of unmarried-partner households.[32] Given the sensitivity of social science research funding to issues that have captivated the political imagination, there have also been a predictable number of studies investigating the

---

27. *See, e.g.*, Nancy S. Landale & Katherine Fennelly, *Informal Unions Among Mainland Puerto Ricans: Cohabitation or an Alternative to Legal Marriage?*, 54 J. MARRIAGE & FAM. 269 (1992); R.S. Oropesa, *Normative Beliefs About Marriage and Cohabitation: A Comparison of Non-Latino Whites, Mexican Americans, and Puerto Ricans*, 58 J. MARRIAGE & FAM. 49 (1996); R. Kelly Raley, *A Shortage of Marriageable Men? A Note on the Role of Cohabitation in Black-White Differences in Marriage Rates*, 61 AM. SOC. REV. 973 (1996).

28. *See, e.g.*, Alfred DeMaris & K. Vaninadha Rao, *Premarital Cohabitation and Subsequent Marital Stability in the United States: A Reassessment*, 54 J. MARRIAGE & FAM. 178 (1992); Elizabeth Thomson & Ugo Colella, *Cohabitation and Marital Stability: Quality or Commitment?*, 54 J. MARRIAGE & FAM. 259 (1992); Joshua R. Goldstein & Catherine T. Kenney, *Marriage Delayed or Marriage Forgone? New Cohort Forecasts of First Marriage for U.S. Women*, 66 AM. SOC. REV. 506 (2001).

29. *See, e.g.*, Anne E. Winkler, *Economic Decision-making by Cohabitors: Findings Regarding Income Pooling*, 29 APPLIED ECON. 1079 (1997); Julie Brines & Kara Joyner, *The Ties That Bind: Principles of Cohesion in Cohabitation and Marriage*, 64 AM. SOC. REV. 333 (1999); Marin Clarkberg et al., *Attitudes, Values, and Entrance into Cohabitational Versus Marital Unions*, 74 SOC. FORCES 609 (1995).

30. Sanjiv Gupta, *The Effects of Transitions in Marital Status on Men's Performance of Housework*, 61 J. MARRIAGE & FAM. 700 (1999); Scott J. South & Glenna Spitze, *Housework in Marital and Nonmarital Households*, 59 AM. SOCIOL. REV. 327 (1994).

31. *See, e.g.*, Brines & Joyner, *supra* note 29; Sarah Avellar & Pamela J. Smock, *The Economic Consequences of the Dissolution of Cohabiting Unions*, J. MARRIAGE & FAM. 315 (2005).

32. *See, e.g.*, Susan L. Brown, *Family Structure and Child Well-Being: The Significance of Parental Cohabitation*, 66 J. MARRIAGE & FAM. 351 (2004); Wendy D. Manning et al., *The Relative Stability of Cohabiting and Marital Unions for Children*, 23 POPULATION RES. & POL'Y REV. 135 (2004); Jay D. Teachman, *The Childhood Living Arrangements of Children and the Characteristics of Their Marriages*, 25 J. FAM. ISSUES 86 (2004).

relationship between cohabitation and nonmarital pregnancy and between cohabitation and the receipt of welfare and reform of the welfare system.[33]

Research now being published includes cross-national data, combining U.S. and Canadian datasets with large cross-national surveys done by Eurobarometer and by the UN Economic Commission for Europe.[34] Today, therefore, we are in a position to interpret the data that have been produced both in cross-temporal and cross-national perspective, to see both trends and differences—differences among nations and among different groups within heterogeneous nations such as the United States.

⁂ 3. What Social Science Has Told Us about Cohabitation

This section describes findings of the social science research done in the last several decades about the following issues: (1) the length of cohabiting unions compared to marriage; (2) the economics of cohabiting relationships; (3) the quality of these relationships; (4) the correlation between cohabitation and domestic violence; and (5) the impact of cohabitation on children resident in these households.

3.1 Duration of Cohabiting Unions

The duration of cohabiting unions is a topic that has attracted a great deal of attention, for a variety of reasons. Duration presumably relates to the quality of these relationships for the partners, and it clearly relates to the stability of living arrangements for any children in their household. Statistics about union length are also important to comparisons between cohabitation and marriage. For my purposes, moreover, the average length of cohabiting relationships is relevant to designing appropriate legal remedies for cohabitants.

---

33. *See, e.g.*, Wendy D. Manning & Nancy S. Landale, *Racial and Ethnic Differences in the Role of Cohabitation in Premarital Childbearing*, 58 J. MARRIAGE & FAM. 63 (1996); Robert A. Moffitt et al., *Beyond Single Mothers: Cohabitation and Marriage in the AFDC Program*, 35 DEMOGRAPHY 259, 264–65 (1998).

34. *See, e.g.*, Kathleen Kiernan, *Redrawing the Boundaries of Marriage*, 66 J. MARRIAGE & FAM. 980 (2004); Patrick Heuveline & Jeffrey M. Timberlake, *The Role of Cohabitation in Family Formation: The United States in Comparative Perspective*, 66 J. MARRIAGE & FAM. 1214 (2004).

The statistics most frequently used to debate these issues are those that appeared in the 1989 Bumpass and Sweet article, to the effect that two-thirds of cohabiting unions last less than one year, only one-third make it through two years, and only one in ten is intact after five.[35] Median duration was reported as 1.3 years (Bumpass refers to 1.5 years in later articles), and cohabitants who subsequently marry were reported to be almost twice as likely to divorce as others who did not cohabit prior to marriage.[36] Authors of social science and law articles have built on these statistics, while drawing their own differing conclusions. For example, one 1996 article by two social scientists entering the debate about how cohabitation is similar to or different from marriage concluded from these statistics that a nontrivial number of cohabiting unions constitute a permanent alternative to marriage:

> [F]or one tenth of cohabitors, it is a long-term relationship that seldom ends in marriage. . . . In the majority of cases, cohabitation shares many of the qualities of marriage. . . . [F]or a nontrivial proportion of cohabitors, it is a permanent living arrangement, a replacement for marriage.[37]

Prominent scholars undertaking the social science research declared that cohabitation was a family form that was here to stay. In his 1990 Presidential Address to the Population Association of America, Larry Bumpass described cohabitation as a long-term, cross-national trend and recommended that social policy be directed at ameliorating any negative consequences rather than attempting to turn back the tide.[38] Others—especially those writing in the law review literature—have drawn an opposite conclusion: that cohabitation is short-lived, unstable, and should not be given any encouragement or legal protection as a result.[39]

---

35. Bumpass & Sweet, *supra* note 20, at 620.

36. *Id.* at 621; *see also* Larry L. Bumpass, *What's Happening to the Family? Interactions Between Demographic and Institutional Change*, 27 DEMOGRAPHY 483, 487 (1990) (describing median as 1.5 years). Another article describes the average duration as about 1 and 3/4 years. Allan V. Horwitz & Helen Raskin White, *The Relationship of Cohabitation and Mental Health: A Study of a Young Adult Cohort*, 60 J. MARRIAGE & FAM. 505, 509 (1998).

37. Susan L. Brown & Alan Booth, *Cohabitation Versus Marriage: A Comparison of Relationship Quality*, 58 J. MARRIAGE & FAM. 668, 668–69 (1996).

38. Bumpass, *supra* note 36, at 493.

39. *See, e.g.*, Duncan, *supra* note 23, at 1005–06, 1024–25.

Scholars reached somewhat varying conclusions about whether cohabitation constituted a new family form. One early and frequently cited article, based on the 1972 high school data, proclaimed that cohabitation was more like being single than a marriage-like family form.[40] Its authors examined the childbearing expectations, marriage plans, employment status, home ownership, and self-descriptions of respondents in the 1972 dataset through its 1986 cycle and concluded that "cohabitation should be viewed in the same context as the rise of premarital intercourse, increases in out-of-wedlock childbearing, and declines in parental authority," all of which they saw as resulting from trends to increasing individualism and secularism in the United States.[41] Most of the cohabitants studied in the data upon which they were relying, however, were still quite young, largely excluding long-term cohabitants and those with children.[42]

It is important to examine both the data upon which the conclusions of these authors rested and the definition of longevity of a cohabiting relationship used in each study. The NSFH findings defined the duration of cohabitation by measuring the period from inception of the relationship until it ended either in marriage or dissolution.[43] One may obviously quarrel with using this measure as the touchstone of stability. Can one say that a cohabitating union that ended in marriage dissolved? The NSFH data showed that fully 60 percent of first cohabitations were likely to end in marriage, with 25 percent of cohabitants marrying within a year and 50 percent of them within three years.[44] A more recent article indicates that the percent ending in marriage within three years dropped to about 33 percent in the 1990s.[45]

By contrast, data from the Centers for Disease Control (CDC), based on the 1995 National Survey of Family Growth, set up the definition of longevity differently.[46] Under the CDC definition, marriage does not constitute

---

40. Rindfuss & VandenHeuvel, *supra* note 17, at 707, 721–22.

41. *Id.* at 722.

42. *Id.* at 721, 723.

43. Bumpass & Sweet, *supra* note 20, at 620.

44. *Id.* at 621.

45. Andrew J. Cherlin, *The Deinstitutionalization of American Marriage*, 66 J. MARRIAGE & FAM. 848, 849 (2004) (citing P.J. Smock & S. Gupta, *Cohabitation in Contemporary North America*, *in* JUST LIVING TOGETHER: IMPLICATIONS OF COHABITATION ON FAMILIES, CHILDREN, AND SOCIAL POLICY 53 (A. Booth & A.C. Crouter eds., 2002).

46. U.S. DEP'T OF HEALTH AND HUMAN SERVICES, CENTERS FOR DISEASE CONTROL AND PREVENTION, NAT'L CENTER FOR HEALTH STATISTICS, COHABITATION, MARRIAGE,

dissolution; the cohabiting union is only dissolved if the couple subsequently divorces.[47] Using this definition, the probability that a woman's first cohabitation will dissolve within three years is 39 percent and 49 percent within five years.[48] This definition leads to different conclusions about the stability of the partners' relationship, if half are still together, married or not, after five years. Nonetheless, even after adding together the time of cohabitation and of marriage, there is still a significantly greater hazard of dissolution for a cohabitation than a marriage.[49] (The divorce rate has hovered at about 50 percent since 1980.[50])

These rates diverge from patterns in other areas of the industrialized world. In the United Kingdom and in Quebec, cohabitation is longer in duration; a recent large-scale survey in the United Kingdom, for example, showed that the average duration of cohabiting unions had increased to six and one-half years, with the median more than four years.[51] The median duration of cohabitation by previously unmarried women aged fifteen to forty-four in France is 4.28 years.[52]

The rate of instability in the United States may even be increasing. A 2000 article by Larry Bumpass and Hsien-Hen Lu, based on Cycle 5 of the National Survey of Family Growth (NSFG), found a substantial increase in

---

DIVORCE, AND REMARRIAGE IN THE UNITED STATES: DATA FROM THE NATIONAL SURVEY OF FAMILY GROWTH (2002) [hereinafter CDC].

47. *Id.* at 7.

48. *Id.* at 14, 17 (Figure 17).

49. *See also* DeMaris & Rao, *supra* note 28, at 189.

50. U.S. CENSUS BUREAU, NUMBER, TIMING, AND DURATION OF MARRIAGES AND DIVORCES: 2001 4 (2003). *See also* William M. Pinsof, *The Death of "Till Death Us Do Part": The Transformation of Pair-Bonding in the 20th Century,* 41 FAM. PROCESS 135, 142–43 (2002) (concluding that a 50 percent divorce rate fits "the evolved human level of monogamous marital stability"). The probability that a first marriage will end in divorce by the twentieth year is reported by this author to be .48 for non-Hispanic whites, .63 for blacks, and .52 for Hispanics. *Id.* at 139.

51. Of those surveyed in the United Kingdom., 47 percent had been together five years or more and 23 percent over ten years. Anne Barlow & Grace James, *Regulating Marriage and Cohabitation in 21st Century Britain,* 67 MOD. L. REV. 143, 154, 159 (2004); Celine Le Bourdais & Évelyne Lapierre-Adamcyk, *Changes in Conjugal Life in Canada: Is Cohabitation Progressively Replacing Marriage?,* 66 J. MARRIAGE & FAM. 929, 934 (2004) (reporting that cohabitations in Quebec are of longer duration and less likely to turn into marriage).

52. Heuveline & Timberlake, *supra* note 34, at 1223 (reporting a range of median duration from 1.78 years in Switzerland to 4.28 years in France).

the instability of cohabiting unions.[53] The change reported by Bumpass and Lu resulted from a decreasing probability of cohabitants marrying their cohabiting partner; marriages following cohabitation also appeared to have become less stable.[54]

An important point that can be missed in the aggregate data is that the stability, like the rate, of cohabitation differs by subgroups of the population. The average duration of a cohabiting union is longer for persons who have previously been married and for senior adults.[55] CDC data also show that women who are older at the start of a cohabiting union (twenty-five or over) are less likely to experience disruption of the relationship,[56] indicating that at least some of the divorces that statistically would have resulted from early marriage have shifted into the statistics about cohabitation instead.[57] The probability of disruption (under the CDC definition) also varies with the race and economic situation of the cohabitants. At about two years' duration, the probability that an African American woman's first cohabitation will break up begins to exceed that of both Hispanics and non-Hispanic whites and continues to do so by larger and larger margins.[58] By three years, the probabilities of disruption for the three groups are 32 percent for Hispanics, 40 percent for non-Hispanic whites, and 43 percent for non-Hispanic blacks; by five years, the same comparison is 43 percent, 49 percent, and 56 percent; and by ten years 59 percent, 61 percent, and 72 percent.[59]

---

53. Larry Bumpass & Hsien-Hen Lu, *Trends in Cohabitation and Implications for Children's Family Contexts in the United States*, 54 POPULATION STUD. 29, 33 (2000). The National Survey of Family Growth is a periodic survey by the National Center for Health Statistics; Cycle 5 took place in 1995 and consisted of interviews averaging 105 minutes with 10,847 women, ages fifteen to forty-four. *Id.* at 30.

54. *Id.* at 33 (reporting that the proportion of cohabitants who had separated by ending either their cohabitation or subsequent marriage by the five-year mark had increased from 45 percent to 54 percent). *See also* Daniel T. Lichter et al., *Marriage or Dissolution? Union Transitions Among Poor Cohabiting Women*, 43 DEMOGRAPHY 223, 236 (2006) (reporting that one-half of cohabiting unions end within one year and 90 percent by the fifth year).

55. *See also* Brown & Booth, *supra* note 37, at 671; Valarie King & Mindy E. Scott, *A Comparison of Cohabiting Relationships Among Older and Younger Adults*, 67 J. MARRIAGE & FAM. 271, 282–83 (2005).

56. CDC, *supra* note 46, at 16 (Figure 13), 28.

57. R. Kelly Raley & Larry Bumpass, *The Topography of the Divorce Plateau: Levels and Trends in Union Stability in the United States after 1980*, 8 DEMOGRAPHIC RES. 245, 246 (2003).

58. CDC, *supra* note 46, at 15 (Figure 12).

59. *Id.* at 49 (Table 15).

Raley and Bumpass, using data from the 1995 NSFG, confirm this variability of duration by groups within the population. Indeed, their analysis shows a 15 percent increase in the instability of first unions for African American women between the 1980–86 and 1987–94 cohorts, a slight increase in instability for non-Hispanic white women, and a decrease for Hispanic women, whose unions appear to be lasting longer.[60] The probability of disruption is also higher in communities with high unemployment. Combining these two variables, 76 percent of African American cohabitants in communities of high unemployment break up within ten years, as compared with 57 percent of non-Hispanic whites living in areas of low unemployment.[61] In addition, the probability that a first cohabitation will transition to marriage within five years is 75 percent for non-Hispanic white women, 61 percent for Hispanic women, and 48 percent for African American women.[62] In short, if you are older, a member of the dominant racial or ethnic group, and economically stable, you are more likely to make a long-term success of either cohabitation or marriage.[63]

In sum, the received wisdom about the duration and stability of cohabiting unions upon which law reviews, many social scientists, and most popularized literature have relied is in fact oversimplified. Reality is much more complicated. It depends who is cohabiting, how old they are, and what their life circumstances may be, particularly their economic well-being. Despite all these qualifications, it remains true that cohabitation is likely to be shorter in duration on average than marriage and thus more likely to result in disruption of the household unit.[64] Scholars have debated whether the characteristics of persons attracted to cohabitation make them break up (the selection hypothesis), whether the institution itself is inherently unstable, or whether the

---

60. Raley & Bumpass, *supra* note 57, at 251–52 (Table 2).

61. CDC, *supra* note 46, at 17 (Figure 17) (defining disruption as a breakup either of the cohabitation or of the subsequent marriage).

62. *Id.* at 12.

63. The probability that a first marriage in a black low-income community will break up within ten years is 56 percent, compared with 23 percent for high-income non-Hispanic whites. *Id.* at 20 (Figure 27).

64. For the population as of 2001, first marriages that ended in divorce lasted a median of eight years. NUMBER, TIMING, AND DURATION OF MARRIAGES AND DIVORCES, *supra* note 50, at 9.

experience of cohabitation leads to instability.[65] For all the paper spent on this debate, there is no definitive answer. It is clear that cohabitation by persons who are not very good prospects for marriage explains some of the difference, but this may be for a variety of reasons. Some cohabitants may be difficult or disturbed people who cannot sustain a relationship. Others may not want to commit very deeply to another human being, or—perhaps more common—one member of the pair does not. Some may be persons whose present circumstances rule out marriage but who under other circumstances would be good prospects for marriage, such as men who are unemployed (perhaps semi-permanently so). On the other hand, other groups of cohabitants may not have characteristics that would select for instability. Some may be women who evaluate the men in their community as too risky for marriage, although it is their ideal. Other individuals may simply prefer a relationship without the historical baggage, especially the gender role baggage, of marriage, yet be just as committed to their partners. Others simply fall into the arrangement and then do not feel any need to change its parameters, whether from inertia or satisfaction with it.[66] And some, as we have seen in the cases described in Chapter 2, may cohabit rather than marry because they recognize that they are benefiting individually from the set-up economically, even at the cost of the other partner.

This is far from an exhaustive list of possibilities. The point I am making is that the instability of cohabitation as an institution says something about the people involved in it and less about the institution itself. What it says about the people involved, moreover, is extremely varied. The selection debate is fundamentally irrelevant to my inquiry about the appropriate legal treatment of cohabitation under U.S. law. If people fail to sustain long-term cohabiting unions, the following questions are more important than why they got themselves into this situation to begin with: How should the legal system address the situations of persons affected when these relationships fail? Would a different legal environment perhaps stabilize some of these unions, even leading some of the partners to marry? I will soon turn to these

---

65. *See, e.g.,* Thomson & Colella, *supra* note 28, at 259–60 (describing literature on selection up to that date); Brines & Joyner, *supra* note 29, at 333–34; Smock, *supra* note 25, at 6–7.

66. *See, e.g.,* Wendy M. Manning & Pamela J. Smock, *Measuring and Modeling Cohabitation: New Perspectives From Qualitative Data,* 67 J. MARRIAGE & FAM. 989, 1000 (2005) (describing couples as sliding or drifting into cohabitation rather than making a deliberate decision).

questions, after discussing other important aspects of the dynamics of the institution of cohabitation.

3.2. The Economics of Cohabiting Relationships

The economics of cohabitation are important to decisions about its appropriate legal treatment in a number of ways, including (1) the management of money within the union, to wit, whether and how the partners share their income; (2) the impact of cohabitation upon the economic well-being of the parties; and (3) the division of labor within the relationship. All of these are relevant to both the logic and the justice of the way the law treats cohabitants during their unions and when they dissolve.

3.2.1. Management of Money Within Cohabiting Relationships

The management of money within cohabiting households is clearly relevant to their legal treatment. If they keep their incomes separate, cohabitants act more like single persons and will be hurt less economically if their unions dissolve. If, by contrast, they pool their incomes, cohabiting unions lead to substantial economic interdependence and potentially dire consequences upon their dissolution. Numbers of early studies concluded, on scant evidence, that cohabitants did not pool their resources the way married couples did and thus should be treated as separate individuals rather than as an economic unit.[67] Law review authors leapt upon the generalization that cohabitants did not pool their incomes to justify denial of legal remedies to them upon dissolution, on the ground that they were not economically interdependent during their relationships.[68]

More sophisticated recent studies about how cohabitants manage money within their relationships call into question the earlier generalizations and

---

67. *See, e.g.,* Winkler, *supra* note 29, at 1089 (basing conclusion on inferences from female cohabitants' labor supply). *See also* Sharon Sassler & James McNally, *Cohabiting Couples' Economic Circumstances and Union Transitions: A Re-examination Using Multiple Imputation Techniques*, 32 Soc. Sci. Res. 553, 556 (2003).

68. *See, e.g.,* Duncan, *supra* note 23, at 1007; Marsha Garrison, *Is Consent Necessary? An Evaluation of the Emerging Law of Cohabitant Obligation*, 52 UCLA L. Rev. 815, 840, 845–46, 875 (2005).

the conclusions drawn from them. It is true that cohabitants are somewhat less likely than married couples to pool their income.[69] However, a majority of both cohabitants and married couples do in fact maintain joint finances. A comparative study of the internal economic relationships of married and cohabiting couples in the United States and Sweden found that only 47.9 percent of cohabitants in Sweden and 45.7 percent in the United States kept their money separate.[70] In other words, the majority, including almost 55 percent of those in the United States, did join their incomes. Another large-scale U.S. study reported that 73 percent of married couples and 52 percent of cohabitants shared income in a common pot even if they did not pool every cent. An additional 24 percent split expenses on a fifty-fifty basis although they did not pool their income, yielding an overall 75.3 percent of cohabitants who were substantially interdependent economically (versus 83.2 percent of married couples in the study).[71]

Yet another study reports that there is no difference at all in the allocative system employed by married and cohabiting couples if they have a biological child.[72] Further examination reveals that the difference between cohabitants with biological and nonbiological children in the family unit may be small and that male cohabitants' incomes are available to their partners even in families where the men have no biological relationship to the children.[73] (Fathers in those families may allocate their budgets differently, however, spending more on adult goods and less on child-related goods such as education.[74])

---

69. *See, e.g.*, Carolyn Vogler, *Cohabiting Couples: Rethinking Money in the Household at the Beginning of the Twenty First Century*, 53 Soc. Rev. 1, 12–13 (2005).

70. Kristen R. Heimdal & Sharon K. Houseknecht, *Cohabiting and Married Couples' Income Organization: Approaches in Sweden and the United States*, 65 J. Marriage & Fam. 525, 533 (2003). The comparable percentages for married couples were 30.1 percent in Sweden and 17.4 percent in the United States. *Id.* at 532. In Sweden, cohabitants not only have the protections given to all individuals by the social welfare state but are also entitled to allocation of their accumulated property upon dissolution. *See id.* at 527.

71. Catherine Kenney, *Cohabiting Couple, Filing Jointly? Resource Pooling and U.S. Poverty Policies*, 53 Fam. Relations 237, 243–45 (2004). Kenney relies on the Fragile Families and Child Wellbeing Study, an ongoing study of a birth cohort of unmarried parents and their children in U.S. cities with populations of more than 200,000; this data is therefore not representative but suggestive.

72. Vogler, *supra* note 69, at 13.

73. Kenney, *supra* note 71, at 244.

74. Thomas DeLeire & Ariel Kalil, *How Do Cohabiting Couples With Children Spend Their Money?*, 67 J. Marriage & Fam. 286, 290, 294 (2005) (finding that cohabiting-parent families spend less on education and on housing than married-parent families but more on

In short, despite the comparatively brief duration of cohabiting unions in the United States and the lack of legal protections for them, which make income sharing very risky, the majority of cohabitants do share their incomes nonetheless. A large-scale survey of cohabiting couples in the United Kingdom that involved qualitative interviews showed similar results. Despite the variety of types of relationships and commitments described to them, the authors of that study found that there was "clear evidence of financial dependence and interdependence during relationships, particularly where there are children."[75]

As these studies show, about half of cohabitants still do keep their money separate rather than pooling it, with each contributing to the joint household in some way. This behavior appears more rational from a strictly economic point of view, given the lack of legal protection given to long-term investments in cohabiting unions. One scholar points out that economic behavior following a principle of strict equality of contribution—a fifty-fifty division of all expenses, dollar for dollar, rather than "from each according to his ability, to each according to his need"[76]—may be the quite rational result of this legal insecurity. In other words, many cohabitants may keep their money separate because the legal status of cohabitation is unprotected, rather than, as some have suggested, cohabiting because of an individualistic predisposition that leads them both to cohabit and to maintain separate finances.[77]

If two cohabitants' contributions to the household are both monetary and their incomes roughly equal, there may be no reason to worry about the possibility of exploitation or vulnerability if their relationship ends. Reality, again, is not so simple. An ideology of equality, defined as equal contribution, may

---

child care). Research comparing the consumer decision making of cohabiting and married couples is in its infancy but seems to indicate that men and women in cohabiting relationships make their purchasing decisions together, while married couples make them separately. *See* Nabil Razzouch et al., *A Comparison of Consumer Decision-making Behavior of Married and Cohabiting Couples*, 24 J. CONSUMER MARKETING 264 (2007). Married and cohabiting couples are similar in the interdependence of their planning for retirement, however. Steven E. Mock & Steven W. Cornelius, *Profiles of Interdependence: The Retirement Planning of Married, Cohabiting, and Lesbian Couples*, 56 SEX ROLES 793, 799 (2007).

75. Anne Barlow & Grace James, *Regulating Marriage and Cohabitation in 21st Century Britain*, 67 MOD. L. REV. 143, 156 (2004).

76. Karl Marx, *Critique of the Gotha Progam, in* THE MARX-ENGELS READER 388 (Robert C. Tucker ed., 1972).

77. Brines & Joyner, *supra* note 29, at 350–51.

mask substantial inequality if the male and female partners' incomes are not equal.[78] In fact, women not only earn less on average than men but are also more likely to spend what they earn for food and other household needs rather than on themselves, leading the author of one study to comment:

> [A]s long as spending on the home and family is constructed as the woman's responsibility, allocative systems in which money is kept partly or completely separate can easily end up in practice operating rather like the traditional housekeeping allowance system, except that the female partner uses her own earnings rather than being given an allowance by the male partner.[79]

Other scholars point out that women's care of and connection with children disadvantage them in bargaining with men for the best deal.[80] In short, we need to be concerned about exploitation and vulnerability whether cohabitants pool their resources or not.

Finally, it is important to note, as with almost every topic discussed thus far, that cohabitants' management of money may differ by group. There is evidence, for example, that the greater economic uncertainty of the fathers of Puerto Rican children may make them less likely to pool their resources than other groups.[81] Less than 40 percent of cohabiting Puerto Rican fathers either pool their income or pay for all the household expenses.[82] Married fathers within this community are much more likely to pool their income than cohabiting fathers are but also more likely simply to pay all the family's expenses themselves, which appears to reflect patriarchal family structures in Latin America.[83]

---

78. Vogler, *supra* note 69, at 20.

79. *Id.* at 23.

80. *See* Andrew J. Cherlin, *Toward a New Home Socioeconomics of Union Formation, in* THE TIES THAT BIND: PERSPECTIVES ON MARRIAGE AND COHABITATION 126, 133 (Linda J. Waite ed., Aldine De Gruyter Dimensions 2000) ("women do not bargain as far toward the margins of their power as men do," quoting Paul England & Barbara Stanek Kilbourne, *Markets, Marriage, and Other Mates: The Problem of Power, in* BEYOND THE MARKETPLACE 163, 171 (Roger Friedland & A.F. Robertson eds., 1990)).

81. R.S. Oropesa et al., *Income Allocation in Marital and Cohabiting Unions: The Case of Mainland Puerto Ricans*, 65 J. MARRIAGE & FAM. 910, 911, 914 (2003).

82. *Id.* at 923.

83. *Id.* at 922–23.

3.2.2. The Impact of Cohabitation Upon the Economic
Well-being of the Partners and their Children

It should be clear by now that cohabitation can have a substantial effect upon the economic welfare of the partners and their children, who receive the economies of sharing living space as well as contributions from an additional person's income. Female cohabitants contribute more to the family income than do wives: one study reported that women cohabitants earn 90 percent of their partners' income, while wives earn 60 percent.[84] Thus, men gain in most cohabiting relationships by being relieved of the necessity of being the family's sole support: female cohabitants make substantial financial contributions to the household and may even give more than their share (as many African American mothers living with unemployed men may do). Economic equality between cohabitants appears to stabilize cohabitation, while it may destabilize marriage.[85]

Women and children gain also by addition of a cohabitant's income to the household. One recent study comparing the effects of marriage and cohabitation on total family income concluded that women gain a virtually identical income premium from either cohabitation or marriage—a gain of roughly 55 percent in needs-adjusted total family income.[86] Yet another study reports that children whose parents have divorced experience an increase of about $6,000 in their median adjusted family income if their custodial parent either remarries or cohabits.[87] In other words, remarriage and cohabitation are equivalent in their ability to restore family income to pre-divorce levels.

In short, it is clear that cohabitants become economically interdependent during their unions. This doubtless leads to changes in economic behavior on the part of the partners. Women like Mrs. Hewitt and Mrs. Friedman obviously relied over the course of their long-term cohabiting relationships not only on their partner's income but also on the assumption that his income would be available for the needs of their families in the long run. Trusting in this arrangement, which looks naïve only in retrospect, neither woman made

---

84. Brines & Joyner, *supra* note 29, at 341.

85. *Id.* at 347–48.

86. Audrey Light, *Gender Differences in the Marriage and Cohabitation Income Premium*, 41 DEMOGRAPHY 263, 279 (2004).

87. Donna Ruane Morrison & Amy Ritualo, *Routes to Children's Economic Recovery after Divorce: Are Cohabitation and Remarriage Equivalent?*, 65 AM. SOC. REV. 560, 570 (2000).

other provisions to protect herself economically in the future.[88] As a result, the dissolution of their unions had a catastrophic effect upon their welfare. A good deal has been written about the economic consequences of divorce for women, in particular about how women's post-divorce income declines precipitously compared to that of men, leaving many women and children in an impoverished state.[89] More recent studies show that the dissolution of a cohabiting relationship has a comparable effect upon the economic welfare of women and children, leaving a substantial number of former cohabitants—about 30 percent—in poverty.[90] Women cohabitants lose about one-third of their household income—more than cohabiting men do—at the end of their relationships, leaving them with levels of household income similar to that of divorced women.[91] The reasons for this impoverishment are similar—women's lower average earnings in the marketplace and their much greater likelihood of having custody of children.[92] Indeed, some scholars suggest that cohabiting women are less likely than divorced women to get child support awards even though they are equally entitled to them.[93] The impact is particularly severe upon African American and Hispanic women.[94]

3.2.3. Division of Household Labor Between Cohabitants

As previously discussed, cohabitants are more likely than other couples to both work outside the home, a pattern increasingly typical of all families in the United States; and cohabiting women bring more income into the household economy than do wives. In these dual-worker couples, how do cohabitants compare with married couples with respect to their division of labor

---

88. *See supra* at 31–33, 56–57.

89. See, e.g., Karen C. Holden & Pamela J. Smock, *The Economic Costs of Marital Dissolution: Why Do Women Bear a Disproportionate Cost?*, 17 ANN. REV. SOC. 51 (1991).

90. Avellar & Smock, *supra* note 31, at 323.

91. *Id.* at 324.

92. *Id.* at 325.

93. Claire M. Kamp Dush & H. Elizabeth Peters, *The Economic Impact of Cohabitation Dissolution versus Marital Dissolution in Fragile Families*, Mar. 2007 (draft in possession of author). Ironically, they may have more of a continuing relationship with the fathers of their children, however, and continue to receive various in-kind contributions. *Id.*

94. Avellar & Smock, *supra* note 31, at 324.

within the household? Is it based less on gender and more on equality or some notion of equity between the partners?

Early studies showed that cohabitants were less likely to divide household labor along gender lines than married couples.[95] This topic continues to attract a good deal of academic interest, with later studies confirming that cohabitation is associated with a more equal division of housework than marriage, although women still contribute more than men in both types of union.[96] Indeed, one study of twenty-two nations, including the United States, showed that couples that cohabit and then marry seem to take their more equal division of housework into the marriage with them.[97] Another study found that men who planned to marry their cohabiting partners spent even more hours on housework than men who had not formed such plans, though the presence or absence of such plans made no difference to women's contribution of housework.[98] Thus, some sort of egalitarianism appears to infect men who cohabit more than those who marry.

Scholars have hypothesized that couples, married or not, divide work between them according to a number of factors, including time availability (the partner with more free time does more housework), relative resources (the partner with more economic power can buy his or her way out of housework), or gender ideology (individuals with more traditional gender ideology divide household labor by gender, assigning repetitive and labor-intensive tasks to women).[99] These factors do not act independently of one another, however, because an individual's gender socialization—that is, the development of his or her expectations about gender roles earlier in life—has an important impact on both time availability and resources.[100] In other words,

---

95. *See, e.g.*, Scott J. South & Glenna Spitze, *Housework in Marital and Nonmarital Households*, 59 Am. Sociol. Rev. 327, 340 (1994) (reporting gender gap among married couples as greater than that among cohabiting couples); Sanjiv Gupta, *The Effects of Transitions in Marital Status on Men's Performance of Housework*, 61 J. Marriage & Fam. 700, 708 (1999) (reporting that transition from cohabitation to marriage does not affect men's or women's housework time).

96. *See* Jeanne A. Batalova & Philip N. Cohen, *Premarital Cohabitation and Housework: Couples in Cross-national Perspective*, 64 J. Marriage & Fam. 743, 753 (2002).

97. *Id.*

98. Teresa Ciabattari, *Cohabitation and Housework: The Effects of Marital Intentions*, 66 J. Marriage & Fam. 118, 123 (2004).

99. *See* Shannon N. Davis, et al., *Effects of Union Type on Division of Household Labor: Do Cohabiting Men Really Perform More Housework?*, 28 J. Fam. Issues 1246, 1248–49 (2007).

100. Mick Cunningham, *Gender in Cohabitation and Marriage: The Influence of Gender Ideology on Housework Allocation Over the Life Course*, 26 J. Fam. Issues 1037, 1055 (2005).

women who have been socialized to assume that the majority of childcare and other housework will fall on them may choose careers that are less time-consuming and often less remunerative.

The effect of gender ideology on the division of labor apparently differs according to whether the couple is married or cohabiting, however. One study reported "a positive association between early gender egalitarianism and subsequent levels of men's relative participation in stereotypically female housework for cohabitors, and the magnitude of this relationship did not vary by gender," but this relationship between gender ideology and household labor did not hold true for married men.[101] The author concludes from the data that while men and women cohabitants are "equally able to put their gender ideology into practice," married women are not; he suggests that some women may choose cohabitation over marriage for this reason.[102] The results of cross-national studies are consistent with these findings. In a study of 17,636 individuals in twenty-eight nations (primarily developed nations), cohabiting men reported doing more housework than married men, and cohabiting women reported doing less than married women.[103] The division of labor in both married and cohabiting couples was influenced by the partners' time availability and their relative resources, with the relative financial contributions of the partners being a key factor in all twenty-eight countries.[104] However, gender ideology had more influence on the way cohabiting couples divided household work than on married couples, that is, "[e]galitarian ideologies are more likely to translate into egalitarian divisions of household labor when present in cohabiting relationships than in marriages."[105] Again, a certain egalitarianism appears to be inherent in cohabitation but not in marriage.

Many couples today, if they can afford to, address inequities that arise in domestic work by hiring other people to do it. Unsurprisingly, the proclivity of all couples to outsource domestic tasks relates to the partners' incomes, but for cohabiting couples, only the woman's earnings are positively related to spending on outsourcing household tasks traditionally classified as women's work. The author of the study finding this correlation concludes

---

101. *Id.* at 1057.

102. *Id.*

103. Davis et al., *supra* note 99.

104. *Id.* at 1265–66.

105. *Id.* at 1267.

that "cohabiting men are apparently less inclined than married men to use their personal income to reduce their partner's domestic burden, [but] they do share housework more equally."[106]

These studies about how couples divide labor within cohabiting relationships are important not just for what they say about the economics of their unions. Satisfaction with the household division of labor has repeatedly been shown to be an important factor in couples' evaluation of the quality of their relationships—especially to women's positive feelings about it—and hence presumably to their longevity.[107] We turn now to the literature comparing cohabitants and married couples on the reported quality of their relationships.

3.3 Quality of the Relationship

There is by now a large literature recounting the supposed benefits of marriage for individuals' physical and mental health. These studies demonstrate that being married correlates with higher earnings, less depression, less alcoholism, less violence, and more all-around happiness.[108] All of these correlations are subject to questions about what is cause and what is effect. Persons in better economic circumstances are more likely than others to get married in the first place; and being economically secure correlates to better physical and mental health.[109] Many scholars believe that the enhanced well-being of married couples compared to cohabitants rests upon their higher

---

106. Judith Treas & Esther De Ruijter, *Earnings and Expenditures on Household Services in Married and Cohabiting Unions*, 70 J. MARRIAGE & FAM. 796, 803 (2008).

107. *Cf.* Galena Kline Rhoades et al., *Premarital Cohabitation, Husbands' Commitment, and Wives' Satisfaction with the Division of Household Contributions*, 40 MARRIAGE & FAM. REV. 5, 6 (2006) and articles cited therein. *See also* Bryndl E. Hohmann-Marriott, *Shared Beliefs and the Union Stability of Married and Cohabiting Couples*, 68 J. MARRIAGE & FAM. 1015, 1025 (2006) (reporting that it is only when the two partners hold dissimilar beliefs about division of labor that it destabilizes their unions).

108. *See* LINDA J. WAITE & MAGGIE GALLAGHER, THE CASE FOR MARRIAGE: WHY MARRIED PEOPLE ARE HAPPIER, HEALTHIER, AND BETTER OFF FINANCIALLY (2000). For a summary of the benefits of marriage, *see* Linda J. Waite, *The Family as a Social Organization: Key Ideas for the Twenty-first Century*, 29 CONTEMP. SOC. 463, 465 (2000).

109. *See, e.g.*, Frederick J. Zimmerman & Wayne Katon, *Socioeconomic Status, Depression, Disparities, and Financial Strain: What Lies Behind the Income-Depression Relationship?*, 14 HEALTH ECON. 1197, 1197 (2005); Betty M. Kennedy et al., *Socioeconomic Status and Health Disparity in the United States*, 15 J. HUM. BEHAV. IN THE SOCIAL ENV'T 13 (2007).

socioeconomic status.[110] Even after controlling for socioeconomic status, however, there still seems to be evidence that being married does confer benefits.[111] What about cohabitation? The record is mixed.

There are numerous studies comparing the mental health of cohabiting partners with that of married couples and many differing axes along which they are compared. Scholars have asked cohabitants questions about their overall happiness, their levels of depression, and consumption of alcohol, as well as about their opinions of the quality of their relationships in general. One thing that does appear clear from repeated studies is that the differences between marriage and cohabitation are not simply the result of selection effects, that is, cohabitants are not more depressed than married people just because more unhappy or depressed people choose to cohabit instead of marry.[112] Cohabitants as a group are more depressed than married people in general, but they are less depressed than single persons.[113] Scholars attempting to discern the reasons for these differences have come up with numerous hypotheses, based on married individuals' greater social resources (supportive networks) and better self-concepts (seeing oneself as fulfilling a socially approved role),[114] expectations and perceptions of equity in the relationship,[115] the fact that marriage is more "institutionalized" (accompanied by clear social norms about conduct within it),[116] and differences in levels of commitment

---

110. See Susan L. Brown, *The Effect of Union Type on Psychological Well-Being: Depression Among Cohabitors Versus Marrieds*, 41 J. HEALTH & SOC. BEHAV. 241, 243 (2000) and articles cited therein.

111. See, e.g., Steven Stack & J. Ross Eshleman, *Marital Status and Happiness: A 17-Nation Study*, 60 J. MARRIAGE & FAM. 527, 534 (1998) (reporting that marriage was 3.4 times more closely associated with the variance of happiness than was cohabitation, in part because of health and economic benefits and in part due to emotional support).

112. See, e.g., Kathleen A. Lamb et al., *Union Formation and Depression: Selection and Relationship Effects*, 65 J. MARRIAGE & FAM. 953, 960 (2003); Kristen Marcussen, *Explaining Differences in Mental Health Between Married and Cohabiting Individuals*, 68 SOC. PSYCH. Q. 239, 253 (2005); Claire M. Kamp Dush & Paul R. Amato, *Consequences of Relationship Status and Quality for Subjective Well-being*, 22 J. SOC. & PERS. RELATIONSHIPS 607, 624 (2005); Brown, *supra* note 110, at 252–53.

113. See, e.g., Susan L. Brown et al., *The Significance of Nonmarital Cohabitation: Marital Status and Mental Health Benefits Among Middle-Aged and Older Adults*, 60B. J. GERONTOLOGY S21, S.24 (2005); Kamp Dush & Amato, *supra* note 112, at 622–23 (re younger persons).

114. See, e.g., Marcussen, *supra* note 112, at 241–42.

115. *Id.* at 242–43.

116. Steven L. Nock, *A Comparison of Marriages and Cohabiting Relationships*, 16 J. FAM. ISSUES 53, 55–56 (1995).

and stability between marriage and cohabitation.[117] Some, if not all, of these factors should have a diminishing effect with the passage of time, as cohabitation has become widely accepted. Indeed, one empirical study published in 2005 shows that cohabitants do not report lower levels of self-esteem than married persons,[118] a result one would expect with decreasing stigmatization of cohabitation. Moreover, as families, neighbors, and friends become more accustomed to cohabiting couples, there is no reason to expect that the supportive social networks available to cohabitants would be inadequate.

The results of the numerous studies comparing the quality of the relationships of cohabiting and married couples are not only confusing about cause and effect but also conflicting.[119] For example, one study comparing the mental health of young adult cohabitants with that of unmarried and married persons found no differences between cohabitants and others in levels of depression but did report more alcohol problems among cohabiting men.[120] The authors also noted that "[h]igh levels of financial need are especially likely to be related to alcohol problems among cohabiting men."[121] So, are these men drinking heavily because they are cohabiting or because they are economically stressed? Or, more likely, are they both cohabiting and drinking because of their economic situation? This example illustrates the types of interpretive problems that accompany these correlations and comparisons.

By contrast to this study reporting no differences in levels of depression, another study, based on NSFH data, shows that cohabitants report substantially higher levels of depression than their married counterparts, even when controlling for sociodemographic factors.[122] The longer the duration of cohabitation, the more the depression, which the author attributes to higher levels of relationship instability.[123] Another oft-cited 1995 article by Steven L. Nock, also based on NSFH data, found that there was no significant

---

117. Marcussen, *supra* note 112, at 243.

118. *Id.* at 252.

119. *See also* Laura Stafford, et al., *Married Individuals, Cohabiters, and Cohabiters Who Marry: A Longitudinal Study of Relational and Individual Well-being*, 21 J. Soc. & Pers. Relationships 231, 236 (2004) (describing conflicting studies about depression and cohabitation).

120. Allan V. Horwitz & Helen Raskin White, *The Relationship of Cohabitation and Mental Health: A Study of a Young Adult Cohort*, 60 J. Marriage & Fam. 505, 510–11 (1998).

121. *Id.* at 511.

122. *Id. See also* Brown, *supra* note 110, at 247, 253.

123. *Id.* at 247–48.

difference between married and cohabiting couples on frequency of disagreements but that cohabitants reported significantly lower levels of happiness.[124] Nock argued that the poorer quality of cohabitants' relationships was caused by lack of institutionalization and the concomitant lack of clear normative standards governing cohabitation.[125] Another major study using NSFH data is consistent with Nock's finding that cohabitants reported poorer relationship quality than their married counterparts, even when controlling for relationship duration and demographic characteristics but found that cohabitants with plans to marry did not differ significantly from married couples on reported relationship quality.[126] Since nearly 75 percent of cohabitants report plans to marry (though only 53 percent actually do),[127] this substantially undercuts generalizations about cohabitation and the quality of relationships. If a majority of cohabitants enjoy this higher relationship quality even prior to marriage (because a majority plan to marry), the experience of marriage could not be responsible for the reported differences.[128]

On the other hand, cohabitants who do not marry may experience an escalation of conflict according to one study.[129] (Perhaps this is because they disagree over whether to marry or not.) Yet the same study reports that "[c]loser inspection reveals that some long-term cohabitors enjoy levels of relationship quality that are not unlike those of their counterparts who marry."[130] The intact unions that this scholar studied in the two-wave NSFH data were only those that had survived as long as seven years, a very select group, given that only one in ten lasts beyond five years according to that dataset; and she admits that "[a] less select group of cohabitors may have higher relationship quality, on average, both before and after marriage."[131]

---

124. Steven L. Nock, *A Comparison of Marriages and Cohabiting Relationships*, 16 J. FAM. ISSUES 53, 69 (1995).

125. *See id.* at 55–56.

126. Brown & Booth, *supra* note 37, at 677. Brown's later research demonstrated that cohabitants' assessment of the quality of their relationships was, not surprisingly, associated with their odds of separating or of marrying. *See* Brown, *supra* note 19, at 843.

127. Susan L. Brown, *Moving From Cohabitation to Marriage: Effects on Relationship Quality*, 33 SOC. SCI. RES. 1, 2 (2004); Bumpass & Lu, *supra* note 53, at 33.

128. Brown, *supra* note 127, at 16.

129. *Id.* at 17.

130. *Id.*

131. *Id.*

Yet another analysis of the NSFH data, this time by scholars of communications rather than sociologists or demographers, concluded that the transition to marriage played little role in cohabitants' frequency of conflict or relational satisfaction.[132] Instead, they found that long-term married persons were more satisfied than cohabitants who married and cohabitants who married were more satisfied than long-term cohabitants, which the authors interpreted as lending support to the selectivity thesis.[133] In short, the results of these studies conflict. The two just described, for example, say, variously, that cohabitation may or may not be correlated with increased depression as compared to marriage and that long-term cohabitants enjoy either higher or lower relationship quality. Moreover, most of these analyses were based on the 1987–88 NSFH study; and we know that as cohabitation becomes more common, it is less vulnerable to selection effects in general.[134]

Despite conflicting studies and confusion about how to interpret the results, we do know a few things. Some proportion of cohabitants are unhappy with their relationships and may be depressed, and their dissatisfaction may be related to the insecurity and instability of cohabitation. Where does this get us? There is no evidence that simply shifting the same individuals into marriage, were that possible, would result in increasing their happiness quotients or protecting them against depression. What one article notes about the economic benefits of marriage may be true here as well: "[T]he benefits of marriage observed for people who are, in fact, married would not necessarily accrue to those who are not."[135] This generalization is confirmed by an empirical study investigating the consequences of cohabitation or marriage for single mothers, the group targeted by the 1996 welfare reforms, which saw marriage as a way to rescue these mothers and their children from poverty. Marriage, the study's authors report, may in fact be substantially worse for the mental and physical health of these women than remaining single, in part because marrying would expose them to their

---

132. Stafford et al., *supra* note 119, at 243.

133. *Id.* at 243–44.

134. *See, e.g.,* Brenda Wilhelm, *Changes in Cohabitation Across Cohorts: The Influence of Political Activism*, 77 Soc. Forces 289, 296 (1998); Dorien Manting, *The Changing Meaning of Cohabitation and Marriage*, 12 Eur. Soc. Rev. 53, 63 (1996).

135. Pamela J. Smock & Wendy D. Manning, *Living Together Unmarried in the United States: Demographic Perspectives and Implications for Family Policy*, 26 L. & Pol'y 87, 103 (2004), citing Pamela J. Smock et al., *The Effect of Marriage and Divorce on Women's Economic Well-Being*, 64 Am. Soc. Rev. 794 (1999).

group's statistically very high risk of divorce, with all its economic and psychosocial distress.[136] Again, the aggregate statistics about relationship quality may mask significant group differences.

Finally, if cohabiting relationships are not of as high a quality as marriages, what implications does that have for the legal treatment of cohabitation? If some of the distress is caused by insecurity, giving legal rights to cohabitants might in fact improve the quality of their relationships. Even if it did not, it does not follow that the persons involved in unhappy relationships are less deserving of legal protection that those who are not; and they may in fact need it more.

3.4. Domestic Violence and Cohabitation

A persisting relationship has been reported between cohabitation and levels of serious domestic violence, including murder of the female partner (femicide), in the United States, Canada, and Australia.[137] It is important to examine the evidence on this issue with care and to deconstruct many of the statistics, especially the data used in the earliest studies on this issue. Some of the studies appear to present conflicting results, at least as to some aspects of the problem, and others present the interpreter with apparent anomalies. At the end, it remains unclear why levels of violence are higher among cohabitants than among married couples. Scholars have explored a number of hypotheses, such as selection bias and lack of institutionalization, but no definitive answer has emerged. Moreover, with the passage of time, the rates of violence among cohabiting and married couples appear to be converging, although it is not yet clear whether they will ultimately become the same.

The earliest studies correlating domestic violence and cohabitation took place at a time when cohabitation was much less common than it is today,

---

136. Kristi Williams et al., *For Better or For Worse? The Consequences of Marriage and Cohabitation for Single Mothers*, 86 SOCIAL FORCES 1481, 1502–05 (2008).

137. *See, e.g.*, Kersti Yllo & Murray A. Straus, *Interpersonal Violence Among Married and Cohabiting Couples*, 30 FAM. REL. 339 (1981) (U.S.); Douglas A. Brownridge, *Understanding Women's Heightened Risk of Violence in Common Law Unions: Revisiting the Selection and Relationship Hypotheses*, 10 VIOLENCE AGAINST WOMEN 626 (2004) (Canada); Todd K. Shackelford & Jenny Mouzos, *Partner Killing by Men in Cohabiting and Marital Relationships: A Comparative, Cross-National Analysis of Data From Australia and the United States*, 20 J. INTERPERSONAL VIOLENCE 1310 (2005) (Australia and United States).

yet they continue to be cited. One, based on a 1976 survey, included only forty cohabitants in its randomized sample of 2,143 heterosexual coupled adults between the ages of eighteen and seventy.[138] That study concluded that the rate of violence among cohabitants was higher than among married persons, but cohabitants over the age of thirty, divorced women, those with high incomes, and those who had been together more than ten years had very low rates of violence, less than their married counterparts.[139] In an early but oft-cited article, Jan E. Stets and Murray A. Straus reported that cohabitants were twice as likely as married persons to be victims of domestic violence.[140] This 1989 study was based on 237 cohabitants and 5,005 married couples, a much lower statistical proportion than would be obtained if a randomized sample were run today.[141] It found violence to be both more common and more severe among cohabitants—35 percent of cohabiting couples versus 15 percent of married couples reported a physical assault during the previous year.[142]

A 1998 article points out that, when Stets's and Straus's data is controlled for age, the differential assault rate changes to 36 percent of married couples versus 40 percent of cohabiting couples, not as striking a difference.[143] This makes sense, given that victims of domestic violence tend to be disproportionately young. Department of Justice statistics show that the highest rates of intimate partner violence affect women between the ages of sixteen and twenty-four.[144]

---

138. Yllo & Straus, *supra* note 137, at 342.

139. *Id.* at 345.

140. Jan E. Stets & Murray A. Straus, *The Marriage License as a Hitting License: A Comparison of Assaults in Dating, Cohabiting, and Married Couples, in* VIOLENCE IN DATING RELATIONSHIPS: EMERGING SOCIAL ISSUES 33, 38 (Maureen A. Pirog-Good & Jan E. Stets eds., 1989). *See also* MARTIN DALY & MARGO WILSON, HOMICIDE 213–15 (1988) (reporting higher rates of victimization in common law marriages in Canada between 1974 and 1983); Nicky Ali Jackson, *Observational Experiences of Intrapersonal Conflict and Teenage Victimization: A Comparative Study Among Spouses and Cohabitors*, 11 J. FAM. VIOLENCE 191, 197 (1996) (reporting that cohabitors among 1985 National Family Violence Resurvey encountered more violence than spouses given similar patterns of childhood victimization).

141. Stets & Straus, *supra* note 140, at 36. Cohabitants were less than 5 percent of the sample, whereas they made up 9 percent of coupled households in the 2000 census. U.S. CENSUS BUREAU, MARRIED-COUPLE AND UNMARRIED-PARTNER HOUSEHOLDS: 2000 3 (2003).

142. Stets and Straus, *supra* note 140, at 38.

143. Lynn Magdol et al., *Hitting Without a License: Testing Explanations for Differences in Partner Abuse Between Young Adult Daters and Cohabitors*, 60 J. MARRIAGE & FAM. 41, 53 (1998); *see also* Stets & Straus, *supra* note 142, at 42 (Figure 2.3).

144. BUREAU OF JUSTICE STAT., U.S. DEP'T OF JUSTICE, INTIMATE PARTNER VIOLENCE 4 (Figure 6), App. (Table 5) (2000, rev'd 1/31/02) (reporting that highest rates of intimate violence

With twenty-five as the median age of first marriage for women today, a larger proportion of the intimate partners affected by violence are likely to be cohabitants. The rate of domestic violence is also higher among subgroups of the population who are more likely to cohabit, such as lower-income persons.[145] It is possible, of course, that socioeconomic distress is responsible to some extent for both the domestic violence and the cohabitation. We also know, as discussed in the previous chapter, that the potential for violence is one reason that low-income mothers cohabit rather than marry.

A more recent study disaggregates the statistics on intimate partner violence according to the length of time a cohabiting couple has been together, finding that the rates of violence for relationships up to one year in duration are fairly similar to those for couples married for the same period, but that the two diverge significantly by five years.[146] The authors explain this pattern with a selection bias theory, one based not on differences between those who select themselves into cohabitation or marriage but rather on those who select themselves out of each status. As we have seen, cohabitants who are employed, more highly educated, and more highly paid are also more likely to get married, transforming a group that was once fairly heterogeneous in its characteristics into an increasingly homogenous group of cohabitants with the passage of time. The group left when five years have passed thus includes a larger proportion of those with characteristics—lower income, unemployment, and

---

affected women aged sixteen to twenty-four) [hereinafter BJS 2002]. Later BJS statistics show that the highest rate of all from 2001–05 was among women aged twenty to twenty-four. BUREAU OF JUSTICE STAT., U.S. DEP'T OF JUSTICE, INTIMATE PARTNER VIOLENCE IN THE UNITED STATES 2007 [hereinafter BJS 2007 INTIMATE PARTNER VIOLENCE], *Average annual nonfatal intimate partner victimization rate, by gender and age, 2001–2005* (2007), *available at* http://www.ojp.usdoj.gov/bjs/intimate/ipv.htm.

145. BJS 2007 INTIMATE PARTNER VIOLENCE, *supra* note 144, *Average annual nonfatal intimate partner victimization rate, by income and gender, 2001–2005* (reporting rates of domestic violence at 12.71 per 1000 for females in households with income less than $7500; 6.2 per 1000 for incomes from $7500 to $24,999; 5.2 per 1000 for incomes from $25,000 to $49,999; and 2.0 per 1000 for incomes of $50,000 or more. Previously, African Americans had higher rates of domestic violence than Anglo Americans, but the average annual rate of the two groups had virtually converged by 2005. *Id., Nonfatal intimate partner victimization rate per 1,000 persons age 12 or older by gender and race, 1993–2005*).

146. Catherine T. Kenney & Sara S. McLanahan, *Why Are Cohabiting Relationships More Violent Than Marriages?*, 43 DEMOGRAPHY 127, 132 (Table 1) (2006) (relying on an NSFH sample interviewed between March 1987 and May 1988). *But see* DOUGLAS A. BROWNRIDGE, VIOLENCE AGAINST WOMEN: VULNERABLE POPULATIONS 52 (2009) (reporting that two of the three datasets studied in Canada showed significantly higher rates of violence reported by cohabitants than by married women, even at one year).

lower education—that are themselves positively associated with domestic violence.[147] At the same time, married persons subject to domestic violence select themselves out of marriage by divorcing; not surprisingly, there is a positive correlation between marital violence and divorce.[148] Thus, a certain type of selection bias—a selecting out bias—might explain the different rates of violence in cohabiting versus married couples after a certain period of time.

Official estimates based on statistics of violent crimes in the United States show that married women are less at risk of domestic violence than women who are unmarried: 1.2 per 1,000 married women were victims of non-lethal domestic violence between 2001 and 2005, versus 5.5 per 1,000 never-married women.[149] However, the Bureau of Justice Statistics (BJS) category "never-married women" includes intimates who are not in fact living together, so it is not coextensive with cohabitants. Further, by far the highest rates of victimization—51.1 per 1,000—are among divorced (10.4 per 1,000) and separated (40.7 per 1,000) women.[150] Although some cohabitants would fall into the marital status divorced, most divorced and all separated women can be seen as a subcategory of married women and are presumably being abused by the same man from whom they are separated rather than by a post-divorce cohabitant.[151] Thus, these statistics do not unproblematically support the frequent generalization that domestic violence is more common among cohabitants than among married couples.

There may also be underreporting of violence among married couples, perhaps because a battered spouse feels she has more to lose by reporting her husband to the criminal authorities. If the married couple are immigrants who have not yet attained legal residency status, a wife would have an additional disincentive to report the violence to the authorities.[152] However, one

---

147. Kenney & McLanahan, *supra* note 146, at 136–37.

148. *Id.*

149. BJS 2007 INTIMATE PARTNER VIOLENCE, *supra* note 144, *Average annual nonfatal intimate partner victimization rate, by gender and marital status, 2001–2005.*

150. *Id.*

151. Severe battery is known to be most common when women separate from their abusers. *See, e.g.,* Martha R. Mahoney, *Legal Images of Battered Women: Redefining the Issue of Separation,* 90 MICH. L. REV. 1, 61–68 (1991) (describing the more intense violence that greets women who attempt to leave as separation assault).

152. Even though her own immigration status may be considered separately from that of her husband in cases of domestic violence under provisions of the Violence Against Women Act, this process may be daunting for an immigrant woman to negotiate, and she may

study of physical violence among Hispanic subgroups reveals that women of Mexican origin report significantly higher rates of domestic violence than Puerto Rican women do, even though the latter need not worry about citizenship issues.[153] In short, both the level of violence and the level of reporting may vary by subgroups.

An apparent discrepancy between reports given by young male and female cohabitants is more difficult to explain, with cohabiting women more likely to report the presence of violence in their relationship (the reporter may be either the victim or perpetrator) than cohabiting men are, who do not appear from studies based on self-reporting to differ from married men in their perpetration of violence.[154] Clearly some kind of bias in the self-reporting is at work here. This is not surprising, given that the women are more likely to be reporting victimization and the men that they have been the perpetrators of violence.[155]

There is fairly solid evidence that the most severe type of domestic violence, femicide, is more common among cohabitants than among married couples. A number of studies have reported a higher murder rate among unmarried intimate partners, but the disparity between married and unmarried couples seems to be getting narrower with time. One astonishing study of the FBI homicide database for 1976 to 1994 reported that women in cohabiting relationships were almost nine times more likely to be killed by their partners than women in marital relationships and that the rates were higher for middle-aged than for younger cohabitants.[156] This is surprising, given the disparity with the BJS statistics on non-lethal violence cited, which showed that domestic violence was 4.58 times more frequent among a group that included all unmarried women and not just cohabitants than among

---

also be heavily dependent upon her husband's language skills and employment. *See* 8 U.S.C.A. § 1229b(b)(2). *See also* Michelle J. Anderson, *A License to Abuse: The Impact of Conditional Status on Female Immigrants*, 102 YALE L.J. 1401 (1993).

153. Sonia M. Frias & Ronald J. Angel, *The Risk of Partner Violence Among Low-Income Hispanic Subgroups*, 67 J. MARRIAGE & FAM. 552, 559 (Table 2), 561 (2005).

154. Susan L. Brown & Jennifer Roebuck Bulanda, *Relationship Violence in Young Adulthood: A Comparison of Daters, Cohabitors, and Marrieds*, 37 GERONTOLOGY 73, 79, 85 (2008).

155. Women are the overwhelming majority of victims of domestic violence. *See* BJS 2002, *supra* note 144, at 1.

156. Todd K. Shackelford, *Cohabitation, Marriage, and Murder: Woman-Killing by Male Romantic Partners*, 27 AGGRESSIVE BEHAV. 284, 287–88 (2001) (reporting femicide rates as highest for ages thirty-five to sixty-four).

married women.[157] BJS homicide statistics report the following rates for 2005: 4.04 per 100,000 intimate homicides for wives and ex-wives and 5.50 per 100,000 for the broad category "girlfriend," which would include noncohabiting intimate partners as well, so the rate of murder among the two groups seems to be converging.[158] The rates for all categories of both lethal and nonlethal violence have also been steadily decreasing over the last decades.[159]

Nonetheless, the statistics do provide some support for the generalization that cohabitants are subject to more severe types of violence than married women, even if the differences between the two groups are growing less stark with the passage of time. Studies carried out in Australia and Canada have also demonstrated disparities in femicide between married and cohabiting women. A study carried out in Australia showed even higher rates of partner-killing of cohabitants (4.7 per million married women killed by their partners per year versus 44.9 per million cohabitants killed, or 9.5 times higher).[160]

Canadian studies also confirm a much higher rate of intimate violence and femicide among cohabitants in that country, reporting that cohabitants were twice as likely as married women to report experiencing violence and six times as likely to be killed by their partners than married persons between 1991 and 2000.[161] One Canadian study compared this rate favorably with previous Canadian findings that cohabitants were nine times as likely as married women to become victims of intimate homicide, hypothesizing that the rates were converging as cohabitation became more common and thus selection bias had decreased.[162] Subsequent studies by the same author based on statistics from 2004 show a continuation of this trend. He reports

---

157. The Bureau of Justice Statistics also reported that of all women murder victims from 1976 to 1996, 18.9 percent were killed by husbands versus 9.4 percent by nonmarried intimate partners. BUREAU OF JUSTICE STAT., U.S. DEP'T OF JUSTICE, VIOLENCE BY INTIMATES: ANALYSIS OF DATA ON CRIMES BY CURRENT OR FORMER SPOUSES, BOYFRIENDS, AND GIRLFRIENDS 6 (1998). These are percentages, however, not rates; and there are many more married than nonmarried in the total number.

158. BUREAU OF JUSTICE STAT., DEP'T OF JUSTICE, HOMICIDE TRENDS IN THE U.S.: INTIMATE HOMICIDE (2007) [hereinafter BJS 2007 INTIMATE HOMICIDE], *Intimate Homicide Rates per 100,000 Population by Victim Race, Gender, and Relationship, available at* http://www.ojp.usdoj.gov/bjs/homicide/intimates.htm#intgrel.

159. *See id., Homicides of intimates by gender of victim, 1976–2005;* BJS 2007 INTIMATE PARTNER VIOLENCE, *supra* note 144, *Nonfatal intimate partner victimization rate, 1993–2005.*

160. Shackelford & Mouzos, *supra* note 137, at 1315–16.

161. Brownridge, *supra* note 137, at 627, 645.

162. *Id.* at 645–48.

that the rates of domestic violence were decreasing faster for cohabitants than for married women in Canada and may soon converge.[163]

Attempts to explain the differential rates of violence between cohabiting and married couples have not been very satisfying. One early hypothesis was that cohabitants were more socially isolated, but a 1991 study testing this theory found that cohabitants were in fact more, rather than less, likely than married persons to be linked with and supported by their family and friends.[164] More recent explanations have focused upon the insecurity of the cohabiting relationship, without either the institutionalization of marriage and its norms or its obstacles to easy exit from the relationship; authors suggest that the resulting insecurity may call forth compensatory domineering violence by insecure males.[165] These explanations are consonant with a good deal of modern literature about the psychology of men who batter women, which emphasize a need for control arising from the abuser's insecurity.[166] The author of one study comparing domestic violence against married, separated or divorced, and cohabiting women living in public housing in Canada opines that poverty and unemployment may have something to do with their high rates of abuse as well, as "men who feel they are unable to live up to gender expectations [of being the primary breadwinner] are more likely to abuse their partners compared to men whose ability to conform affirms their masculinity and sense of control."[167] So the real-world insecurity of the men who abuse may be exacerbated by their perceptions of the insecurity of their relationship.

The precise connection between domestic violence and cohabitation remains somewhat mysterious. Anomalies present themselves, such as the fact that rates of domestic violence have been decreasing in both the United States and Canada over the period when the rate of cohabitation has been going up.[168] In Canada, moreover, the lowest rates of domestic violence

---

163. BROWNRIDGE, *supra* note 146, at 48.

164. Jan E. Stets, *Cohabiting and Marital Aggression: The Role of Social Isolation*, 53 J. MARRIAGE & FAM. 669, 676 (1991).

165. *See, e.g.*, Shackelford, *supra* note 156, at 290; Brownridge, *supra* note 137, at 647.

166. *See, e.g.*, NEIL S. JACOBSON & JOHN M. GOTTMAN, WHEN MEN BATTER WOMEN: NEW INSIGHTS INTO ENDING ABUSIVE RELATIONSHIPS 38 (1998) (emphasizing batterers' need to control their partners based on personal insecurity).

167. Walter S. DeKeseredy et al., *Which Women Are More Likely to Be Abused? Public Housing, Cohabitation, and Separated/Divorced Women*, 21 CRIMINAL JUSTICE STUD. 283, 289 (2008).

168. Brownridge, *supra* note 137, at 631; BJS 2007 INTIMATE HOMICIDE, *supra* note 158, *Nonfatal violent victimization rate by victim-offender relationship and gender, 1993–2005*

coexist, in Quebec, with the highest rate of cohabitation.[169] This gap between Quebec and the rest of Canada appears to be increasing with time.[170] Attempts to explain this discrepancy emphasize the fact that cohabitation is much more widespread and of more long standing in Quebec, thus placing that section of the country into a later phase of acceptance of this conduct.[171] This theory would indicate that rates of domestic violence and rates of cohabitation may in fact vary inversely.

Whatever the connection between union type and violence, it is clear that intimate partner violence remains a serious problem among cohabiting couples. If substantial numbers of cohabitants are killed by their partners in the United States every year,[172] this fact needs to be taken into account in any consideration about how cohabitants should be treated by the law. Ironically, this is one area in which U.S. law has almost entirely assimilated cohabitants to married couples: the domestic violence laws in virtually every state already include persons cohabiting or residing in the same household within their protections.[173] On the other hand, if other legal changes were to contribute to increased stability in cohabiting relationships, it is possible that they would give birth to less violence.

3.5. Impact of Cohabitation on Children

As soon as the NSFH data were available, the presence of children in cohabiting households became evident. Bumpass, Sweet, and Cherlin reported that four out of every ten cohabiting couples had children present.[174] This fact did

---

(reporting that rate of intimate partner violence fell from 9.8 to 3.6 per 1000 women over the period from 1993 to 2005).

169. Brownridge, *supra* note 137, at 648.

170. BROWNRIDGE, *supra* note 146, at 53 (Table 4.8).

171. *Id.* at 52–53.

172. One study reported that 2000 cohabiting women were killed by their partners in the United States between 1976 and 1994. Shackelford, *supra* note 156, at 285. More recent BJS statistics indicate that between 685 and 716 "boyfriends and girlfriends," a substantial number of whom may be cohabitants, were killed by their intimate partners each year from 2001–05. BJS 2007 INTIMATE HOMICIDE, *supra* note 158, *Homicides of intimates by relationship of victim to the offender, 1976–2005*, and data underlying the chart.

173. *See* Ruth Colker, *Marriage Mimicry: The Law of Domestic Violence*, 47 WM. & MARY L. REV. 1841, 1888–98 (App. B) (2006).

174. Larry L. Bumpass et al., *The Role of Cohabitation in Declining Rates of Marriage*, 53 J. MARRIAGE & FAM. 913, 919 (1991).

not surprise the authors, as they noted that, among this group, 20 percent of cohabitants were still together after five years.[175] The 1990 Census confirmed this 40 percent figure, comparing it with 46 percent of married-couple households that include children under eighteen.[176] By the time of the 2008 Population Survey by the Census Bureau, the number of children living in opposite-sex cohabitant households was estimated at almost 4.2 million, almost 6 percent of all children in the United States.[177] About half of these children are the biological children of the cohabitants, and about half are the children of one of the cohabitants, typically of the woman.[178] These numbers, based on a snapshot of the population at one particular time, may underestimate the impact of cohabitation on children, as others report that two of every five children in the United States will spend time in a cohabiting household before the age of sixteen.[179]

It thus became obvious that many of the children born outside of marriage in the United States were not, in fact, living in single-parent families.[180] The numbers differ dramatically by race and ethnic group. A 1996 study reported that 8 percent of Puerto Rican children, 5 percent of Mexican American and Black children, and 3 percent of non-Hispanic white children live in cohabiting families.[181] A 2003 study reported that more Puerto Rican

---

175. *Id.*

176. MARRIED-COUPLE AND UNMARRIED-PARTNER HOUSEHOLDS, *supra* note 141, at 10.

177. U.S. CENSUS BUREAU, CURRENT POPULATION SURVEY, 2008 ANNUAL SOCIAL AND ECONOMIC SUPPLEMENT, *Table C3. Living Arrangements of Children Under 18 Years and Marital Status of Parents: 2008*, *available at* http://www.census.gov/population/www/ socdemo/hh-fam/cps2008.html [hereinafter CPS 2008]; *see also* Wendy D. Manning & Daniel T. Lichter, *Parental Cohabitation and Children's Economic Well-Being*, 58 J. MARRIAGE & FAM. 998, 1008 (1996) (reporting 2.2 million, or 3.5 percent of all children in 2000).

178. *See, e.g.*, Gregory Acs & Sandi Nelson, "Honey, I'm Home." Changes in Living Arrangements in the Late 1990s, Urban Institute New Federalism National Survey of America's Families B-38; ROSE M. KREIDER & JASON FIELDS, LIVING ARRANGEMENTS OF CHILDREN:2001 5 (Table 2) (U.S. Census Bureau 2001). The 2008 CPS indicated that the proportion living with two biological parents versus one biological parent remained constant at about 50 percent. See CPS 2008, supra note 177, Table C3.

179. Bumpass & Lu, *supra* note 53, at 35.

180. Before this reality sank in, studies did not distinguish between single and cohabiting mothers of nonmarital children. Robert A. Moffitt et al., *Beyond Single Mothers: Cohabitation and Marriage in the AFDC Program*, 35 DEMOGRAPHY 259, 259 (1998).

181. Manning & Lichter, *supra* note 177, at 1002–03.

children were born to cohabiting parents (37 percent) than to either married couples or single mothers.[182]

Early studies examined the role of cohabitation in the rise of nonmarital childbearing.[183] Again, the impact differed by subgroup. While 59 percent of Puerto Rican and 40 percent of Mexican American nonmarital births are to women in cohabiting unions, confirming a positive connection between cohabitation and childbearing, cohabitation appears to have minimal effect upon the childbearing of African Americans, who have the highest rate of nonmarital births but relatively few of the children are born into cohabiting couples.[184] The authors of one study concluded that cohabitation had a significant effect on the rate of pregnancy among unmarried Puerto Rican women but that "the recent growth in cohabitation plays little role in explaining the dramatic increase in nonmarital childbearing among African American women."[185] Perhaps more important to the children involved, Puerto Rican children are much more frequently born into a two-parent unit—one in which their mothers regard themselves as married, and the addition of their unmarried father's presence adds to the family income.[186]

It is now well established that cohabitation has economic benefits for these children, although the extent of the benefit varies with the resources of the adult partners. A cohabitant's contribution to the household can be very important to many households, especially to the 25 percent of children in cohabiting families whose mothers receive public assistance.[187]

In contrast to these early studies exploring the statistics about children in cohabiting unions and the possible relationship to the rise in nonmarital births, more recent studies have focused upon the significance of these facts

---

182. R.S. Oropesa et al., *Income Allocation in Marital and Cohabiting Unions: The Case of Mainland Puerto Ricans*, 65 J. MARRIAGE & FAM. 910, 911, 914 (2003).

183. *See, e.g.*, Wendy D. Manning & Nancy S. Landale, *Racial and Ethnic Differences in the Role of Cohabitation in Premarital Childbearing*, 58 J. MARRIAGE & FAM. 63 (1996). This topic is still of interest to some scholars. *See, e.g.*, Sharon Sassler & Anna Cunningham, *How Cohabitors View Childbearing*, 51 SOCIOL. PERSPS. 3 (2008) (describing how many people no longer view marriage as a prerequisite to childbirth); Shannon N. Davis, *Premarital Cohabitation, Gender Ideologies, and Timing of First Marital Birth*, 34 INT'L J. SOCIOL. FAM. 1 (2008); Cynthia Osborne, *Marriage Following the Birth of a Child Among Cohabiting and Visiting Parents*, 67 J. MARRIAGE & FAM. 14 (2005).

184. Manning & Landale, *supra* note 183, at 63, 74.

185. *Id.* at 73–74.

186. *Id.* at 66; Oropesa et al., *supra* note 182, at 1006.

187. Oropesa et al., *supra* note 182, at 1003.

for the welfare of the children involved. Official poverty statistics do not take into account the income of cohabitants living in the household, and doing so makes a dramatic difference. Between 1990 and 2000, for example, the percent of cohabiting couples went up from 3.5 to 5.5; over that same period, the percent of children living in poverty within these couples decreased from 43.3 to 39.7 according to the official statistics; but the percent living in poverty fell from 25.1 percent to 20.1 percent if the cohabiting partner's income was taken into account.[188] In other words, almost half of these children were living in poverty according to the official statistics in 1990, but only one-quarter were living in poverty if both cohabitants' incomes were taken into account. This does not lift all these children out of poverty—a substantial number remained below the poverty line—but it does mark a substantial improvement in their economic situations. The actual economic benefit probably lies somewhere between the two assumptions because not all cohabitants pool all their income or share on an equal basis. Still, cohabitation does improve the lives of a substantial number of children, at least economically.

The economic impact varies by race and ethnic group and possibly by the relation of a child to the cohabiting father as well. One study based on 1999 data shows that the decline in poverty is greatest for white children, less so for African American children, and almost non-existent for Hispanic children.[189] In apparent conflict with these findings, an earlier study indicated that Puerto Rican children born into informal unions benefit the most economically from cohabitation, with a gain of 51 percent over the resources that would be available to them in a single-female-parent family.[190] The conflicting data underline how important it is not to consider Hispanics as a single category. Puerto Rican children may well benefit greatly from the economics of cohabitation, while Mexican American and other Hispanic children do not benefit as much.

The study relying on data from 1999 explored whether children living in cohabiting households with their biological fathers or those living with a man who is the mother's partner but not their biological father benefit more

---

188. Daniel T. Lichter et al., *Child Poverty Among Racial Minorities and Immigrants: Explaining Trends and Differentials*, 86 Soc. Sci. Q. 1037, 1046 (Table 2) (2005).

189. Wendy D. Manning & Susan Brown, *Children's Economic Well-Being in Married and Cohabiting Parent Families*, 68 J. Marriage & Fam. 345, 357–58 (2006).

190. Oropesa et al., *supra* note 182, at 1006.

economically from the partner's presence. While studies have shown that stepparents in married couples tend to invest less in their nonbiological children than biological parents do, the opposite may in fact be true for children in cohabiting couples.[191] Fifty-eight percent of children living with nonbiological fathers are reclassified as nonpoor when the cohabitant's income is taken into account, whereas only 40 percent of those living with their biological cohabiting father are reclassified. The authors surmise that mothers who cohabit after already having children by another man are much more selective in choosing a partner with good economic prospects.[192] Moreover, as we've seen in the last chapter, his poor economic prospects may be one of the reasons the woman did not marry her child's father in the first place. However, when measures of economic hardship such as food insecurity and housing insecurity are taken into account, there is not a significant difference between two-biological-parent and stepparent cohabiting families in the aggregate.[193] The effect of the child's relatedness to the cohabitant also appears to vary by race and ethnic group, with one study reporting that "Black children living with cohabiting two biological parents fare significantly better than Black children living with cohabiting stepparents."[194]

All of these economic benefits are based on comparing children in cohabiting families with those in single-parent families. Those in families with two married parents do better on all these measures, if one assumes (not always realistically) that married couples always pool all of their income.[195] Again, this does not mean that the same benefits would accrue to the children living in cohabiting households if their parents could somehow be persuaded to marry. Their parents are disproportionately non-white and less well-paid on the average than parents who are already married; marriage *per se* will not make any difference in that.[196]

The most serious problem for children living in cohabiting households—and it is a very big problem for children—is that these unions are less stable than marriages. This difference means not only that the economic advantages they enjoy may not be long lasting but also that the transitions they

---

191. Manning & Brown, *supra* note 189, at 347, 358.

192. *Id.* at 358.

193. *Id.* at 359.

194. *Id.*

195. *Id.* at 346–47.

196. *Id.* at 360.

confront may cause many problems for them. Transitions in childhood living arrangements are very stressful for children; and the more transitions, the more stress.[197] The risk of a disruptive transition is much greater for children born to cohabiting parents, even if their parents subsequently marry, than for those born to married parents:

> [T]he risk of parental disruption is 292% greater among children whose cohabiting parents do not marry than children born to married parents and 151% greater among children whose cohabiting parents marry than children born into marriage. . . .[198]

Fifteen percent of these children will experience the end of their parents' relationship by the time they are one (versus 4 percent of children of married parents), 50 percent by the time they are five (versus 15 percent of children of married parents), and two-thirds by the time they are ten.[199] Again, the likelihood of disruption varies by subgroup, with 40 percent of Hispanic and non-Hispanic white children born to cohabiting couples and 60 percent of comparable African American children confronting this loss by age five.[200] Non-Hispanic white children born to cohabiting couples whose parents subsequently marry have rates of stability similar to those in married-couple families, while Black and Hispanic children do not.[201]

A major study of more recent birth cohorts confirms the higher risk of instability faced by children of cohabiting parents, finding that children born to cohabiting versus married parents have a 184 percent higher risk of their parents separating by the time they are three years old.[202] The authors found this to be true across all racial and ethnic groups, even when accounting for economic and other factors.[203] While some part of the difference in instability between married and cohabiting couples may be attributable to economic

---

197. *See, e.g.,* Manning et al., *supra* note 32, at 136; Jay D. Teachman, *The Childhood Living Arrangements of Children and the Characteristics of Their Marriages,* 25 J. FAM. ISSUES 86, 91 (2004), and articles cited therein.

198. Manning et al., *supra* note 32, at 151.

199. *Id.* at 146.

200. *Id.*

201. *Id.* at 151.

202. Cynthia Osborne et al., *Married and Cohabiting Parents' Relationship Stability: A Focus on Race and Ethnicity,* 69 J. MARRIAGE & FAM. 1345, 1361 (2007).

203. *Id.*

factors, there may also be effects of family complexity; that is, many cohabitants have been previously married and thus live in blended families, a source of instability even in marriages.[204]

There are now many studies about the long-term effects of parental cohabitation on children, a topic of particular interest since around 2004, when multiple studies began to emerge from the academy. This undertaking is still in its infancy, in part because of its recency but primarily because there are so many different outcome measures one can examine (school performance, parents' reports of child well-being, and juvenile delinquency are just a few) as well as a plethora of different factors to which those outcomes could be related, such as the economic situation of the child's household, parenting skills, age of the parent, age of the child, length of the cohabiting relationship and its quality, whether the child is the biological or nonbiological child of one cohabitant, and so on. Most of these factors relate in turn to other factors, generating no shortage of hypotheses; and there are many different comparisons that can be made as well—to children raised by single mothers; children raised by both parents who are married; children whose parents remarry; or children living in blended families, with siblings of their parent's partner, either married or unmarried. Needless, to say, this generates a lot of grist for the academic mill.

Moreover, many of the studies available so far reach conflicting results. Children who live in cohabiting stepfamilies may or may not experience less time with their stepfather than with a married stepfather, may or may not receive more parental supervision than if their parent had remarried, may or may not have lower achievement academically, and may or may not have more behavioral or emotional problems than those in remarried families.[205] Studies based on parental reports indicate no difference between psychological well-being and attitude toward school between adolescents in cohabiting or remarried stepfamilies; problems that existed were unrelated to parental marital status.[206] Other studies of adolescents see things differently. One 2003 study, based on interviews in 1995 with both students in grades 7 through 12 and their parents, reports that teens living with cohabiting

---

204. *Id.* at 1347.

205. *See* Marion C. Willetts & Nick G. Maroules, *Parental Reports of Adolescent Well-Being: Does Marital Status Matter?*, 43 J. DIVORCE & REMARRIAGE 129, 133 (2005) (describing multiple conflicting studies on all these topics).

206. *Id.* at 144.

stepparents confront a variety of disadvantages compared with those living with two biological married parents, such as higher delinquency scores and lower grades.[207] However, most of these differences are explained by socio-economic factors like income, race, ethnicity, and parent's education, and these children do better on these measures than teens living with single mothers.[208] One study found that the type of impact of cohabitation is likely to vary with the age of the child at the time it occurs, with adolescents experiencing more emotional and behavioral problems and six- to eleven-year-olds experiencing lower levels of engagement in school, after controlling for parental economic resources.[209]

What else do we "know" so far?

- Single mothers who live with a cohabitant spend more time with their children than if they were unpartnered, limited only by their hours of employment.[210]
- Cohabiting fathers spend somewhat less time with and are generally less invested in their children, both biological and step, than married fathers.[211] This would seem to indicate that marriage is more important to the father-child relationship than biology; but these fathers' lower involvement may relate to having biological children of their own from previous unions—and the child living in the cohabiting union also has another father who may play a role in his or her life.
- Adolescent girls living in cohabiting families are likely to have sex earlier, have greater odds of teenage childbirth, and are less likely to graduate from high school than children of married parents, an effect not explained by the higher instability of cohabiting families and not varying according

207. Wendy D. Manning & Kathleen A. Lamb, *Adolescent Well-Being in Cohabiting, Married, and Single-Parent Families*, 65 J. MARRIAGE & FAM. 876, 885–86, 888 (2003).

208. *Id.* at 891.

209. Brown, *supra* note 32, at 364. It is important to control for parental economic resources because parental income has been shown to account for 50 percent of the negative effects of divorce upon children. Smock & Manning, *supra* note 135, at 94.

210. Sarah M. Kendig & Suzanne M. Bianchi, *Single, Cohabiting, and Married Mothers' Times With Children*, 70 J. MARRIAGE & FAM. 1228, 1239 (2008).

211. Sandra L. Hofferth & Kermyt G. Anderson, *Are All Dads Equal? Biology Versus Marriage as a Basis for Paternal Investment*, 65 J. MARRIAGE & FAM. 213, 230 (2003).

to whether they live with two biological parents or with one biological parent and one stepparenting cohabitant.[212]

- Children who live with cohabiting mothers are reported to have lower grades and be less likely to graduate from high school than those living in stable two-parent families (and possibly than children in divorced and/or remarried families too), but the authors of this study report that this disadvantage may result from the higher levels of instability in their family relationships or lower educational expectations of their mothers.[213]

One final example from recent research: there are no differences in outcomes for children of cohabiting parents in kindergarten apart from a lag in reading skills compared to five-year-olds in married two-parent families, once the following factors are controlled: child characteristics, economic factors, household stability, depressive symptoms of the mother, and parenting practices.[214] This is a very long list of variables to control, and some but not all of them may correlate independently with cohabitation. In short, based upon the multiple variables involved and the conflicting studies, it is impossible to reach any definitive conclusions about the precise effects of cohabitation upon children.

What is the bottom line? Children who live in families with both their parents, in which neither parent dies or divorces the other during their childhood, are best off in all sorts of ways. That is clear, but the implications of it are not. At least one law review author has concluded from these studies that the government's efforts to promote marriage are therefore well worth it.[215] Others conclude from the same evidence that marriage-promotion efforts are ill-advised, either because they direct the government's support to children who are already advantaged in other ways[216] or because it would be better simply to teach the individuals who are parents norms of parental

---

212. Ronald E. Bulanda & Wendy D. Manning, *Parental Cohabitation Experiences and Adolescent Behavioral Outcomes*, 27 POPULATION RES. & POL'Y REV. 593, 613 (2008).

213. R. Kelly Raley et al., *Maternal Cohabitation and Educational Success*, 78 SOCIOL. EDUC. 144, 158, 160 (2005).

214. Julie E. Artis, *Maternal Cohabitation and Child Well-Being Among Kindergarten Children*, 69 J. MARRIAGE & FAM. 222, 232 (2007).

215. Robin Fretwell Wilson, *Evaluating Marriage: Does Marriage Matter to the Nurturing of Children?*, 42 SAN DIEGO L. REV. 848 (2005).

216. Laura S. Adams, *Privileging the Privileged? Child Well-Being as a Justification for State Support of Marriage*, 42 SAN DIEGO L. REV. 881 (2005).

responsibility directly, no matter what their marital status.[217] The terms of the debate typically are whether the state should be supporting marriage between heterosexual adults and subsidizing it by law, or whether it should withdraw support and subsidies from marriage in general.[218] There is a third alternative, which I explore in the next chapters: to extend the protections and supports given to married couples to cohabitants with children as well.

One of the most important lessons from this burgeoning literature is that the negative impacts experienced by children of cohabiting couples are largely shared with children of single parents and children living with parents who had divorced and remarried. Living in a married stepfamily can be just as harmful to children as living in a cohabiting parent household:

> [R]esiding outside a two-biological-parent married family can be negatively related to children's well-being. . . .[R]egardless of whether a parent remarries or forms a cohabiting stepfamily, child outcomes are similar.[219]

Given that a large number of American children no longer live in married families with their biological parents,[220] public policy needs to be premised upon this reality and to focus upon improving the conditions encountered by these children in their real-world settings, which are relatively unstable and fraught with problems that improved economic resources and better legal protection might alleviate.

3.6. What We Know: A Summary

Let us summarize what generalizations we can safely draw from the social science literature before drawing any conclusions about how the legal system should treat cohabitants. First, we know that there were at least 13.6 million Americans in opposite-sex unmarried couple households in the year 2008.

---

217. Kimberley A. Yuracko, *Does Marriage Make People Good or Do Good People Marry?*, 42 SAN DIEGO L. REV. 889 (2007).

218. *See* Wilson, *supra* note 215, at 850–51.

219. Brown, *supra* note 32, at 364.

220. U.S. CENSUS BUREAU, CHILDREN AND THE HOUSEHOLDS THEY LIVE IN: 2000 9 (2004) (reporting that approximately two-thirds lived in married-couple family groups in 2000); *see also* CPS 2008, *supra* note 177, at Table C3 (about 67 percent of children live with both married parents).

The rate of growth of heterosexual cohabitation has been very rapid; and for a variety of reasons (economics, age cohort maturation, and intergenerational attitudinal change), it will continue to grow. These facts are not easy to alter.

Second, we know that the groups involved are extremely varied. While unmarried cohabitation has spread throughout all social and economic groups, it is most pronounced among lower-income people, African Americans, Hispanic Americans (especially Puerto Ricans), and divorced persons. Most of these unions are short in term, with the median duration less than two years. By the most conservative estimates, however, at least 10 percent are long term, and this number may be increasing. If we include those who have transformed their unions into marriage, four out of ten couples are still together after ten years. Nonetheless, cohabiting unions are significantly less stable than marriage, and the percentage of cohabitants who ultimately marry is decreasing. Cohabitation is less stable if the partners are young and/or poor, which many are.

Third, cohabitants are somewhat less gender-specialized in their households than married people, though married couples are also decreasingly so; female cohabitants are less confined to traditional gender roles both inside and outside of the household, and they contribute more to its finances. Although cohabitants are less likely than married couples to pool their income, the majority do so nonetheless; and virtually all of them do so if they have a child together. As several have commented, cohabitation is a different type of union than marriage,[221] but it still involves substantial economic interdependence for most cohabitants, with an accompanying potential for exploitation during the relationship and vulnerability at its dissolution.

Fourth, some cohabitants—those without plans to marry—are less satisfied with their relationships than married persons. Cohabitants may experience more depression, though the evidence is somewhat mixed on this score. Cohabiting women are more likely to be victims of domestic violence than

---

221. Sassler & McNally, *supra* note 67, at 574 ("a different kind of union"); Le Bourdais & Lapierre-Adamcyk, *supra* note 51, at 940 (describing cohabitation and marriage as two different forms of conjugal engagement). Bumpass et al. have called cohabitation "a family status, but one in which levels of certainty about the relationship are lower than in marriage." Bumpass et al., *supra* note 174, at 926. Perhaps most accurately, Brown and Booth name it a "complex family form," to indicate the variety of types of unions—long- and short-term, with and without children—contained within it. Brown & Booth, *supra* note 37, at 668.

are married women, and their children thus more likely to live in a household where it is present.

Finally, many children will live in cohabiting relationships at some point in their lives, and the lack of stability and other problems may have a negative impact upon their emotional and educational development. On the other hand, cohabitation yields a substantial income premium for a mother who would otherwise be a single or divorced parent, and economic resources can alleviate some of the negative effects of parental separation on children. In general, both partners and their children would be better off in long-term marriages. But this is not the world in which we live, for a variety of reasons unrelated to whether legal protection is granted to cohabitation or not— economic factors, gender role change, and higher expectations of marriage, for example.[222]

ℳ 4. Implications of the Social Science Findings

What are the implications of all this social science data for the legal treatment of cohabitation? As described in the introductory chapter, I believe that protection for persons who are left in a vulnerable position when family relationships fail is at the core of the values underlying our system of family law. While our legal rules also favor respecting the autonomy of individuals and protecting the public fisc by privatizing many obligations, when values conflict, I believe that rules designed to protect persons in the position of Mrs. Hewitt and Mrs. Friedman should be given priority. The social science findings set out throughout this chapter, considered in light of these values, support the extension of legal protections to cohabitants, for a number of reasons.

First, cohabitation is often, though not always, less stable than marriage, more likely to involve domestic violence, and involves substantial economic interdependence. A large number of cohabitants are poor, come from disadvantaged racial or ethnic minorities, and have children. All of these are powerful reasons to recognize their unions for purposes of government

---

222. For a description of the changes in expectations of marriage over time, culminating in the modern expectation of a personally fulfilling and emotionally satisfying relationship, *see, e.g.*, Cherlin, *supra* note 45, at 852–53; *see also* Marcia Carlson et al., *Union Formation in Fragile Families*, 41 DEMOGRAPHY 237, 242 (2004).

benefits, to extend a variety of legal remedies upon the ending of their relationships, and to grant them rights against third parties. Indeed, the instability complained of with respect to cohabitation is itself a strong reason to
provide rights to property and support upon dissolution of these relationships, so long as the relationship has lasted a certain period of time or has
produced a child. If, as recent studies indicate, cohabitants are more likely to
merge their finances than to keep them separate, and the presence of a
cohabitant in the household adds substantially to the ability of an otherwise
single mother to support her child, we need to worry about vulnerability of
the parties if the relationship ends. Legal remedies for the custodial parent
(most likely the mother)—remedies beyond the child support she can presumably command from the child's biological father—can be very important
for the welfare of the children involved.

To date, there is only one area of law where all states have concluded that
cohabitants should be treated identically to married couples—the provision
of criminal and civil remedies for domestic violence.[223] The ability to get an
order of protection, however, is only one part of the protection that abused
women require. The lack of legal remedies for cohabitants can place abused
women in a very difficult situation: they can escape the household only if
they are willing to give up any share in the couple's accumulated property
and any hope of financial support.

Failure to extend legal protection to cohabitants is highly gendered in
its effects not only because women are more often the victims of domestic
violence; they are also likely to be in a weaker bargaining position within
their relationships because of their lack of economic power relative to their
partners. If there are children in the household, the female partner is typically disadvantaged in the marketplace by caring for them and also disadvantaged within the internal economy of the partnership by her unequal
financial contribution. A joint account system based on equal contributions
results in the partner with more income being able to keep more for himself,
either for consumption or for investment; and there is no protection for the
partner whose contributions consisted of housework and child care or who
spent her own wages on the needs of the family and children. Her investments

---

223. *See* Judith A. Smith, *Battered Non-Wives and Unequal Protection-Order Coverage: A Call for
Reform*, 23 YALE L. & POL'Y REV. 93, 103–04 (2005) (reporting that virtually every state's
domestic violence legislation protects cohabitants). *See also* Margaret M. Mahoney,
Forces Shaping the Law of Cohabitation For Opposite Sex Couples, 7 J. LAW & FAM. STUD.
135, 193–95 (2005).

in the relationship will not be protected unless legal rules similar to those applied at the end of marriage are applied to her as well.

There is also reason to believe that women are more subject to exploitation within cohabiting relationships than men because of their differing levels of commitment to the relationship. This concern was voiced in the earliest literature on the subject. In a 1978 article, Eleanor Macklin noted the "tendency for cohabiting females to have higher commitment scores than their male counterparts."[224] Commitment was measured both by personal dedication to continuing the relationship and by the behavioral changes one makes in one's life that make it likely one will continue the relationship.[225] If one partner is more committed than the other, the one less willing to walk away from the relationship is vulnerable to exploitation; and the one who has committed more behaviorally is likely to be hurt more by its termination.

The NSFH data showed that at least one of the cohabiting partners expected to marry in 90 percent of cases but that the partners frequently disagreed on the subject.[226] Women cohabitants were more likely to see the union as leading to marriage.[227] A higher proportion of cohabiting women than of cohabiting men indicated that their economic security, emotional security, and overall happiness would be greater if they were married.[228] It seems justified to assume that the woman partner is more often the one arguing or hoping for marriage.

A 2004 study comparing couples who had cohabited prior to marriage with those who had not cohabited found that females who had cohabited were more dedicated to their partner and to the relationship than those who had not, while men who had cohabited were less committed.[229] The authors concluded that cohabitation appeared to select "for men—but not women— who are . . . less dedicated to their relationships."[230] A subsequent study

---

224. Eleanor D. Macklin, *Nonmarital Heterosexual Cohabitation: A Review of the Recent Literature*, 1 MARRIAGE & FAM. REV. 6 (Mar./Apr. 1978).

225. *Id.* at 5.

226. Bumpass, *supra* note 36, at 487 (reporting that in 90 percent of cohabiting couples studied, one partner expected to marry); Rindfuss & VandenHeuvel, *supra* note 17, at 707, citing an unpublished paper by Bumpass et al., from 1989 (reporting disagreement between partners concerning marriage).

227. Rindfuss & VandenHeuvel, *supra* note 17, at 711.

228. Bumpass et al., *supra* note 174, at 921.

229. Scott M. Stanley et al., *Maybe I Do: Interpersonal Commitment and Premarital or Nonmarital Cohabitation*, 25 J. FAM. ISSUES 496, 509 (Table 2) (2004).

230. *Id.* at 513.

appears to confirm the conclusion that women cohabitants are more committed to the relationship than are their male counterparts.[231] These persistent gender differences in commitment have an obvious potential for exploitation and vulnerability.

For all these reasons, in addition to the presence of children in so many cohabiting households, the primary concern of our family law rules should be with the interdependency and vulnerability caused by cohabitation; and legal remedies should be directed at alleviating the effects of these problems. Extending rather than restricting legal recognition to cohabitants is the way to do so.

The next chapter examines the experience of other countries, nations comparable to the United States which have designed remedies intended to pursue these goals.

---

231. *See* Galena Kline Rhoades et al., *Pre-engagement Cohabitation and Gender Asymmetry in Marital Commitment*, 20 J. FAM. PSYCHOL. 553 (2006).

FIVE

Treatment of Cohabitation in Other Nations

WHILE THE UNITED STATES HAS BEEN STRUGGLING OVER whether to give any legal rights to heterosexual cohabitants, other developed countries have for the most part been extending to opposite-sex unmarried couples the remedies available to married couples. These legal changes have often occurred, as in France and The Netherlands, in response to the movement for gay rights. Yet in other countries, such as Canada, rights have first been extended to heterosexual cohabitants and subsequently extended to same-sex couples. By 2009, an array of legal arrangements existed.

In designing a system to address the legal rights of cohabitants, each country is required to make several fundamental choices. The first is whether to adopt a system under which couples opt in to the new legal status (as, for example, by entering a Pacte Civil de Solidarité, or PACS, in France) or a system in which the status is thrust upon them after a certain period of time, the birth of a child, or other qualifying criteria have been met (as happens for unregistered couples in Canada and some Australian states). This is similar to the distinction described in Chapter 2 between systems based either on contract or on status in various parts of the United States.

Second, a country may choose to address unmarried couples' rights through the legislature or the courts, or by some combination of legislation and case law. Whichever way it chooses to proceed, it may do so either in a comprehensive or piecemeal fashion. In federal systems such as Canada and Australia, where jurisdiction over rights affecting the family is split between two levels of government, statutes and case law may be necessary both at a federal level and in individual states and provinces. To date, almost every country enacting reforms on cohabitation has proceeded with piecemeal reform to some extent, extending the definition of spouse in certain statutes and for the receipt of certain social benefits and then proceeding to broaden the benefits offered. We have seen a similar, though very preliminary, piecemeal process at work in the United States in the extension of unemployment compensation benefits to an unmarried partner in some states and of the right to sue for loss of consortium or negligent infliction of emotional distress in others. In most industrialized countries, which typically have much more extensive social welfare systems than the United States, a good deal of this development has taken place prior to passage of more comprehensive reforms, that is, by broadening the definition of who is entitled to benefits under a particular law. In this way, unmarried partners were entitled to many benefits in The Netherlands and France even before passage of the Dutch Registered Partnership Act or the PACS, and common law widows received benefits in England after World War I even though common law marriage was not recognized. More comprehensive legal reforms have occurred only during the last few decades.

This chapter explores the way in which six countries have addressed the issue of cohabitants' rights. Three come from the common law tradition, where much of the law emerged from decisions of the courts—England, Canada, and Australia; two of those—Canada and Australia—have federal systems of government, while England represents a unitary, or nonfederal, common law system. Three countries have civil law systems, where codes or statutes are the official source of law: France, The Netherlands, and Sweden.[1] With respect to each country and tradition examined, I discuss both how its particular system of legal treatment of cohabitation has developed and how it seems to be working. After examining each, the overarching question is which, if any, if these systems would provide a good model for the United States. Or is the context in each of the other settings so different that systems developed there would be unlikely to take root on U.S. soil?

A caveat is in order. This area of the law is in constant flux; an accurate description today may be outdated by tomorrow. Moreover, many nations other than the six to be discussed have developed responses to the legal problems faced by unmarried couples. The United States is in fact one of the few that have extended almost no remedies to cohabitants. The six nations I discuss here therefore serve primarily as possible models of different types of legal regimes on cohabitation and allow us to assess the advantages and disadvantages of each approach as a model for the United States.

---

1. Spain also has a federal system, which has resulted in the development of the law of cohabitants' rights in certain parts of the country and not in others, as well as the development of certain protections under national law. *See* Blanca Rodriquez Ruiz, *Recognizing the Rights of Unmarried Cohabitants in Spain: Why Not Treat Them Like Married Couples?*, 2 I-CON 669, 676–82 (2004); *see also Stable Pair Relationships, Act 10 of 1998* (Spain), *available at* http://www20.gencat.cat/docs/Justicia/Documents/ARXIUS/doc_10614500_1.pdf.

🎕 1. England: Nonrecognition and Piecemeal Benefits

Unlike the United States, England has been addressing the issue of cohabitants' rights for some time.[2] A limited number of rights were extended to opposite-sex couples early in the twentieth century, even before the rates of cohabitation began to soar. Between 1976 and 1998, the proportion of unmarried women under fifty who were cohabiting grew from 9 percent to 29 percent, more than tripling in about two decades.[3] By 2002, 70 percent of all first partnerships in England were cohabitations, and 25 percent of all unmarried people between the ages of sixteen and fifty-nine were cohabiting.[4] Cohabitation lasts longer in England than in the United States, with an average duration of about six and a half years.[5] Several studies of cohabitants in England have shown that the partners report a high level of commitment to one another, comparable to that of married couples.[6] Surveys report that a majority of respondents would favor legal reforms that would treat cohabitants as though they were married, and most cohabitants in fact believe they are already entitled to be treated as though married after some period of time, despite the fact that England has not recognized common law marriage since 1753.[7]

---

2. This section is about England and Wales but not the United Kingdom as a whole. Scotland has its own separate legal system. On the cohabitants' issue, Scotland recognized common law marriage until it was abolished in the Family Law Act of 2006. *See* THE FAMILY LAW SCOTLAND ACT, 2006, c. 19 (Scot.), *available at* http://www.opsi.gov.uk/legislation/scotland/acts2006/pdf/asp_20060002_en.pdf. *See also* FIONA GAVIN ET AL., COHABITATION (W. Green & Son 2005); Ian Dey & Fran Wasoff, *Protection, Parity, or Promotion: Public Attitudes to Cohabitation and the Purposes of Legal Reform*, 29 L. & POL'Y 159 (2007).

3. John Haskey, *Cohabitation in Great Britain: Past, Present and Future Trends—and Attitudes*, 103 POPULATION TRENDS 4, 7 (2001).

4. Anne Barlow, *Cohabitation Law Reform—Messages from Research*, 14 FEMINIST LEG. STUD. 167, 172–73 (2006) (citing Office for National Statistics 2005).

5. Anne Barlow et al., *Just a Piece of Paper? Marriage and Cohabitation*, *in* BRITISH SOCIAL ATTITUDES: THE 18TH REPORT 14 (Park et al. eds., Sage 2001).

6. Haskey, *supra* note 3, at 7; Simon Duncan et al., *Why Don't They Marry? Cohabitation, Commitment and DIY Marriage*, *in* MARRIAGE AND COHABITATION 60–61 (Alison Diduck ed., Ashgate 2008).

7. Anne Barlow, *Regulation of Cohabitation, Changing Family Policies and Social Attitudes: A Discussion of Britain Within Europe*, 26 L. & POL'Y 57, 73 (2004); Anne Barlow & Grace James, *Regulating Marriage and Cohabitation in 21st Century Britain*, 67 MODERN L. REV. 143, 161–62 (2004).

Over the past decade or so, the legal rights of cohabiting couples have become a prominent issue in England, with British academics and the government engaging in numerous studies of cohabitation. Both the Law Society (the national bar association) and the Law Commission (an independent body set up by Parliament to review the law and recommend reforms) undertook studies and issued reports. However, when the Civil Partnership Act was passed in 2004, it extended all the rights of married couples to same-sex couples who registered as partners but left the situation of opposite-sex couples to future reform. This section describes the historical process in which these changes and this debate have taken place.

England first extended legal rights to cohabitants near the beginning of the twentieth century. As early as 1906, the Workman's Compensation Act recognized unmarried couples as a unit for compensation, setting a precedent for paying benefits to unmarried dependents of an employed person.[8] After World War I, the government paid separation allowances to cohabitants who were being supported by a soldier, and unmarried "wives" received pensions.[9] A cohabitant's income was also taken into account when welfare benefits were calculated, based on a presumption of support by the cohabitant even in the absence of a legal obligation to provide it.[10] In typically piecemeal fashion, cohabitants were excluded from the Fatal Accidents Act of 1976 (the equivalent of state wrongful death legislation allowing suits for damages against a third party in the United States), but the act was amended in 1982 to extend this remedy to cohabitants.[11] When special remedies were designed for domestic violence, however, they were immediately extended to cohabitants, including the remedy of excluding the legal owner of a home from his or her own property to protect a cohabiting partner.[12] A cohabitant, unlike a spouse, does not have a right to inherit upon his or her partner's death, but the Inheritance (Provision for Family and Dependants) Act of 1975 gave cohabitants who had lived with their deceased partner at least two years prior to his or her death the right to apply for financial provision if they

---

8. Rebecca Probert, *Cohabitation in Twentieth Century England and Wales: Law and Policy*, 26 L. & POL'Y 13, 15, 17 (2004).

9. *Id.*

10. *Id.* at 20; Barlow & James, *supra* note 7, at 147.

11. Probert, *supra* note 8, at 22–23.

12. *Id.* at 22.

were not adequately provided for under a will.[13] Their claims, however, were limited to ones for reasonable maintenance.

With the exception of these benefits extended piecemeal by statute, opposite-sex cohabitants in England lack most of the rights of married couples. A cohabiting father does not acquire parental responsibility for his child automatically at birth. He can acquire it by signing a parental responsibility agreement with the mother's consent, but only about 5 percent of fathers do so.[14] Upon dissolution of their relationships, cohabitants have no right to the property distribution and maintenance available to married couples on divorce. The courts have no jurisdiction to order this kind of relief on the breakdown of a cohabiting relationship; they have no discretion to adjust the property of cohabitants at all.[15]

Cohabitants' rights to the family home have attracted the most attention from British lawmakers. If that home is rented, cohabitants have been given rights by statute to retain the lease or to transfer a residential tenancy upon dissolution of the relationship or death of their partner, rights that can be very important for staying in subsidized council housing or continuing under rent control.[16] However, in almost 60 percent of all cohabitations in England, the couple's home is owned rather than rented, with 44 percent of these homes titled in the name of only one partner; fewer than 10 percent of cohabitants draft any kind of contract governing their ownership interests in the property.[17] In the absence of a contract or joint ownership, under British law, like American, cohabitants who separate must resort to costly litigation to have a beneficial interest, or trust, declared by the court. In England, this has typically required the nonowner cohabitant to prove the existence of

---

13. Barlow, *Regulation of Cohabitation, supra* note 7, at 71.

14. *Id.* at 68.

15. THE LAW COMMISSION, SHARING HOMES: A DISCUSSION PAPER 76 (2002), *available at* http://www.lawcom.gov.uk/docs/lc278(1).pdf [hereinafter LAW COMMISSION, SHARING HOMES]. In fact, English courts have only had jurisdiction to make a discretionary redistribution of assets upon divorce since 1973; prior to that, they could only grant periodic maintenance payments. Anne Barlow, *Cohabiting Relationships, Money and Property: The Legal Backdrop*, 37 J. SOCIO-ECON. 502, 505 (2008).

16. Haskey, *supra* note 3, at 71 (in some instances, the cohabitant is required to have lived with the tenant for twelve months before death); *see also* Anne Barlow, *Rights in the Family Home—Time for a Conceptual Revolution?, in* NEW PERSPECTIVES ON PROPERTY LAW, HUMAN RIGHTS AND THE HOME 54–57 (Alastair Hudson ed., Cavendish Publishing 2004).

17. *Id.* at 67; *see also* Barlow et al., *supra* note 5, at 16.

what is called a common intention constructive trust, either express or implied from the fact that the nonowner cohabitant made direct contributions to the purchase price.[18] The court must also find that both parties intended that the property be held in partial trust for the nonowner. Moreover, Britain has traditionally not recognized contracts between cohabitants, although this is changing.[19]

Some British scholars argue that the family home is a unique kind of property, as a shared space in which there is a joint emotional as well as financial investment, "the focal point of family life, the place where partnering is anchored and where parenting takes place."[20] Anne Barlow and Craig Lind have argued that the family home should not be treated under standard tenets of property law but instead under family law, proposing adoption of a modified system of community property under which a nonowner cohabitant would gain an increasing interest in the family home over time—10 percent each year up to 50 percent, or even more if the nonowner is the primary caretaker of children in the home.[21] Although the government has not taken up this radical suggestion, both the Law Society and the Law Commission have issued reports relevant to the subject.

The Law Society's study of the issue was occasioned by the highly publicized 1983 case, *Burns v. Burns*.[22] Mrs. Burns had lived with Mr. Burns for nineteen years, and the couple had two children, but the house where they lived for seventeen of those years was titled in his name only. Because she had been a traditional homemaker and caretaker of the children rather than working in the paid economy, Mrs. Burns had made no financial contribution toward purchase of the house. As a result, the court held that it had no jurisdiction to assign any interest in their home to her at the ending of their relationship. If the law were to be changed, the court said, this was a matter for Parliament.

The problem in the *Burns* case, as the Law Society recognized in its report, was that the common intention necessary to establish a trust is very rarely stated expressly, and trust law does not recognize the nonfinancial

---

18. Barlow, *supra* note 16, at 61–62.

19. ANNE BARLOW, COHABITANTS AND THE LAW 14 (3d ed. Butterworths 2002).

20. Barlow, *supra* note 16, at 68–69.

21. *Id.* at 73–75; *see also* Anne Barlow & Craig Lind, *A Matter of Trust: The Allocation of Rights in the Family Home*, 19 LEG. STUD. 468 (1999).

22. [1984] 1 All ER 244 (EWCA Civ.) (Eng.).

contributions of a cohabitant, such as homemaking and child care.[23] Acknowledging the injustice involved in a case like that of Mrs. Burns, the Law Society recommended that the courts be given authority to adjust the property interest in a family home under certain circumstances—when a couple had cohabited for two years or had a child together, and one side had gained an economic advantage from the contributions of the other, including contributions such as those made by a parent in maintaining the home and raising the children. In line with the limited purpose of a trust to disgorge benefits that had unjustly enriched one party at the expense of another, there would be no adjustment if neither party had been advantaged or disadvantaged by the relationship.[24] The Law Society went on to make additional recommendations for a limited and temporary right to maintenance for cohabitants who were economically disadvantaged at the end of their relationship, a number of limited exemptions from transfer or inheritance taxes, and the right to seek an order for sharing of pensions upon separation.[25] At base, however, the Law Society report favored extending remedies to cohabitants under only very limited circumstances.

The Law Commission's charge from Parliament was limited to considerations involved in the sharing of homes, but it extended to all persons sharing homes, not just cohabitants.[26] The Commission reviewed the problems under current English law with respect to this issue and also surveyed new legal arrangements to handle these problems in Canada, Australia, and New Zealand.[27] Its report acknowledged that the requirements for proving a beneficial interest under a trust were not suited to the realities of cohabitation and caused long, uncertain, and costly litigation. In the end, however, it concluded that it was not possible to devise a statutory scheme that would work fairly across the diversity of situations under which people shared homes; it closed with a recommendation that the courts ease up on the requirements for constructive trusts and that cohabitants become more aware of their rights and make express written agreements concerning their intentions.[28]

---

23. THE LAW SOCIETY, COHABITATION: THE CASE FOR CLEAR LAW: PROPOSALS FOR REFORM ¶¶ 91–92 (2002).

24. *Id.* at ¶¶ 95–96, 101–102, 104.

25. *Id.* at ¶¶ 111–113.

26. LAW COMMISSION, SHARING HOMES, *supra* note 15.

27. *Id.* at ¶¶ 2.1–2.114, 4.1–4.29.

28. *Id.* at 85.

In short, the Law Commission essentially gave up on the attempt to reform the law to address the particulars of this problem, in large part because it was determined to maintain the unique character of marriage.[29]

At this point, Parliament proceeded to address the situation of same-sex couples by passing the Civil Partnership Act of 2004 and referred the remaining problems of opposite-sex cohabitants and of same-sex couples who did not register for further study. Those problems were seen as limited to those of the cohabitants vis-à-vis one another at the end of their relationship rather than as including broader rights against third parties or the state. The result of this referral was the publication of another enormous report by the Law Commission, circulated for comment in 2006 and published in final form in 2007.[30]

Despite the efforts of the Law Lords to provide a framework for cohabitants' cases under the doctrine of constructive trust,[31] the Law Commission concluded that current law was inadequate to provide a comprehensive solution because it offered no assistance to couples who did not own their homes or other capital assets, and it did not apply to pensions.[32] Relying heavily on social scientific studies of cohabitation in England and other Commonwealth countries, it recommended passage of "a new statutory scheme designed specifically for cohabitants on separation," applicable to couples that lived together and either had a child together or had cohabited for a minimum period.[33] The report suggested that Parliament set a minimum period from two to five years but give courts discretion to deviate from it if the period set was greater than two years.[34] The minimum duration requirement was rationalized both as reducing unmeritorious claims and as selecting for relationships likely to be characterized by commitment that merited legal protection.[35] Cohabitants would be allowed to opt out of the statutory

---

29. *Id.* at ¶¶ 5.42–5.45.

30. THE LAW COMMISSION, COHABITATION: THE FINANCIAL CONSEQUENCES OF RELATIONSHIP BREAKDOWN (2007), *available at* http://www.lawcom.gov.uk/docs/lc307.pdf [hereinafter LAW COMMISSION, COHABITATION].

31. *See, e.g.*, Stack v. Dowden, [2007] UKHL 17, [2007] 2 WLR 831. The House of Lords is the highest court in England, but the judicial task is performed by a specially selected group of judges rather than by hereditary peers.

32. LAW COMMISSION, COHABITATION, *supra* note 30, at ¶ 2.16.

33. *Id.* at ¶ 1.2.

34. *Id.* at ¶ 3.56.

35. *Id.* at ¶¶ 3.39–3.40.

system by entering into a contract to that effect.[36] To reduce confusion about this issue, the Commission recommended that Parliament specify that cohabitants' contracts were not contrary to public policy and thus were enforceable.[37]

The Law Commission settled on an opt-out rather than an opt-in system because of its concern for vulnerable persons who might for a variety of reasons fail to register for an opt-in scheme:

> [A]n opt-in scheme is likely to leave too many economically vulnerable people facing unjustified hardship on separation. The factors that led to their economic vulnerability are all too likely to be the same factors that led them to agree with an economically stronger partner not to opt in, meant that they failed to convince their partner to opt in, or led them to be understandably ignorant of the law, in the first place.[38]

It settled on a simple definition of cohabitation as "living as a couple in a joint household" rather than relying on a marriage analogy (such as "living in a marriage-like relationship") because living as a couple in a joint household was easily understood and easy to apply. For similar reasons it rejected including a checklist of statutory factors for courts to consider (while nonetheless discussing several factors that were relevant, such as the existence of a sexual relationship).[39]

To obtain financial relief following separation, a cohabitant would be required to prove:

1. that his or her partner had retained an economic benefit, in the form of capital, income, or earning capacity that had been acquired or enhanced; or

2. that the applicant had sustained an economic disadvantage, in the form of a diminution of savings or earnings lost, past and future, as a result of contributions he or she had made to the parties' shared lives, including nonfinancial contributions such as child care.[40]

---

36. *Id.* at ¶ 5.56.

37. *Id.* at ¶ 5.8.

38. *Id.* at ¶ 2.91.

39. *Id.* at ¶¶ 3.13–3.22.

40. *Id.* at ¶¶ 4.33–4.36.

The court (the Commission thought family court was the most appropriate forum to adjudicate these claims[41]) was charged with using a "principled discretion" to adjust the retained benefit by reversing it; if after doing so, the applicant would still suffer an economic disadvantage, that disadvantage was to be shared equally by the parties.[42] The factors guiding the court's discretion in this respect included, among other things, the welfare of any children affected, the needs and obligations of each party, and the resources each party had or was likely to have in the future.[43]

This adjustment was to be carried out through lump sum payments or installments, property transfers, property settlements, orders for sale, and pension sharing, but periodic payments were not available except for child support.[44] In short, contributions would be reimbursed only where they had resulted in a retained benefit in the form of property, profits, savings, and the like, or an economic disadvantage, such as a loss of future earning capacity or failure to secure a pension or make other savings or investments.[45] In no event should the court place the applicant in a stronger economic position for the foreseeable future than the respondent; and an economically stronger party would not be allowed to pursue an economic disadvantage claim based on contributions he or she had made.[46] Thus, the purpose of the new provisions, although embodied in a statute that would be administered in family court, was similar to the goals underlying the constructive trust doctrine—to disgorge benefits bestowed by one party on the other in reliance on their relationship—quite a different principle from those underlying the law of marriage and divorce, which emphasize equitable sharing of gains and losses as well as provision for the needs of an economically weaker party.

In addition, the Law Commission recommended two main changes in the provision for cohabitants included in the Inheritance (Provision for Family and Dependants) Act of 1975. First, it proposed that the definition of a cohabitant be made consistent between that act and the proposed law covering dissolutions, thus allowing a cohabitant to apply under the Inheritance Act if living in the same household at the time of the partner's death and the two

---

41. *Id.* at ¶ 4.118.

42. *Id.* at ¶ 4.37.

43. *Id.* at ¶ 4.38.

44. *Id.* at ¶ 4.40.

45. *Id.* at ¶¶ 4.45, 4.52, 4.60.

46. *Id.* at ¶¶ 4.65, 4.75.

either had been living together for the preceding two years or had a child together.[47] Second, it recommended that the reasonable financial provision a court was allowed to award a cohabitant not be interpreted simply in terms of what the surviving cohabitant might need for his or her maintenance but also in light of what the applicant might have received if they had separated instead of been parted by death.[48]

These recommendations were issued by the Law Commission in July 2007, and by late 2009, no bill had been passed by Parliament to put them into effect. Commentators have suggested both that they go too far and that they do not go far enough. While supporting the family law approach to remedies and the opt-out system, Rebecca Probert comments that the new system is really no more generous than the current property law remedies and will not give appropriate credit to domestic contributions, thus failing to address the potential for injustice at the end of cohabiting relationships.[49] She argues, as well, that provision for a bereaved cohabitant should be more generous than what he or she could expect if the parties separated.[50] She concludes that the new scheme would place cohabitants who had given up work to look after children in a position closer to the outcome they could expect under divorce law but that some cohabitants would be better off under the current treatment under the law of trusts.

Other feminist scholars object to the replacement of the property law remedy with the opt-out family-law-based system proposed. Anne Bottomley has argued that the types of remedies proposed by the Law Commission are directed to the plight of Mrs. Burns, the financially vulnerable homemaker-mother, a model that no longer reflects reality.[51] Instead, she maintains, the more typical cohabitants of today and tomorrow will be like Mrs. Oxley in *Oxley v. Hiscock*—an older, divorced woman with money of her own and children from a previous union for whom she wants to protect her assets, in short, a woman who is not economically dependent on a man.[52]

---

47. *Id.* at ¶ 6.26.

48. *Id.* at ¶ 6.43.

49. R.J. Probert, *A Review of Cohabitation: The Financial Consequences of Relationship Breakdown, Law Com. No. 307 (HMSO 2007)*, 41 FAM. L.Q. 521, 528–29 (2007).

50. *Id.* at 535.

51. Anne Bottomley, *From Mrs. Burns to Mrs. Oxley: Do Co-habiting Women (Still) Need Marriage Law?*, 14 FEMINIST LEG. STUD. 181 (2006).

52. *Id.* at 188–95; *see also* Oxley v. Hiscock, [2004] EWCA (Civ.) 546, [1]-[75], [2005] FAM. 211 (Eng.).

Mrs. Oxley had contributed to the purchase of a house that was titled in her partner's name; her lawyer advised against this, but she responded in a letter that she knew Mr. Hiscock well enough to trust him.[53] After living together in this house for some ten years, their relationship ended, and the house was sold; Mr. Hiscock treated Mrs. Oxley's contribution to it as a loan, while she saw it as establishing a beneficial joint ownership. The trial court apparently agreed and awarded her the equivalent of half the proceeds from the sale, and Mr. Hiscock appealed. The appellate court reversed. Analyzing the case under the law of common intention constructive trusts, it awarded Mrs. Oxley 40 percent instead, based on the parties' respective initial contributions and the fact that they had pooled their resources to pay household expenses, including the mortgage.[54] Bottomley regards this outcome as just and contends that, if the law of trusts were applied more flexibly and opened up to considerations of reliance and expectation as well as contribution, it would protect Mrs. Burns as well.[55] Another feminist legal scholar agrees that the law of constructive trusts provides a better remedy for cohabitants, so long as it is reformulated to take account of women's typical contributions; she prefers it because trust law reinforces the notion of the woman's rights as proprietary instead of consigning the outcome to the discretion of a judge.[56]

Who has the better of this argument? Whether the Law Commission's recommendations go too far or not far enough surely relates to what the appropriate goals are and what persons the law seeks to protect. The Commission's specified goal was to design protections for economically vulnerable cohabitants when their relationships ended. While the world of the future may consist of many more Mrs. Oxleys, Mrs. Burns certainly is an appropriate object for legal protection in the present. It is a mistake to assume an equality that does not yet exist. There are still many Mrs. Burnses today according to the statistics—cohabitants of low income and little property, many of them with children. As for the Mrs. Oxleys, they can simply opt out of any new system by contract if they wish and negotiate other terms for themselves.

---

53. Bottomley, *supra* note 51, at 189.

54. *See* Oxley, [2005] FAM. at 249.

55. Bottomley, *supra* note 51, at 204–05.

56. Simone Wong, *Trust(s) and Intention in Resolving Disputes over the Shared Family Home,* 56 N. IRE. LEG. Q. 105, 116 (2005).

More important, the remedies proposed by the Law Commission simply do not offer adequate protection for the majority of cohabitants, those without property to adjust, who need maintenance under the same circumstances as ex-wives. The remedy suggested by the Law Commission is also very complex and requires family court judges to analyze cases according to principles that not only are unfamiliar to them but also seem similar to the factors applicable in a divorce while actually being quite different, a situation sure to confuse.

Finally, there are problems inherent in the piecemeal process of reform the English have followed. Reforms have responded to specific problems and establish ad hoc, often partial, solutions to them. If cohabitants happen to confront a problem the law has addressed, such as recovery for the wrongful death of a partner, suitable remedies are available; if the problem that arises has not yet been the subject of political attention, they are out of luck. Pursuit of a comprehensive and principled approach to the legal issues faced by cohabitants is a preferable way to proceed. What appears to make parliamentarians and law commissioners reluctant to do so is their unwillingness to give cohabitants too many of the rights accorded to married couples, which would, they believe, diminish the unique status of marriage, a topic that will be addressed at some length in the next chapter.

In many ways, cohabitants are better off now in England than in the United States. Being a unitary rather than a federal system, reform of a particular law, such as the workers' compensation or inheritance statute, benefits everyone who cohabits, not just the citizens of one state. Moreover, many essential benefits, such as health insurance, are provided by the British state to all citizens; these benefits do not depend on marital status or employment, as in the United States. For the same reasons, English reform efforts may not be an appropriate model for the United States, even if they did offer adequate protection to cohabitants.

On the other hand, if legislation based on the Law Commission's recommendations is passed by Parliament, some cohabitants could be much better off when their relationships terminate than cohabitants constrained to rely upon equitable remedies in the United States. Until that happens, English law is not that much ahead of the law in some American states with respect to the protection of cohabitants. The main difference—and it is an important one—is that the issue has been given a great deal more public discussion on that side of the ocean. More political attention and public resources have been directed toward attempting to grapple with the very real problems faced by the increasing number of cohabiting opposite-sex couples. This in itself should be a model for the United States.

✌ 2. Canada: The New Common Law Marriage?

Canada has been part of the worldwide trend toward cohabiting relationships, although their incidence varies from province to province. The 2006
Census reported that 2.8 million people, 10.8 percent of the total population,
were what are referred to in Canada as "common-law partners"; 42.5 percent
of them were in their late twenties and early thirties.[57] The fastest-growing
sector, however, was among people forty and older.[58] The pattern in the
province of Quebec, especially among French speakers, is unique, with
cohabitation having largely replaced marriage for over half the population.
The 2006 Census reported 2,731,635 cohabitants in Canada as a whole and
12,470,400 married couples; by contrast, in Quebec there were 2,361,855 married couples and 1,221,855 cohabitants, 52% of all couples.[59] Characteristics
of cohabitants in Quebec do not differ significantly from those of married
persons, and their unions are more stable, longer in duration, and more likely
to involve children than elsewhere in Canada.[60] Some attribute Quebec's
uniqueness to the widespread rejection by young people there of Catholic
social doctrines on marriage and sexuality and the church's refusal to allow
lay participation in decision making after the liberal reforms of Vatican II.[61]

The Canadian government has been attempting to address the legal problems of cohabitants for a long time. Courts, legislatures, provincial law reform
commissions, and the federal Law Commission have struggled with these
issues. As in England, the process of reform has been piecemeal both in its
procedures and results, but it is a great deal further along the road toward
making cohabitation the equivalent of marriage. Unlike in many other countries, that road did not begin with the demand of same-sex couples for recognition but instead with constitutional challenges brought by opposite-sex
couples under the equal rights provisions of the Canadian Charter of Rights

---

57. STATISTICS CANADA, REPORT ON THE DEMOGRAPHIC SITUATION IN CANADA: 2005 AND
    2006 70 (2008).

58. *Id.*

59. STATISTICS CANADA, LEGAL MARITAL STATUS, COMMON LAW STATUS, FOR THE
    POPULATION 15 YEARS AND OVER, 2006 CENSUS, *available at* http://www12.statcan.gc.
    ca/english/census06/data/topics/ (Marital Status).

60. *See* Don Kerr et al., *Marriage and Cohabitation: Demographic and Socioeconomic Differences
    in Quebec and Canada*, 33 CAN. STUD., *in* POPULATION 83, 108 (2006).

61. *See, e.g.,* Benôit Laplante, *The Rise of Cohabitation in Quebec: Power of Religion and Power
    over Religion*, 31 CAN. J. SOCIOL. 1 (2006).

and Freedoms. The trend, moreover, has been to recognize cohabitants' rights on the basis of status, defined by the duration of the relationship, rather than of contract.[62]

Since the 1970s, a number of provinces in Canada had been gradually extending some of the protections of their family law statutes to unmarried heterosexual couples.[63] For example, the 1978 Family Law Reform Act in Ontario extended support rights to this group on dissolution of their relationships, while excluding them from property distribution.[64] In a 1993 report, the Ontario Law Reform Commission recommended still more:

> When two persons have lived together in a relationship of some permanence, interdependence, and emotional importance to both of them, and that partnership comes to an end, the law should ensure a fair sharing of the assets that they acquired during the time they were together, a fair disposition of the family home and a fair consideration of support if one party is likely to suffer economic hardship as a result of participation in the relationship. The intent is to prevent the economic exploitation of one by the other . . . It is likely that one or both partners have assumed that the relationship will be permanent and that the assets they have acquired are likely to be intermingled.[65]

Because it was unfair for an individual partner to profit under these circumstances and the state then be left with responsibility for taking care of the economically weaker cohabitant, the Commission recommended that the Ontario Family Law Act change its definition of spouse for all purposes to include heterosexual cohabitants who had lived together for three years or had a child.[66] The act was amended, but only to require treatment as spouses for purposes of postrelationship support.

Canadian courts were also confronting cohabitants' legal problems at the end of their relationships in cases brought to claim property rights based, as

62. Susan B. Boyd & Claire F.L. Young, *"From Same-Sex to No Sex"?: Trends Towards Recognition of (Same-Sex) Relationships in Canada*, 1 SEATTLE J. SOC. JUST. 757, 760 (2003).

63. *Id.*

64. Winifred Holland, *Intimate Relationships in the New Millenium: The Assimilation of Marriage and Cohabitation?*, 17 CAN. J. FAM. L. 114, 128–29 (2000).

65. ONTARIO LAW REFORM COMMISSION, REPORT ON THE RIGHTS AND RESPONSIBILITIES OF COHABITANTS UNDER THE FAMILY LAW ACT 3 (1993).

66. *Id.* at 61.

in other common law countries, upon the doctrines of unjust enrichment and constructive trust.[67] In a 1993 case involving a woman who had lived with her partner for more than twelve years, during which she had cared for their children and done all the housework without pay, the Supreme Court actually awarded the family home to her at the end of their relationship although it was titled in the male partner's name and he had paid the mortgage.[68] Departing from the British trust model based on monetary contributions, the court found that "there is no logical reason to distinguish domestic services from other contributions" and that "her services helped preserve the property and saved the man large sums of money which he used to pay off his mortgage and to purchase a houseboat and a van."[69] In other words, it recognized both nonmonetary and indirect contributions to the acquisition of property. Thus, cohabitants in Canada have a more extensive property remedy under the constructive trust doctrine than they enjoy in England. It is nonetheless an onerous burden to be required to undertake the expense of litigation to prove the elements of a trust, causing the Canadian Law Commission later to remark that "it is a tool beyond the reach of many people."[70]

The 1990s were marked by a series of constitutional cases brought to challenge the exclusion of unmarried couples from the benefits received by those who were married. Section 15 of the Canadian Charter of Rights and Freedoms contains a very broad equal protection and equal benefit of the laws provision that has been interpreted quite broadly by the courts. Unlike jurisprudence under the U.S. Bill of Rights, Canadian courts look to the historical context to determine whether a discriminatory legal classification perpetuates negative stereotypes and fails to achieve its acknowledged purpose to "protect and promote human dignity."[71] In *Miron v. Trudel* (1995), a cohabitant brought a Section 15 challenge to exclusion from his partner's insurance policy because they were not legally married.[72] The couple had lived together for more than four years and had two children when he was

---

67. Holland, *supra* note 64, at 142–43.

68. Peter v. Beblow, [1993] 1 S.C.R. 980 (Can.).

69. *Id.* at 1003.

70. Law Commission of Canada, Beyond Conjugality: Recognizing and Supporting Close Personal Adult Relationships 115 (2001) [hereinafter Beyond Conjugality].

71. *See* Hon. Claire L'Heureux-Dubé, *It Takes A Vison: The Constitutionalization of Equality in Canada*, 14 Yale J. L. & Feminism 363, 366–69 (2002).

72. Miron v. Trudel, [1995] 2 S.C.R. 418 (Can.).

injured in an accident. The insurance policy terms were standard terms prescribed by the Canadian Insurance Act, which the plaintiff challenged as violating Section 15 of the Charter by discriminating based on marital status. The Supreme Court agreed, holding that marital status was a prohibited ground upon which to discriminate because it touched the dignity and worth of an individual in ways similar to other recognized grounds of discrimination, possessed characteristics associated with social disadvantage and prejudice, and was, though not immutable, often beyond the individual's control.[73] Under the Charter, the burden then shifted to the state to justify the law by showing its connection to an acceptable state goal. The *Miron* court, pointing to the fact that the Ontario Family Law Act imposed spousal support upon cohabitants after three years or the birth of a child, found that the function of the insurance legislation under challenge was clearly to support families when a member was injured and that marital status was not a good indicator of support.[74] It therefore held that discrimination based on marital status—that is, the status of a couple not being married—was constitutionally prohibited by Section 15 of the Charter.[75]

After *Miron v. Trudel*, various provinces raced to revise their laws to survive a similar Charter-based challenge. A cohabitant brought suit in Alberta based on *Miron* to obtain support at the end of a 29-year relationship.[76] The trial court agreed that the definition of spouse under the Alberta Domestic Relations Act must be changed to include common-law partners, a straightforward application of the holding in *Miron v. Trudel*. The appellate court agreed but thought that the matter should be referred to the legislature for definition of a qualifying relationship, pointing out that the qualifying period varied in other provinces, from one year in Nova Scotia and Newfoundland, to three years in Ontario and New Brunswick, to five in Manitoba.[77] It concluded, nonetheless, that "Promoting marriage as the sole form of legally recognized relationship in the face of this statistical evidence [about cohabitation in Canada] thus arguably does not reflect social reality and may not amount to

---

73. *Id.* at 497–98.

74. *Id.* at 499, 504–06.

75. For a contrasting definition of marital status by the courts of some U.S. states, *see* North Dakota Fair Housing Council v. Peterson, 625 N.W.2d 551 (N.D. 2001) (holding that marital status means divorced, widowed, or separated, rather than married or unmarried).

76. Taylor v. Rossu, [1998] 216 A.R. 348 (Can.).

77. *Id.* at 359–63, 372.

a pressing and substantial objective."[78] Further, the exclusion of cohabitants from the law failed the rational connection test because it had neither increased the number of marriages nor discouraged cohabitation and also was not rationally connected to the statutory goal of relieving dependency at the end of a relationship.[79] The legislature in Alberta, a conservative province, amended its law to include support rights for opposite-sex cohabitants "if there has been a 'marriage-like' relationship where the partners have had a child or cohabited for three years."[80] In 1999, same-sex cohabitants also succeeded in a Section 15 challenge against their exclusion from the support provisions of the Ontario Family Law Act based on sexual orientation.[81]

One of the most important results of *Miron v. Trudel* was the passage of the Modernization of Benefits and Obligations Act in 2000 by the Canadian federal Parliament, which changed the definition of spouse in all federal laws to include unmarried cohabitants.[82] The new status is called "common-law partners," a somewhat odd term for a status bestowed by statute rather than emerging from the common law. The act states that it "extends benefits and obligations to *all* couples who have been cohabiting in a conjugal relationship for at least one year, in order to reflect values of tolerance, respect and equality, consistent with the *Canadian Charter of Rights and Freedoms*."[83] Thus, for example, the Old Age Security Act was revised to include common-law partners for all purposes, including survivors' benefits, under the social security system.[84] Common-law partners are also treated as though married under the income tax laws.[85] In 2001, the Law Commission of Canada issued its report *Beyond Conjugality*, recommending that every law be evaluated according to

---

78. *Id.* at 386.

79. *Id.* at 386–87.

80. Nicholas Bala, *Canada: Court Decisions on Same-Sex and Unmarried Partners, Spousal Rights and Children, in* INTERNATIONAL SURVEY OF FAMILY LAW 43, 49 (Andrew Bainham ed., Cambridge Univ. Press 2001).

81. M. v. H., [1999] 2 S.C.R. 3 (Can.).

82. MODERNIZATION OF BENEFITS AND OBLIGATIONS ACT, 2000 S.C., Chap. 12 (Can.). *See* BEYOND CONJUGALITY, *supra* note 70, at 14–15.

83. MODERNIZATION OF BENEFITS AND OBLIGATIONS ACT, *supra* note 82 (emphasis in original).

84. *Id.,* Ch. 12, §§ 192–206.

85. Berend Hovius, *Property Rights for Unmarried Cohabitants in Canada*, [2006] INT'L FAM. L. 29 (2006). Marital status is less important to taxation in Canada than the United States, however, because the personal income tax is based on individual rather than marital units in Canada. Holland, *supra* note 64, at 144.

the "fit" between its purpose and the category of persons covered and that many of the benefits extended to cohabitants be extended to nonconjugal relationships that involve caring and interdependence as well.[86]

A number of provinces also established domestic partnership or civil union schemes open to both opposite- and same-sex partners; they vary in the benefits they confer. The first, in Nova Scotia, set up a limited civil union system under which cohabitants who register as domestic partners are given the rights and obligations of married couples under the province's family property statute.[87] Quebec passed a broader civil union law than that in Nova Scotia, under which same- and opposite-sex cohabitants who register receive the rights and obligations of married persons under family law as well as rights pertaining to health care and adoption.[88] (Quebec has the only civil law system in Canada, and thus common law remedies such as constructive trusts are not available to the many unregistered cohabitants who live there.) In Alberta, an Adult Interdependent Relationships Act was passed in 2002, allowing conjugal and nonconjugal couples who have lived in an interdependent relationship for three years (or less if they have a child) to enter into written interdependent relationship contracts with one another, after which they become eligible for support, damages in the case of wrongful death, and inheritance, but no property rights.[89] Unregistered cohabitants were already eligible for support after three years or the birth of a child under the 1999 statute described earlier.

In 2002, the rush to equivalence between cohabitation and marriage came to a sudden halt with the Supreme Court's decision of *Walsh v. Bona*.[90] This case was a challenge to Nova Scotia's total exclusion of unmarried couples from its Matrimonial Property Act prior to passage of the new civil union law. Everyone expected the challenge to succeed based on the precedent of *Miron v. Trudel* and its prohibition of discrimination based on marital status. However, the Supreme Court held that exclusion from marital property

---

86. BEYOND CONJUGALITY, *supra* note 70. *See* Nancy D. Polikoff, *Ending Marriage As We Know It*, 32 HOFSTRA L. REV. 201, 205–17 (describing the methodology recommended by BEYOND CONJUGALITY and attempting to apply it to American law). The Law Commission was defunded by the Conservative Government in 2006 and no longer exists.

87. Martha Bailey, *Regulation of Cohabitation and Marriage in Canada*, 26 L. & POL'Y 153, 155 (2004).

88. *Id.* at 162–63.

89. *Id.* at 163–64.

90. Walsh v. Bona, [2002] 4 S.C.R. 325 (Can.).

rights legislation did not constitute discrimination because it did not affect the dignity of cohabitants. Upon marriage, it said, couples are presumed to have consented to enter a scheme of deferred sharing of property, including the family home, but cohabitants have not done so.[91] The decision elicited a spirited dissent from Justice L'Heureux-Dubé, who had written one of the concurring opinions in *Miron v. Trudel.* The purposes of spousal support, the subject of *Miron,* and of marital property distribution, the subject of *Walsh,* were fundamentally the same, she said—to meet the financial needs of a partner upon termination of a relationship.[92] Moreover, the deferred sharing embodied in the marital property system is intended to recognize the contributions of both partners, including the contributions of a homemaker like Susan Walsh, and to lessen the burden of dependency imposed upon the public fisc by those left in a vulnerable economic position if the couple separated. Hence, she argued, there was no principled reason upon which to distinguish the issue in *Walsh* from that in *Miron* under the Charter.[93] Most commentators think she was correct and that the *Walsh* decision marked a sharp departure from prior jurisprudence under the Charter as part of a general turn to the right in Canadian politics.[94]

Despite the outrage of Justice L-Heureux-Dubé and many others, provinces that had not already extended property remedies to cohabitants (which Saskatchewan and Manitoba had done) or enacted civil union schemes extending property rights to registered partners were not constitutionally required to do so.[95] Thus, in Ontario, for example, cohabitants must rely on the law of constructive trusts for any property adjustment at the end of their relationships, or they can enter into a contract specifying their property rights vis-à-vis one another.[96] In Nova Scotia, Manitoba, and Quebec, cohabitants who register as partners or enter civil unions obtain property rights vis-à-vis one another, and in the Northwest Territories and Nunavut,

---

91. *Id.* at 359.

92. *Id.* at 403, 406–08.

93. *Id.* at 415–16, 425–26.

94. *See, e.g.,* Heather Conway & Philip Girard, *"No Place Like Home": The Search for a Legal Framework for Cohabitants and the Family Home in Canada and Britain,* 30 QUEEN'S L.J. 715, 727 (2005) and sources cited therein.

95. Bailey, *supra* note 87, at 162–63.

96. Hovius, *supra* note 85, at 30–31.

Saskatchewan, and Manitoba, the province's family law property rules cover unmarried couples.[97]

In sum, cohabitants in Canada receive a mélange of rights depending upon their place of residence. All are entitled to support at the end of their relationships based on the holding in *Miron v. Trudel* but to property remedies only where the province has changed its statute concerning matrimonial property, which few have done. For property rights, cohabitants in common law provinces must resort to the constructive trust doctrine, but that doctrine has been developed by the courts to address their situation more adequately than under English law. As for rights against third parties and the state, it depends upon whether the issue is governed by federal or provincial law—if by federal statute, all the benefits available to married couples are extended to cohabitants of one year or longer; otherwise, it depends upon the statutes of the particular province. In addition, several provinces have opposite-sex domestic partnerships that offer a range of benefits to partners who register but exclude those who do not. In short, one might say that Canada is a veritable laboratory of differing experiments in its approach to the law of cohabitants' rights.

Nonetheless, cohabitants are clearly much better protected in Canada than in either the United States or England, although there are some basic gaps in that protection concerning property distribution upon separation, and a great deal depends upon where one lives. The decision of *Walsh v. Bona* was a major setback, but there appears to be an overall trend toward assimilation of cohabitation to marriage after a required period of duration. Some feminists have been critical of this approach based upon its tendency and probable intent to privatize benefits as the welfare state has been retrenched in recent years.[98] In other words, as public benefits are cut, the responsibility for former partners is placed on the shoulders of their ex-cohabitants. This is true to some extent, but the Canadian reforms have also benefited many people, especially vulnerable women and children, and given them benefits beyond those available simply in private law, such as those against third parties and the state. Privatization of benefits is not, moreover, the only argument for extending rights to cohabitants.

---

97. *Id.* at 33.

98. *See, e.g.,* Mary Jane Mossman, *Conversations About Families in Canadian Courts and Legislatures: Are There "Lessons" for the United States?*, 32 HOFSTRA L. REV. 171, 173–74 (2003); Boyd & Young, *supra* note 62, at 776–81.

Indeed, the rationale based on privatization of benefits and protection of the public fisc may provide a potentially effective argument for extension of similar family law benefits to cohabitants in the United States, precisely because the argument appeals to political conservatives. Canada is an apt model for the United States for a number of reasons. Both countries have federal systems, with family law consigned to the states or provinces, and both have a common law system with fairly similar marriage and divorce laws. A major difference, however, is the notion of substantive equality embedded in the Canadian Charter of Rights and Freedoms, as opposed to the limited version of rights under the current interpretation of the U.S. Constitution, which makes it difficult to mount an effective legal argument, based on equal protection, for treating unmarried couples like those who are married.[99]

Certain remedies in Canada were extended first to opposite-sex couples and later extended to same-sex partners on equality grounds, while in the United States, the movement toward extending any sort of rights to cohabitants has largely been directed at the legal problems of same-sex couples. Perhaps that is simply a first step, with rights for opposite-sex couples to follow. At any rate, the piecemeal procedure and results of the Canadian reforms are likely to be the way the United States will proceed, both because of its federal system and its conservative, pragmatic approach to legal reform.

✎ 3. *De Facto* Relationships in Australia

Cohabitation has grown rapidly down under, much as it has in other countries. Heterosexual cohabiting couples increased in Australia from 6 percent of all couples in 1986 to 12.4 percent in 2001.[100] The rate of increase slowed a bit from 2001 to 2006, but the number of cohabitants increased by 25 percent over that period, and by 2006, *de facto* couples made up 15 percent of all couples.[101] The median age of males in these *de facto* relationships

---

99. *See supra* at 68.

100. Catherine Caruana, *Relationship Diversity and the Law*, 63 FAM. MATTERS 60–65 (2002).

101. AUSTRALIAN BUREAU OF STATISTICS, 1301.0—YEAR BOOK AUSTRALIA, 2008, released Feb. 7, 2008, *available at* http://www.abs.gov.au/ausstats/abs@.nsf/bb8db737e2af84b8-ca2571780015701e/D5F4805AD4C3E03ECA2573D2001103E0?opendocument.

was 35.3 and that of females was 33.3.[102] About 20 percent of those who cohabited between 1990 and 1994 were still together five years later.[103] The high rates of cohabitation in Australia may be due, at least in part, to the fact that indigenous Australians, or Aborigines, have a long history of consensual partnerships; cohabiting is three times more common among indigenous than among nonindigenous Australians (35.8 percent versus 11.7 percent).[104]

Australia responded relatively early to the legal problems of opposite-sex cohabitants with reforms on a state-by-state basis. The Australian constitution confers jurisdiction over disputes arising out of married relationships upon the federal government but leaves relationships between unmarried couples to the states.[105] However, jurisdiction over children, both marital and nonmarital, lies with the federal Family Court.[106] So Australian cohabitants may be required to go to both federal and state court to resolve all the issues that arise at the end of their relationships.

Legal reform concerning cohabitants has proceeded differently in Australia than in Canada because the Australian constitution contains no Bill of Rights or other guarantee of equality. Thus, constitutional litigation as a route to reform, as happened under the Canadian Charter of Rights and Freedoms, has not been a viable option in Australia. As a result, reforms have been carried out almost exclusively through legislation.[107] By the same token, however, Australian legislatures have not been bound by a rigid interpretation of equality such as that developed under the equal protection clause in the United States, where courts have rejected the extension of rights to cohabitants on the grounds that they are not similarly situated to married couples.[108]

Before the passage of new laws, the Australian courts, like those in other common law countries, attempted to deal with situations of injustice that arose between *de facto* partners under the law of trusts. In one famous 1987

---

102. *Id.*

103. Ken Dempsey & David de Vaus, *Who Cohabits in 2001? The Significance of Age, Gender, Religion and Ethnicity*, 40 J. SOCIOL. 157, 161 (2004).

104. *Id.* at 169.

105. Lindy Willmott et al., *De Facto Relationships Property Adjustment Law—A National Direction*, 17 AUSTRALIAN J. FAM. LAW 37 (2003).

106. Carauna, *supra* note 100, at 60–61.

107. Reg Graycar & Jenni Milbank, *From Functional Family to Spinster Sisters: Australia's Distinctive Path to Relationship Recognition*, 24 J. L. & POL'Y 121, 124 (2007).

108. *Id.* at 157.

case, *Baumgartner v. Baumgartner*, the High Court of Australia established that property titled in the name of one cohabitant to which both had contributed was subject to a constructive trust in favor of the partner not holding title, thus giving rise to what was known as a Baumgartner trust.[109] However, in the *Baumgartner* case, both cohabitants had contributed financially to acquisition of the property at issue. Both partners worked, and each month Mrs. Baumgartner turned over her income to the household bank account, out of which payments on the mortgage were made. Although some allowance was made for the three months during which she did not work due to the birth of the couple's child, her ultimate share of the family home was based upon the proportion she had contributed to the couple's pooled income. This precedent would not be available to a cohabitant whose partner had made all the mortgage payments himself.

Australian commentators, like those in the United States, England, and Canada, have remarked upon the inconvenience of using equitable remedies such as the constructive trust in cohabitant cases because of the lengthy, complex, and expensive legal services required; the uncertainty of the outcome also makes it very difficult for attorneys to advise clients and to negotiate settlements.[110] Unlike in England, however, Australian law does not require proof of a common intention to create a trust; the trust is imposed as a matter of equity rather than one of presumed agreement.[111] Australian case law about trusts in cohabitants' cases has been developed further since the *Baumgartner* case, to include in-kind as well as purely financial contributions and to presume equality of contribution after a long-term relationship. Nevertheless, the trust remedy remains inferior to treatment a spouse could expect under the Australian Family Law Act, which takes future need into consideration.[112]

In response to these limitations under the case law, state after state in Australia has passed legislation dealing with the property relationships of *de facto* couples, with New South Wales (where Sydney is located) the first to do so. The New South Wales Law Commission undertook an inquiry in 1981 that resulted in a 1983 report recommending new legislation for property

---

109. Baumgartner v. Baumgartner (1987), 164 C.L.R 137 (Austl.).

110. Ian Kennedy, *The Legal Position of Cohabitees in Australia and New Zealand*, INT'L FAM. L. 238, 239, Nov. 2004.

111. *Id.*

112. *Id.* at 241.

division upon the termination of heterosexual *de facto* relationships.[113] The result was passage of the New South Wales De Facto Relationships Act in 1984. The current version of that act defines a *de facto* relationship as two adults living together as a couple who are not married or related to one another and applies to maintenance as well as property.[114] While cohabitation is required, a specific time period (two years) applies only to property distribution and inheritance.[115]

Unlike systems in Canada that define cohabitation simply by a specified duration, cohabitants in Australia are required to establish the nature of their relationship by proof of a list of factors prescribed by the legislature. This generally requires a court determining whether parties qualify as a *de facto* couple to take into account such factors as the duration of the relationship, the nature and extent of common residence, the existence of a sexual relationship, the degree of financial dependence or interdependence and financial support between the parties, their ownership, use, and acquisition of property, the degree of mutual commitment to a shared life, the care and support of children, performance of household duties, the couple's reputation, and other public aspects of the relationship.[116] In short, Australian law requires a mini-trial to establish the nature of a couple's relationship before the partners can claim any remedies that may be available. Moreover, the factors required to be proved clearly reflect the model of heterosexual marriage.[117]

Although the De Facto Relationships Act in New South Wales began as a contribution-based property distribution scheme, revisions to it have gradually expanded the rights given to *de facto* couples.[118] Between 2001 and 2006, every other Australian state also passed legislation applying to *de facto* couples. These statutes vary both in their scope and in their definition of the group covered. While some are primarily property acts, others place qualifying cohabitants into a position similar to that of married couples

---

113. Graycar & Millbank, *supra* note 107, at 125–27.

114. *Id.* at 133.

115. *Id.*

116. Kennedy, *supra* note 110, at 241.

117. Simone Wong, *Property Regimes for Home-sharers: The Civil Partnership Bill and Some Antipodean Models*, 26 J. SOC. WELFARE & FAM. L. 361, 372 (2004)

118. Graycar & Millbank, *supra* note 107, at 127.

upon breakdown of their relationships.[119] Several include same-sex couples in their coverage, and two also include persons in caring but nonconjugal relationships.[120] In about one-third of the states, the provisions for property distribution approximate those that would be applied to married couples upon divorce by taking future needs into account as well as past contributions.[121] The Tasmanian Relationships Act of 2003, for example, takes the following non-exclusive list of factors into account in allocating a cohabiting couple's property when they separate:

    a. Financial and nonfinancial contributions to the acquisition, conservation, and improvement of the property
    b. The financial resources of both parties
    c. Contributions of each party, including services as a homemaker
    d. The nature and duration of the parties' relationship[122]

Partners are not eligible for property adjustment or other remedies under this statute unless they have cohabited continuously for at least two years or have a child in common.[123] If these requirements are satisfied, however, the partners' remedies *inter se* are comparable to those of married couples. Queensland and Western Australia are similar to Tasmania in taking future needs as well as past contributions to acquisition of property into account in allocating it at the end of a relationship.[124]

    The breadth of these remedies contrasts with the more restrictive ones available in New South Wales, Victoria, and the Northern Territory, where a court will only consider the parties' contributions in allocating the couple's property at the point of dissolution, not their future needs or any other issues influencing their financial position.[125] In addition, most other states provide

---

119. *See* Jenni Millbank, *Domestic Rifts: Who Is Using the Domestic Relationships Act 1994 (ACT)?*, 14 AUSTRALIAN FAM. L.J. 163, 165–66 (2000) (describing differences between treatment of property distribution under *de facto* relationship acts and under the Family Law Act).

120. Statutes in New South Wales, Western Australia, the Northern Territory, Tasmania, the Australian Capital Territory, and South Australia included same-sex couples as of 2007. Graycar & Millbank, *supra* note 107, at 132–35. Statutes in the Australian Capital Territory and Tasmania extend beyond conjugal relationships. *Id.* at 147–50.

121. *See* Willmott et al., *supra* note 105, at 39–40.

122. TASMANIAN RELATIONSHIPS ACT, 2003, § 40 (1) (Austl.).

123. *Id.* at § 37 (1)-(2).

124. Willmott et al., *supra* note 105, at 39–40.

125. *Id.* at 8.

only for property adjustment at the end of a cohabiting relationship and do not allow an award of maintenance—the exact opposite of the situation in Canada, where support is universally available but property distribution is not.[126]

Maintenance is available under the Tasmanian act at the end of a relationship if one cohabitant's earning capacity has been adversely affected by the relationship; the statute includes a long list of factors to be weighed by the judge, resembling those applied to married couples under the Family Law Act.[127] In other states, maintenance may be unavailable or limited. In New South Wales, a party is eligible for maintenance only if unable to work because of needing to care for a child under twelve (or a handicapped child under sixteen) or has lost his or her earning capacity as a result of the relationship and is prepared to undergo training to recover it.[128]

An unusual feature of the Australian system for cohabitants is the coexistence of both a status-based regime and a registration scheme for opposite-sex domestic partners.[129] In Tasmania, for example, partners may evade both the durational requirement and the onerous in-court proof of qualification as a *de facto* couple by registering a deed of relationship.[130] Unlike in Europe, however, the overwhelming preference in Australia is for conferring rights upon cohabitants based on status instead of registration. In the words of an Australian feminist scholar, "This preference for a presumption-based

---

126. Caruana, *supra* note 100, at 64. *See id.* at 63 for a chart detailing what benefits are available to same-sex, opposite-sex, and other relationships in the various Australian states.

127. The Tasmanian Relationships Act provides that the following factors be taken into account in deciding about maintenance on dissolution of a cohabiting relationship: income; property and financial resources of each partner; their physical and mental capacity for employment; financial needs and obligations of each; responsibility of either partner to support other persons; terms of the property distribution; any payments as child maintenance, whether the recipient is the custodian of a minor child; age and health of each partner; a reasonable standard of living; extent to which maintenance would increase the party's earning capacity by enabling him or her to study; extent to which the partner contributed to the income, earning capacity, and property of the other partner; length of their relationship; extent to which the relationship affected the party's earning capacity; and any other relevant factor. TASMANIAN RELATIONSHIPS ACT, *supra* note 122, at § 47(1).

128. NEW SOUTH WALES, DE FACTO RELATIONSHIPS ACT, 1984, Pt. III, § 27(1)(a)–(b) (Austl.).

129. New Zealand also has a dual system, with a liberal *de facto* relationships act extending both property rights and maintenance to cohabitants after three years if they qualify and an opt-in system by which they may register their relationships. *See* Graycar & Millbank, *supra* note 107, at 141–42; Kennedy, *supra* note 110, at 242–43.

130. Wong, *supra* note 117, at 367.

approach recognized that those most vulnerable are also those least likely to formally register their relationships and legal affairs."[131]

In addition to rights against one another under state law, *de facto* couples in Australia enjoy a variety of rights comparable to those given married couples under both federal and state laws that simply include them within the coverage of an act or redefine who is a spouse for purposes of the particular legislation. Cohabitants are, for example, treated the same as married couples for purposes of taxation, social security, pensions, immigration, bankruptcy, and workers' compensation.[132] Contracts between cohabitants are also recognized in Australia.[133]

Finally, the Australian federal government agreed in 2002 to accept referrals concerning heterosexual *de facto* couples from the states.[134] Several states have referred these matters to the federal government for decision, where they will be covered by the Family Law Act rather than by the more limited provisions of state *de facto* relationship laws, and commentators see this as the wave of the future.[135] So, for example, in 2003, the legislature of New South Wales referred financial matters arising out of the breakdown of *de facto* relationships, including both property distribution and maintenance, to the federal government.[136] As a result, cohabitants in New South Wales can have all aspects of their dissolution cases heard by the federal courts under the provisions of law applied to married couples.

In sum, Australian law gives opposite-sex cohabitants the rights of married couples in many respects, and it does so without assimilating the two statuses. Rather than simply directing that cohabitants who fall within the qualifying definition be treated as though they were married, it doles out remedies piecemeal, primarily aimed at resolving disputes at the end of cohabiting relationships. Finally, it imposes on the courts the burden of deciding the nature of a couple's relationship by reference to a list of factors, an approach destined to yield inconsistent results, results that may reflect

---

131. Graycar & Millbank, *supra* note 107, at 131.

132. Kennedy, *supra* note 110, at 243.

133. Willmott et al., *supra* note 105, at 39.

134. Kennedy, *supra* note 110, at 240.

135. NEW SOUTH WALES, COMMONWEALTH POWERS (DE FACTO RELATIONSHIPS) ACT, 2003, §§ 1, 3 (Austl.).

136. Kennedy, *supra* note 110, at 241.

the biases of particular judges. Because of these substantial limitations, it does not provide a good model for the United States.

✄ 4. The Netherlands: A Cafeteria Approach to Cohabitants' Rights

The Netherlands offers a cafeteria of choices for opposite-sex couples. They may marry, register as domestic partners with virtually all the rights of married couples, or enter into a relatively formalized contract with an attorney. Even if they pursue none of these options, they still receive many of the same benefits as married couples under Dutch law. The story of how this polyglot system came into existence is interesting.

The system of registered partnership established in The Netherlands in 1998 had its origins in the movement for gay and lesbian rights. After deciding in 1990 that exclusion of gays and lesbians from the benefits attendant upon marriage was not discriminatory under current law, the Supreme Court invited the legislature to consider the issue.[137] The parliament established a committee to investigate, known as the Kortmann Committee. Its 1991 report recommended the establishment of two different types of registration: one that would have public law effects (tax, social security, and the like) and another that would confer the incidents of marriage under family law upon a registered couple.[138] Initially, opposite-sex couples were excluded from the proposed law.[139] After debate over whether their exclusion would itself be discriminatory, the Registered Partnership and Adaptation Act that ultimately passed and went into effect in 1998 included both same- and opposite-sex couples.[140] Everyone seemed to accept that equality of treatment required this result.[141]

---

137. Ian Sumner, *Transformers—Marriages in Disguise?*, Mar. 2003 INT'L FAM. L. 15 (2003).

138. Wendy Schrama, *Registered Partnership in The Netherlands*, 13 INT'L J. L., POL'Y & FAM. 315, 317 (1999).

139. *Id.* at 318; *see also* Sumner, *supra* note 137, at 15.

140. BRAM VAN DIJK & YVONNE SCHERF, MINSTRY OF JUSTICE, REGISTERED PARTNERSHIP IN THE NETHERLANDS: A QUICK SCAN (1999).

141. Interview with Ian Sumner, in Utrecht, Neth. (June 28, 2004).

The 1998 law was basically an amalgam of several laws amending the Civil Code and numerous other statutes.[142] A status called Registered Partnerships was inserted into the Dutch Civil Code as Title 5A, directly after Title 5, Marriage.[143] Couples may enter the new status in a civil ceremony similar to that required for marriage in The Netherlands, after which a certificate of partnership would be included in a government register.[144] The legal consequences are virtually indistinguishable from those of marriage, including community of property, the right to support and maintenance, sharing of household debt, the inheritance and pension rights of a spouse, alimony, familial relationship, and treatment as a married couple in all other fields of law, such as taxation and social security.[145] The only differences relate to custody of children; the father of a child born to registered partners is not automatically related to the child but can recognize the child and obtain joint custody.[146] In addition, a partnership differs from marriage in that it can be terminated by mutual consent without going to court, so long as the couple has a notary (a notary is an attorney in The Netherlands) sign their agreement making provision for maintenance of the economically weaker partner, distribution of property under the Dutch community of property rules, and division of pension rights.[147] Married couples in The Netherlands may obtain a no-fault divorce based on the petition of one of the spouses alleging irretrievable breakdown of the marriage, but they cannot do so without going to court, with its consequent delay.[148]

From its effective date in January 1998 through the end of 2000, 3,398 gay couples, 2,973 lesbian couples, and—to the surprise of many—4,433 opposite-sex couples entered into registered partnerships in The Netherlands.[149]

---

142. YUVAL MERIN, EQUALITY FOR SAME-SEX COUPLES 114 (Univ. of Chicago Press 2002).

143. *See* FAMILY LAW LEGISLATION OF THE NETHERLANDS: A TRANSLATION INCLUDING BOOK 1 OF THE DUTCH CIVIL CODE, PROCEDURAL AND TRANSITIONAL PROVISIONS AND PRIVATE INTERNATIONAL LAW LEGISLATION 36, 51 (Ian Sumner & Hans Warendorf eds., Intersentia 2003) [hereinafter DUTCH CIVIL CODE].

144. Schrama, *supra* note 138, at 319. According to Merin, the ceremony is different in that the partners take no oath to each other but simply consent in front of the registrar and sign the deed of partnership to be entered in the register. MERIN, *supra* note 142, at 116.

145. Schrama, *supra* note 138, at 319–20. *See also* VAN DIJK & SCHERF, *supra* note 140, at 8.

146. Schrama, *supra* note 138, at 320. Domestic partners are also excluded from international adoptions. Interview with Wendy Schrama, in Utrecht, Neth. (June 28, 2004).

147. Schrama, *supra* note 138, at 321–22; *see also* MERIN, *supra* note 142, at 119.

148. *See* DUTCH CIVIL CODE, Tit. 9, § 2, arts. 150–51, *supra* note 143, at 80.

149. MERIN, *supra* note 142, at 115.

According to a study by the Ministry of Justice, those who registered as partners in the first year the status was available were older, less religious, and better educated than married couples.[150] In 1998 there was a pent-up demand for status recognition on the part of gay and lesbian couples, but in 1999 and 2000, the total same-sex registrations outnumbered those of opposite-sex couples only by about 300 a year.[151]

In 2001, a law allowing same-sex couples to marry in The Netherlands went into effect, but the registered partnership law was not repealed.[152] Although the decision to maintain both statuses is still under consideration, the fact that partnerships had proved so popular with heterosexuals led the government to continue that status even though the group whose demands had occasioned its establishment could now marry.[153] Thereafter, opposite-sex couples entering registered partnerships substantially outnumbered same-sex couples—in the first year alone, there were 2,691 male-female registrations and only 651 gay and lesbian registrations.[154] In 2007, there were 6,804 new partnership registrations by opposite-sex couples (out of 7,330 total), demonstrating that there is a continuing demand for the status.[155] Interviews soon after the registered partnership law went into effect reported that, while some of the opposite-sex couples entering partnerships were doing so because of an aversion to the institution of marriage, most said they did so because of financial reasons, because it was less binding than marriage or because it was quicker and less expensive.[156] However, their actual knowledge of the legal consequences of partnership was rather limited.

When the act allowing same-sex marriage was passed, the Dutch Civil Code was amended to allow couples to convert partnerships into marriage by drawing up an instrument of conversion and to convert marriages into partnerships by consent simply by notifying the Registrar of Births, Deaths, Marriages and Registered Partnerships of their joint desire to do so.[157] Many attributed the

---

150. Van Dijk & Scherf, *supra* note 140, at 16–19.

151. Sumner, *supra* note 137, at 19.

152. *Id.* at 15.

153. Interview with Ian Sumner, *supra* note 141.

154. Sumner, *supra* note 137, at 19.

155. Statistics Netherlands, *Marriages and partnership registrations, available at* http://statline.cbs.nl/StatWeb/publication/?DM=SLEN&PA=37772ENG&D1=35-47&D2=0, 50-57&LA=EN&VW=T.

156. Van Dijk & Scherf, *supra* note 140, at 21–25.

157. DUTCH CIVIL CODE, Tit. 5, § 5a (conversion of marriage into partnership); Tit. 5A, art. 80g (conversion of partnership into marriage), *supra* note 143, at 49, 53.

huge jump in registration of opposite-sex partners in 2002 (from 2,691 in 2001 to 6,764 in 2002) to the availability of this option, which in essence made a form of administrative divorce available to married couples: they could convert their marriages into partnerships and then dissolve the partnerships by agreement over a 24-hour period, thus evading both the waiting period for divorce and the necessity of going to court to obtain one.[158] Despite these statistics, the Minister of Justice did not believe that the possibility of conversion increased the divorce rate but only made the process simpler.[159] In dissolving either a marriage or a partnership, the couple must draw up an agreement providing for property, maintenance, pensions, and the like, which probably necessitates consulting an attorney in any event.[160] The conversions of marriages into partnerships slowed down after the initial period during which this possibility was available.[161] Nonetheless, as of March 1, 2009, the law was changed to no longer permit conversion of a marriage into a registered partnership.[162]

Domestic partnerships are not the only option for opposite-sex couples who do not wish to marry in The Netherlands. They may choose instead to enter into a cohabitation contract, which only has legal consequences between the two of them but can be designed to contain whatever provisions they would like; however, the contract must be formally drawn up by a notary.[163] Therein, apparently, lies the rub. To draw up a cohabitation contract is much more expensive than entering a registered partnership; it can cost hundreds of Euros to have a customized agreement drawn up by a notary instead of using the standardized, cheap, and quick procedure for a partnership.[164] For this

---

158. Sumner, *supra* note 137, at 17. *See also* Ian Sumner & Caroline Forder, *Bumper Issue: All You Ever Wanted to Know About Dutch Family Law (And Were Afraid to Ask),* in THE INTERNATIONAL SURVEY OF FAMILY LAW 2003 267–68 (Andrew Bainham ed., Jordan Publishing 2003); Ian Sumner, *Dissolution of Registered Partnerships: Excursion in Conversion,* Nov. 2004 INT'L FAM. L. 231–32.

159. Katharina Boele-Woelki, *Registered Partnership and Same-Sex Marriage in The Netherlands,* in LEGAL RECOGNITION OF SAME-SEX COUPLES IN EUROPE 50 (Katharina Boele-Woelki & Angelika Fuchs eds., Intersentia 2003).

160. *Id.* at 48.

161. While 5,425 marriages were converted into opposite-sex partnerships in 2004, the number had dropped to 3,141 by 2007. Statistics Netherlands, *supra* note 155.

162. E-mail from Kees Waaldijk, Senior Lecturer, University of Leiden Law School, to Cynthia Grant Bowman, Dorothea S. Clarke Professor of Law, Cornell Law School (Aug. 7, 2009, 10:04 a.m.) (on file with author).

163. Boele-Woelki, *supra* note 159, at 41.

164. Interview with Kees Waaldijk, Senior Lecturer, University of Leiden Law School, E.M. Meijers Institute of Legal Studies, Leiden, Neth. (July 19, 2004).

reason, many preferred the partnership route when it became available.[165] As in other countries, only a small minority of opposite-sex cohabitants had in fact drawn up cohabitation contracts prior to passage of the partnership law. While more than 50 percent of same-sex couples had contracts, only 16 percent of opposite-sex couples interviewed in one study had done so.[166]

Even if they enter into neither a contract nor a partnership, Dutch cohabitants are protected by a great deal of legislation anyway. From the 1970s on, cohabitants were increasingly given rights and duties similar to those of married couples under laws concerning rents and tenancy, social security and income tax, state pensions, immigration, and death duties.[167] For example, after cohabiting for six months in a year, cohabitants may choose to be taxed jointly, and after two years, they gain the right to retain a partner's tenancy upon dissolution or death.[168] Moreover, antidiscrimination legislation passed in 1994 made it illegal for an employer or provider of goods and services to discriminate based on whether a couple was married or unmarried.[169] Most of these legal changes resulted indirectly from litigation by cohabitants. Courts in The Netherlands are not allowed to consider constitutional questions (this is regarded as a violation of separation of powers), but when Dutch courts have found that a particular distinction did not constitute discrimination between married and unmarried couples under the existing law, the legislature has typically been quick to pass legislation to abolish whatever classification was challenged in the lawsuit.[170] It has done so out of a general assumption on the part of the Dutch that it is unfair to discriminate on this basis, even though it may not be illegal.[171]

In short, cohabitants in The Netherlands receive a great deal of protection unavailable to cohabitants in the United States even if they do not register as partners. To obtain the protections of the family law system, however, they must register. Unregistered cohabitants unprotected by a contract will be left without remedies against one another if their relationships dissolve. On the other hand, The Netherlands is a country with an extensive social welfare

---

165. Van Dijk & Scherf, *supra* note 140, at 21.

166. *Id.* at 20.

167. Merin, *supra* note 142, at 112.

168. Interview with Wendy Schrama, *supra* note 146.

169. Merin, *supra* note 142, at 113.

170. Interview with Wendy Schrama, *supra* note 146.

171. *Id.*

system that provides support both to individuals and to couples, married or unmarried. The Dutch social welfare system is not only very comprehensive but also confers benefits on individuals rather than attaching them to marital status.[172] Thus, for example, a cohabitant does not need to worry about health insurance tied to the employment of his or her partner either during or after their relationship.

A problem with the Dutch system and others like it is that the status of registered partner may not be recognized by other countries. Thus, if a registered couple should move to another European country, their union may not be considered valid. This raises a number of questions, such as whether a registered partner could simply marry someone else in the other country.[173]

Would the Dutch legal treatment of cohabitants be a good model for the United States? It would not, in part because of the absence in the United States of the comprehensive social welfare system available to the Dutch. One of my main concerns in evaluating any system has been its impact upon vulnerable parties at the end of a cohabiting relationship. A system that depends upon registration or contract, as the system in The Netherlands does, would leave those who do not register in an extremely vulnerable position. They are taken care of, as individuals, by the Dutch social welfare system, receiving health care, pensions, and basic income supports; but no such safety net exists in the United States. And, as previously discussed, those who do not register or enter into contracts are likely to be the most vulnerable of the vulnerable. For this reason, any system dependent upon voluntary registration is inadequate to protect cohabitants in the United States.

🕭 5. France: Concubinage and the Pacte Civil de Solidarité

Outside of Scandinavia, France has the largest percentage of cohabitants in Europe.[174] One study based on the 1994 wave of the European Community

---

172. Nancy G. Maxwell, *Opening Civil Marriage to Same-Gender Couples: A Netherlands-United States Comparison*, 18 ARIZ. J. INT'L & COMP. L. 141, 206 (2001).

173. *See, e.g.*, Caroline Forder, *An Undutchable Family Law: Partnership, Parenthood, Social Parenthood, Names and Some Article 8 ECHR Case Law, in* THE INTERNATIONAL SURVEY OF FAMILY LAW 1997 259, 263 (Andrew Bainham ed., Martinus Nijhoff Publishers 1999); Sumner, *supra* note 137, at 19–21.

174. *See* Kathleen Kiernan, *Cohabitation in Western Europe*, 96 POPULATION TRENDS 25, 24 (Table 1) (1999); Matthijs Kalmijn, *Explaining Cross-national Differences in Marriage*,

Household Panel, a large-scale longitudinal study carried out by the European Union, reported that 19.7 percent of all women between the ages of twenty and twenty-four in France were cohabiting, and so were 25.9 percent of all women aged twenty-five to twenty-nine.[175] By the end of the millennium, one in six heterosexual couples in France was unmarried.[176] One factor in this high rate of cohabitation may be the relatively high age of marriage in France compared to many European countries and the United States—29.7 years for men and 27.7 for women in 1998, although it is hard to separate cause from effect in this.[177]

There is a long history of so-called *unions libres*, or free unions, in France, but the Napoleonic Code regarded cohabitants as legal strangers: "They don't want law, law pays no regard to them."[178] As in other countries, the trend to increasing rates of cohabitation started with the working class and was related to difficulty finding stable employment.[179] As growing numbers of cohabitants faced legal problems, France dealt with those problems under the law of concubinage. *Concubins*, the French term for cohabitants, were opposite-sex couples sharing a sexual relationship and a common life of some stability, duration, and public acknowledgement.[180]

In response to issues arising when cohabitants' relationships dissolved, French courts developed a jurisprudence somewhat similar to that under the constructive trust doctrine in common law countries, with causes of action based on *société de fait*, or *de facto* partnership, and *enrichissement sans cause*, or unjust enrichment.[181] Under the law pertaining to *de facto* partnership, a cohabitant was entitled to be reimbursed for whatever he or

Cohabitation, and Divorce in Europe, 1990–2000, 61 POPULATION STUD. 243, 249 (Table 1) (2007).

175. Maria Iacovou, *Regional Differences in the Transition to Adulthood*, 580 ANNALS AM. ACAD. POLIT. & SOC. SCI. 40, 55 (Table 3) (2002).

176. Rebecca Probert, *From Lack of Status to Contract: Assessing the French* Pacte Civil de Solidarité, 23 J. SOC. WELFARE & FAM. L. 257, 259 (2001).

177. Claude Martin & Irène Théry, *The PACS and Marriage and Cohabitation in France*, 15 INT'L J. L., POL'Y & FAM. 135, 136 (2001).

178. *Id.* at 142.

179. Catherine Villeneuve-Gokalp, *From Marriage to Informal Union: Recent Changes in the Behaviour of French Couples*, 3 POPULATION 81, 95–102 (1991).

180. CAROLINE MÉCARY & FLORA LEROY-FORGEOT, QUE SAIS-JE?: LE PACS 84 (Presses Universitaires de France 2000).

181. Martin & Théry, *supra* note 177, at 142.

she had contributed to the partnership; if they had both actively participated in acquiring the property, the law then considered it to be held by the two as partners.[182] The cause of action for unjust enrichment, on the other hand, required that one party confer a benefit upon the other that it was unjust to allow the second party to retain. Litigation brought on this basis was unlikely to yield a satisfactory result for a typical cohabitant. In one case involving an 18-year relationship, for example, the court found no unjust enrichment because the female partner did not contribute more than would be a reasonable contribution to the costs of their common life.[183] In other words, she had already enjoyed the benefits during the relationship. Concubines were not one another's heirs and were even limited in the amount they could leave one another by will if a testamentary provision deprived family members of what was regarded as their fair share.[184] Concubines did, however, have a cause of action for the wrongful death of a cohabitant and could sue for damages arising out of the rupture of their relationship.[185]

Cohabitants also had a number of public law rights. They were able to get a residency permit for an immigrant partner and were entitled to make health decisions for a disabled partner.[186] They were covered under a partner's health insurance after having lived together for twelve months if they were totally dependent upon the partner, although this benefit became meaningless after a 1998 reform extended universal health insurance to everyone on an individual basis.[187] There could be a downside to treatment as a couple as well, as a partner's income was taken into account in calculating social welfare benefits. For example, caretakers of children receive a family allowance in France, but a cohabitant would lose the additional allowance given to a single mother.[188] Opposite-sex cohabitants were also entitled to transfer of a lease held by a partner who either left the premises or died.[189]

Same-sex cohabitants were excluded from these benefits. The growing strength of the movement for gay and lesbian rights in the 1980s and 1990s

---

182. MÉCARY & LEROY-FORGEOT, *supra* note 180, at 92.

183. *Id.* at 95–96.

184. *Id.* at 100–101.

185. *Id.* at 106–08.

186. *Id.* at 104, 106.

187. *Id.* at 112–13; Martin & Théry, *supra* note 177, at 143.

188. MÉCARY & LEROY-FORGEOT, *supra* note 180, at 115–16.

189. *Id.* at 110–11.

focused public attention upon the human problems that resulted from their lack of these rights. In particular, the AIDS epidemic publicized the plight of cohabitants who were evicted from a couple's accommodations upon the death of their partner if the title or lease was in the deceased partner's name.[190] Same-sex cohabitants brought suit under the law of concubinage to be allowed to stay on in the lodging under these circumstances, but the Court of Cassation held in 1989 and again in 1997 that same-sex cohabitants were not included within the protections of the law of concubinage.[191] The result was a campaign that culminated in passage of the Pacte Civil de Solidarité, or Civil Solidarity Pact, popularly known as the PACS.

As the demand to reform the law concerning same-sex cohabitants grew louder, it finally reached the ears of the National Assembly. Bills to establish some kind of civil partnership were submitted, debated, amended, and resubmitted in 1997 and 1998.[192] One of the original drafts would have assimilated partners to married couples with respect to both community of property and inheritance.[193] The bill that finally emerged, however, was a compromise between conservative and liberal forces; and it distinguished between partnership and marriage in a number of ways, including removing any right of inheritance for partners and changing the default property regime from community of property to co-ownership.[194] The French legislature passed the compromise bill on November 15, 1999, establishing the PACS, a status somewhere in between a contract and a civil union. Opposite-sex couples were included within its coverage. Thus, as in The Netherlands, the current French system of rights for opposite-sex cohabitants was an unanticipated by-product of the movement for gay and lesbian rights.

To distinguish the new status from civil marriage, which is performed in a ceremony before the mayor at the town hall, a PACS is entered by registering it with the town clerk, a minor official.[195] Although the clerk then causes

---

190. Xavier Tracol, *The Pacte Civil de Solidarité*, *in* LEGAL RECOGNITION OF SAME-SEX COUPLES IN EUROPE (Katharina Boele-Woelki & Angelika Fuchs eds., Intersentia 2003); Martin & Théry, *supra* note 177, at 140.

191. MÉCARY & LEROY-FORGEOT, *supra* note 180, at 9, 110–12; Martin & Théry, *supra* note 177, at 146–47.

192. Martin & Théry, *supra* note 177, at 147–50.

193. *Id.* at 148.

194. *Id.* at 149.

195. Apparently a number of powerful mayors were refusing to perform gay marriages. Wilfried Rault, *The Best Way to Court. The French Mode of Registration and Its Impact on*

the registration to be noted on the birth certificates of each partner, the sexes of the partners are not recorded.[196] This confidentiality is apparently a reaction to the sad French history of rounding up and deporting homosexuals during World War II.[197] The contract, or pact, which the couple gives to the registrar can be entirely individualized; the two can set out whatever arrangements they wish in it concerning property, support, and other terms of their relationship. However, 98 percent of partners sign a one-line contract simply stating that they are entering into a PACS under the law of November 15, 1999.[198]

In the absence of other provisions in their individual pact, the 1999 law provided that the partners' property would be assumed to be jointly owned, and that they were jointly liable for their household debts.[199] While partners were entitled to succeed to tenancies and given health insurance and social security protections, they were excluded from both pension rights and inheritance.[200] After a certain period of time, they received some tax breaks, including the right to file joint returns and to avoid onerous inheritance taxes.[201] Their union was defined as a contract between two persons to organize their common life.[202] They were exhorted to render mutual aid and support to one another, but the manner of doing so was to be spelled out in their pact rather than in the law itself.[203] Other minor benefits included certain employment law rights, such as the right to vacations at the same time, to transfer if one's partner was transferred to another location, to family leaves, and the like.[204]

---

the Social Significance of Partnerships, in SAME-SEX COUPLES, SAME-SEX PARTNERSHIPS, AND HOMOSEXUAL MARRIAGES: A FOCUS ON CROSS-NATIONAL DIFFERENTIALS 27, 29 (Marie Digoix & Patrick Festy eds., Ined 2004). Couples entering a PACS compensate for the mundane nonceremony by placing announcements in the newspaper, showing up for the registration with many people and in distinctive clothes, and throwing private parties with their own ceremonies. Id. at 32.

196. Martin & Théry, supra note 177, at 151.

197. Interview with Caroline Mécary, Attorney, in Paris, France (July 1, 2005).

198. Tracol, supra note 190, at 79; Interview with Caroline Mécary, supra note 197.

199. Martin & Théry, supra note 177, at 150; Tracol, supra note 190, at 73–74.

200. Martin & Théry, supra note 177, at 150–51; Tracol, supra note 190, at 74.

201. Probert, supra note 176, at 259.

202. CODE CIVIL [C. CIV.] art. 515-1 (Katharina Boele-Woelki & Angelika Fuchs eds., Intersentia 2003) (Fr.).

203. Id. at art. 515-4.

204. MÉCARY & LEROY-FORGEOT, supra note 180, at 72–73.

At the same time, the new law included concubinage as a separate legal status, defined as "a *de facto* union characterized by a common life of stability and continuity, between two persons, of different sex or the same sex, who live as a couple."[205] Thus, the preexisting law governing cohabitants was both recognized as continuing to exist alongside the new status and extended to apply to same-sex couples as well.

A PACS differs from a marriage in how it can be terminated. Unilateral no-fault divorce is unavailable in France, so that it may take a long time to get divorced if one party does not consent.[206] A PACS can be terminated immediately, either by consent or if one of the parties marries; it can also be terminated with three months notice in the absence of mutual consent.[207] However, a form of damage remedy apparently remains available to all cohabitants and partners for harms caused by rupture of their relationship.[208] While most people assume that termination of a PACS is much easier than a divorce, if the partners have children, they face the difficulty of undergoing litigation in two different court systems to resolve all the issues—one to end the PACS and determine the terms of property settlement and/or damages and another to deal with the custody, care, and support of children.[209]

Being a compromise, the provisions of the PACS law continued to be debated after it was passed, especially the delay in receiving income tax benefits and the exclusion of partners from inheritance.[210] Some persons interviewed soon after entering into a PACS early in the existence of the new status, wished that the PACS were treated more like marriage; others wanted to maintain its distinctiveness and the freedom from traditional marriage.[211] A report commissioned by the Ministry of Justice and published in November 2004 recommended a number of changes after five years of experience with the PACS, including:

- spelling out the obligations included in mutual aid and support
- redefining the liability for mutual debts so as to make them not more onerous than those of spouses, who are not liable for excessive expenditures

---

205. CODE CIVIL [C. CIV.] art. 515-8 (Fr.) (translation by author).

206. *See* CODE CIVIL [C. CIV.] art. 237-40 (Fr.).

207. *Id.* at art. 515-7.

208. Martin & Théry, *supra* note 177, at 78–79.

209. Probert, *supra* note 176, at 261; Interview with Caroline Mécary, *supra* note 197.

210. GÉRARD IGNASSE, LES PACSÉS: ENQUÊTE SUR LES SIGNATAIRES D'UN PACTE CIVIL DE SOLIDARITÉ 94 (L'Harmattan 2002).

211. *Id.* at 94–97.

- changing the default property regime to separate property rather than co-ownership
- adding specificity about the possibility of compensation at termination of the relationship for damages arising out of a partner's contribution to the couple's common life
- abolishing the delay for abatement of gift taxes
- adopting an income tax regime identical to that for spouses, that is, with automatic joint filing status
- extending more employment rights so that partners were assimilated to married couples in this respect
- extending workers' compensation coverage
- conferring pension rights after a ten-year period of cohabitation[212]

Some of these reforms had been passed by 2009, including changing the default property regime from joint to separate ownership, automatic joint income taxation, and redefinition of the partners' joint liability for debts to align it with that of spouses.[213] The Ministry of Justice report also pointed to the need to educate the public about the differences between marriage and partnership and the desirability of partners drawing up more detailed contracts (although it was also concerned that the procedure for entering a PACS not become too costly as a result of the need to make extensive use of legal representation).[214]

Although debate may have ensued over its provisions, the PACS proved extremely popular with heterosexual cohabitants in France. By September 2004, 131,651 pacts had been concluded, and 15,641 had been dissolved, 11 percent of them by the partners' marriage, 81 percent by agreement, and less than 5 percent unilaterally.[215] After the first three years, there had been very few legal disputes resulting from dissolution of the new partnerships.[216]

---

212. MINISTRY OF JUSTICE, REPORT, LE PACTE CIVIL DE SOLIDARITÉ: REFLEXIONS ET PROPOSITIONS DE REFORME (2004).

213. Le Régime Patrimonial des Pacsés, LE MONDE, Oct. 7, 2007; Mariage ou Pacs, les Limites de L'harmonisation, LE MONDE, Nov. 25, 2007 (concerning changes in tax treatment); CODE CIVIL [C. CIV.] art. 515-4 (Fr.). (changing liability for debts and excluding manifestly excessive expenses).

214. MINISTRY OF JUSTICE, REPORT, supra note 212, at 7–8.

215. Id. at 5.

216. Daniell Borrillo & Eric Fassin, The PACS, Four Years Later: A Beginning or an End?, in SAME-SEX COUPLES, SAME-SEX PARTNERSHIPS, AND HOMOSEXUAL MARRIAGES: A FOCUS ON CROSS-NATIONAL DIFFERENTIALS 19, 23 (Marie Digoix & Patrick Festy eds., Ined 2004).

According to the National Institute for Statistics and Economics Studies, 106,000 new PACS were registered during the first three quarters of 2008, with almost 140,000 expected for the year as a whole, making the ratio of PACS to marriages one to two.[217] Although it is prohibited to record the sexes of the persons entering into a PACS, the Institute estimated (typically these estimates have been based on inquiries by journalists) that 94 percent of the PACS in 2008 were between opposite-sex couples.[218] In short, the PACS has become an extremely popular institution in France, competing with marriage. Yet there continues to be a political will to maintain the distinction between it and marriage, which presumably underlies some of the key differences such as the exclusion of partners from inheritance, joint adoption, and automatic fatherhood status (an unmarried father must officially recognize his child within the first year of its life to obtain joint custody).[219]

It is unlikely that the PACS would be similarly suited to the United States. This is so in part for reasons similar to those discussed in connection with the Dutch model. Both France and The Netherlands have social welfare systems that protect individuals who do not register their partnerships. In both countries, cohabiting couples also receive many benefits under various laws even if they do not register. This would not be so in the United States. And even in France, as commentary in *Le Monde* points out, only marriage truly protects a vulnerable party at the end of a relationship.[220]

Moreover, the PACS and concubinage regimes as currently constituted are excessively complicated and not fully understood by most people. They result in a strange hierarchy of differing rights, depending upon whether one marries, enters a PACS, or lives with a partner informally. One needs to understand what benefits or obligations fall under the PACS law and which under the law of concubinage. Of course, French law may move toward an equivalence of the benefits and obligations of PACS and marriage, as seems

---

217. *Naissances, décès, mariages: la France en chiffres selon l'Insee,* Jan. 13, 2009, *available at* http//www.insee.fr.

218. *Id.*

219. MÉCARY & LEROY-FORGEOT, *supra* note 180, at 10; *see also* Daniel Borrillo & Kees Waaldijk, *Major Legal Consequences of Marriage, Cohabitation and Registered Partnership for Different-sex and Same-sex Partners in France, in* MORE OR LESS TOGETHER: LEVELS OF LEGAL CONSEQUENCES OF MARRIAGE, COHABITATION AND REGISTERED PARTNERSHIPS FOR DIFFERENT-SEX AND SAME-SEX PARTNERS: A COMPARATIVE STUDY OF NINE EUROPEAN COUNTRIES 93–102, *available at* http://www-same-sex.ined.fr/publica_doc125.htm (charting all the legal rights and obligations available in France in a comparative study with other nations).

220. *Mieux Vaut Être Marié En Cas de Séparation,* LE MONDE, June 25, 2006.

to have been happening. One of the advantages of an assimilationist approach to cohabitants' rights is that the incidents attached to the status are clear, at least to the extent that people know what marriage entails legally.

Finally, the process by which the new French law came into being was very different from the manner in which law reform is likely to take place in the United States. The process was piecemeal but unique—that is, after a broad national debate on cohabitants' rights, the national legislature passed a bill containing what was to be a comprehensive treatment of the issue; after its passage, the new law has been amended piecemeal year by year, with all of the changes so far in the direction of making the PACS more like marriage. Quite apart from the fact that the law governing cohabitants could never be reformed by the national legislature under the U.S. Constitution, reform in America is much more likely to take place piecemeal by treating one issue after another, such as happened in Canada.

6. Sweden and Neutrality Between Cohabitation and Marriage

Sweden has a long history of informal cohabitation. The practice was common among both rural and urban working-class people even before the beginning of the twentieth century.[221] The tradition appears to have been strongest in the sparsely populated north of the country.[222] Cohabitation is still widespread. About 50 percent of all couples are unmarried in Sweden, the highest rate in all of Europe.[223] In fact, until quite recently Swedish statistics did not even distinguish between married and unmarried couples.[224] It is estimated that there were about 1.2 million cohabitants in Sweden in 2002,

---

221. *See* MARY ANN GLENDON, THE TRANSFORMATION OF FAMILY LAW: STATE, LAW, AND FAMILY IN THE UNITED STATES AND WESTERN EUROPE 273-74 (Univ. of Chicago Press 1989); D. Bradley, *Unmarried Cohabitation in Sweden: A Renewed Social Institution?*, 11 J. LEG. HIST. 300, 301–03 (1990) (tracing the practice of cohabitation further back than the nineteenth century).

222. Anders Agell, *The Swedish Legislation on Marriage and Cohabitation: A Journey Without a Destination* 9, 17, *in* SCANDINAVIAN STUDIES IN LAW, Vol. 24 (Folke Schmidt ed., Almqvist & Wiksell 1980).

223. GÖREN LIND, COMMON LAW MARRIAGE: A LEGAL INSTITUTION FOR COHABITATION 788–89 (Oxford Univ. Press 2008).

224. Ulla Björnberg, *Cohabitation and Marriage in Sweden—Does Family Form Matter?*, 15 INT'L J. L., POL'Y & FAM. 350, 351 (2002).

out of a population of some 8.8 million total.[225] More than 50 percent of children are born to unmarried parents.[226] And fully 90 percent of Swedish cohabitants consider their relationships to be comparable to marriage.[227]

It is therefore not at all surprising that Sweden was one of the first nations to begin to adapt its system of laws to the legal problems of cohabitants. A drive for increased legal recognition of unmarried couples arose out of the openly socialist and feminist goals of the Swedish Social Democratic Party in the 1930s, influenced especially by Gunnar and Alva Myrdal; ironically, their policies were intended to increase both the rate of marriage and the birthrate.[228] The aim was to encourage childrearing in modern egalitarian families by socializing many of its costs, while also making women economically independent of and equal to men.[229] In pursuit of these goals, by the 1970s, the Swedish government established well-equipped and attractive child care facilities staffed by trained teachers, as well as after-school centers and vacation care for children up to the age of twelve, with the costs heavily subsidized by the state or free. In addition, Swedish parents are entitled to paid family leave for the first year of their child's life, and children's allowances are paid regardless of marital status.[230]

The principles underlying the Swedish socialist-feminist family policies were laid out in a 1968 report by Alva Myrdal:

> The point of departure must be that every adult is responsible for his/her own support. Benefits previously inherent in married status should be eliminated or transferred to children.[231]

---

225. Åke Saldeen, *Sweden: Cohabitation Outside Marriage or Partnership, in* THE INTERNATIONAL SURVEY OF FAMILY LAW 2005 EDITION 503 (Andrew Bainham ed., Jordan Publishing 2005).

226. Björnberg, *supra* note 224, at 351.

227. Agell, *supra* note 222, at 18.

228. *See* Allan Carlson, *Deconstruction of Marriage: The Swedish Case*, 44 SAN DIEGO L. REV. 153, 155–59 (2007).

229. *Id.* at 156–57.

230. *See, e.g.*, RUTH SIDEL, WOMEN & CHILDREN LAST: THE PLIGHT OF POOR WOMEN IN AFFLUENT AMERICA 180–87 (Penguin 1986). *See also* Linda Haas, *Family Policy in Sweden*, 17 J. FAM. & ECON. ISSUES 47, 80–85 (1996) (describing the continued commitment of the Swedish government to high-quality subsidized day care for all children despite economic downturn and the replacement of the Social Democrats by a more conservative government).

231. Carlson, *supra* note 228, at 161, quoting THE WORKING GROUP ON EQUALITY, TOWARDS EQUALITY: THE ALVA MYRDAL REPORT 82 (1971).

The report argued that no preference should be given by the state to any form of cohabitation, referring by this term to both married and unmarried couples.[232] The Swedish government translated these goals into what is known as the principle of neutrality, described by the Ministry of Justice in 1969 as requiring that all legislation be neutral as to different forms of living together, so as to allow everyone the freedom of choice to construct their personal lives for themselves without any influence by the state.[233] Thus, as one author reported in 1980, "an effort to secure factual uniform treatment irrespective of marital status has for the last two decades been a guideline in the legislation in different areas within social and tax law."[234]

This guideline resulted in substantial changes in the laws affecting both cohabitation and marriage. One author argues that the most important change was the abolition of joint income tax returns in 1971; since then, all of the notoriously high income taxes in Sweden have been calculated on an individual basis, ending the treatment of married couples as economic units, a reform that benefits two-income couples and penalizes traditional one-breadwinner families.[235] In addition, joint marital liability for debts was abolished, with the goal of giving spouses increased independence of one another.[236] At the same time, benefits enjoyed by married couples, including widows' pensions, housing allowances, and the right to sue for loss of a breadwinner, were extended to cohabitants who were living together in circumstances resembling marriage (or, for some benefits, who had a child).[237] Apart from the need of an unmarried father to register his paternity, there are no distinctions between married and unmarried parents with respect to their children—their rights of custody and obligations of support are identical.[238] Other benefits available to cohabitants in Sweden include exemption from inheritance taxes, ease of getting residency and citizenship for a foreign partner, the right

---

232. *Id.*, quoting THE WORKING GROUP ON EQUALITY, at 38.

233. Agell, *supra* note 222, at 21.

234. *Id.* at 23.

235. Carlson, *supra* note 228, at 162–63.

236. *Id.* at 166.

237. Agell, *supra* note 222, at 28–31. *See also* David Bradley, *The Development of a Legal Status for Unmarried Cohabitation in Sweden*, 18 ANGLO-AM. L. REV. 322, 323–25 (1989).

238. Agell, *supra* note 222, at 33–34.

to refuse to testify against one another, and status as next-of-kin for medical and other purposes.[239]

The reforms based on the principle of neutrality culminated in passage of the Cohabitees (Joint Homes) Act in 1987.[240] A new but similar edition of the same act went into effect in 2003.[241] Cohabitees are defined by the current statute as two persons who live together on a permanent basis as a couple and have a joint household.[242] The impact of the legislation is to make a kind of marital property out of any dwelling and furnishings that have been acquired for a cohabiting couple's joint use, even if they are owned by only one of the two. Neither may sell this property without the other's consent; and if they separate, one of the cohabitees may apply to the court for division of the property or the right to remain in the joint home.[243] After household debts have been deducted, there is a presumption that this property will be equally divided between the two.[244] If one cohabitant dies, the other is to receive a specified amount out of the property pertaining to their joint home.[245] Similar principles apply to rented housing, and the person with greater need (typically the custodian of children) is entitled to take over use of the dwelling, rented or owned.[246] Although these provisions can be altered by a contract between the cohabitants, almost no cohabitants in fact make

---

239. Hans Ytterberg & Kees Waaldijk, *Major Legal Consequences of Marriage, Cohabitation and Registered Partnerships for Different-sex and Same-sex Partners in Sweden, in* MORE OR LESS TOGETHER, *supra* note 219.

240. The 1987 Cohabitees (Joint Homes) Act had antecedents in 1973 legislation giving courts the power to make orders affecting cohabitants' homes, including rights to transfer the tenancy upon termination of a marriage-like cohabiting relationship. Bradley, *supra* note 237, at 325.

241. *See Cohabitees and Their Joint Homes–A Brief Presentation of the Cohabitees Act* 2 (Aug. 2003), *available at* http://www.sweden.gov.se/sb/d/574/a/16218.

242. *Id.* at 4. Having a joint household is interpreted by Swedish courts in terms of time, the presence of children, and sharing of housekeeping expenses. Anne Barlow, *Regulation of Cohabitation, Changing Family Policies and Social Attitudes: A Discussion of Britain Within Europe*, 26 L. & POL'Y 57, 62 (2004).

243. *Cohabitees and Their Joint Homes*, *supra* note 241, at 5–7.

244. *Id.* at 8.

245. *Id.* at 9.

246. *Id.* at 10. On provisions of the Cohabitees (Joint Homes) Act, *see also* Björnberg, *supra* note 224, at 352; GLENDON, *supra* note 221, at 276; Bradley, *supra* note 237, at 324–33.

either a contract or a will.[247] Moreover, certain provisions cannot be altered by contract if the couple has minor children in the home.[248]

These changes in the Swedish law governing marriage and cohabitation do not obliterate the differences between the two. Cohabitants, for example, cannot inherit in the absence of a will, and they are not entitled to support at the end of their relationships except for care of their children.[249] Moreover, the property provisions described above apply only to particular assets—homes acquired for joint use—and not to any other assets or property acquired during the cohabitants' relationship.[250] However, as Mary Ann Glendon has pointed out, neither inheritance nor property other than a home is important for most Swedish couples today.[251] Given the very high tax rates, few couples have substantial assets other than their home, and few have accumulated assets to bestow upon their heirs. Moreover, continuing support of an ex-partner is very rare in Sweden even upon divorce, given the underlying assumptions about individuals being responsible for their own support.[252] Individuals are assumed to be economically independent and capable of supporting themselves after dissolution of a relationship or the death of a partner, and the state enables them to be independent by providing pension schemes, workers' compensation, and the many benefits of the social welfare system, including housing assistance, universal free health care, and child care. This philosophy assumes full employment, but the Swedish state also provides a basic minimum safety net for all individuals in need. As a consequence, although there continue to be distinctions between the legal treatment of marriage and cohabitation, the Swedish social contract reduces or eliminates any harmful effects of those differences.

Despite erasure of the impact of differences between the legal status of cohabitants and that of married couples, the majority of cohabitants surveyed in Sweden in 1999 expected to get married at some point: the proportion who at age thirty expected to be married within five years was 75 percent.[253]

---

247. Björnberg, *supra* note 224, at 355.

248. Bradley, *supra* note 237, at 328.

249. *See Cohabitees and Their Joint Homes, supra* note 241, at 11.

250. Bradley, *supra* note 237, at 331.

251. GLENDON, *supra* note 221, at 275.

252. Carlson, *supra* note 228, at 164.

253. Eva Bernhardt, *Cohabitation or Marriage? Preferred Living Arrangements in Sweden* 4 (2004), *available at* http://www.oif.ac.at/sdf/sdf04-04-bernhardt.pdf.

About one-third did not have any current plans to marry, with those in very long-term relationships the most likely to have no plans.[254] Those who were highly educated, older, and lived in metropolitan areas were more likely to expect to marry, but parenthood did not play a role in their decision to wed.[255]

The Swedish Cohabitees Act applies to both opposite- and same-sex couples. However, in 1995, a system of registered partnerships with rights comparable to those of married couples was established for same-sex couples, which was superseded in 2009 by the availability of same-sex marriage.[256] The legislature considered extending the registered partnerships to opposite-sex couples as well but rejected the option of requiring registration for all cohabitants as a condition of their equal (or neutral) treatment, even though it would simplify the identification of a cohabiting relationship. It opted instead to retain the current system of protections for all cohabitants, specifically because those most in need of protection would be unlikely to register.[257] These benefits and obligations are instead imposed upon cohabitants without their consent.

These features of Swedish law have caused one knowledgeable observer of cohabitation law in Europe to conclude that Sweden is the only European country that has responded to new family forms "by taking a deliberately functional approach based on social needs."[258] Although Sweden has created a tiered system, placing marriage above cohabitation in the order of relationships, Anne Barlow maintains that:

> Sweden has created a legal framework where the tiering is transparent, relatively easy to identify and understand while at the same time providing adequate family law-style regulation for other functionally identified informal families in line with the protective aims of family law.[259]

In short, the model of cohabitation law adopted by Sweden appears to fulfill the underlying purposes of family law, at least in that context.

---

254. *Id.*

255. *Id.*

256. Carlson, *supra* note 228, at 167.

257. Saldeen, *supra* note 225, at 505.

258. Barlow, *supra* note 16, at 61.

259. *Id.* at 63.

Would the Swedish model work as well in the United States? The answer to this question is clearly no. The transformation of family law in Sweden arose out of and is linked in necessary ways to a major socialization of that society that is unimaginable in the near future in the United States. Swedish law would not adequately protect vulnerable cohabitants if it did not coexist with national health insurance, universally available child care, and the many, comprehensive income-support mechanisms of the Swedish social welfare state and its national commitment to the substantive equality of women. None of these preconditions exist in the United States at present and, given the very high rates of taxation required to fund them, are not feasible in the present political climate. In short, it is still important, whatever one's ideological preferences may be, to privatize many of the costs of protecting vulnerable family members in the United States.

In sum, none of the six models described in this chapter provides a perfect model for the United States to follow in reforming its own legal treatment of cohabitants, although the Canadian system comes perhaps the closest. The English system is inadequate in its protections for cohabitants. The Australian system is better but still not comprehensive in its protections and requires cumbersome proof of factors to establish that a couple is in a *de facto* relationship. The systems in France and The Netherlands depend at least in part upon registration, and the vulnerable parties the law on cohabitation should seek to protect are the least likely to register. Finally, both in France and The Netherlands and to a much greater extent in Sweden, a variety of social welfare measures that do not exist in the United States protect cohabitants who do not register in the first two and fill in whatever gaps exist in the protections available in Sweden. That is true to some extent in Canada as well.

Despite the fact that none of these models is perfect, they do illustrate the great variety of ways in which states can protect cohabitants, and perhaps some aspects can borrowed from them. In the next chapter, I outline and discuss specific recommendations for what might be an ideal system for the United States.

SIX SIX

A New Law for Cohabitants in the United States

IN THIS CHAPTER, I make specific recommendations for how the law governing cohabitation in the United States should be changed. The discussion in the previous five chapters was a necessary precondition for a number of reasons. First, reforms in the law should be made in light of the goals of our family law system and its underlying priorities. As set forth in the introductory chapter, the priority should be to protect persons made vulnerable as a result of the family relationships in which they live and to extend benefits and impose responsibilities as necessary to this goal. The benefits provided may also help stabilize cohabiting relationships and thus improve the lives of people living in cohabitant households, especially children. It is also important to allow a couple not desiring to undertake commitments to one another to avoid doing so, and not to cast the net so wide that short-term cohabitants or those unlikely to have developed mutual dependencies will be caught in it. This is not always possible. When these goals conflict, I argue that priority should be given to protection of the vulnerable.

Second, reforms should be designed in light of what we know about the history of cohabitation and its legal treatment in the United States, the subject of Chapters 1 and 2. The lesson to be derived from that story is that the approaches to the legal problems of cohabitants adopted thus far have not been successful either in preventing exploitation of the weaker party in these relationships or in promoting the goals of family law to protect the vulnerable and to stabilize family units.

Third, it is important to take into account empirical data about the groups that make up the majority of cohabitants in the United States and to consider why they cohabit instead of marrying, the subject of Chapter 3. We now have a great deal of social scientific data about the institution of cohabitation in the United States—its instability as compared to marriage (also an unstable institution, but less so), the economic interdependence of most cohabitants, the quality of their relationships, the potential for violence, and the impact of cohabitation on children living in these family units. These data and their

221

implications for the law, discussed in Chapter 4, lead me to conclude that legal protections for cohabitants should be substantially increased.

The experience of other countries, the subject of Chapter 5, provides information about different models of legal treatment of cohabitation and how each model has been working in a particular context. This discussion reveals that the United States is almost unique in its failure to provide substantial protections for unmarried couples in an era when cohabitation has become common. U.S. law must be designed for the local context, one in which cohabitation is widespread but the state has not undertaken to build the safety nets that exist in other nations for persons who are disadvantaged in the market. As a result, it is necessary to privatize welfare functions that might elsewhere be the responsibility of the state and to extend to cohabitants public support systems now available only to married persons.

In light of the research described in this book, I have reached a number of other conclusions.

First, a legal system requiring cohabitants to register in order to obtain any protections will not fulfill the family law goals I have articulated. The most vulnerable cohabitants are the ones least likely to register, and the United States does not have a social welfare system adequate to take care of those who fall through the cracks.

Second, a system based upon status rather than upon contract or property law is most appropriate for this setting. Contract-based remedies have been tried and found wanting, even in California, the state of *Marvin v. Marvin*, because intimate partners typically do not make contracts, and any implied agreements are difficult to prove in court. Moreover, property law or equitable remedies are not designed to fulfill the functions underlying family law. They are also cumbersome, expensive, and yield inconsistent results.

Third, the manner in which the status of cohabitant is defined should be simple, not requiring proof under a long list of factors, with all the attendant costs for both the litigant and the court system.

Fourth, the legal treatment of cohabitants should be comprehensive rather than piecemeal. A qualifying couple should enjoy the same rights and be subject to the same obligations as a married couple for all purposes, rather than simply for property distribution and support, as some have suggested.[1]

---

1. *See, e.g.*, Elizabeth Scott, *Marriage, Cohabitation and Collective Responsibility for Dependency*, 2004 U. CHI. LEGAL F. 225 (2004) (arguing for maintaining the privileged position of

I reach this conclusion because most cohabitants in the United States do not have accumulated property to distribute and are unable to pay adequate support. For these persons, to be treated as married by the state and third parties can be much more important—to have status as survivors under the social security laws, for example, and as litigants in tort cases. It is interesting to note that most of these rights against third parties have been extended by statute to cohabitants in virtually all of the other countries surveyed in Chapter 5, and these statutes were passed without controversy, in some cases a decade or more ago. A comprehensive approach is also preferable because it is impossible to tell in advance what statutory benefit or other legal treatment will prove critical to the welfare of a cohabiting couple and the children in their household. Moreover, treating cohabitants differently for different purposes is administratively burdensome. By contrast, the legal incidents of marriage are well settled and thus easily understood and applied by the courts.

Finally, it is clear from the diversity of groups that cohabit in the United States that no one-size-fits-all model will suffice. A number of options should be available, and the choice of opting out should be accessible to all.

※ 1. Recommendations for Reform of U.S. Law

The legal remedies provided to cohabitants in the United States should be multiple and layered. My recommendations include three layers: (1) domestic partners who have been together two years or have a child should be treated as though they were married; (2) the ability to contract out of these obligations should be easily available for couples who do not wish to be treated as though they were married; and (3) a system for registration as domestic partners should be provided, accompanied by all the benefits and burdens of marriage unless the partners design their own individual contract delimiting their rights vis-à-vis one another.

---

marriage but extending improved contract-based remedies to cohabitants). *See also* Milton C. Regan, Jr., *Calibrated Commitment: The Legal Treatment of Marriage and Cohabitation*, 76 NOTRE DAME L. REV. 1435, 1450–61 (2001) (arguing for the protection of vulnerable parties on a claim-by-claim basis, extending rights in certain categories of cases and not others).

1.1. Imposition by Law of Quasi-marital Status on Cohabitants After Two Years or a Child

After they have been living together for two years or have a child, a cohabiting couple should be treated by the law as though they were married. This status would be imposed on a couple without their consent, similar to the proposal of the American Law Institute.[2] The ALI remedies are presumptively available to individuals who have cohabited for a state-defined period and who act jointly with respect to household management or have a common child; others may establish that they are domestic partners through proof of a number of factors having to do with intimacy and interdependence.[3] My proposal is different in two important ways. First, it eliminates the proof-by-factors method of establishing partnership and substitutes the nondiscretionary approach of "two years or a child." This approach is preferable both because a factors approach makes too much work for the court system and, more importantly, because it gives too much discretion to judges, who have often shown bias against cohabitants' rights when deciding cohabitation contract cases.[4]

Second, the ALI Principles provide only divorce-style remedies upon dissolution of the relationship, including property distribution and maintenance, and no rights against third parties or the state. These are most useful to relatively well-off couples who have property or income to share after separating their households. My approach, by contrast, treats the couple as though they were married for all purposes, thus entitling them to inheritance; rights to sue for wrongful death, negligent infliction of emotional distress, and loss of consortium; rights to social security survivors benefits, workers' compensation, and taxation as a coupled unit; and rights in the private sphere such as eligibility for family health insurance, next-of-kin status

---

2. *See* AMERICAN LAW INSTITUTE, PRINCIPLES OF THE LAW OF FAMILY DISSOLUTION: ANALYSIS AND RECOMMENDATIONS, §§ 6.04–6.06, 4.09–4.10, 5.04 (2002) [hereafter ALI PRINCIPLES 2002]. In this sense, the recommended system is also similar to the imposition in Canada of an obligation of support at the end of a cohabiting relationship.

3. *Id.* at § 6.03 (7).

4. *See, e.g.,* Cynthia Grant Bowman, *Legal Treatment of Cohabitation in the United States,* 26 L. & POL'Y 119, 126–27 (2004). It would still be necessary to allow the use of a factors approach for the presumably small number of people who are not really cohabitants yet are caught in the new net of obligation, but the burden of proof would be on a presumed cohabitant to show that he or she is not in fact a cohabitant under the factors prescribed.

in hospitals, and the like. Given the information we have about the groups who most often cohabit, these rights are likely to be of most value to them.

I have chosen two years as the period of time after which cohabitation will be transformed into a quasi-marriage for a number of reasons. This is a time period frequently employed by cohabitation regimes in other countries and recommended by others who have studied the question.[5] More important, statistics concerning cohabitation in the United States indicate that this durational requirement will eliminate large numbers of cohabitants who may not wish or intend legal consequences to be visited upon their relationships. Extrapolating from figures in the Census Bureau's 2008 Annual Social and Economic Supplement, there were almost 6.8 million opposite-sex unmarried-couple households in 2008 and so about 13.6 million individual cohabitants.[6] Taking the NSFH figures on duration from the 1989 Bumpass and Sweet article (which may be low), only about 33 percent of all cohabitants make it past the two-year mark.[7] This group thus probably included about 4.5 million people in 2008. That is a considerable number of individuals who would be affected by this or any policy directed at their legal issues, particularly considering that at least 40 percent of their households contain children.[8] But the two-year period would weed out large numbers of short-term cohabitants, some nine million people in 2008. Supported by the knowledge that

5. *See, e.g.*, ANNE BARLOW, COHABITANTS AND THE LAW 100, 109 (3d ed. Butterworths 2001) (two-year period used for British Inheritance Act claims and Fatal Accident claims); Martha Bailey, *Regulation of Cohabitation and Marriage in Canada*, 26 L. & POL'Y 153, 162 (2004) (two-year period for inheritance and property claims in Saskatchewan); Gostlin v. Kergin, 3 B.C.L.R. 2d 264 (B.C. Ct. App. 1986) (two-year period for maintenance claims in British Columbia); Lindy Willmott et al., *De Facto Relationships Property Adjustment Law—A National Direction*, 17 AUSTRALIAN J. FAM. L. 37, 38 (2003) (two-year period or a child to qualify as *de facto* couple for purposes of property distribution in Queensland, Tasmania, and Western Australia); TASMANIA, RELATIONSHIPS ACT 2003 (No. 44 of 2003), Pt. 5, § 37(1) (two-year period for financial adjustment and maintenance in Tasmania). *See also* Grace Ganz Blumberg, *Cohabitation Without Marriage: A Different Perspective*, 28 UCLA L. Rev. 1125, 1166 (1981) (recommending the two years or a child test for maintenance, property division, and inheritance in an article preceding the ALI Principles by more than twenty years).

6. U.S. CENSUS BUREAU, CURRENT POPULATION SURVEY, 2008 Annual Social and Economic Supplement, *Table UC1. Opposite Sex Unmarried Couples by Labor Force Status of Both Partners: 2008*, *available at* http://www.census.gov/population/www/socdemo/hh-fam/cps2008.html [hereafter CPS 2008].

7. Larry L. Bumpass & James A. Sweet, *National Estimates of Cohabitation*, 26 DEMOGRAPHY 615, 620 (1989).

8. CPS 2008, *supra* note 6, *Table UC3. Opposite Sex Unmarried Couples by Presence of Biological Children Under 18: 2008*.

most cohabitants do commingle their finances, it is reasonable to presume economic interdependence after two years together.

Attachment of these rights upon the birth of a child should need no explanation. A common child presumptively entwines the obligations of the two parents, and studies show that cohabitants with children are identical to married couples in their income-sharing behavior.[9] Even though the custodial parent is entitled to child support regardless of marital status if the union dissolves, this provision provides inadequate protection. The amount awarded in child support is typically insufficient to support most children,[10] and such awards provide no support for the custodial parent, thus indirectly affecting the welfare of the child. By contrast, a married custodial parent is entitled upon divorce to property distribution and possibly alimony, which can be critical to the well-being of his or her child, and is typically awarded possession of the family home as well. A cohabiting custodial parent is entitled to none of this, and the child's welfare is injured by a parent's diminished economic condition. Moreover, a long-term cohabitant who has been the primary caretaker of children who are now adults is without any remedy at all; all of her investment in the household can be lost if the couple's assets are titled in her partner's name.[11] And those assets are likely to be titled in his name if he has brought in more money to the household while she has invested in caretaking and spent most of her wages on the family.

Some scholars suggest that a variety of equitable, contractual, and property law remedies are adequate to address situations like this.[12] I disagree, for

---

9. Carolyn Vogler, *Cohabiting Couples: Rethinking Money in the Household at the Beginning of the Twenty First Century*, 53 SOC. REV. 1, 13 (2005).

10. *See* MARY BECKER ET AL., FEMINIST JURISPRUDENCE: TAKING WOMEN SERIOUSLY 700 (3d ed. 2007).

11. *See* Anne Barlow & Grace James, *Regulating Marriage and Cohabitation in 21st Century Britain*, 67 MOD. L. REV. 143, 148–49 (2004).

12. *See, e.g.,* Marsha Garrison, *Is Consent Necessary? An Evaluation of the Emerging Law of Cohabitant Obligation*, 52 UCLA L. REV. 815, 891–94 (2005). Professor Garrison also suggests that we revive common law marriage. *Id.* at 887–88. I have been a prominent supporter of reviving common law marriage in the past, for reasons similar to those that now drive my proposals for protection of cohabitants. *See* Cynthia Grant Bowman, *A Feminist Proposal to Bring Back Common Law Marriage*, 75 OR. L. REV. 709 (1996). The world, however, has been moving in the opposite direction, and several states have abolished common law marriage since I wrote that article. At any rate, without redefinition, the doctrine would not protect many cohabitants today because it requires that the couple hold themselves out to the world as husband and wife, while modern cohabiting couples neither feel the need to do so nor think of themselves that way.

a number of reasons. Contractual remedies require an agreement by both parties, work best where the two are of roughly equal bargaining power, can be difficult to prove if oral, and have often been interpreted by the courts to exclude contributions that are not easily monetized, so that homemakers' contributions are rarely reimbursed.[13] Remedies based in property law or equity, such as unjust enrichment, *quantum meruit*, and constructive trusts, are similar in this last respect. The typical situation in which they may be of use to cohabitants is where one party has contributed specific amounts of money to the accumulation of property titled in the name of the other partner.[14] These causes of action do not remedy the more typical situation where a female cohabitant contributes to household expenses, devotes labor to her partner's business, or simply takes care of the house and children.[15] This is precisely the area of human behavior that family law, not property law, is designed to address.[16]

Moreover, remedies under property and contract law apply only to the two parties; they cannot confer benefits against third parties or the state. As I've noted above, for many cohabiting couples, there will be no accumulated property to divide; and thus a variety of other benefits are much more important to their welfare, in particular, benefits designed to address situations of dependency, such as workers' compensation and social security survivors' benefits. A long-term caretaking cohabitant would be without any of these support systems if his or her partner died and would not inherit their home and property in the absence of a will. Yet empirical studies show that most cohabitants want a substantial share, if not all, of their estates to go to their partners upon their death even though they fail to make wills, which is the only way this intention can currently be effectuated (except in New Hampshire, with its system of quasi-common law marriage that arises only upon the death of a cohabitant).[17]

---

13. *See* Bowman, *supra* note 4, at 126–29.

14. *See id.* at 123–24.

15. *See, e.g.,* Ann Laquer Estin, *Unmarried Partners and the Legacy of* Marvin v. Marvin: *Ordinary Cohabitation*, 76 NOTRE DAME L. REV. 1381, 1395 (2001).

16. Scholars of equitable remedies also question whether they are appropriate in marriage-like relationships, especially with respect to domestic services. Emily Sherwin, *Love, Money, and Justice: Restitution Between Cohabitants*, 77 U. COLO. L. REV. 711, 729–30 (2006).

17. *See* Mary Louise Fellows et al., *Committed Partners and Inheritance: An Empirical Study*, 16 L. & INEQUALITY 1, 38 (1998); N.H. REV. STAT. ANN. § 457: 39 (2001) (providing that

For all of these reasons, a quasi-marital status should be imposed upon cohabiting couples whose unions have lasted two years or who have a child. To avoid this result, a couple would need to agree to take action before their relationship had lasted more than two years or a child was born. For couples in which the partners disagree, with one partner desiring commitment and the other possibly wanting to take advantage of his partner's contributions while avoiding any obligation, I believe this result is appropriate.

1.2. The Ability of Cohabitants to Contract Out of Obligations

Second, I would allow couples an easily and effectively available option to contract out of undertaking obligations to one another. Setting the terms of cohabitation (or even of marriage) by contract is now allowed by almost every state, although these contracts only affect rights between the two parties. In this case, they would be provided with an opportunity to opt out of being treated as married not just under family law but for all purposes. This proposal would shift the burden from requiring people to contract in to these commitments to requiring cohabitants who wish to avoid commitment to contract out before two years have elapsed. If both agree to opt out, a simple, standardized form should be available, to be notarized and filed with a court without the assistance of a lawyer. It would, of course, be preferable if both parties were advised of the rights they would be giving up, but this is not always required even for premarital contracts waiving legal rights.[18] A pamphlet explaining those rights in simple language should accompany the opt-out form to be filed. Problems arising from the parties' inability to predict the vulnerability and dependency that frequently arise over the course of an intimate relationship will remain; but if the parties agree upon this course of action, these problems should be tolerated in the interest of respecting their autonomy.[19]

---

persons cohabiting and reputed to be husband and wife for three years before the death of one party shall be deemed to have been legally married).

18. *See, e.g.,* Simeone v. Simeone, 581 A.2d 162 (Pa. 1990).

19. If a cohabitant is coerced into signing the contract, it can be challenged under contract law as invalid due to force or duress or as an unconscionable contract when the other partner attempts to enforce it.

If the two partners disagree, this provision gives the party desiring commitment substantial bargaining power. Given what we know about the differing inclinations of women and men for commitment,[20] this will often be the woman; but either party could be in a weaker economic situation or more vulnerable for some other reason. Parties wanting to avoid commitment would then be put to the choice of terminating the relationship and losing whatever advantages they derive from it or having a changed status and its obligations imposed upon them. This system may drive some to leave cohabiting relationships when they might not otherwise have done so. This is not necessarily a bad thing. Some of them—those who are violence-prone or unable to form long-term intimate relationships, for example—would be better left outside marriage-like relationships in general.

What may happen if obligations are imposed upon a commitment-phobic person? Violence is a possible response. But it is also possible, given what we know about the psychology of batterers and the insecurity underlying much of domestic violence, that the increased security this legal change gives to a relationship will lead to a diminution of violence. Moreover, by extending family law remedies to long-term cohabitants, we may also create the conditions under which victims of violence are enabled to leave a cohabiting relationship and rebuild their lives, aided by benefits now provided only to married couples, including economic assistance from the former cohabitant.

1.3. A System of Registration for Domestic Partnerships

Third, I advocate allowing cohabitants to register as domestic partners at any time prior to their two-year anniversary if they wish to do so—entering a domestic partnership similar in many respects to that available since 2005 to same-sex couples and to heterosexuals over the age of sixty-two in California.[21] This would allow opposite-sex couples who want to avoid the religious or gender-based assumptions of traditional marriage to enter into a status with

---

20. *See supra* at 171–72; *see also* Carol Smart, *Stories of Family Life: Cohabitation, Marriage and Social Change*, 17 CAN. J. FAM. L. 20, 39 (2000) (describing how male cohabitants in England placed more emphasis on maintaining their independence, while female cohabitants felt they were already very committed, even if privately).

21. *See* California Domestic Partner Rights and Responsibilities Act, CAL. FAM. CODE § 297.5 (2005).

both its benefits and its burdens, such as the duty of support and common ownership of property. The experience of other countries shows that such a system, although appearing to be superfluous for persons able to marry, is very popular with opposite-sex cohabitants. Although the domestic partnership system parallel to marriage in The Netherlands was set up initially to accommodate gay couples, heterosexuals outnumbered the same-sex couples who registered even before same-sex marriage became available there; heterosexual couples have also been attracted by the Pacte Civil de Solidarité in France since its inception.[22]

This type of domestic partnership would have as its default provision—the terms of the partnership if the partners do not draw up an individual partnership agreement—both responsibility for mutual support during and at the end of the couple's relationship and equitable sharing of property at its end, thus addressing the complaint leveled at some local partnership arrangements that partners are given the benefits of marriage without its burdens. It would thus be similar to the system of registered partnerships in The Netherlands in its default provision but would allow couples to design their own contract, as in France, if they wish to avoid the full impact of family law remedies *inter se*. They would nonetheless be treated as if married by the state and third parties.

2. The Impact of the Proposed Reforms on Marriage

A number of legal scholars argue that we should not give legal protection to cohabitation or give it only very limited protection because to do so will

---

22. *See, e.g.,* Wendy M. Schrama, *Registered Partnership in The Netherlands*, 13 INT'L J. LAW, POL'Y & FAM. 315, 322 (1999) (reporting that one-third of the registrants in the first year were heterosexual); Katharina Boele-Woelki, *Registered Partnership and Same-Sex Marriage in The Netherlands*, in LEGAL RECOGNITION OF SAME-SEX COUPLES IN EUROPE 47 (Katharina Boele-Woelki & Angelika Fuchs eds., Intersentia 2003) (reporting that heterosexual partners far exceeded same-sex partners through 2002); Suzanne Daley, *French Couples Take Plunge That Falls Short of Marriage*, N.Y. TIMES, Apr. 8, 2000, at A3 (reporting that about 40 percent of the 14,000 couples entering PACS in the first four months were heterosexual). *See also* Marion C. Willetts, *An Exploratory Investigation of Heterosexual Licensed Domestic Partners*, 65 J. MARRIAGE & FAM. 939 (2003) (describing motivations reported by heterosexuals who registered as domestic partners in Ann Arbor, Michigan; Madison, Wisconsin; Minneapolis, Minnesota; and Seattle, Washington, which included to obtain economic benefits and to enter an ideological alternative to marriage that was open to both straight and gay couples).

harm the institution of marriage, which is seen as the societal ideal.[23] Writers involved in the movement to promote marriage also press this argument.[24] Because this objection is so widespread, it is important to confront it when arguing for an extension of cohabitants' legal rights. In this section, I begin by deconstructing the argument that in order to protect marriage, we must not give legal recognition to any other type of conjugal union or any benefits to cohabitants. I then discuss historical and comparative evidence showing that extending such recognition and benefits is unlikely to harm marriage and may in fact benefit it in the long run.

2.1. Incentives and Marriage

The argument that to give legal status to cohabitants will harm marriage is based upon several assumptions. First, it assumes that the provision of legal rights has an impact on individuals' decisions whether to marry or to cohabit and thus on the overall rate of marriage, and consequently that refusal to recognize cohabitation will lead those who would otherwise cohabit to get married instead. Authors making this argument also assume that marriage by many of the people who are currently cohabiting would remedy the bad effects that often seem to accompany their cohabitation. Arguments to this effect are seriously flawed in a number of respects.

First, legal incentives do not seem to affect people's private behavior in this way. Indeed, most people are unlikely even to know what their legal rights and obligations are with respect to marriage, at least until they get divorced. Many Puerto Rican women in informal unions regard their unions as marriages and may even report them as such, though they in fact have none of the legal protections of marriage.[25] Indeed, many people in the United States believe, mistakenly, that the law treats cohabitants as though they were married after a certain period of time, although common law marriage

---

23. *See, e.g.,* William C. Duncan, *The Social Good of Marriage and Legal Responses to Non-Marital Cohabitation*, 82 OR. L. REV. 1001, 1031 (2003); Scott, *supra* note 1.

24. *See, e.g.,* Maggie Gallagher, *Rites, Rights, and Social Institutions: Why and How Should the Law Support Marriage?*, 18 NOTRE DAME J. L. ETHICS & PUB. POL'Y 225, 238–40 (2004).

25. Nancy S. Landale & Katherine Fennelly, *Informal Unions Among Mainland Puerto Ricans: Cohabitation or an Alternative to Legal Marriage?*, 54 J. MARRIAGE & FAM. 269, 272, 275, 278–79 (1992) (respondents were allowed to classify their relationships themselves).

is recognized only in a decreasing handful of states.[26] A large-scale survey in the United Kingdom in 2000 revealed the widespread existence of a common law marriage myth there. Despite the fact that common law marriage was abolished in England in 1753, over half the respondents thought that living together for a period (varying, in their opinions, from six months to six years) gave cohabitants the same rights as married couples.[27] Cohabitants in this survey were quizzed about their reasons for entering a cohabiting relationship. The differing legal consequences of cohabitation and marriage played no role in their decision making, leading the authors of the study to comment upon the "astonishing lack of awareness about the different legal consequences of unmarried as opposed to married cohabitation."[28] Americans do not appear to be more knowledgeable about their legal rights in this respect than the British.

Moreover, if the proclivity to marry were directly related to the legal status of cohabitation, there would presumably be a positive correlation between the rate of cohabitation and legal rights given to cohabitants. The opposite has been true. The rate of cohabitation has risen dramatically in the United States despite the fact that cohabitants have been offered very few rights and treated punitively in many states. The behavior of some groups of cohabitants also directly contradicts the presumed influence of these legal incentives. For example, alimony was regularly terminated in the past when an ex-spouse receiving it cohabited, yet divorced persons have been one of the groups most likely to cohabit.[29] So if legal and financial disincentives are supposed to

---

26. ALI PRINCIPLES 2002, *supra* note 2, Ch. 6 (Overview) (concerning common law marriage myth in the United States). *See* GÖRAN LIND, COMMON LAW MARRIAGE: A LEGAL INSTITUTION FOR COHABITATION 8–12 (Oxford Univ. Press 2008) (discussing which states still recognize common law marriage and which do not).

27. Barlow & James, *supra* note 11, at 161–63.

28. *Id.* at 161. For a more detailed exposition of British cohabitants' beliefs about their legal rights, *see* ANNE BARLOW ET AL., COHABITATION, MARRIAGE AND THE LAW: SOCIAL CHANGE AND LEGAL REFORM IN THE 21ST CENTURY 27-47 (Hart Pub'g 2005). *See also* Mary Hibbs et al., *Why Marry? Perceptions of the Affianced*, 31 FAM. LAW 197, 200–03 (2001) (reporting, based on a survey of engaged couples in England, that the legal consequences of marriage were not among their reasons for planning to marry and that most of them had little idea, or mistaken ideas, about the consequences of marriage).

29. *See* IRA MARK ELLMAN ET AL., FAMILY LAW: CASES, TEXT, PROBLEMS 485–86 (3d ed.1998) (discussing traditional rule terminating alimony upon cohabitation but reporting that the more recent trend is to examine the financial impact of the cohabitation on the party receiving support and thus her financial need before making this decision).

discourage cohabitation and encourage marriage, experience shows that they have not worked.

We now have a number of studies, primarily in the context of welfare reform, about the impact of legal incentives more generally upon the rate of marriage. These studies show that welfare programs designed to encourage marriage have had no statistically significant effect on the marriage rate.[30] Indeed, one study suggests that entry into marriage is inversely related to federal welfare initiatives that have drastically limited payment of benefits to unmarried mothers.[31] Another study concludes that reduced public welfare benefits are negatively associated with the probability of marriage for African American never-married mothers.[32] These results are consistent with evidence that variations in welfare benefits do not affect the nonmarital birth rate.[33] Human beings apparently do not regulate behavior as private as union formation and childbirth in response to incentives from the state.[34]

Even assuming that people did think and act in response to legal incentives concerning these matters, the incentive structure provided by the current legal treatment of cohabitation in the United States is perverse. By not imposing any legal obligations on cohabitants, the stronger partner economically is given an incentive *not* to marry, because to do so would mean being required to share his or her property upon dissolution of the

---

30. *See, e.g.,* LISA A. GENNETIAN & VIRGINIA KNOX, STAYING SINGLE: THE EFFECTS OF WELFARE REFORM POLICIES ON MARRIAGE AND COHABITATION 14–23 (MRDC 2003) (providing a meta-analysis of studies on fourteen different U.S. welfare programs and concluding that they did not affect marriage or cohabitation); Robert A. Moffitt et al., *Beyond Single Mothers: Cohabitation and Marriage in the AFDC Program,* 35 DEMOGRAPHY 259 (1998) (reporting on a variety of state experiments with incentive structures).

31. Marianne P. Bitler et al., *The Impact of Welfare Reform on Marriage and Divorce,* 41 DEMOGRAPHY 213, 232 (2004) (finding that TANF has led fewer, rather than more, women to marry).

32. McKinley L. Blackburn, *Welfare Effects on the Marital Decisions of Never-Married Mothers,* 35 J. HUMAN RESOURCES 116 (2000) (finding that for black never-married mothers, higher benefits are associated with higher rather than lower rates of marriage).

33. Kathryn Edin, *What Do Low-Income Single Mothers Say about Marriage?,* 47 SOC. PROBLEMS 112, 113 (2000); *see also* Lucy A. Williams, *The Ideology of Division: Behavior Modification Welfare Reform Proposals,* 102 YALE L.J. 719, 739–40 (1992).

34. A notable exception appears to be the enormous one-year increase in marriages in Sweden in 1989—from 522.9 per 100,000 in 1988 to 1,277.3 per 100,000 in 1989 and then back down to 471.2 per 100,000 in 1990—in response to a significant pension-based incentive to marry. William N. Eskridge Jr. et al., *"Nordic Bliss? Scandinavian Registered Partnerships and the Same-Sex Marriage Debate,* ISSUES IN LEGAL SCHOLARSHIP", Single-Sex Marriage (2004), at 5 n. 29, 43, *available at* http://www.bepress.com/ils/iss5/art4.

relationship and possibly to support the former partner in the short or long run. Except in the state of Washington, no such obligation currently exists for cohabitants in the absence of a contract, thus presumably encouraging calculating and manipulative people to take advantage of partners who are weaker, more trusting, or self-deluding about their partner's intentions. Assuming that legal incentives ever affect behavior, any legal remedies proposed should take this perverse incentive into account.

Finally, whether people act in ignorance of their rights or not, and whether their behavior is influenced by economic incentives or not, their decisions about whether to marry may respond to some deeper level of rationality. The lower-income women interviewed by Kathryn Edin, for example, may not respond to incentives structured into public assistance law, but they are acting rationally in their decisions not to link their fates to men who may endanger their own survival and happiness and that of their children.[35] And why should the law want them to act differently? If, as the social science seems to show, some male cohabitants are commitment-averse or violence-prone, should we encourage them to marry? It is unlikely that the institution of marriage would of itself transform them into persons able to sustain long-term, productive, and peaceful relationships. Thus, even if we could somehow transport them into the institution of marriage, doing so would not promote the ideals for which marriage is valued in the first place. Moreover, in light of the statistics about the inexorable increase in cohabitation in the United States, designing our law to encourage cohabitants to marry could result in sacrificing the good in a futile search for the best—that is, trying to encourage marriage at all costs rather than supporting and potentially stabilizing the unions in which people actually live. Moreover, as the next section shows, stable cohabiting relationships often can lead to marriage, so improving the legal treatment of cohabitants might actually increase the marriage rate.

2.2. Cross-historical and Cross-national Comparisons

It is helpful to look at some comparative statistics in deciding whether to worry about the impact of cohabitation on marriage. More than 90 percent

---

35. *See also* Smart, *supra* note 22, at 49 (emphasizing, based upon interviews with cohabitants in England, that the relationships many women choose depend upon their alternatives in a world of limited choice, their self-concept, and their expectations about the quality of heterosexual relationships).

of every female cohort in the United States since the mid-1800s (when records began to be kept) has eventually married.[36] Virtually all young people plan to marry at some time; and 90 percent are still likely to do so, though the likelihood varies by race and ethnic group.[37] Interviews of American adolescents (7th, 9th, and 11th grade students) between 2001 and 2004 showed that three-quarters of them had definite or probable expectations to marry in the future, even though half of them also expected to cohabit at some time as well.[38] The vast majority of Americans are committed to marriage and express a preference for it as the ideal, even when they are not married themselves.[39] As one author tracing trends from the 1960s through the 1990s commented:

> One very important continuity is the strong emphasis and commitment given to marriage, children, and family life in America today.... Americans overwhelmingly believe that marriage is a lifetime relationship that should not be terminated except under extreme circumstances.[40]

Nonetheless, many scholars apparently still believe that people will cohabit instead of marrying if the law makes cohabitation as good as marriage in terms of public benefits and warn that we need to be careful about the supposedly vulnerable institution of marriage. One, Lynn D. Wardle, points to early Bolshevik family law as an object lesson in the risks of tinkering with our law in this way.[41] After the Bolshevik Revolution of 1918, divorce

---

36. Joshua R. Goldstein & Catherine T. Kenney, *Marriage Delayed or Marriage Forgone? New Cohort Forecasts of First Marriage for U.S. Women*, 66 AM. SOC. REV. 506, 507 (2001).

37. Larry L. Bumpass, *What's Happening to the Family? Interactions Between Demographic and Institutional Change*, 27 DEMOGRAPHY 483, 488 (1990) (reporting, based on NSFH data, that all plan to marry and 90 percent are likely to marry). *See also* Goldstein & Kenney, *supra* note 36, at 511 (reporting that about 90 percent of all American women in the cohorts born in the 1950s and 1960s will marry).

38. Wendy D. Manning et al., *The Changing Institution of Marriage: Adolescents' Expectations to Cohabit and to Marry*, 69 J. MARRIAGE & FAM. 559, 571–72 (2007). Girls were more likely to expect to marry than boys, and African American adolescents had (realistically) lower marriage expectations than white adolescents. *Id.* at 572.

39. *See, e.g.*, Marin Clarkberg, *The Price of Partnering: The Role of Economic Well-Being in Young Adults' First Union Experiences*, 77 SOC. FORCES 945, 946 (1999); Arland Thornton & Linda Young-DeMarco, *Four Decades of Trends in Attitudes Toward Family Issues in the United States: The 1960s Through the 1990s*, 63 J. MARRIAGE & FAM. 1009, 1017–19, 1030 (2001).

40. Thornton & Young-DeMarco, *supra* note 39, at 1030.

41. Lynn D. Wardle, *The "Withering Away" of Marriage: Some Lessons from the Bolshevik Family Law Reforms in Russia, 1917–1926*, 2 GEO. J. L. & PUB. POL'Y 469 (2004).

was liberalized and unilateral divorce allowed; civil marriage was mandated; illegitimacy was abolished as a legal category; and in 1926, marital benefits were extended to *de facto* couples.[42] Yet after one of the most drastic experiments in, as Wardle calls it, "leveling marriage with *de facto* cohabitation,"[43] there is no evidence that marriage was seriously harmed as an institution in the former Soviet Union. Statistics for Belarus, Russia, and the Ukraine, for example, show that in 1980 there were 10.1 marriages per thousand population in Belarus, 10.6 in Russia, and 9.3 in the Ukraine, compared to 10.5 in the United States, 7.4 in the United Kingdom, and 5.7 in Italy that same year.[44] In short, marriage is a very durable institution. The rates of marriage in all of these countries had dropped by 2001, especially in Belarus, Russia, and the Ukraine (to 6.9 per thousand in Belarus and Russia and 5.6 in the Ukraine), but this was not in response to any changes in their family law.[45] The rate of marriage appears to have fallen in the countries of the former Soviet Union in response to their unfavorable economic situations, which we know from history bear a prominent relationship to rates of marriage.

The comparisons of most immediate interest for the subject of this book are those between the United States and countries similar to the United States that have extended legal protections to cohabiting couples, such as the ones discussed in Chapter 5. Research shows that extending rights to cohabitants has not harmed marriage in those countries. A study of marriage rates in various Australian states before and after their legislation extending rights to *de facto* couples, for example, showed no evidence of a correlation between the fall in the marriage rate and introduction of that legislation.[46] Moreover, scholars familiar with the situation in France report that "Birthrates have not collapsed, and marriage itself seems to have been, if anything, reinforced by the new option offered with the [PACS]."[47]

---

42. *Id.* at 473.

43. *Id.* at 477.

44. U.N. Econ. Commission for Europe, *Trends in Europe and North America*, Pt. 2, Ch.2, § 2.4: Trends in marriage and divorce, *available at* http://www.unece.org/stats/trend/register.htm.

45. *Id.* The comparable rates had also fallen in the United States to 8.4 per 1000, in the United Kingdom to 5.1 per 1000, and in Italy to 4.5. *Id.*

46. Kathleen Kiernan et al., *Cohabitation Law Reform and Its Impact on Marriage: Evidence from Australia and Europe*, 2007 INT'L FAM. L. 71, 72.

47. Daniel Borrillo & Eric Fassin, *The* PACS, *Four Years Later: A Beginning or an End?*, *in* SAME-SEX COUPLES, SAME-SEX PARTNERSHIPS, AND HOMOSEXUAL MARRIAGES: A FOCUS ON CROSS-NATIONAL DIFFERENTIALS 19, 23 (Marie Digoix & Patrick Festy eds., Ined 2004).

In The Netherlands, opposite-sex couples have been able to choose since 1998 between marriage and registration as domestic partners with virtually all the rights of marriage.[48] Yet between 2002 and 2003, the rate of cohabitation to marriage in The Netherlands was identical to that in England, where legal protections for cohabitants are vastly inferior: 25 percent of unions in both countries were cohabitations.[49] In Sweden, cohabitation has been accepted for the longest period of time and is given very favorable treatment by the government.[50] Yet Eurobarometer surveys show that 90 percent of Swedish young people report being in favor of marriage, and 61.2 percent of cohabiting women aged fifteen to forty-four in Sweden eventually marry their partners, compared with 48 percent in the United States.[51] In other words, giving positive legal treatment to cohabitation does not seem to discourage marriage and may in fact encourage it.

In France, where the Pacte Civil de Solidarité allows cohabitants who register to receive some of the benefits of marital status, approximately equal proportions of cohabitants end their cohabitation by marrying as in the United States: 46.3 percent in France and 48 percent in the United States.[52] Whether they ultimately marry or separate, however, cohabiting unions in the two countries vary dramatically in duration, with a median of 4.28 years in France and about 1.5 in the United States.[53] Moreover, although half of coupled Swedish men and women between the ages of thirty and thirty-nine are cohabitants rather than married, 70 percent of Swedish 17-year-olds live

---

48. *See* Boele-Woelki, *supra* note 22, at 45–48.

49. Kathleen Kiernan, *Redrawing the Boundaries of Marriage*, 66 J. MARRIAGE & FAM. 980, 981 (2004).

50. *See* Anne Barlow, *Regulation of Cohabitation, Changing Family Policies and Social Attitudes: A Discussion of Britain Within Europe*, 26 L. & POL'Y 57, 61–62 (2004); Hans Ytterberg, *"From Society's Point of View, Cohabitation Between Two Persons of the Same Sex Is a Perfectly Acceptable Form of Family Life": A Swedish Story of Love and Legislation, in* LEGAL RECOGNITION OF SAME-SEX PARTNERSHIPS: A STUDY OF NATIONAL, EUROPEAN AND INTERNATIONAL LAW 427, 429 (Robert Wintemute & Mads Andenaes eds., Hart Publishing 2001).

51. Kiernan, *supra* note 49, at 980; Patrick Heuveline & Jeffrey M. Timberlake, *The Role of Cohabitation in Family Formation: The United States in Comparative Perspective*, 66 J. MARRIAGE & FAM. 1214, 1223 (Table 2) (2004) (61.2 percent of Swedish cohabitants marry).

52. *Id.* at 1223 (Table 2).

53. *Id.* (substituting the median duration in the social science literature described above for that in Heuveline's Table 2).

with both their biological parents.[54] This makes a great deal of difference to the children affected by these unions.

The expected probability of exposure to at least one maternal cohabitation by age sixteen is about 40 percent in France, followed by about 34 percent in the United States.[55] Given these probabilities, the law should consider what is best for the children involved if they cannot all be raised by married biological parents, as is decreasingly the case even for those born to married couples today. To grow up where cohabiting unions last a long time and have the highest probability of transition into marriage appears best in this second-best world. On this measure, children in the United States have perhaps the worst of all possible worlds, in which the probability of exposure to parental cohabitation is very high, the median duration is brief, less than one half of cohabiting couples marry, and protections for cohabitants are slim.

The best case scenario is presented in Sweden, with its lengthy tradition of cohabitation and very generous legal treatment of cohabitants, where the median duration of cohabitation is 3.44 years and there is a 61.2 percent rate of transition to marriage.[56] The authors of one comparative study opine that it is precisely because cohabitation has become virtually indistinguishable from marriage in Sweden that more people eventually do marry.[57] Another interpretation might be that, where cohabiting couples are made more secure by the extension of legal benefits to them, that very security can increase the possibility of their subsequent marriage. And even if they do not marry, extension of those benefits to cohabitants might make many of their unions more stable.

In sum, offering legal recognition and support to cohabitants and making their lives easier does not appear to discourage marriage, and in fact the opposite may be true.

---

54. *See, e.g.*, Kiernan, *supra* note 49, at 982 (reporting that the proportion of those cohabiting and married among 30- to 39-year-old men and women was 48 percent to 52 percent); Eskridge et al., *supra* note 34, at 7.

55. Heuveline & Timberlake, *supra* note 51, at 1224 (Figure 2).

56. *Id.* at 1223 (Table 2).

57. *Id.* at 1225. Similarly, in parts of Canada where common law unions are interpreted as imposing support and in some cases property obligations, people may be less reluctant to marry than in Quebec, because they know that they will have to share their resources either way. *See* JEAN DUMAS & ALAIN BÉLANGER, REPORT ON THE DEMOGRAPHIC SITUATION IN CANADA 1996: CURRENT DEMOGRAPHIC ANALYSIS, PT. II: COMMON-LAW UNIONS IN CANADA AT THE END OF THE 20TH CENTURY 80 (Statistics Canada 1997), *available at* http://www.statcan.gc.ca/bsolc/olc-cel/olc-cel?catno=91-209-X&CHROPG=1&lang=eng.

⅜ 3. The Impact of the Proposed Reforms on Various Groups of Cohabitants

Of more importance to me than speculation about the effects these legal reforms might have on the institution of marriage is to analyze the impact they would have upon the people who cohabit in the United States and their children. To assess this, it is necessary once again to break down the overall category of cohabitants into the groups described in Chapter 3 as including large numbers of cohabitants in the United States. The groups on that list included:

1. young singles sharing quarters for reasons of convenience and economy;
2. young adults cohabiting as some sort of trial marriage;
3. working-class couples without resources for a wedding or a home of their own;
4. low-income mothers, many of whom are African American and some of whom are receiving public assistance;
5. Puerto Rican couples in traditional consensual unions, often with children of the union;
6. divorced persons either screening candidates for remarriage or seeking an alternative to marriage; and
7. older persons cohabiting for convenience, economy, or because they have no particular reason to marry and some disincentives to do so.

Let us examine how the rules I have proposed would affect each of these groups.

Young single people who are essentially in a dating relationship that involves sharing a residence would need to split up or draw up a contract by the end of two years of cohabitation to avoid having quasi-marital obligations imposed upon them. Should we be willing to tolerate this effect of the new legal rules? In fact, it could be beneficial to force these young people seriously to face, after two years together, what they want their obligations to one another to be in the future. So long as they agree, the two will be able to opt out of having legal consequences imposed upon them by filing the simple standardized opt-out agreement described above. A necessary precondition, of course, is that the potential legal consequences of inaction must be widely publicized. Perhaps a few television comedies about the unintended consequences of ignoring this new law would be effective; it seems like a good subject for a Seinfeld-type episode. Moreover, as discussed above, the younger cohabitants are, the less stable their relationships are.[58] Thus many, if not most, of these unions will have dissolved by the two-year deadline. Perhaps the others ought to dissolve as well if the partners cannot agree whether they want to opt out or not. Similarly, young adults cohabiting prior to marriage or as some sort of trial marriage would need to decide about the success or failure of their trial within a two-year period or opt out of the legal consequences of continuing it.[59]

What would be the impact on low-income mothers who are receiving contributions to their support and that of their children from cohabitants? Most of these unions are also very short term, and in-depth interviews such as those done by sociologist Kathryn Edin indicate that the women involved are wary of longer term connections with the men involved. These cohabitants could nonetheless have obligations imposed upon them if they remain together for two years or more. If the man is employed, this would give the woman a right to support from him both during the relationship and after it ends; the new status would also give both of them access to a variety of government benefits and rights against third parties that currently attach only to marital status. All of that is to the good. If, however, the man has a tenuous connection to the labor force, the woman could end up with obligations of support to him if she does not evict him in time. Two things alleviate my concern about this possibility. First, the women that Edin and her colleagues interviewed were very attuned to the possibility of exploitation by a nonproductive male and determined to protect themselves and their children from this long-term prospect. Second, if a quasi-marital status were thrust upon them, the remedies applied upon dissolution of marriages would typically protect these women, for example, by allocating property on the basis of factors such as a party's contribution to the household.

Many of the Puerto Rican couples in consensual unions, most of them with children, already think of themselves as married. Cohabitation typically results in a 51 percent gain to their household income, indicating both that

---

58. U.S. Dep't of Health and Human Services, Centers for Disease Control and Prevention, Nat'l Center for Health Statistics, Cohabitation, Marriage, Divorce, and Remarriage in the United States: Data from the National Survey of Family Growth 16 (Table 13) (2002) (correlating age at start of cohabitation with probability of breakup).

59. Perhaps the provision of an option to renew for an additional one or two years should be provided to give more psychological flexibility to those unsure of their intentions; if no action were taken, the option would expire.

the partners and their children benefit from the relationship and that their finances have become intertwined. It is appropriate to extend the benefits and the continuing support obligations of marriage to these couples. To do so would also give them and their children the protection of workers' compensation law, for example, standing to sue for relational injuries such as loss of consortium and negligent infliction of emotional distress, social security survivors' benefits, and access to important benefits such as family health insurance.

Divorced persons cohabiting either to screen possible candidates for remarriage or seeking an alternative to marriage would need to contract out of further obligations if they did not wish to incur them after two years. The experience of having gone through a divorce is a great sensitizer to legal rights and obligations; and these people would likely be wary enough to opt out if they do not wish to undertake obligations to one another, provided that these consequences have been widely publicized. Given that such major legal reforms would not be passed without a period of noisy public debate, the general public would be likely to have received a good deal of education about them before they went into effect.

Older persons cohabiting for convenience, economy, or because they have no particular reason to marry and some reasons not to do so are similar to divorced persons in some of these respects. Often a main objection to marriage for these groups is raised by their bonds to children from previous unions (or by those adult children themselves). Inheritance by a cohabitant could pose a particular problem for the elderly, but they, like divorced persons, can draft wills to address their concern for their children. They would need to do this whether they were married or had a quasi-marital status thrust upon them by the passage of time. Without reforms of this type, elderly people may be in a particularly vulnerable position at the end of a cohabiting relationship. If they have joined their households and incomes as an economic survival strategy, the consequences can be dire if one partner can simply leave a two-year relationship without any legal remedy being available to the other partner.[60]

---

60. One author suggests that elderly couples would do best under a statewide civil union scheme, under which they would not lose their benefits from prior spouses under social security, Medicare, and Medicaid. John R. Schleppenbach, *Strange Bedfellows: Why Older Straight Couples Should Advocate for the Passage of the Illinois Civil Union Act*, 17 ELDER L.J. 31, 51–53 (2009).

In sum, the legal remedies I outline here benefit, on balance, each of the main groups I have described. There is no perfect fit between legal remedy and reality, but I am convinced that this system of legal treatment of cohabitants is the best under the circumstances. It imposes obligations after a period of time but also allow couples to opt out if they agree to do so. Some may nonetheless be caught by legal obligations they did not anticipate and did not intend. The partner who at the moment of dissolution would prefer to avoid all obligations to a long-term partner may face responsibilities he or she does not desire to undertake. In some cases, their desires and intentions may have been different at an earlier period in the relationship, before it reached the point of breakdown. This is no different from the situation at the end of a marriage, where the member of a divorcing couple from whom support is sought often seeks to avoid obligations that were contemplated at its inception and which he or she would have welcomed if the union were ongoing. Or perhaps the cohabitant never wanted to be bound in this way. In that situation, there is a direct conflict between that person's freedom of choice and the protection of their partner from the vulnerability that follows the ending of a long-term relationship. The priority of our legal system under these circumstances should be to protect the vulnerable.

Conclusion

AMERICANS ARE FOND OF THINKING that their country is unique, and to some extent this is true. Among other unique characteristics, the United States is the only industrialized democracy that privatizes such a large proportion of its social welfare functions. Under these circumstances, only comprehensive reform of the legal treatment of cohabitation would be truly adequate, and it should be the ideal. But the United States Constitution, with its delegation of family law to the states, makes this impossible. It is necessary instead to pursue reforms like those I suggest on a state-by-state basis and perhaps on a statute-by-statute basis on the federal level as well.[11] It is nonetheless important to have an ideal at which to aim and by which reforms can be measured. If reform proceeds on a piecemeal and incremental basis, as seems likely, individual reforms can be evaluated according to whether they will obstruct or further that ideal.

If forced to choose a second-best course of action in reforming the law governing cohabitants, the Canadian experience provides the best guide. Canada, like the United States, has a federal system, so reform of cohabitation law there required working on the level of both national and provincial governments, and province by province as well. Lacking the basic social welfare system available in Canada, replication of the current Canadian system would not provide adequate protection for cohabitants in the United States. But it would be a distinct improvement—and a start.

---

1. Before the dispute over same-sex marriage, federal law had always looked to state law for its definition of a spouse, thus, for example, entitling a common law spouse to federal benefits if he or she lived in a state recognizing that status. The federal Defense of Marriage Act prohibits doing so in the case of a same-sex spouse. 1 U.S.C. § 7 (2000) ("the word 'spouse' refers only to a person of the opposite sex who is a husband or a wife"). However, there is currently nothing preventing the passage of a federal statute similar to that in Canada, providing that qualifying opposite-sex cohabitants shall be included within the definition of a spouse for the purpose of all federal laws.

Realizing that all the reforms I recommend are unlikely to take place in the near future, I invite the American public and policymakers nonetheless to embark upon a national debate about these issues, such as has happened in England, Canada, and other countries. What are the goals we strive to promote through our family law rules? Should they apply to persons who have chosen to live together without getting married? If not, why not, in light of the information we now have about cohabitation in the United States?

I end on a personal note. When I think of legal remedies, I often use a former legal clinic client as a touchstone—a woman in her late thirties, a victim of domestic violence who had cohabited with her partner for fifteen years, staying home and raising their two children. She did eventually leave her abuser, but she could not afford to take her children with her. She had to move in with her mother in order to survive. The legal system I have proposed here would have protected her. It would have allowed her to sue for an equitable share of the couple's house and accumulated property. Indeed, she might not have had to leave the house in the first place, even though it was titled in her partner's name. She could have sued for maintenance in addition to child support. She would have been entitled to an interest in her partner's pension and eventually in his social security benefits. In the United States today, only the law of the state of Washington would entitle her to any portion of these benefits. The remedies I have outlined here would have allowed her some dignity and security after a 15-year relationship, and they would have enabled her children to be raised by a nonabusive parent. This seems to me to be a better and more constructive outcome, an outcome that is healthier both for the individuals involved and the country in which they live.

References

Adams, Laura S. 2005. Privileging the Privileged? Child Well-Being as a Justification for State Support of Marriage. *San Diego Law Review* 42: 881–88.

Agell, Anders. 1980. The Swedish Legislation on Marriage and Cohabitation: A Journey Without a Destination. In *Scandinavian Studies in Law*, edited by Folke Schmidt. Almqvist and Wiksell, Stockholm.

American Law Institute. 2002. *Principles of the Law of Family Dissolution: Analysis and Recommendations.* Lexis Nexis, New York.

Anderson, Michelle J. 1993. A License to Abuse: The Impact of Conditional Status on Female Immigrants. *Yale Law Journal* 102: 1401–30.

Arafat, Ibithaj, and Betty Yorburg. 1973. On Living Together without Marriage. *Journal of Sex Research* 9: 97–106.

Artis, Julie E. 2007. Maternal Cohabitation and Child Well-Being Among Kindergarten Children. *Journal of Marriage and Family* 69: 222–36.

Avellar, Sarah, and Pamela J. Smock. 2005. The Economic Consequences of the Dissolution of Cohabiting Unions. *Journal of Marriage and Family* 67: 314–27.

Axinn, William G., and Arland Thornton. 2000. The Transformation in the Meaning of Marriage. In *The Ties that Bind: Perspectives on Marriage and Cohabitation*, edited by Linda J. Waite. Aldine De Gruyter, New York.

Bailey, Martha. 2004. Regulation of Cohabitation and Marriage in Canada. *Law and Policy* 26: 153–75.

Bala, Nicholas. 2001. Canada: Court Decisions on Same-Sex and Unmarried Partners, Spousal Rights and Children. In *International Survey of Family Law*, edited by Andrew Bainham. Jordan Publishing, Bristol.

Barlow, Anne. 2002. *Cohabitants and the Law.* Butterworths, London.

Barlow, Anne. 2004. Regulation of Cohabitation, Changing Family Policies and Social Attitudes: A Discussion of Britain Within Europe. *Law and Policy* 26: 57–86.

Barlow, Anne. 2004. Rights in the Family Home—Time for a Conceptual Revolution? In *New Perspectives on Property Law, Human Rights and the Home*, edited by Alastair Hudson. Cavendish Publishing, London.

Barlow, Anne. 2006. Cohabitation Law Reform—Messages from Research. *Feminist Legal Studies* 14: 167–80.

Barlow, Anne. 2008. Cohabiting Relationships, Money and Property: The Legal Backdrop. *Journal of Socio-Economics* 37: 502–18.

Barlow, Anne, and Craig Lind. 1999. A Matter of Trust: The Allocation of Rights in the Family Home. *Legal Studies* 19: 468–88.

Barlow, Anne, and Grace James. 2004. Regulating Marriage and Cohabitation in 21st Century Britain. *Modern Law Review* 67: 143–76.

Barlow, Anne, et al. 2001. Just a piece of paper? Marriage and Cohabitation. In *British Social Attitudes the 18th Report*, edited by Alison Park et al. Sage Publications Ltd., London.

Barlow, Anne, et al. 2005. *Cohabitation, Marriage and the Law: Social Change and Legal Reform in the 21st Century*. Hart Publishing, Oxford.

Batalova, Jeanne A., and Philip N. Cohen. 2002. Premarital Cohabitation and Housework: Couples in Cross-national Perspective. *Journal of Marriage and Family* 64: 743–55.

Becker, Gary S. 1981. *A Treatise on the Family*. Harvard University Press, Cambridge.

Becker, Mary. 2001. Family Law in the Secular State and Restrictions on Same-Sex Marriage: Two Are Better Than One. *University of Illinois Law Review* 2001: 1–56.

Bernhardt, Eva. 2004. *Cohabitation or Marriage? Preferred Living Arrangements in Sweden*. http://www.oif.ac.at/sdf/sdf04-04-bernhardt.pdf.

Bernstein, Anita. 2003. For and Against Marriage: A Revision. *Michigan Law Review* 102: 129–66.

Bitler, Marianne P., et al. 2004. The Impact of Welfare Reform on Marriage and Divorce. *Demography* 41: 213–36.

Björnberg, Ulla. 2001. Cohabitation and Marriage in Sweden—Does Family Form Matter? *International Journal of Law, Policy, and Family* 15: 350–62.

Blackburn, McKinley L. 2000. Welfare Effects on the Marital Decisions of Never-Married Mothers. *Journal of Human Resources* 35: 116–42.

Bloomfield, Maxwell. 1976. *American Lawyers in a Changing Society, 1776–1876*. Harvard University Press, Cambridge.

Blumberg, Grace Ganz. 1981. Cohabitation Without Marriage: A Different Perspective. *UCLA Law Review* 28: 1125–180.

Boele-Woelki, Katharina. 2003. Registered Partnership and Same-Sex Marriage in The Netherlands. In *Legal Recognition of Same-Sex Couples in Europe*, edited by Katharina Boele-Woelki and Angelika Fuchs. Intersentia Publishing, Oxford.

Booth, Alan, and Ann C. Crouter, eds. 2002. *Just Living Together: Implications of Cohabitation on Families, Children, and Social Policy*. L. Erlbaum Associates, Mahwah, NJ.

Booth, Alan, and David Johnson. 1988. Premarital Cohabitation and Marital Success. *Journal of Family Issues* 9: 255–72.

Borah, Woodrow, and Sherburne F. Cook. 1966. Marriage and Legitimacy in Mexican Culture: Mexico and California. *California Law Review* 54: 946–1008.

Borrillo, Daniel, and Eric Fassin. 2004. The PACS, Four Years Later: A Beginning or an End? In *Same-sex Couples, Same-sex Partnerships, and Homosexual Marriages: A Focus on Cross-national Differentials*, edited by Marie Digoix and Patrick Festy. Ined, Paris.

Borrillo, Daniel, and Kees Waaldijk. Major Legal Consequences of Marriage, Cohabitation and Registered Partnership for Different-sex and Same-sex Partners in France. In *More Or Less Together: Levels of Legal Consequences of Marriage,*

Cohabitation and Registered Partnerships for Different-sex and Same-sex Partners: A Comparative Study of Nine European Countries. 2005. Ined, available at http://www-same-sex.ined.fr/publica_doc125.htm.

Bottomley, Anne. 2006. From Mrs. Burns to Mrs. Oxley: Do Co-habiting Women (Still) Need Marriage Law? *Feminist Legal Studies* 14: 181–211.

Bowman Craig A., and Blake M. Cornish. 1992. Note, A More Perfect Union: A Legal and Social Analysis of Domestic Partnership Ordinances. *Columbia Law Review* 92: 1164–211.

Bowman, Cynthia Grant. 1996. A Feminist Proposal to Bring Back Common Law Marriage. *Oregon Law Review* 75: 709–81.

Bowman, Cynthia Grant. 2004. Legal Treatment of Cohabitation in the United States. *Law and Policy* 26: 119–51.

Bowman, Cynthia Grant. 2007. Social Science and Legal Policy: The Case of Heterosexual Cohabitation. *Journal of Law and Family Studies* 9: 1–52.

Boyd, Susan B., and Claire F.L.Young. 2003. "From Same-Sex to No Sex"?: Trends Towards Recognition of (Same-Sex) Relationships in Canada. *Seattle Journal of Social Justice* 1: 757–93.

Bradley, David. 1989. The Development of a Legal Status for Unmarried Cohabitation in Sweden. *Anglo-American Law Review* 18: 322–34.

Bradley, David. 1990. Unmarried Cohabitation in Sweden: A Renewed Social Institution? *Journal of Legal History* 11: 301–03.

Brines, Julie, and Kara Joyner. 1999. The Ties That Bind: Principles of Cohesion in Cohabitation and Marriage. *American Sociological Review* 64: 333–56.

Brown, J. Brian, and Daniel T. Lichter. 2004. Poverty, Welfare, and the Livelihood Strategies of Nonmetropolitan Single Mothers. *Rural Sociology* 69: 282–301.

Brown, Susan L. 2000. The Effect of Union Type on Psychological Well-Being: Depression Among Cohabitors Versus Marrieds. *Journal of Health and Social Behavior* 41: 241–55.

Brown, Susan L. 2000. Union Transitions Among Cohabitors: The Significance of Relationship Assessments and Expectations. *Journal of Marriage and Family* 62: 833–46.

Brown, Susan L. 2004. Family Structure and Child Well-Being: The Significance of Parental Cohabitation. *Journal of Marriage and Family* 66: 351–67.

Brown, Susan L. 2004. Moving From Cohabitation to Marriage: Effects on Relationship Quality. *Social Science Research* 33: 1–19.

Brown, Susan L., and Alan Booth. 1996. Cohabitation Versus Marriage: A Comparison of Relationship Quality. *Journal of Marriage and Family* 58: 668–78.

Brown, Susan L., and Jennifer Roebuck Bulanda. 2008. Relationship Violence in Young Adulthood: A Comparison of Daters, Cohabitors, and Marrieds. *Gerontology* 37: 73–87.

Brown, Susan L., et al. 2005. The Significance of Nonmarital Cohabitation: Marital Status and Mental Health Benefits Among Middle-Aged and Older Adults. *Journal of Gerontology* 60B: S21–S29.

Brown, Susan L., et al. 2006. Cohabitation Among Older Adults: A National Portrait. *Journal of Gerontology* 61B: S71–S79.

Brown, Susan L., et al. 2008. Generational Differences in Cohabitation and Marriage in the U.S. *Population Research and Policy Review* 27: 531.

Brownridge, Douglas A. 2004. Understanding Women's Heightened Risk of Violence in Common-Law Unions: Revisiting the Selection and Relationship Hypotheses. *Violence Against Women* 10: 626–51.

Brownridge, Douglas A. 2009. *Violence Against Women: Vulnerable Populations.* Routledge, New York.

Bulanda, Ronald E., and Wendy D. Manning. 2008. Parental Cohabitation Experiences and Adolescent Behavioral Outcomes. *Population Research and Policy Review* 27: 593–18.

Bumpass, Larry L. 1990. What's Happening to the Family? Interactions Between Demographic and Institutional Change. *Demography* 27: 483–98.

Bumpass, Larry, and Hsien-Hen Lu. 2000. Trends in Cohabitation and Implications for Children's Family Contexts in the United States. *Population Studies* 54: 29–41.

Bumpass, Larry L., and James A. Sweet. 1989. National Estimates of Cohabitation. *Demography* 26: 615–25.

Bumpass, Larry L., et al. 1991. The Role of Cohabitation in Declining Rates of Marriage. *Journal of Marriage and Family* 53: 913–27.

Callan, Megan E. 2003. The More, The Not Marry-er: In Search of a Policy Behind Eligibility for California Domestic Partnerships. *San Diego Law Review* 40: 427–59.

Canada. Law Commission. 2001. *Beyond Conjugality: Recognizing and Supporting Close Personal Adult Relationships.*

Canada National Statistics Agency. 2006. *Legal Marital Status, Common Law Status, for the Population 15 Years and Over, 2006 Census.*

Canada National Statistics Agency. 2008. Report on the Demographic Situation in Canada: 2005 and 2006.

Carbone, June. 2005. The Legal Definition of Parenthood: Uncertainty at the Core of Family Identity. *Louisiana Law Review* 65: 1295–344.

Carlile, Alisha M. 2005. Like Family: Rights of Nonmarried Cohabitational Partners in Loss of Consortium Actions. *Boston College Law Review* 48: 391–421.

Carlson, Allan. 2007. Deconstruction of Marriage: The Swedish Case. *San Diego Law Review* 44: 153–71.

Carlson, Marcia. 2004. Union Formation in Fragile Families. *Demography* 41: 237–61.

Carroll, Ginny. 1989. Marriage by Another Name. *Newsweek*, July 24: 46.

Caruana, Catherine. 2002. Relationship Diversity and the Law. *Family Matters* 63: 60–65.

Casad, Robert C. 1978. Unmarried Couples and Unjust Enrichment: From Status to Contract and Back Again. *Michigan Law Review* 77: 47–62.

Casper, Lynne M., et al. 2000. How Does POSSLQ Measure Up? Historical Estimates of Cohabitation. *Demography* 37: 237–245.

Chambers, David L. 1996. What If? The Legal Consequences of Marriage and the Legal Needs of Lesbian and Gay Male Couples. *Michigan Law Review* 95: 447–91.

Cherlin, Andrew J. 2000. Toward a New Home Socioeconomics of Union Formation. In *The Ties that Bind: Perspectives on Marriage and Cohabitation*, edited by Linda J. Waite. Aldine De Gruyter, New York.

Cherlin, Andrew J. 2004. The Deinstitutionalization of American Marriage. *Journal of Marriage and Family* 66: 846–81.

Chevan, Albert. 1996. As Cheaply as One: Cohabitation in the Older Population. *Journal of Marriage and Family* 58: 656–67.

Christensen, Craig W. 1977. Legal Ordering of Family Values: The Case of Gay and Lesbian Families. *Cardozo Law Review* 18: 1299–416.

Ciabattari, Teresa. 2004. Cohabitation and Housework: The Effects of Marital Intentions. *Journal of Marriage and Family* 66: 118–25.

Clark, Homer H., Jr. 1988. *The Law of Domestic Relations in the United States*. 2nd ed. West Publishing Company, St. Paul.

Clark, Scott H. 2005. Utah Prefers Married Couples. *Saint Thomas Law Review* 18: 215–26.

Clarkberg, Marin. 1999. The Price of Partnering: The Role of Economic Well-Being in Young Adults' First Union Experiences. *Social Forces* 77: 945–68.

Clarkberg, Marin, et al. 1995. Attitudes, Values and Entrance into Cohabitational versus Marital Unions. *Social Forces* 74: 609–32.

Clayton, Richard R., and Harwin L. Voss. 1997. Shacking Up: Cohabitation in the 1970s. *Journal of Marriage and Family* 39: 273–83.

Closen Michael L., and Joan E. Maloney. 1995. The Health Care Surrogate Act in Illinois: Another Rejection of Domestic Partners' Rights. *Southern Illinois University Law Journal* 19: 479–522.

Colker, Ruth. 2006. Marriage Mimicry: The Law of Domestic Violence. *William and Mary Law Review* 47: 1841–98.

Conway, Heather, and Philip Girard. 2005. "No Place Like Home": The Search for a Legal Framework for Cohabitants and the Family Home in Canada and Britain. *Queen's Law Journal* 30: 715–71.

Cunningham, Mick. 2005. Gender in Cohabitation and Marriage: The Influence of Gender Ideology on Housework Allocation Over the Life Course. *Journal of Family Issues* 26: 1037–61.

Cunningham, Mick, and Arland Thornton. 2005. The Influence of Union Transitions on White Adults' Attitudes Toward Cohabitation. *Journal of Marriage and Family* 67: 710–20.

Cunningham, Mick, and Arland Thornton. 2007. Direct and Indirect Influences of Parents' Marital Instability on Children's Attitudes Toward Cohabitation in Young Adulthood. *Journal of Divorce and Remarriage* 46: 125–43.

Dagan, Hanoch. 2004. *The Law and Ethics of Restitution*. Cambridge University Press, Cambridge.

Dalton, Susan E. 2001. Protecting Our Parent-Child Relationships: Understanding the Strengths and Weaknesses of Second-Parent Adoption. In *Queer Families, Queer Politics: Challenging Culture and the State*, edited by Mary Bernstein and Renate Reimann. Columbia University Press, New York.

Daly, Martin, and Margo Wilson. 1988. *Homicide*. Aldine de Gruyter, New York.

Davis, Shannon N. 2008. Premarital Cohabitation, Gender Ideologies, and Timing of First Marital Birth. *International Journal of the Sociology of the Family* 34: 1–18.

Davis, Shannon N., et al. 2007. Effects of Union Type on Division of Household Labor: Do Cohabiting Men Really Perform More Housework? *Journal of Family Issues* 28: 1246–272.

DeKeseredy, Walter S., et al. 2008. Which Women Are More Likely to Be Abused? Public Housing, Cohabitation, and Separated/Divorced Women. *Criminal Justice Studies* 21: 283–93.

DeLeire, Thomas, and Ariel Kalil. 2005. How Do Cohabiting Couples With Children Spend Their Money? *Journal of Marriage and Family* 67: 285–94.

DeMaris, Alfred. 1984. A Comparison of Remarriages with First Marriages on Satisfaction in Marriage and Its Relationship to Prior Cohabitation. *Family Relations* 33: 443–49.

DeMaris, Alfred, and K. Vaninadha Rao. 1992. Premarital Cohabitation and Subsequent Marital Stability in the United States: A Reassessment. *Journal of Marriage and Family.* 54: 178–90.

Dempsey, Ken, and David de Vaus. 2004. Who Cohabits in 2001? The Significance of Age, Gender, Religion and Ethnicity. *Journal of Sociology* 40: 157–78.

Dey, Ian, and Fran Wasoff. 2007. Protection, Parity, or Promotion: Public Attitudes to Cohabitation and the Purposes of Legal Reform. *Law and Policy* 29: 159–82.

Dubler, Ariela R. 2000. Wifely Behavior: A Legal History of Acting Married. *Columbia Law Review* 100: 957–1021.

Duncan, Simon. 2008. Why Don't They Marry? Cohabitation, Commitment and DIY Marriage. In *Marriage and Cohabitation*, edited by Alison Diduck. Ashgate, London.

Duncan, William C. 2003. The Social Good of Marriage and Legal Responses to Non-Marital Cohabitation. *Oregon Law Review* 82: 1001–32.

Duncan, William C. 2004. Marital Status and Adoption Values. *Journal of Law and Family Studies* 6: 1–18.

Edin, Kathryn. 2000. What Do Low-Income Single Mothers Say about Marriage? *Social Problems* 47: 112–33.

Edin, Kathryn, and Maria Kefalas. 2005. *Promises I Can Keep: Why Poor Women Put Motherhood before Marriage*. University of California Press, Berkeley.

Ellman, Ira Mark. 1989. The Theory of Alimony. *California Law Review* 77: 40–77.

Ellman, Ira Mark, et al. 1998. *Family Law: Cases, Text, Problems*. 3rd ed. West Group, New York.

Elwert, Felix. 2006. *Cohabitation, Divorce, and the Trial Marriage Hypothesis*. Ph.D. dissertation, Harvard University, Department of Sociology, Cambridge.

Ertman, Martha M. 2001. The ALI Principles' Approach to Domestic Partnership. *Duke Journal of Gender Law and Policy* 8: 107–17.

Eskridge, William N. Jr., et al. 2004. "Nordic Bliss? Scandinavian Registered Partnerships and the Same-Sex Marriage Debate. In *Issues in Legal Scholarship, Single-Sex Marriage*. http://www.bepress.com/ils/iss5/art4.

Estin, Ann Laquer. 2001. Unmarried Partners and the Legacy of Marvin v. Marvin: Ordinary Cohabitation. *Notre Dame Law Review* 76: 1381–408.

Falco, Melanie C. 2004. The Road Not Taken: Using the Eighth Amendment to Strike Down Criminal Punishment for Engaging in Consensual Sexual Acts. *North Carolina Law Review* 82: 723–58.

Fellows, Mary Louise et al. 1998. Committed Partners and Inheritance: An Empirical Study. *Law and Inequality* 16: 1–94.

Fine, David R., and Mark A. Fine. 1992. Learning from Social Sciences: A Model for Reformation of the Laws Affecting Stepfamilies. *Dickinson Law Review* 97: 49–81.

Fineman, Martha L. 1981. Law and Changing Patterns of Behavior: Sanctions on Non-Marital Cohabitation. *Wisconsin Law Review* 1981: 275–332.

Flood, John A. 1982. The Rights of a Mexican Concubine Under Arizona Workmen's Compensation Law. *Arizona Journal of International and Comparative Law* 1: 259–70.

Forder, Caroline. 1999. An Undutchable Family Law: Partnership, Parenthood, Social Parenthood, Names and Some Article 8 ECHR Case Law. In *The International Survey of Family Law*, edited by Andrew Bainham. Martinus Nijhoff Publishers, The Hague.

France. Institut national de la statistique et des études économiques. 2009. Bilan Demographique 2008, *Deux Mariages Pour un PACS*, available at http://www. insee.fr/fr/themes/document.asp?ref_id=ip1220#inter4.

France. Ministry of Justice. 2004. *Report, Le Pacte Civil de Solidarité: Reflexions et Propositions de Réforme.*

Franke, Katherine M. 1999. Becoming a Citizen: Reconstruction Era Regulation of African American Marriages. *Yale Journal of Law and the Humanities* 11: 251–308.

Franke, Katherine M. 2004. The Domesticated Liberty of *Lawrence v. Texas. Columbia Law Review* 104: 1339–426.

Frias, Sonia M., and Ronald J. Angel. 2005. The Risk of Partner Violence Among Low-Income Hispanic Subgroups. *Journal of Marriage and Family* 67: 552–64.

Friedman, Lawrence M. 1985. *A History of American Law.* 2nd ed. Simon and Schuster, New York.

Gallagher, Maggie. 2004. Rites, Rights, and Social Institutions: Why and How Should the Law Support Marriage? *Notre Dame Journal of Law, Ethics, and Public Policy* 18: 225–42.

Garrison, Marsha. 2005. Is Consent Necessary? An Evaluation of the Emerging Law of Cohabitant Obligation. *UCLA Law Review* 52: 815–98.

Gavin, Fiona, et al. 2005. *Cohabitation.* W. Green & Son, Edinburgh.

Gennetian, Lisa A., and Virginia Knox. 2003. Staying Single: The Effects of Welfare Reform Policies on Marriage and Cohabitation. *Manpower Demonstration Research Corporation* 2003: 14–23.

Gibson-Davis, Christina M., et al. 2005. High Hopes But Even Higher Expectations: The Retreat From Marriage Among Low-Income Couples. *Journal Marriage and Family* 67: 1301–12.

Glendon, Mary Ann. 1989. *The Transformation of Family Law: State, Law, and Family in the United States and Western Europe.* University of Chicago Press, Chicago.

Goldstein Joshua R., and Catherine T. Kenney. 2001. Marriage Delayed or Marriage Forgone? New Cohort Forecasts of First Marriage for U.S. Women. *American Sociological Review* 66: 506–19.

Gorback, Michael Jay. 2002. Negligent Infliction of Emotional Distress: Has the Legislative Response to Diane Whipple's Death Rendered the Hard-Line Stance of *Elden* and *Thing* Obsolete? *Hastings Law Journal* 54: 273–309.

Gordon, Katherine C. 1998. Note, The Necessity and Enforcement of Cohabitation Agreements: When Strings Will Attach and How to Prevent Them—A State Survey. *Brandeis Law Journal* 37: 245–57.

Graycar, Reg, and Jenni Milbank. 2007. From Functional Family to Spinster Sisters: Australia's Distinctive Path to Relationship Recognition. *Journal of Law and Policy* 24: 121–64.

Gronvold-Hatch, Rebecca. 1995. *Aging and Cohabitation*. Garland Publishing, New York.

Grossberg, Michael. 1985. *Governing the Hearth: Law and the Family in Nineteenth-Century America*. University of North Carolina Press, Chapel Hill.

Gupta, Sanjiv. 1999. The Effects of Transitions in Marital Status on Men's Performance of Housework. *Journal Marriage and Family* 61: 700–11.

Haas, Linda. 1996. Family Policy in Sweden. *Journal of Family and Economic Issues* 17: 47–92.

Hall, Kermit L. 1989. *The Magic Mirror: Law in American History*. Oxford University Press, New York.

Haskey, John. 2001. Cohabitation in Great Britain: Past, Present and Future Trends—and Attitudes. *Population Trends* 103: 4–25.

Heimdal, Kristen R., and Sharon K. Houseknecht. 2003. Cohabiting and Married Couples' Income Organization: Approaches in Sweden and the United States. *Journal of Marriage and Family* 65: 539–49.

Hein, Jonathan Andrew. 2000. Caring for the Evolving American Family: Cohabiting Partners and Employer Sponsored Health Care. *New Mexico Law Review* 30: 19–42.

Heuveline, Patrick, and Jeffrey M. Timberlake. 2004. The Role of Cohabitation in Family Formation: The United States in Comparative Perspective. *Journal of Marriage and Family* 66: 1214–30.

Hibbs, Mary, et al. 2001. Why Marry? Perceptions of the Affianced. *Family Law* 31: 197–207.

Hofferth, Sandra L., and Kermyt G. Anderson. 2003. Are All Dads Equal? Biology Versus Marriage as a Basis for Paternal Investment. *Journal of Marriage and Family* 65: 213–32.

Hohmann-Marriott, Bryndl E. 2006. Shared Beliefs and the Union Stability of Married and Cohabiting Couples. *Journal of Marriage and Family* 68: 1015–28.

Holden, Karen C., and Pamela J. Smock. 1991. The Economic Costs of Marital Dissolution: Why Do Women Bear a Disproportionate Cost? *Annual Review of Sociology* 17: 51–78.

Holland, Winifred. 2000. Intimate Relationships in the New Millenium: The Assimilation of Marriage and Cohabitation? *Canadian Journal of Family Law* 17: 114–68.

Horwitz Allan V., and Helen Raskin White. 1998. The Relationship of Cohabitation and Mental Health: A Study of a Young Adult Cohort. *Journal of Marriage and Family* 60: 505–14.

Hovius, Berend. 2006. Property Rights for Unmarried Cohabitants in Canada. *International Family Law* 2006: 29–34.

Hunter, Andrea G. 2006. (Re)Envisioning Cohabitation: A Commentary on Race, History, and Culture. In *Race, Work, and Family in the Lives of African Americans*, edited by Marlese Durr and Shirley A. Hill. Rowman & Littlefield Publishers, Lanham, MD.

Iacovou, Maria. 2002. Regional Differences in the Transition to Adulthood. *Annals of the American Academy of Political and Social Science* 580: 40–69.

Ignasse, Gérard. 2002. *Les PACSé-e-s: Enquête sur les Signataires d'un Pacte Civil de Solidarité.* L'Harmattan, Paris.

Jackson, Nicky Ali. 1996. Observational Experiences of Intrapersonal Conflict and Teenage Victimization: A Comparative Study Among Spouses and Cohabitors. *Journal of Family Violence* 11: 191–203.

Jacobson, Neil S., and John M. Gottman. 1998. *When Men Batter Women: New Insights into Ending Abusive Relationships.* Simon & Schuster, New York.

Kalmijn, Matthijs. 2007. Explaining Cross-national Differences in Marriage, Cohabitation, and Divorce in Europe 1990–2000. *Population Studies* 61: 243–63.

Kamp Dush, Claire M., and H. Elizabeth Peters. 2007. The Economic Impact of Cohabitation Dissolution Versus Marital Dissolution in Fragile Families. Draft in possession of author.

Kamp Dush, Claire M., and Paul R. Amato. 2005. Consequences of Relationship Status and Quality for Subjective Well-being. *Journal of Social and Personal Relationships* 22: 607–27.

Kandoian, Ellen. 1987. Cohabitation, Common Law Marriage, and the Possibility of a Shared Moral Life. *Georgia Law Journal* 75: 1829–73.

Karst, Kenneth L. 1980. The Freedom of Intimate Association. *Yale Law Journal* 89: 624–92.

Kay, Herma Hill, and Carol Amyx. 1977. *Marvin v. Marvin*: Preserving the Options. *California Law Review* 65: 937–77.

Kendig, Sarah M., and Suzanne M. Bianchi. 2008. Single, Cohabiting, and Married Mothers' Times With Children. *Journal of Marriage and Family* 70: 1228–40.

Kennedy, Betty M., et al. 2007. Socioeconomic Status and Health Disparity in the United States. *Journal of Human Behavior in the Social Environment* 15: 13–23.

Kennedy, Ian. 2004. The Legal Position of Cohabitees in Australia and New Zealand. *International Family Law* 2004: 238–43.

Kenney, Catherine. 2004. Cohabiting Couple, Filing Jointly? Resource Pooling and U.S. Poverty Policies. *Family Relations* 53: 237–47.

Kenney, Catherine T., and Sara S. McLanahan. 2006. Why Are Cohabiting Relationships More Violent Than Marriages? *Demography* 43: 127–40.

Kerr, Don, et al. 2006. Marriage and Cohabitation: Demographic and Socioeconomic Differences in Quebec and Canada. *Canadian Studies in Population* 33: 83–117.

Kiernan, Kathleen. 1999. Cohabitation in Western Europe. *Population Trends* 96: 25–32.

Kiernan, Kathleen. 2004. Redrawing the Boundaries of Marriage. *Journal of Marriage and Family* 66: 980–87.

Kiernan, Kathleen, et al. 2007. Cohabitation Law Reform and Its Impact on Marriage: Evidence from Australia and Europe. *International Family Law* 2007: 71–74.

King, Valarie, and Mindy E. Scott. 2005. A Comparison of Cohabiting Relationships Among Older and Younger Adults. *Journal of Marriage and Family* 67: 271–85.

Koegel, Otto E. 1922. *Common Law Marriage and Its Development in the United States.* J. Byrne & Co., Washington.

Krause, Harry D. 1971. *Illegitimacy, Law and Social Policy.* Bobbs-Merrill, Indianapolis.

Lamb, Kathleen A., 2003. Union Formation and Depression: Selection and Relationship Effects. *Journal of Marriage and Family* 65: 953–62.

Landale, Nancy S. 1991. Patterns of Entry into Cohabitation and Marriage Among Mainland Puerto Rican Women. *Demography* 28: 587–607.

Landale, Nancy S., and Katherine Fennelly. 1992. Informal Unions Among Mainland Puerto Ricans: Cohabitation or an Alternative to Legal Marriage? *Journal of Marriage and Family* 54: 269–80.

Laplante, Benôit. 2006. The Rise of Cohabitation in Quebec: Power of Religion and Power over Religion. *Canadian Journal of Sociology* 31: 1–24.

Le Bourdais, Celine, and Évelyne Lapierre-Adamcyk. 2004. Changes in Conjugal Life in Canada: Is Cohabitation Progressively Replacing Marriage? *Journal of Marriage and Family* 66: 929–42.

L'Heureux-Dubé, Claire, Hon. 2002. It Takes A Vision: The Constitutionalization of Equality in Canada. *Yale Journal of Law and Feminism* 14: 363–75.

Lichter, Daniel T., et al. 2005. Child Poverty Among Racial Minorities and Immigrants: Explaining Trends and Differentials. *Social Science Quarterly* 86: 1037–59.

Lichter, Daniel T., et al. 2006. Marriage or Dissolution? Union Transitions among Poor Cohabiting Women. *Demography* 43: 223–40.

Light, Audrey. 2004. Gender Differences in the Marriage and Cohabitation Income Premium. *Demography* 41: 263–84.

Lind, Göran. 2008. *Common Law Marriage: A Legal Institution for Cohabitation.* Oxford University Press, New York.

Lynd, Paul R. 2000. Domestic Partner Benefits Limited to Same-Sex Couples: Sex Discrimination Under Title VII. *William and Mary Journal of Women and Law* 6: 561–610.

Lyness, Judith L., et al. 1972. Living Together: An Alternative to Marriage. *Journal of Marriage and Family* 34: 305–11.

Macklin, Eleanor D. 1972. Heterosexual Cohabitation Among Unmarried College Students. *The Family Coordinator* 21: 463–72.

Macklin, Eleanor D. 1978. Nonmarital Heterosexual Cohabitation: A Review of the Recent Literature. *Marriage and Family Review* 1: 1–12.

MacNamara, Donald E. J., and Edward Sagarin. 1977. *Sex, Crime, and the Law.* The Free Press, New York.

Magdol, Lynn, et al. 1998. Hitting Without a License: Testing Explanations for Differences in Partner Abuse Between Young Adult Daters and Cohabitors. *Journal of Marriage and Family* 60: 41–85.

Mahoney, Margaret M. 2005. Forces Shaping the Law of Cohabitation For Opposite Sex Couples. *Journal of Law and Family Studies* 7: 135–95.

Mahoney, Martha R. 1991. Legal Images of Battered Women: Redefining the Issue of Separation. *Michigan Law Review* 90: 1–94.

Manning, Wendy D., and Daniel T. Lichter. 1996. Parental Cohabitation and Children's Economic Well-Being. *Journal of Marriage and Family* 58: 998–1010.

Manning, Wendy D., and Kathleen A. Lamb. 2003. Adolescent Well-Being in Cohabiting, Married, and Single-Parent Families. *Journal of Marriage and Family* 65: 876–93.

Manning, Wendy D., and Nancy S. Landale. 1996. Racial and Ethnic Differences in the Role of Cohabitation in Premarital Childbearing. *Journal of Marriage and Family* 58: 63–77.

Manning, Wendy D., and Pamela J. Smock. 2005. Measuring and Modeling Cohabitation: New Perspectives From Qualitative Data. *Journal of Marriage and Family* 67: 989–1002.

Manning, Wendy D., and Susan Brown. 2006. Children's Economic Well-Being in Married and Cohabiting Parent Families. *Journal of Marriage and Family* 68: 345–62.

Manning, Wendy D., et al. 2004. The Relative Stability of Cohabiting and Marital Unions for Children. *Population Research and Policy Review* 23: 135–59.

Manning, Wendy D., et al. 2007. The Changing Institution of Marriage: Adolescents' Expectations to Cohabit and to Marry. *Journal of Marriage and Family* 69: 559–75.

Manting, Dorien. 1996. The Changing Meaning of Cohabitation and Marriage. *European Sociological Review* 12: 53–65.

Marcussen, Kristen. 2005. Explaining Differences in Mental Health Between Married and Cohabiting Individuals. *Social Psychology Quarterly* 68: 239–57.

Martin, Claude, and Irène Théry. 2001. The PACS and Marriage and Cohabitation in France. *International Journal of Law, Policy, and Family* 15: 135–58.

Martin, Teresa Castro. 2002. Consensual Unions in Latin America: Persistence of a Dual Nuptiality System. *Journal of Comparative Family Studies* 33: 35–55.

Maxwell, Nancy G. 2001. Opening Civil Marriage to Same-Gender Couples: A Netherlands-United States Comparison. *Arizona Journal of International Law and Comparative Law* 18: 141–207.

McClain, Linda C. 2003. Intimate Affiliation and Democracy: Beyond Marriage? *Hofstra Law Review* 32: 379–421.

McManus, Mike, and Harriet McManus. 2008. *Living Together: Myths, Risks & Answers*. Howard Books, New York.

Mécary, Caroline, and Flora Leroy-Forgeot. 2000. *Que Sais-je?: Le PACS*. Presses Universitaires de France, Paris.

Merin, Yuval. 2002. *Equality for Same-Sex Couples*. University of Chicago Press, Chicago.

Millbank, Jenni. 2000. Domestic Rifts: Who Is Using the Domestic Relationships Act 1994 (ACT)? *Australian Family Law Journal* 14: 163–66.

Mock, Steven E., and Steven W. Cornelius. 2007. Profiles of Interdependence: The Retirement Planning of Married, Cohabiting, and Lesbian Couples. *Sex Roles* 56: 793–800.

Moffitt, Robert A. 2000. Female Wages, Male Wages, and the Economic Model of Marriage: The Basic Evidence. In *The Ties that Bind: Perspectives on Marriage and Cohabitation*, edited by Linda J. Waite. Aldine De Gruyter, New York.

Moffitt, Robert A., et al. 1998. Beyond Single Mothers: Cohabitation and Marriage in the AFDC Program. *Demography* 35: 259–78.

More Or Less Together: Levels of Legal Consequences of Marriage, Cohabitation and Registered Partnerships for Different-sex and Same-sex Partners: A Comparative Study of Nine European Countries. 2005. Ined, http://www-same-sex.ined.fr/publica_doc125.htm.

Morrison, Donna Ruane, and Amy Ritualo. 2000. Routes to Children's Economic Recovery after Divorce: Are Cohabitation and Remarriage Equivalent? *American Sociological Review* 65: 560–80.

Mossman, Mary Jane. 2003. Conversations About Families in Canadian Courts and Legislatures: Are There "Lessons" for the United States? *Hofstra Law Review* 32: 171–200.

Nimkoff, Meyer F. 1947. *Marriage and the Family*. Houghton Mifflin Co., Boston.

Nock, Steven L. 1995. A Comparison of Marriages and Cohabiting Relationships. *Journal of Family Issues* 16: 53–76.

Note. 1978. Fornication, Cohabitation, and the Constitution. *Michigan Law Review* 77: 252–306.

Oldham, J. Thomas. 2001. Lessons from *Jerry Hall v. Mick Jagger* Regarding U.S. Regulation of Heterosexual Cohabitants or, Can't Get No Satisfaction. *Notre Dame Law Review* 76: 1409–34.

Ontario Law Reform Commission. 1993. *Report on The Rights and Responsibilities of Cohabitants under the Family Law Act.*

Oppenheimer, Valerie Kincade. 2000. The Continuing Importance of Men's Economic Position in Marriage Formation. In *The Ties that Bind: Perspectives on Marriage and Cohabitation*, edited by Linda J. Waite. Aldine De Gruyter, New York.

Oropesa, R.S. 1996. Normative Beliefs About Marriage and Cohabitation: A Comparison of Non-Latino Whites, Mexican Americans, and Puerto Ricans. *Journal of Marriage and Family* 58: 49–62.

Oropesa R.S., and Bridget K. Gorman. 2000. Ethnicity, Immigration, and Beliefs about Marriage as a "Tie That Binds." In *The Ties that Bind: Perspectives on Marriage and Cohabitation*, edited by Linda J. Waite. Aldine De Gruyter, New York.

Oropesa, R.S., et al. 2003. Income Allocation in Marital and Cohabiting Unions: The Case of Mainland Puerto Ricans. *Journal of Marriage and Family* 65: 910–26.

Osborne, Cynthia. 2005. Marriage Following the Birth of a Child Among Cohabiting and Visiting Parents. *Journal of Marriage and Family* 67: 14–26.

Osborne, Cynthia, et al. 2007. Married and Cohabiting Parents' Relationship Stability: A Focus on Race and Ethnicity. *Journal of Marriage and Family* 69: 1345–66.

Parr, Gavin M. 1999. What Is a "Meretricious Relationship"?: An Analysis of Cohabitant Property Rights under *Connell v. Francisco*. *Washington Law Review* 74: 1243–73.

Phillips, Julie A., and Megan M. Sweeney. 2005. Premarital Cohabitation and Marital Disruption Among White, Black, and Mexican American Women. *Journal of Marriage and Family* 67: 296–314.

Pinsof, William M. 2002. The Death of "Till Death Us Do Part": The Transformation of Pair-Bonding in the 20th Century. *Family Process* 41: 135–57.

Pleck, Elizabeth H. *Shacking Up: Cohabitation and the Sexual Revolution, 1962-1990*. Unpublished manuscript on file with author.

Ploscowe, Morris. 1951. *Sex and the Law*. Prentice-Hall, New York.

Polikoff, Nancy D. 2003. Ending Marriage As We Know It. *Hofstra Law Review* 32: 201–32.

Polikoff, Nancy D. 2008. *Beyond (Straight and Gay) Marriage: Valuing All Families under the Law*. Beacon Press, Boston.

Posner Richard A., and Katharine B. Silbaugh. 1996. *A Guide to America's Sex Laws*. University of Chicago Press, Chicago.

Probert, Rebecca. 2001. From Lack of Status to Contract: Assessing the French Pacte Civil de Solidarité. *Journal of Social Welfare and Family Law* 23: 257–69.

Probert, Rebecca. 2004. Cohabitation in Twentieth Century England and Wales. *Law and Policy* 26: 13–32.

Probert, R.J. 2007. A Review of Cohabitation: The Financial Consequences of Relationship Breakdown Law Com. No. 307 (HMSO 2007). *Family Law Quarterly* 41: 521–37.

Raley, R. Kelly. 1996. A Shortage of Marriageable Men? A Note on the Role of Cohabitation in Black-White Differences in Marriage Rates. *American Sociological Review* 61: 973–83.

Raley, R. Kelly. 2000. Recent Trends and Differentials in Marriage and Cohabitation. In *The Ties that Bind: Perspectives on Marriage and Cohabitation*, edited by Linda J. Waite. Aldine De Gruyter, New York.

Raley, R. Kelly, and Larry Bumpass. 2003. The Topography of the Divorce Plateau: Levels and Trends in Union Stability in the United States after 1980. *Demographic Research* 8: 245–60.

Raley, R. Kelly, et al. 2005. Maternal Cohabitation and Educational Success. *Sociological Education* 78: 144–64.

Rault, Wilfried. 2004. The Best Way to Court. The French Mode of Registration and Its Impact on the Social Significance of Partnerships. In *Same-sex Couples, Same-sex Partnerships, and Homosexual Marriages: A Focus on Cross-national Differentials*, edited by Marie Digoix and Patrick Festy. Ined, Paris.

Razzouch, Nabil, et al. 2007. A Comparison of Consumer Decision-making Behavior of Married and Cohabiting Couples. *Journal of Consumer Marketing* 24: 264–74.

Regan, Milton C., Jr. 2001. Calibrated Commitment: The Legal Treatment of Marriage and Cohabitation. *Notre Dame Law Review* 76: 1435–66.

Reppy, William A. Jr. 1984. Property and Support Rights of Unmarried Cohabitants: A Proposal for Creating a New Legal Status. *Louisiana Law Review* 44: 1677–723.

Rhoades, Galena H. 2007. *A Longitudinal Study of Cohabiting Couples' Reasons for Cohabitation, Relationship Quality, and Psychological Well-Being*. Ph.D. dissertation, University of Denver, Dept of Psychology.

Rhoades, Galena Kline. 2006. Pre-engagement Cohabitation and Gender Asymmetry in Marital Commitment. *Journal of Family Psychology* 20: 553–60.

Rhoades, Galena Kline, et al. 2006. Premarital Cohabitation, Husbands' Commitment, and Wives' Satisfaction with the Division of Household Contributions. *Marriage and Family Review* 40: 5–22.

Rindfuss, Ronald R., and Audrey VandenHeuvel. 1990. Cohabitation: A Precursor to Marriage or an Alternative to Being Single? *Population and Development Review* 16: 703–26.

Robbennolt Jennifer K., and Monica Kirkpatrick Johnson. 1999. Legal Planning for Unmarried Committed Partners: Empirical Lessons for a Preventive and Therapeutic Approach. *Arizona Law Review* 41: 417–57.

Saldeen, Åke. 2005. Sweden: Cohabitation Outside Marriage or Partnership. In *The International Survey of Family Law 2005 Edition*, edited by Andrew Bainham. Jordan Publishing, Bristol.

Sassler, Sharon. 2004. The Process of Entering into Cohabiting Unions. *Journal of Marriage and Family* 66: 491–505.

Sassler, Sharon, and Anna Cunningham. 2008. How Cohabitors View Childbearing. *Sociological Perspectives* 51: 3–28.

Sassler, Sharon, and James McNally. 2003. Cohabiting Couples' Economic Circumstances and Union Transitions: A Re-examination Using Multiple Imputation Techniques. *Social Science Research* 32: 553–78.

Sawyer, Christopher D. 2003. Practice What You Preach: California's Obligation to Give Full Faith and Credit to the Vermont Civil Union. *Hastings Law Journal* 54: 727–50.

Schlam, Lawrence. 2007. Third-Party "Standing" and Child Custody Disputes in Washington: Non-Parent Rights—Past, Present, and Future? *Gonzaga Law Review* 43: 391–61.

Schleppenbach, John R. 2009. Strange Bedfellows: Why Older Straight Couples Should Advocate for the Passage of the Illinois Civil Union Act. *Elder Law Journal* 17: 31–59.

Schoen, Robert. 1992. First Unions and the Stability of First Marriages. *Journal of Marriage and Family* 54: 281–84.

Schrama, Wendy M. 1999. Registered Partnership in The Netherlands. *International Journal of Law, Policy, and Family* 13: 315–27.

Scott, Elizabeth. 2004. Marriage, Cohabitation and Collective Responsibility for Dependency. *University of Chicago Legal Forum* 2004: 225–64.

Shackelford, Todd K. 2001. Cohabitation, Marriage, and Murder: Woman-Killing by Male Romantic Partners. *Aggressive Behavior* 27: 284–91.

Shackelford, Todd K., and Jenny Mouzos. 2005. Partner Killing by Men in Cohabiting and Marital Relationships: A Comparative, Cross-National Analysis of Data from Australia and the United States. *Journal of Interpersonal Violence* 20: 1310–24.

Sherwin, Emily. 2006. Love, Money, and Justice: Restitution Between Cohabitants. *University of Colorado Law Review* 77: 711–37.

Sherwin, Robert Veit. 1949. *Sex and the Statutory Law in all 48 States*. Oceana Publications, New York.

Sidel, Ruth. 1986. *Women & Children Last: The Plight of Poor Women in Affluent America*. Penguin Group, New York.

Simerman, Anne E. 1993. The Right of a Cohabitant to Recover in Tort: Wrongful Death, Negligent Infliction of Emotional Distress and Loss of Consortium. *University of Louisville Journal of Family Law* 32: 531–50.

Sirjamaki, John. 1953. *The American Family in the Twentieth Century.* Harvard University Press, Cambridge.

Smart, Carol. 2000. Stories of Family Life: Cohabitation, Marriage and Social Change. *Canadian Journal of Family Law* 17: 20–53.

Smith, Judith A. 2005. Battered Non-Wives and Unequal Protection-Order Coverage: A Call for Reform. *Yale Law and Policy Review* 23: 93–162.

Smock, Pamela J. 2000. Cohabitation in the United States: An Appraisal of Research Themes, Findings, and Implications. *Annual Review of Sociology* 26: 1–20.

Smock, Pamela J., and Wendy D. Manning. 1997. Cohabiting Partners' Economic Circumstances and Marriage. *Demography* 34: 331–41.

Smock Pamela J., and Wendy D. Manning. 2004. Living Together Unmarried in the United States: Demographic Perspectives and Implications for Family Policy. *Law and Policy* 26: 87–117.

Smock, Pamela J., et al. 2005. "Everything's There Except Money": How Money Shapes Decisions to Marry Among Cohabitors. *Journal of Marriage and Family* 67: 680–96.

Snyder, Anastasia R., and Diane K. McLaughlin. 2006. Economic Well-being and Cohabitation: Another Nonmetro Disadvantage? *Journal of Family and Economic Issues* 27: 562–82.

South, Scott J., and Glenna Spitze. 1994. Housework in Marital and Nonmarital Households. *American Sociological Review* 59: 327–47.

Stacey, Judith. 1990. *Brave New Families: Stories of Domestic Upheaval in Late Twentieth Century America.* University of California Press, Berkeley.

Stack, Steven, and J. Ross Eshleman. 1998. Marital Status and Happiness: A 17-Nation Study. *Journal of Marriage and Family* 60: 527–36.

Stafford, Laura Susan, et al. 2004. Married Individuals, Cohabiters, and Cohabiters Who Marry: A Longitudinal Study of Relational and Individual Well-being. *Journal of Social and Personal Relationships* 21: 231–48.

Stanley, Scott M., et al. 2004. Maybe I Do: Interpersonal Commitment and Premarital or Nonmarital Cohabitation. *Journal of Family Issues* 25: 496–519.

Statistics Netherlands. 2008. *Marriages and Partnership Registrations.*

Stets, Jan E. 1991. Cohabiting and Marital Aggression: The Role of Social Isolation. *Journal of Marriage and Family* 53: 669–80.

Stets, Jan E., and Murray A. Straus. 1989. The Marriage License as a Hitting License: A Comparison of Assaults in Dating, Cohabiting, and Married Couples. In *Violence in Dating Relationships: Emerging Social Issues*, edited by Maureen A. Pirog-Good and Jan E. Stets. Praeger, New York.

Stone, Donald H. 1990. Just Molly and Me and Baby Makes Three—Or Does It? Child Custody and the Live-In Lover: An Empirical Study. *Pace Law Review* 11: 1–62.

Storrow, Richard F. 2006. Rescuing Children from the Marriage Movement: The Case Against Marital Status Discrimination in Adoption and Assisted Reproduction. *University of California Davis Law Review* 39: 305–70.

Svarer, Michael. 2004. Is Your Love in Vain? Another Look at Premarital Cohabitation and Divorce. *Journal of Human Resources* 39: 523–35.

Sweden. 2003. *Cohabitees and Their Joint Homes—a Brief Presentation of the Cohabitees Act.*

Teachman, Jay. 2003. Premarital Sex, Premarital Cohabitation, and the Risk of Subsequent Marital Dissolution Among Women. *Journal of Marriage and Family* 65: 444–55.

Teachman, Jay D. 2004. The Childhood Living Arrangements of Children and the Characteristics of Their Marriages. *Journal of Family Issues* 25: 86–111.

TenBroek, Jacobus. 1965. California's Dual System of Family Law: Its Origin, Development, and Present Status. *Stanford Law Review* 17: 614–82.

Thomson, Elizabeth, and Ugo Colella. Cohabitation and Marital Stability: Quality or Commitment? *Journal of Marriage and Family* 54: 259–67.

Thornton, Arland, and Linda Young-DeMarco. 2001. Four Decades of Trends in Attitudes Toward Family Issues in the United States: The 1960s Through the 1990s. *Journal of Marriage and Family* 63: 1009–37.

Thornton, Arland, et al. 2007. *Marriage and Cohabitation*. University of Chicago Press, Chicago.

Tracol, Xavier. 2003. The Pacte Civil de Solidarité. In *Legal Recognition of Same-Sex Couples in Europe*, edited by Katharina Boele-Woelki and Angelika Fuchs. Intersentia Publishing, Oxford.

Treas, Judith, and Esther de Ruijter. 2008. Earnings and Expenditures on Household Services in Married and Cohabiting Unions. *Journal of Marriage and Family* 70: 796–805.

Tribe, Lawrence H. 2004. *Lawrence v.* Texas: "The Fundamental Right" That Dare Not Speak Its Name. *Harvard Law Review* 17: 1893–1955.

U.S. Census Bureau. 2000. *Special Reports: Married-Couple and Unmarried-Partner Households*. Washington, D.C.

U.S. Census Bureau. 2003. *Married-Couple and Unmarried–Partner Households: 2000*. Washington, D.C.

U.S. Census Bureau. 2004. *Children and the Households They Live In: 2000*. Washington, D.C.

U.S. Census Bureau. 2004. *Number, Timing, and Duration of Marriages and Divorces*. Washington, D.C.

U.S. Census Bureau. 2009. *Current Population Survey, 2008 Annual Social and Economic Supplement*. Washington, D.C.

U.S. Department of Health and Human Services. Centers for Disease Control and Prevention, Nat'l Center for Health Statistics. 2002. *Cohabitation, Marriage, Divorce, and Remarriage in the United States: Data from the National Survey of Family Growth*. Washington, D.C.

U.S. Department of Justice. Bureau of Justice Statistics. 1998. *Violence by Intimates: Analysis of Data on Crimes by Current or Former Spouses, Boyfriends, and Girlfriends*. Washington D.C.

U.S. Department of Justice. Bureau of Justice Statistics. 2000. *Intimate Partner Violence*. Washington D.C.

U.S. Department of Justice. Bureau of Justice Statistics. 2007. *Homicide Trends in the U.S.: Intimate Homicide*. Washington D.C.

U.S. Department of Justice. Bureau of Justice Statistics. 2007. *Intimate Partner Violence in the United States*. Washington D.C.

United Kingdom. The Law Commission. 2007. *Cohabitation: The Financial Consequences of Relationship Breakdown*.

United Kingdom. The Law Commission. 2002. *Sharing Homes: A Discussion Paper*.

United Kingdom. The Law Society. 2002. *Cohabitation: The Case for Clear Law: Proposals for Reform*.

Villeneuve-Gokalp, Catherine. 1991. From Marriage to Informal Union: Recent Changes in the Behaviour of French Couples. *Population* 3: 81–111.

Vogler, Carolyn. 2005. Cohabiting Couples: Rethinking Money in the Household at the Beginning of the Twenty First Century. *Sociological Review* 53: 1–29.

Waite, Linda J. 2000. The Family as a Social Organization: Key Ideas for the Twenty-first Century. *Contemporary Society* 29: 463–69.

Waite, Linda J., and Maggie Gallagher. 2000. *The Case for Marriage: Why Married People Are Happier, Healthier, and Better Off Financially*. Broadway Books, New York.

Wardle, Lynn D. 2004. The "Withering Away" of Marriage: Some Lessons from the Bolshevik Family Law Reforms in Russia, 1917–1926. *Georgia Journal of Law and Public Policy* 2: 469–522.

Weyrauch, Walter O. 1965. Informal Marriage and Common Law Marriage. In *Sexual Behavior and the Law*, edited by Ralph Slovenko. Thomas, Springfield.

Wilhelm, Brenda. 1998. Changes in Cohabitation Across Cohorts: The Influence of Political Activism. *Social Forces* 77: 289–310.

Willetts, Marion C. 2003. An Exploratory Investigation of Heterosexual Licensed Domestic Partners. *Journal of Marriage and Family* 65: 939–52.

Willetts, Marion C., and Nick G. Maroules. 2005. Parental Reports of Adolescent Well-Being: Does Marital Status Matter? *Journal of Divorce and Remarriage* 43: 129–48.

Williams, Kristi. 2008. For Better or For Worse? The Consequences of Marriage and Cohabitation for Single Mothers. *Social Forces* 86: 1481–511.

Williams, Lucy A. 1992. The Ideology of Division: Behavior Modification Welfare Reform Proposals. *Yale Law Journal* 102: 719–46.

Willmott, Lindy, et al. 2003. De Facto Relationships Property Adjustment Law—A National Direction. *Australian Journal of Family Law* 17: 37–61.

Wilson, Robin Fretwell. 2005. Evaluating Marriage: Does Marriage Matter to the Nurturing of Children? *San Diego Law Review* 42: 847–80.

Wilson, William Julius. 1987. *The Truly Disadvantaged: The Inner City, the Underclass, and Public Policy*. University of Chicago Press, Chicago.

Winkler, Anne E. 1997. Economic Decision-making by Cohabitors: Findings Regarding Income Pooling. *Applied Economics* 29: 1079–90.

Witcher, Phyllis H. 2007. Premarital Cohabitation Increases the Chances of Divorce. In *Divorce*, edited by Christina Fisanick. Greenhaven Press, Detroit.

Wong, Simone. 2004. Property Regimes for Home-sharers: The Civil Partnership Bill and Some Antipodean Models. *Journal of Social Welfare and Family Law* 26: 361–75.

Wong, Simone. 2005. Trust(s) and Intention in Resolving Disputes over the Shared Family Home. *Northern Ireland Legal Quarterly* 56: 105–18.

Xu, Xiaohe, et al. 2006. The Role of Cohabitation in Remarriage. *Journal of Marriage and Family* 68: 261–74.

Yllo, Kersti, and Murray A. Straus. 1981. Interpersonal Violence among Married and Cohabiting Couples. *Family Relations* 30: 339–47.

Ytterberg, Hans. 2001. "From Society's Point of View, Cohabitation Between Two Persons of the Same Sex Is a Perfectly Acceptable Form of Family Life": A Swedish Story of Love and Legislation. In *Legal Recognition of Same-sex Partnerships: A Study of National, European and International Law*, edited by Robert Wintemute and Mads Andenaes. Hart Publishing, Oxford.

Yuracko, Kimberley A. 2005. Does Marriage Make People Good or Do Good People Marry? *San Diego Law Review* 42: 889–94.

Zimmerman, Frederick J., and Wayne Katon. 2005. Socioeconomic Status, Depression, Disparities, and Financial Strain: What Lies Behind the Income-Depression Relationship? *Health Economics* 14: 1197–1215.

Cases

Air Transport Ass'n v. City of San Francisco, 992 F. Supp. 1149 (N.D. Cal. 1998).

Alison D. v. Virginia M., 569 N.Y.S.2d 586 (N.Y. 1991).

Allen v. Storer, 600 N.E.2d 1263 (Ill. App. Ct. 1992).

Arwood v. Sloan, 560 So. 2d 1251 (Fla. Dist. Ct. App. 1990).

Atwater v. Atwater, 309 N.E.2d 632 (Ill. App. Ct. 1974).

Ayala v. Fox, 564 N.E.2d 920 (Ill. App. Ct. 1990).

Ayyoub v. City of Oakland, No. 99-02937 (Cal. State Labor Comm'r, Oct. 27, 1997).

Barker v. Briggs, 544 A.2d 629 (Conn. 1988).

Baumgartner v. Baumgartner (1987), 164 C.L.R 137 (Austl.).

Beal v. Beal, 577 P.2d 507 (Or. 1978).

Binns v. Fredendall, 513 N.E.2d 278 (Ohio 1987).

Bowers v. Hardwick, 478 U.S. 186 (1986).

Brandt v. Brandt, 425 N.E.2d 1251 (Ill. App. Ct. 1981).

Bulloch v. United States, 487 F. Supp. 1078 (1980).

Buness v. Gillen, 781 P.2d 985 (Alaska 1989).

Burns v. Burns, [1984] 1 All ER 244 (EWCA Civ.) (Eng.).

Caban v. Mohammed, 441 U.S. 380 (1979).

Carlson v. Olson, 256 N.W.2d 249 (Minn. 1977).

Childers v. Shannon, 444 A.2d 1141 (N.J. Super. Ct. 1982).

Cleaves v. City of Chicago, 68 F. Supp. 2d 963 (N.D. Ill. 1999).

Collins v. Hoag & Rollins, Inc., 241 N.W. 766 (Neb. 1932).

Commonwealth v. Munson, 127 Mass. 459 (1879).

Coney v. R.S.R. Corp., 563 N.Y.S.2d 211 (N.Y. App. Div. 1990).

Connell v. Francisco, 898 P.2d 831 (Wash. 1995).

Cooper v. French, 460 N.W.2d 2 (Minn. 1990).

Cooper v. Merkel, 470 N.W.2d 253 (S.D. 1991).

Corder v. Cont'l Ill. Bank & Trust Co. of Chicago (*In re* Estate of Enoch), 201 N.E.2d 682 (Ill. App. Ct. 1964).

Costa v. Oliven, 849 N.E.2d 122 (Ill. App. Ct. 2006).

Creasman v. Boyle, 196 P.2d 835 (1948).

Davis v. Davis, 643 So. 2d 931 (Miss. 1994).

Dillon v. Legg, 441 P.2d 912 (Cal. 1968).

Doe v. Duling, 782 F.2d 1202 (4th Cir. 1986).

Dunkin v. Boskey, 98 Cal. Rptr.2d 44 (Cal. Ct. App. 2000).

Dunphy v. Gregor, 642 A.2d 372 (N.J. 1994).

Egan v. Fridlund-Horne, 211 P. 3d 1213 (Ariz. Ct. App. 2009).

Elden v. Sheldon, 758 P.2d 582 (Cal. 1988).

Ellison v. Ramos, 502 S.E.2d 891 (N.C. Ct. App. 1998).

Engel v. Kenner, 926 S.W.2d 472 (Mo. Ct. App. 1996).

Engle v. State, 659 S.E.2d 795 (Ga. Ct. App. 2008).

E.N.O. v. L.M.M., 711 N.E.2d 886 (Mass. 1999).

Evans v. Wall, 542 So. 2d 1055 (Fla. Dist. Ct. App. 1989).

Everett v. Commonwealth, 200 S.E.2d 564 (Va. 1973).

Feliciano v. Rosemar Silver Co., 514 N.E.2d 1095 (Mass. 1987).

Fenton v. Reed, 4 Johns. 52 (N.Y. Sup. Ct. 1809).

Foray v. Bell Atlantic, 56 F. Supp. 2d 327 (S.D.N.Y. 1999).

Friedman v. Friedman, 24 Cal. Rptr. 2d 892 (Cal. Ct. App. 1993).

Frothingham v. Mellon, 262 U.S. 447 (1923).

Glona v. Am. Guar. & Liab. Ins. Co., 391 U.S. 73 (1968).

Goode v. Goode, 396 S.E.2d 430 (W. Va. 1990).

Goodridge v. Dept. of Pub. Health, 798 N.E.2d 941 (Mass. 2003).

Graves v. Estabrook, 818 A.2d 1255 (N.H. 2003).

Hesseltine v. McLaughlin (*In re* McLaughlin's Estate), 30 P. 651 (1892).

Hewitt v. Hewitt, 394 N.E.2d 1204 (Ill. 1979).

Holguin v. Flores, 18 Cal. Rptr.3d 749 (Ct. App. 2004) .

In re Adoption of Carl, 709 N.Y.S.2d 905 (N.Y. Fam. Ct. Queens Co. 2000).

In re Adoption of Joseph, 684 N.Y.S.2d 760 (N.Y. Surr. Ct. Oneida Co. 1998).

In re Custody of Dombrowski (Dombrowski v. Goodright), 705 P.2d 1218 (Wash. Ct. App. 1985).

In re Custody of H.S.H.-K. (Holtzman v. Knott), 533 N.W.2d 419 (Wis. 1995).

In re Estate of Ericksen, 337 N.W.2d 671 (Minn. 1983).

In re Estate of Erlanger, 145 Misc. 19321 (N.Y. Co. Surrogate's Ct.).

In re Estate of Marson, 120 P.3d 382 (Mont. 2005).

In re Estate of Soeder, 220 N.E.2d 547 (Ohio Ct. App. 1966).

In re Jacob, 620 N.Y.S.2d 640 (1994).

In re Jacob, 600 N.E.2d 397 (N.Y. 1995).

In re Jason C., 533 A.2d 32 (N.H. 1987).

In re J. M., 575 S.E.2d 441 (Ga. 2003).

In re L.A.N., 623 S.E.2d 682 (Ga. Ct. App. 2005).

In re Marriage Cases, 183 P.3d 384 (Cal. 2008).

In re Marriage of Cary, 109 Cal. Rptr. 862 (Cal. Ct. App. 1973).

In re Marriage of Cripe, 538 N.E.2d 1175 (Ill. App. Ct. 1989).

In re Marriage of Diehl, 582 N.E.2d 281 (Ill. App. Ct. 1991).

In re Marriage of Freel, 448 N.W.2d 26 (Iowa 1989).

In re Marriage of Hanson, 445 N.E.2d 912 (Ill. App. Ct. 1983).

In re Marriage of Lawver, 402 N.E.2d 430 (Ill. App. Ct. 1980).

In re Marriage of Lindsey, 678 P.2d 328 (Wash. 1984).

In re Marriage of McKeever, 453 N.E.2d 1153 (Ill. App. Ct. 1983).

In re Marriage of Pennington, 14 P.3d 764 (Wash. 2000).

In re Marriage of R.S. and S.S., 677 N.E.2d 1297 (Ill. App. Ct. 1996).

In re Marriage of Roofe, 460 N.E.2d 784 (Ill. App. Ct. 1984).

In re Marriage of Thompson, 449 N.E.2d 88 (Ill. 1983).

In re Meaux, 417 So.2d 522 (La. Ct. App. 1982).

In re Nelson, 825 A.2d 501 (N.H. 2003).

In re Tammy, 619 N.E.2d 315 (Mass. 1993).

Irizarry v. Bd. of Educ. of City of Chicago, 251 F.3d 604 (2001).

Janice M. v. Margaret K., 948 A.2d 73 (Md. 2008).

Jarrett v. Jarrett, 382 N.E.2d 12 (Ill. Ct. App. 1978).

Jarrett v. Jarrett, 400 N.E.2d 421 (Ill. 1979).

Jasniowski v. Rushing, 678 N.E.2d 743 (Ill. App. Ct. 1997).

Johnson v. Calvert, 851 P.2d 776 (Cal. 1993).

Johnson v. Green, 309 S.E.2d 362 (Ga. 1983).

Jones v. Boring Jones, 884 A.2d 915 (Pa. Super. Ct. 2005).

Jordan v. Mitchell, 705 So. 2d 453 (Ala. Civ. App. 1997).

Kaiser v. Fleming, 735 N.E2d 144 (Ill. App. Ct. 2000).

Labine v. Vincent, 401 U.S. 532 (1971).

Lalli v. Lalli, 439 U.S. 1978 (259).

Lawrence v. Texas, 539 U.S. 558 (2003).

Lazzarevich v. Lazzarevich, 200 P.2d 49 (Cal. Ct. App. 1948).

Lehr v. Robertson, 463 U.S. 248 (1983).

Lennon v. Charney, 797 N.Y.S.2d 891 (N.Y. Sup. Ct. 2005).

Leonardis v. Morton Chemical Co., 445 A.2d 45 (N.J. Super. Ct. 1982).

Levy v. Louisiana, 391 U.S. 68 (1968).

Lewis v. Harris, 875 A.2d 259 (N.J. Super. Ct. App. Div. 2005).

Lewis v. Harris, 908 A.2d 196 (N.J. 2006).

Long v. Marino, 441 S.E.2d 475 (Ga. Ct. App. 1994).

Lozoya v. Sanchez, 66 P.3d 948 (N.M. 2003).

Lynch v. Bowen, 681 F. Supp. 506 (N.D. Ill. 1988).

M. v. H., [1999] 2 S.C.R. 3 (Can.).

MacGregor v. Unemployment Ins. Appeals Bd., 689 P.2d 453 (Cal. 1984).

Marriage of Sappington, 462 N.E.2d 881 (Ill. App. Ct. 1984).

Martin v. Ziherl, 607 S.E.2d 367 (Va. 2005).

Marvin v. Marvin, 557 P.2d 106 (Cal. 1976).

Mason v. Dwinnell, 660 S.E.2d 58 (N.C. Ct. App. 2008).

McChesney v. Johnson, 79 S.W.2d 658 (Tex. 1934).

Medley v. Strong, 558 N.E.2d 244 (Ill. App. Ct. 1990).

Meister v. Moore, 96 U.S. 76 (1877).

Metro. Life Ins. Co. v. Johnson, 645 P.2d 356 (Idaho 1982).

Miron v. Trudel, [1995] 2 S.C.R. 418 (Can.).

Mister v. A.R.K. P'ship, 553 N.E.2d 1152 (Ill. App. Ct. 1990).

Morone v. Morone, 413 N.E.2d 1154 (N.Y. 1980).

Multari v. Sorrell, 731 N.Y.S.2d 238 (N.Y. App. Div. 2001).

Norman v. Unemployment Ins. Appeals Bd., 663 P.2d 904 (Cal. 1983).

North Dakota Fair Housing Council v. Peterson, 625 N.W.2d 551 (N.D. 2001).

Oxley v. Hiscock, [2004] EWCA (Civ.) 546, [2005] Fam. 211 (Eng.).

Peter v. Beblow, [1993] 1 S.C.R. 980 (Can.).

Phillips v. Wisconsin Pers. Comm'n, 482 N.W.2d 121 (Wis. Ct. App. 1992).

Pickens v. Pickens, 490 So. 2d 872 (Miss. 1986).

Portee v. Jaffee, 417 A.2d 521 (N.J. 1980).

Powell v. State, 510 S.E.2d 18 (Ga. 1998).

Price v. Howard, 484 S.E.2d 528 (N.C. 1997).

Quilloin v. Walcott, 434 U.S. 246 (1978).

Ram v. Ramharack, 571 N.Y.S.2d 190 (N.Y. Sup. Ct. 1991).

Reep v. Comm'r of Dep't of Employment and Training, 593 N.E.2d 1297 (Mass. 1992)

Roberts v. Roberts (*In re* Roberts' Estate), 133 P.2d 492 (Wyo. 1943).

Salzman v. Bachrach, 996 P.2d 1263 (Colo. 2000).

Schoenhard v. Schoenhard, 392 N.E.2d 764 (Ill. App. Ct. 1979).

Schwegmann v. Schwegmann, 441 So.2d 316 (La. Ct. App. 1983).

Sharp v. Kosmalski, 40 N.Y.2d 119 (N.Y. 1976).

Smith v. North Memphis Sav. Bank, 89 S.W. 392 (Tenn. 1905).

Spafford v. Coats, 455 N.E.2d 241 (Ill. App. Ct. 1983).

Stack v. Dowden, [2007] UKHL 17, [2007] 2 WLR 831

Stahl v. Chuhak (*In re* Estate of Stahl), 301 N.E.2d 82 (Ill. App. Ct. 1973).

Stanley v. Illinois, 405 U.S. 645 (1972).

State v. Brooks, 254 N.W. 374 (Wis. 1934).

State v. Saunders, 381 A.2d 333 (N.J. 1977).

State v. Workers' Comp. Appeals Bd., 156 Cal. Rptr. 183 (Cal. Ct. App. 1979).

Stockey v. Gayden, 280 Cal. Rptr. 862 (Cal. Ct. App. 1991).

Sullivan v. Rooney, 533 N.E.2d 1372 (Mass. 1989).

Sullivan v. Stringer, 736 So. 2d 514 (Miss. Ct. App. 1999).

Taylor v. Rossu, [1998] 216 A.R. 348 (Can.).

Temple v. Meyer, 544 A.2d 629 (Conn. 1988).

Trimble v. Gordon, 430 U.S. 762 (1977).

Troxel v. Granville, 530 U.S. 57 (2000).

Trutalli v. Meraviglia, 12 P.2d 430 (Cal. 1932).

Tumeo v. Univ. of Alaska, No. 4FA-94-43 Civ., 1995 WL 238359 (Alaska Super. Jan. 11, 1995).

Van v. Zahorik, 597 N.W.2d 15 (Mich. 1999).

Vargas v. Vargas (*In re* Estate of Vargas), 111 Cal. Rptr. 779 (Cal. Ct. App. 1974).

Vasquez v. Hawthorne, 33 P.3d 735 (Wash. 2001).

Waage v. Borer, 405 N.W.2d 92 (Wis. Ct. App. 1994).

Walsh v. Bona, [2002] 4 S.C.R. 325 (Can.).

Ward v. Jahnke, 583 N.W.2d 656 (Wis. Ct. App. 1998).

Watts v. Watts, 405 N.W.2d 303 (Wis. 1987).

Watts v. Watts, 448 N.W.2d 292 (Wis. Ct. App. 1989).

Weber v. Aetna Cas. & Sur. Co., 406 U.S. 164 (1972).

Wooldridge v. Wooldridge, 856 So. 2d 446 (Miss. 2003).

Index